The Rocky Road

KT-447-520

By the same author

Only a Game?: The Diary of a Professional Footballer
Unforgettable Fire: The Story of U2
A Strange Kind of Glory: Sir Matt Busby and Manchester United
Keane: The Autobiography (*with Roy Keane*)

The Rocky Road

EAMON DUNPHY

PENGUIN
IRELAND

PENGUIN IRELAND

Published by the Penguin Group
Penguin Ireland, 25 St Stephen's Green, Dublin 2, Ireland
(a division of Penguin Books Ltd)
Penguin Books Ltd, 80 Strand, London WC2R ORL, England
Penguin Group (USA) Inc., 375 Hudson Street, New York, New York 10014, USA
Penguin Group (Canada), 90 Eglinton Avenue East, Suite 700, Toronto, Ontario, Canada M4P 2Y3
(a division of Pearson Penguin Canada Inc.)
Penguin Group (Australia), 707 Collins Street, Melbourne, Victoria 3008, Australia
(a division of Pearson Australia Group Pty Ltd)
Penguin Books India Pvt Ltd, 11 Community Centre,
Panchsheel Park, New Delhi – 110 017, India
Penguin Group (NZ), 67 Apollo Drive, Rosedale, Auckland 0632, New Zealand
(a division of Pearson New Zealand Ltd)
Penguin Books (South Africa) (Pty) Ltd, Block D, Rosebank Office Park,
181 Jan Smuts Avenue, Parktown North, Gauteng 2193, South Africa

Penguin Books Ltd, Registered Offices: 80 Strand, London WC2R ORL, England

www.penguin.com

First published 2013
001

Copyright © Eamon Dunphy, 2013

The moral right of the author has been asserted

All rights reserved
Without limiting the rights under copyright
reserved above, no part of this publication may be
reproduced, stored in or introduced into a retrieval system,
or transmitted, in any form or by any means (electronic, mechanical,
photocopying, recording or otherwise), without the prior
written permission of both the copyright owner and
the above publisher of this book

Set in 12/14.75pt Bembo Book MT Std
Typeset by Jouve (UK), Milton Keynes
Printed in Great Britain by Clays Ltd, St Ives plc

A CIP catalogue record for this book is available from the British Library

ISBN: 978–1–844–88332–5

www.greenpenguin.co.uk

MIX
Paper from
responsible sources
FSC™ C018179

Penguin Books is committed to a sustainable
future for our business, our readers and our planet.
This book is made from Forest Stewardship
Council™ certified paper.

For my mother, Margaret, my father,
Paddy, and my brother, Kevin

While in the merry month of May from my home I started . . .
Saluted father dear, kissed my darling mother . . .
See the lassies smile, laughing all the while
At my curious style, 'twould set your heart a-bubblin'.
Asked me was I hired, wages I required,
I was almost tired of the Rocky Road to Dublin.

From 'The Rocky Road', as sung by Luke Kelly

Contents

Acknowledgements

As will be evident to any reader of this book, I have been very fortunate in my personal and professional life. The same is true of this attempt to tell my story. Many people were indispensable to my endeavours. My agent Peter Straus was patient beyond belief. His guidance was invaluable. Tony Lacey edited the manuscript with great skill. As a young man, Tony bought and published my first book, *Only a Game?*, thirty-seven years ago. The book is still in print. And we remain good friends. Tony is generous, literate and fun. Without him, this book would not have been published.

During the two years it took to complete it, Clodagh Lynam and Michael O'Connor offered constant support. The bad grammar, iffy syntax and faltering narrative, not to mention my bad spelling, were all fixed by Clodagh and Michael. I am indebted to both. At a critical moment, Colm Tóibín offered wise counsel. He was unbelievably generous, for which I am deeply grateful. Hazel Orme did a superb job editing the copy.

Michael McLoughlin and Brendan Barrington of Penguin Ireland have been of enormous assistance, particularly on the home stretch. Andrew O'Rorke of Hayes and Co. legalled my text. Wise, thoughtful and sensitive to the text, Andrew is an exceptional man.

As many authors have noted, the staff at the National Library are unfailingly courteous and efficient. Sue Gogan did much research in the library for me, for which I am very grateful.

John Giles has been my friend, mentor and colleague for a very long time. John made a huge contribution to this book. He has an astonishing memory, which I plundered at will. Liam Brady, a victim of my crazy pen on occasions too numerous to mention, has happily become a very good friend and colleague. His insight into the Charlton era was invaluable. Bill O'Herlihy was helpful in many ways, notably about my flirtation with Garret FitzGerald's Fine Gael.

I'd like to thank Paul Brady and Christy Moore, two of our finest singer-songwriters, for generously allowing me to use their lyrics.

My friends Noel Pearson, PJ Mara, Shane Ross and Oliver Barry still think I'm mad. But they helped refresh my memory of the Horseshoe Bar and other things.

Patrick Guilbaud reminded me of moments we'd shared that I'd forgotten. He was an enthusiastic supporter all the way.

Colleagues Kieran Cunningham, Paddy Agnew, Ger Colleran, Eoin Brannigan, Frank Connelly and Eimear Bradley all helped greatly. As did an old friend, Nicky Coffey, one of Ireland's most astute political journalists.

Dessie Toal's son, John, provided a wonderful photograph of the Dump. Photographers Ray McManus, Derek Speirs and Billy Stickland went out of their way to find many of the evocative images in the book. Alan Manicom, sports editor of the *Reading Post*, kindly produced a photograph of the bullock.

My friend Liz Brennan gave me a lovely photograph of her late husband Shay, Harry Gregg and myself.

Harry Gregg enriched my research with wonderfully vivid memories of Old Trafford during the Busby era. Harry also gave me a splendid photograph of the Manchester United staff from a photoshoot in 1961. Ann and Denise Dunphy were very helpful with photographs and recollections of my family. Paul Rowan of the *Sunday Times* generously allowed me to quote extensively from his excellent book *The Team That Jack Built*.

Sadly, three of the most important people in my life, Tim O'Connor, Aengus Fanning and Dessie Toal, passed away while I was writing the book. I think very fondly of each of them and thank God for their generosity to me.

Finally, I must thank my family. My wife, Jane Gogan, my children, Tim and Colette, and Jane's daughter, Rosie, for their constant love and support.

1. What's in a Name?

On St Patrick's Day 1943 Éamon de Valera addressed the Irish people on Radio Éireann. He had been Taoiseach for eleven years. Dev was the most influential Irishman of his time. More than a mere politician, he was the nation's spiritual and cultural icon. Often derided by Irish intellectuals in the decades that followed, his vision as expressed in 1943 resonated with a majority of the people he led, among them my mother, Margaret.

Two years after Dev's famous speech, my mother would name me after him. If my father, Paddy, had been doing the naming, my given name might well have been Jim, after the charismatic labour leader Jim Larkin. Big Jim was someone my father deeply admired and frequently quoted. The difference between my parents' political preferences was irrelevant when set against the deep love they felt for each other. Paddy would sometimes tease Peg, as he called her, about Dev; she might respond by reminding Dad that Larkin's finest hour, his leadership of the workers during the 1913 Dublin Lockout, had ended in abject failure when, starved and humiliated, the strikers had shuffled back to work for the cruel merchants who had resisted their claims for a decent living wage.

When my brother was born two years after me, my mother named him Kevin after Kevin Barry, the eighteen-year-old medical student executed by the British in 1920. Barry was offered his freedom in return for the names of his fellow volunteers. He refused to give them and was hanged. Another martyr for old Ireland, as a line from a popular ballad about Barry put it.

My mother's background, like that of so many Irish people, was rural, devoutly Catholic and poor. It was at that constituency that Dev's radio speech was aimed:

> The ideal Ireland that we would have, the Ireland that we dreamed of, would be the home of a people who valued material wealth only as a basis for right living, of a people who, satisfied with frugal comfort, devoted their leisure to the things of the spirit – a land whose countryside would

be bright with cosy homesteads, whose fields and villages would be joyous with the sounds of industry, with the romping of sturdy children, the contest of athletic youths and the laughter of happy maidens whose firesides would be forums for the wisdom of serene old age. The home, in short, of a people living the life that God desires that men should live.

Before returning to Dev's homily about the virtues of frugal living (there is some guff about patriotic sacrifice to follow), we should note that he was a massive swindler, a con artist who had robbed thousands of Irish and American people of $250,000, which he had raised to set up the *Irish Press*, a newspaper 'for the people' that he promised would be 'committed to telling the truth in news'.

Founded in 1931, twelve years before the 'Ireland that we dreamed of' speech, the *Irish Press* was primarily an organ of propaganda for Dev's Fianna Fáil (the Soldiers of Destiny) party, an organizational mix of the Moonies and the Mafia that was committed to one thing only: the retention of political power.

The well-meaning investors, most of them domiciled in the United States, which at the time was mired in the Great Depression, were gulled by a simple corporate manoeuvre. Instead of receiving shares in Irish Press Limited they received certificates from Irish Press Corporation, which was registered in the tax-haven state of Delaware. Once Dev had the $250,000, Irish Press Limited issued 60,000 A-class share certificates from Irish Press Corporation. Those pieces of paper were worthless. Control of the publishing company would rest with the owner of the 200 B-class shares, the God-fearing patriot Éamon de Valera. The scam that he 'dreamed of' would not be fully exposed for decades.

Viewed in the context of the share shakedown, the evocative speech of St Patrick's Day 1943 acquires an element of cruel, peculiarly Irish farce:

> . . . with the tidings that make such an Ireland possible, St Patrick came to our ancestors fifteen hundred years ago promising happiness here no less than happiness hereafter. It was the pursuit of such an Ireland that later made our country worthy to be called the Island of the Saints and Scholars. It was the idea of such an Ireland – happy, vigorous, spiritual – that fired the imagination of our poets, that made successive generations of patriotic men give their lives to win political and religious liberty and will urge men in our own and future generations to die, if need be, so

that these liberties be preserved. One hundred years ago, the Young Ire-
landers, by holding up the vision of such an Ireland before the people,
inspired and moved them spiritually as our people had hardly been
moved since the Golden Age of Irish Civilization. Fifty years later, the
founders of the Gaelic League similarly inspired the people of their day.
So later, did the leaders of the Irish Volunteers. *(The IRA!)*

We of this time, if we have the will and active enthusiasm, have the
opportunity to inspire and move our generation in a like manner. We
can do so by keeping this thought of a noble future for our country con-
stantly before our eyes, ever seeking in action to bring that future into
being and ever remembering that it is for our nation as a whole that
future must be sought.

That last reference to 'our nation as a whole' was a sly signal that he had
not forgotten the core principle of the anti-Treaty side in the Civil
War – a united Ireland – for which so many of his comrades had given
their life. This cause, upon which his leadership and the initial legitimacy of the Fianna Fáil Party were founded, had hardly been advanced
during his period as Taoiseach.

The reference to religious liberty was similarly disingenuous: his
God was Catholic; the Ireland that he dreamed of, ruled by Catholic
dogma, was a place that would have been hostile to men like Robert
Emmet, Wolfe Tone and Charles Stewart Parnell, all of whom were
Protestants offering a truly republican vision profoundly at odds with
de Valera's narrow Catholic nationalism.

I have often wondered what drew my mother to Mr de Valera. The
answer may be that he wasn't W. T. Cosgrave, Dev's main political rival
in the 1920s and early 1930s. It is impossible to imagine Cosgrave, a
Dubliner, articulating, as Dev did, the romantic vision of Ireland that so
appealed to a countrywoman.

In the fiction that is Official Irish history, Cosgrave is a revered figure.
He took the pro-Treaty side with Michael Collins and led the first Irish
government when the Irish Free State was formed in 1922. Cosgrave
was a publican before becoming a gunman, or freedom fighter, as these
killers have come to be regarded with the passage of time. My mother
wasn't mad about publicans.

But perhaps her affection for Dev, the pious romantic, was essentially
a rejection of Cosgrave's extreme right-wing politics, which are best

summarized in a letter he wrote to a colleague in 1921, when he was minister for local government.

> As you are aware, people reared in workhouses are no great acquisition to human society. As a rule, their highest aim is to live at the expense of the ratepayers. As a consequence, it would be a decided gain if they took it into their heads to emigrate. When abroad, they are thrown onto their own responsibilities and have to work whether they like it or not.

It would be wrong to conclude from my mother's devotion to Dev and my father's admiration for Larkin that ours was a political home. In fact, politics was rarely mentioned. My parents were too busy surviving to waste time chewing the political fat. Home for the four of us was one room with no hot water or electricity. The house was a one-storey-over-a-basement dwelling on Richmond Road, Drumcondra. The basement was occupied by a family of four. We lived above, across the hall from a childless couple.

Remarkably, I recall no contact between the three families in the fifteen years I spent there. While my father was a genial man, always in good humour, my mother was intensely private. She had no time for what she derisively described as 'gossip'. So the door of our room stayed firmly shut. Her time was spent taking care of Kevin and me and her husband, Paddy, to whom she was so clearly devoted.

Peg was raised in Foynes, County Limerick. As a young teenager she set out for Dublin, finding employment as a nanny/housekeeper for a well-off Dublin family. She left Ireland on only one occasion: on a holiday with her employers to the Isle of Man. Often, while we were growing up, she would regale Kevin and me with the wonders of that trip. The funfair, the cafés, the buzz of the Isle of Man beguiled her, offering a singular glimpse of a world other than the one she, like so many of her generation, inhabited – the world of grinding deprivation and never-ceasing obligation to God, employer, priest or politician.

Yet in our room Peg was happy, sometimes joyously so in the role of mother and wife. She would sing the songs of John McCormack, which she loved, no less because he was a papal count. Another favourite was 'I Dreamt I Dwelt In Marble Halls', the story of a Romany girl who dreamed of living 'with vassals and serfs by my side'. A particularly poignant lyric, given our circumstances.

In our early years on Richmond Road, Peg was happy. There were many reasons, though, to regard the outside world with suspicion or grim hostility. As very young children, my brother and I were shielded from the problems our parents faced on an almost daily basis.

My father worked as a builder's labourer for Macken's, the most rapacious employers in a business notorious for its exploitative bosses. This was brutal work for any man, and particularly for Paddy, a gentle, good-natured soul. He worked six-day weeks except when rain stopped play and labourers entered 'broken time' for which they got no wages. It rains a lot in Ireland.

His daily return to our room was cause for rejoicing. He and Peg would embrace, she enquiring if he was all right, relief on her face that he had survived another day. While he washed off the muck and grime of the building site in the warm water she had heated, Peg would put his dinner on the table. The gaslight flickered, the room now filled with unspoken love and peace.

He would always have the newspapers, the *Irish Independent* and the *Evening Mail*. From a very early age I would grab them to read about the world. Pre-school and pre-friends, except for Kevin, the papers were my only contact with the world outside our room. I devoured them every night from back to front, from sport to politics, gossip and foreign affairs.

Before bed each night, the four of us knelt to say a decade of the rosary. This was no mere ritual, rather an intense expression of gratitude for all the mercies of that day.

It was almost thirty years later that my father told me about the difficulties he and my mother had grappled with after Kevin was born. We were having a drink in Fagan's pub in Drumcondra, his local, a drinking shop that would hit the headlines many years later as the bar where Bertie Ahern and his courtiers hung out. The subject of religion came up. I was by then estranged from, if not downright hostile to, the Catholic Church. Still the story Dad told me – and the emotion he displayed while he did so – has remained indelibly in my mind. With two young children and one room to live in, Peg and Paddy faced a dilemma. There was no space for another body. While our parents slept in the bed, Kevin and I shared a mattress on the floor. That was fine for Kevin and me, but for a couple in their late twenties, sex became a risky business. Should my mother conceive – the purpose of sex, according to Catholic dogma – we were in trouble.

5

Seeking guidance, Peg went to see Father McDonald, the parish priest in Fairview, our nearest church. McDonald was a very visible character on the local landscape. Stern and stocky, he often strode the streets in search of sinners. Young courting couples in nearby Fairview Park might suddenly be confronted by the dog-collared bully who ordered that they stop sinning.

Young people hanging out on street corners – in the early fifties, there was little else to do – were also subject to McDonald's wrath. Sometimes he got physical, his icy stare the precursor to a blow to the head from his meaty fist. He was also known for his sermons in which he hectored his parishioners for sins, real or imagined, they may or may not have committed. It was, it seemed, his mission to instil fear in the community. The impression left was that if you thought he was vengeful, the Creator whose message he was conveying would be much more rigorous when you stood before Him to account for yourself.

History has rendered such creeps a sick joke, but in our time, McDonald and his ilk were no laughing matter. It was to McDonald my mother turned seeking counsel. She was as devout as one could be, a daily mass-goer; a modest woman who sought nothing more than to live her life as God would have it lived.

McDonald treated her with contempt, according to my father. As he listened to her story, McDonald bristled with impatience. Why was she bothering him when the solution to her problem was so obvious? It was clear what she must do: stop having sex with your husband or suffer the pain of mortal sin.

Distressed as much by the callous manner of its delivery as by the message itself, my mother returned home to tell my dad. Reflecting on her pain three decades later, Paddy's eyes filled with tears. My own response was anger, not just for the mother I loved but for generations of Irish women – and men – whose lives were scarred by monsters like McDonald.

The option of moving from our room to somewhere with more space had to be considered. Alas, on a builder's labourer's wages (minus 'broken time'), the only possible alternative was local-authority housing, which posed a major problem for Peg and Paddy.

Both were, at heart, country people. Even though my father had been born in Dublin, his roots were in Kilkenny among the farming stock his parents came from. My paternal grandfather, Martin, was the eldest son of a comfortable farming family. He came to Dublin for love, forfeiting his inheritance to pursue his romantic dream.

Native Dubliners, real Dubs, as they were called, were very unlike their country cousins. The differences were magnified among the less well-off and this was keenly felt, especially by my mother, who often spoke scornfully of 'Jackeens', as real Dubs were dismissively known to proud country people. Real Dubs were coarser. They ate processed food from tins and packets. They couldn't grow cabbages or spuds. They made nothing except noise. The women dressed immodestly, adorned with lipstick and powder, and they kept bad company in pubs and dancehalls.

At times, Peg spun much humour out of the fact that Paddy, Kevin and I were all Jackeens and the lesser for it. But beneath the banter something tangible was in play: a real alienation from what Peg perceived as the bawdy artifice of real Dubs, which was reflected in what they ate, what they wore and how they behaved. At best they were dumb, at worst loathsome.

My father was less judgemental: he got along with people in the way that many men do in pubs, sports clubs or, in his case, on building sites. Paddy suspended disbelief while indulging the male impulse for superficial buddydom.

Now, though, on the important matter of where to live and raise two children, he deferred to my mother. Staying in our room on Richmond Road meant bearing the burden imposed by Father McDonald. The alternative was to apply for local-authority housing in one of the inner-city flat complexes or suburban estates that were expanding around Dublin to accommodate the working class (or, as Peg would sometimes slyly suggest, the work-shy class).

The idea of living among the realest of real Dubs appalled my mother. The flats and estates populated by Jackeens eating from tins and packets or straight from fish 'n' chip shops, wearing garish clothes, powdered and lipsticked and lazy, was not for her, her husband and especially not for Kevin and me.

By contrast with the real or imagined horrors of 'Jackeen' land, Drumcondra was an oasis of genteel respectability. Everybody worked most of the time. The locale was inhabited by junior civil servants, small shopkeepers, the better class of tradesman (printers being the princes), bank tellers, guards and nurses. Crucially, real Dubs were absent, by and large, and even more important was the fact that most at the Richmond Road end of Drumcondra were either country people or, like Paddy, first-generation Dubliners. That we were by far the least well-off mattered less, far less, than the comforting ambience of the neighbourhood.

The clinching point in my parents' deliberations concerned education. St Patrick's National School was less than five minutes' walk from our room. With a renowned teacher-training college attached, St Pat's was believed to be the best national school on the northside of the city. If celibacy was the price of a good education, Peg and Paddy were prepared to pay.

2. Out and About

I started school in September 1950. I was five, shy and small for my age. Our family had lived in what might be best described as contented solitude. Day one was a huge shock. I cried for my mother as soon as she left the school gates; nothing unusual in that. However, I bawled so hysterically that our teacher, Mr Hayden, had to summon her to take me home. Somehow I was coaxed back the following day. After my inauspicious start, things settled down. Looking back, the six years I spent in Mr Hayden's classroom were hugely important. He knew my family circumstances, where we stood socially, relative to my classmates. Initially, he factored this into class work in a nuanced way: the odd word of praise here and there; a short reading from an essay I'd submitted; maybe selecting me to answer a question he knew I had the answer to. His kindness extended to everyone in the class: the insecure or those unable to comprehend were treated with respect. I was a diligent student, others less so; one or two were on a mission to disrupt. It was a normal class, I suppose. Mr Hayden never lost his temper or control.

He was a countryman from Leitrim. His thatch of wild grey hair sprayed ungroomed in all directions. His slightly disorderly appearance contrasted favourably to us with the pinstriped conformity of his peers around the corridors. Not for the last time in my life I found a badly needed ally at just the right moment.

At year's end we got our exam results and a report to take home. In deference to the boys who had struggled, Hayden only announced the top three names. A genius named Bourke, the swot from Central Casting, came first. To my immense pride, I came second and a boy named Michael Tutty finished third. Michael, another swottish type, would later confirm his promise by becoming a senior civil servant in the Department of Finance and subsequently Ireland's energy regulator.

Though still painfully shy outside the classroom, I began to make friends at St Pat's. A boy called Ray Redmond became a particular buddy. Football was the passion we shared. I had been playing with a ball, usually a worn tennis ball, for ever, always on my own on a narrow strip of ground behind our house. We lived on the edge of what was known as Hennessy's Field. Nobody knew who Hennessy was. All we knew was that he never tended his field, which was a jungle full of weeds and nettles. A group of local people had cleared a patch of land close to the road to create some space for kids to play. This was known as the Dump.

The uneven wall bordering the Dump was essential to achieving the objective of mastering the ball. When the ball was struck, the wall returned it speedily at crazy angles. The desired outcome was control with your first touch. Progress was control while turning past an imaginary opponent behind you.

Winter and summer I spent long, lonely hours absorbed in this exercise. Now with Ray Redmond, I went in search of real opposition. Such forays were not without their complications in the early fifties. First you had to find a game you could join. Ray, an extrovert, was the man for that particular task.

Griffith Park, close to St Pat's on the banks of the Tolka river, was usually our best bet. 'The Park', as we knew it, was a wonderful amenity filled with all kinds of possibilities, the most alarming of which to me was the prospect of meeting girls. Incredible though it may seem, at the age of six I had never spoken to a girl. For several years to come, that remained the case.

But it was in the Park that I discovered I could play ball against real opponents, all of whom were bigger, stronger and, at first, more practised than me. The matches were improvised and played with savage intensity. Anyone could participate. There was no upper age limit, although for kids like Ray and me some street cred was required to get into the ball game. Ray had the street cred and it turned out that I had enough game to achieve some status.

With no referee and coats or jumpers for goal posts, the scope for disputes was mighty. For the most part things worked out, justice depending on the karmatic principle that what goes around comes around. If there was a greater conclusion to be drawn from the dispute mechanism used to deliver justice on the streets – Drumcondra's anyway – it was that usually a majority favoured fairness.

Indeed, justice was essential to the proceedings, as was evident on the rare occasions agreement could not be reached. A fair score denied, or dodgy goal awarded, sometimes brought the match to a premature end. 'Fuck it, we're off,' the aggrieved would declare, the Pyrrhic victory that ensued leaving a hollow feeling in the gut of the opponents.

As summer drew to an end and minds focused on the new school year, an added burden was placed on my mother's weekly budget. New clothes were needed. Also, more critically, I would need new school books. The extra money required simply wasn't there. Every week was a battle for survival.

For a couple of reasons, our circumstances were particularly acute. In the poorer parts of the city, where Fate (and Father McDonald) ordained that we belonged, there was at least a certain solidarity in the community: everyone was in it together. In the matter of dress, for example, frayed cuffs and collars were of little or no consequence when your mates were similarly togged out. Ditto patches on the cheap, flimsy flannel trousers we wore before the miracle of denim equalized the game for future generations. Thanks to Penneys and Dunnes Stores, kids' clothes today are both affordable and durable. It is impossible to distinguish between rich and poor on the basis of clothing. In fifties Drumcondra the frayed cuff, patched trouser or darned sock was a sign of poverty.

With two growing children, my mother was in a ceaseless battle. Her problem was compounded by her ban on cheaper convenience foods from packets or tins. Food, or nourishment, as she described it, was the number-one priority for her children and her hard-labouring, adored husband. Fresh vegetables, fruit, good meat and fish were our staples. The room smelt like a bakery with apple and rhubarb pies and home-baked bread in the oven.

Her endless seeking out of quality food, an exercise conducted with missionary zeal, is one of the abiding memories of my childhood. Pre-school, Kevin and I would accompany Peg on her daily shopping expedition. Before the days of supermarkets, the hunt for food consisted of a tour of small shops where the fare on offer was variable to say the least. If, as was the case with Peg, only the best would do, tenacity was required. Many of the small shopkeepers were rogues. Drumcondra's butchers – there were five – were her most persistent foes.

A countrywoman, she knew the difference between good, bad or indifferent cuts of meat. Of course, you couldn't tell just by looking. The proof was in the eating. Beef properly hung and aged tastes an awful lot better. When she was duped, as frequently happened, Peg's wrath was fearsome. Over the years she fell out with all five local butchers. On one memorable occasion, the offending piece of roast beef was returned to its supplier – who happened to be a neighbour on Richmond Road – with the suggestion that he feed it to his own family to see how they'd like it.

Embarrassed at the time, I now marvel at my mother's magnificent defiance of Drumcondra's merchant class. They were, in truth, many of them, bastards. What held for butchering was also true for vegetables and fruit. One of the butchers' favoured strokes concerned minced meat, which was the dish *du jour* when funds were running low. Knowing that what was already minced was rubbish, Peg would order a pound of round steak to be minced in her presence. This was duly done. Alas, what was ground out of the mincer was the usual old rubbish that had been in the machine all along.

An identical trick served to screw people looking for decent fruit and vegetables: behind the handsome triangle of potatoes, apples or cabbages lay the stale, the rotting, the overripe, which, by a manoeuvre worthy of a three-card-trick man, was bagged out of sight of the innocent customer. This ruse would be exposed only when the purchaser got home. As with the butcher, my mother would take the rubbish back and demand the kind of produce on display.

Even the simplest everyday transactions of life were tainted by venality, though the local swindlers cloaked their dishonesty in piety. The churches were packed every Sunday, standing room only, as they sought forgiveness for their sins before duly returning to fumble in their greasy tills on Monday morning.

In the form of Moore Street, the bustling city-centre market, the Irish genius for myth-making (and thieving) scaled epic heights. The street vendors, or hawkers as they were known, were invariably women, representing, it was claimed, the heart and soul of the city, real Dubs. In the fifties, as now, a trip to Moore Street was deemed essential for crooked local politicians – Charlie Haughey was a regular – seeking to curry favour with the People.

Similarly, when Official Ireland's media wanted to gauge the national mood, Moore Street was where they headed. Television and film cameras seemed permanently *in situ* to capture pictures of politicians, international celebrities and local chancers as they strolled among the People. The hard-faced hawkers played their parts to perfection:

'How'ya, Charlie?' they would holler, one eye on the cameras. He would incline his head like royalty and smile benignly, a statesman among his beloved people. Liz Taylor and Richard Burton, Richard Harris, Peter O'Toole and Grace Kelly, all had availed themselves of this landmark photo opportunity. 'How'ya, Liz?' 'How'ya, Richard?' 'How'ya, Grace?' Had Adolf Hitler prevailed in the Second World War – and Official Ireland did little to prevent that outcome – I have no doubt he would have walked the walk down Moore Street. 'How'ya, Adolf?'

For most Dubliners Moore Street was a place to avoid, a film set for politicians on the make and gullible international celebrities. Its denizens survived by selling shite to those desperate for a bargain, and enjoyed their fame as extras in Official Ireland's fictional version of the real Dublin.

In moments of extreme desperation, my mother ventured to this dreadful, dirty place. Late in the day it was conceivable that a bargain might be had, a head of cabbage, some apples, some oranges that were just on the right side of edible. As Peg reached out to touch an item on display, she would receive a sharp rebuke from behind the stall – 'Fuck off back to where you came from, missus, don't touch the produce.' We fucked off back to Drumcondra, where warfare was conducted on more nuanced terms.

In order to get my clothes and books for the new school year my mother went to the lender of last resort in those days, the pawn shop. The only item she had to pledge was Paddy's Sunday suit. I vividly remember her folding the suit, packing it in brown paper secured by twine. Off we headed to Dorset Street, Kevin and I traipsing anxiously by Peg's side. As children often do, we knew instinctively that this was to some degree a humiliating step into the unknown for this proud, defiant countrywoman.

Watches, wedding rings and fancy clocks were the usual offerings accepted by pawnbrokers. What price a Sunday suit from Burtons? As it happened, the gentleman behind the counter, perhaps sensing my mother's distress, was courteous and respectful as he opened the parcel to inspect the pledge. 'How much, ma'am?' he enquired.

'Two pounds,' Peg ventured.

He smilingly assented, explaining the terms and conditions. As transactions go, this one was civil, with immeasurably more integrity at its heart than we were used to in Drumcondra's meat and vegetable bazaars.

Just when we needed to we encountered a decent man. He was Jewish or, in the vile patois of the pious Roman Catholics we lived among, 'a Jewboy'. The respect that man extended to my mother meant even more than the desperately needed couple of pounds.

Outside the classroom, football and reading were my consuming passions. Ray Redmond, extrovert Ray, was the leader of our gang of two. He started to organize pre-class football on Millbourne Avenue, the side street adjacent to St Pat's. All kinds of obstacles had to be overcome to play effective ball: the kerb of the footpath, passers-by, cyclists on their way to work and the ire of shopkeepers whose businesses formed the opposite touchline to the school wall.

Another acute concern in the early fifties was securing a ball to play with. Known as a 'bouncer', the favoured alternative to the tennis ball was half the size and twice as volatile as a proper leather football. They were hard to come by. The kid who owned one was certain to get his game. It was a happy day when you had a bouncer that stayed unburst or unconfiscated by angry residents or grocers. Street soccer required uncommon resourcefulness even before the game began.

The best street players were masters of invention and guile. Seeing Lionel Messi today, you witness the street game at its most beguiling. The shimmies and swivels, the feint, the dummy, the rapid change of pace and direction, the knowledge without looking of where every foe is lurking and every team-mate waiting, the glorious elusiveness, the wit, all being consummated by the stunning final execution of a telling goal. This is the beautiful game of legend. No teacher or coach can impart the imagination and dexterity required to be a master of this art.

3. Holy Ireland

Fifties Dublin was bleak in so many ways. Austerity was the norm for working-class people. Austerity or, worse, the grinding poverty that came with unemployment. Fear was a common emotion: fear that you might lose your job, or that your children would be jobless, would turn to drink or crime, or resort, as so many did, to emigration.

Presiding over all of this was a callous and greedy ruling class, their wickedness redeemed by the weekly visit to the confession box. At Sunday mass, they stuck their tongues out to receive Communion, the sliver of wine-soaked bread that wiped the slate clean. This was the Holy Catholic Ireland that de Valera dreamed of, a nation he governed in close collaboration with the Catholic clergy.

In 1948, this spell was briefly broken in an election when Fianna Fáil lost power. A coalition inter-party government was formed. This new regime incorporated a rump of disillusioned republicans who'd come to the view that the Ireland de Valera dreamed of was a sick parody of the vision many liberty-seeking idealists had given their lives for. But it was headed by a deeply conservative Fine Gael majority who ensured their leader, John A. Costello, would be the new Taoiseach. Many scholars have written about the distinction between Fine Gael and Fianna Fáil. Both asserted their patriotism. Both fought the British. Michael Collins, once a close comrade of Dev's, signed the Treaty with the Brits that split the republican movement. Dev was anti-Treaty, an all-or-nothing man, or so it seemed.

Fine Gael's forerunner party, Cumann na nGaedheal, formed the first Irish government, but a civil war broke out and Collins was murdered, shot in the back. Later, Dev, tiring of the wilderness and the powerlessness, discovered the wonders of democracy, the folly of the gun and the potency of politics. The brutal truth behind the endless republican myth-making, which continues to this day, is that snobbery and prejudice lay at the heart of the arguments dividing Ireland's governing class.

To Fine Gaelers, Fianna Fáil was lower-caste, venal, shamelessly populist and utterly unfit to govern. Fianna Fáil levelled equally grave charges against Fine Gael. The Blueshirts, as Fine Gael were known, in reference to the uniforms worn by an army association linked to them, were the party of the self-regarding cohort in Irish society who believed in their inalienable right to govern, the party of big farmers, the merchant class, fat-cat barristers and others in the professional middle class.

In their damning assessments of each other, the dominant players in Irish politics were accurate. What distinguished Fianna Fáil, ensuring that they were the country's most popular party, was the fantasy that they might some day complete the unfinished business of uniting Ireland.

What might become of the large Protestant community in the six Northern counties 'occupied' by Britain was a particularly intriguing question when viewed in the context of the Irish Constitution drafted by de Valera in 1937. In this document, a 'special position' was reserved for the Roman Catholic Church. Protestantism was 'recognized', whatever that was supposed to mean. This recognition did not extend to allowing Protestants to exercise their civil rights in matters as fundamental as contraception and divorce.

In truth, Dev's constitution was a profoundly discriminatory document, a parody of republicanism. How the constitution could be reconciled with the united Ireland project has never been explained. Some of Fianna Fáil's more ardent supporters favoured the option of 'driving' the hundreds of thousands of northern Protestants 'into the sea'.

The existence of the bigots' charter that was the 1937 constitution did nothing to stem the tide of the republican sentiment that typically found expression in popular rebel ballads, one of the most popular being a song written in the nineteenth century by the nationalist Thomas Davis. 'A Nation Once Again' was sung with lusty relish and not just by drunks at closing time. Davis was a Protestant, ironically, but the people singing his song certainly weren't. Artists as renowned as Count John McCormack, the Dubliners and the Clancy Brothers also recorded the ditty, which, like the constitution, must have alarmed any listening 'Prods':

A Nation once again,
A Nation once again,
And Ireland, long a province, be
A Nation once again!

God is also invoked:

For, Freedom comes from God's right hand
And needs a Godly train;
And righteous men must make our land
A Nation once again.

Such cant never failed to rally the Fianna Fáil troops. They were our Soldiers of Destiny untainted by the original sin of the Peace Treaty with the Brits; Fine Gael could never compete with the true Gaels led by Dev.

Ideologically, there was little between the dominant parties that emerged from the Civil War. The kind of left/right divisions that defined politics in Britain or France did not exist in Ireland. Socialism was regarded as a dangerous, Godless aberration that posed a mortal threat to the Catholic piety embraced by Dev, the constitution and, even more fervently, by Blueshirt leaders like John A. Costello.

The two mass-circulation newspaper groups were avowedly conservative Catholic. And the embryonic broadcasting service Radio Éireann (now RTÉ) was controlled by the government, whose stooges manned the microphones.

Reflecting on the Ireland of 1942, the celebrated writer Frank O'Connor argued that it was impossible to write a normal social novel in this place: 'The moment a writer raises his eyes from the slums and cabins, he finds nothing but a vicious and ignorant middle class, and for aristocracy, the remnants of an English garrison, alien in religion and education. From such material, he finds it almost impossible to create a picture of life . . . A realistic literature is clearly impossible.'

That is why three of Ireland's greatest writers had fled the Ireland de Valera dreamed of. Sharing Frank O'Connor's analyses, Samuel Beckett, James Joyce and Sean O'Casey chose permanent exile from what was in truth a moral, intellectual and political slum. Writers who opted to stay paid with their lives. Brendan Behan, Patrick Kavanagh and Brian O'Nolan drank themselves to death, overwhelmed by the stench of corrupt mediocrity. Alcohol was, as Kavanagh later wrote, the anaesthetic required to function in Dev's dreamland.

The inter-party government of 1948 is remembered for what seems in retrospect a relatively modest reform of the health service. In Britain, Clement Attlee's post-war Labour government had passed legislation to introduce a free-to-all National Health Service. Attlee gave the task of creating the NHS to Aneurin Bevan, his minister for health. Faced by opposition from reactionaries in the medical profession and the media, Bevan, a robust Welsh socialist, deployed his political skills, not least among them a gift for oratory, to ensure the passage of legislation that transformed the lives of ordinary citizens. His radical health legislation was hailed internationally as a victory for social justice. Here was tangible proof that those ordinary citizens who had sacrificed so much to defeat Fascism had not suffered in vain.

The kind of mass labour movement that produced Nye Bevan simply did not exist in Ireland. Generally, those seeking political power gravitated to one or other of two Civil War parties. The result was – and remains – a grotesquely dysfunctional political system.

Noël Browne was appointed minister for health by the inter-party government that took office in 1948. A medical doctor who had lost both his parents to tuberculosis and had himself survived the then killer disease, Browne entered government determined to fix a health system that inflicted the most injustice on people of little or no means. He was one of ten deputies elected to the new Dáil for Clann na Poblachta, a republican socialist party led by Seán MacBride, who had been Chief of Staff of the IRA as recently as 1936. Clann na Poblachta was the third-largest party in government. Fine Gael was the largest grouping, followed by the Labour Party. John A. Costello, a barrister who had flirted with European Fascism a decade earlier, was Taoiseach. William Norton, the Labour Party leader, was Costello's deputy. Norton, it would later emerge, was a member of the Knights of Columbanus, a secret Masonic-style cabal of conservative Catholics. Norton was no Nye Bevan.

As well as exhibiting a fondness for Hitler and Mussolini, expressed openly in a Dáil debate in 1934, Costello was a Catholic extremist. 'I am,' he famously declared, 'an Irishman second, I am a Catholic first, and I accept without qualification in all respects the teaching of the hierarchy and the Church to which I belong.'

Noël Browne had campaigned as a radical and behaved accordingly in office. Inspired by Nye Bevan and Franklin D. Roosevelt's New Deal Democrats, he began to talk about justice and inequality, particularly in the provision of healthcare. He floated the idea of a state-funded health-care system. He introduced free mass screening for tuberculosis. New vaccines and drugs were becoming available to treat not just tuber-culosis but polio and other previously untreatable medical conditions. Who would pay? The state, Browne argued. He began to sell off state assets to purchase drugs for those without the means to pay. Browne was making waves . . . and saving lives. The introduction of strepto-mycin and mass screening reduced the incidence of TB in Ireland dramatically.

Browne's first two years in office saw him emerge as a champion of the dispossessed. My father admired him greatly. To others, not least his government colleagues, Browne was a dangerous radical out of control. Among those others was the Catholic Church, which controlled virtu-ally every hospital and the medical profession, which at the high end was dominated by conservative Catholics. Notions about state-funded healthcare were not exactly original. De Valera's post-war government had introduced a Health Act that broached the question of equality. The trouble with Noël Browne was that he actually began doing things.

Ranged against him was an awesome coalition of politicians, priests, doctors and a media consensus that was, save a couple of contrary commentators, deeply reactionary. In the battle between Them and Us, Irish newspapers were on their side, not ours.

By late 1950 when he published his proposals for the Mother and Child Scheme, I was following Browne's story via the papers and my father's dinner-table recounting of it. As we saw it, this was the tale of one good man, great, according to my dad, fighting a rotten system. Cops and robbers to my innocent mind. Cop and robbers would seem a more precise description.

The Mother and Child Scheme promised free maternity care for all mothers and free healthcare for all children up to the age of sixteen. It was partially designed to combat the infant-mortality rate, which was just about the highest in the developed world. Many more children died of neglect, malnutrition and other diseases in Ireland than, say, in Brit-ain, which was governed by Godless Protestants.

Browne's attempt to tackle this malaise met with savage resistance.

His cabinet colleagues were at first lukewarm about his plans. They soon hardened their position when the majority of Catholic bishops expressed their opposition. As the Church ran the hospitals no change was possible without their support. Doctors also weighed in, fearing loss of income. The opposition was led by the rather sinister Archbishop of Dublin, John Charles McQuaid. McQuaid took his orders from the Vatican. The papal perspective was summed up in an edict from Pope Pius XI: 'It is a fundamental principle of social philosophy, fixed and unchangeable, that one should not withdraw from individuals and commit to the community what they can accomplish by their own enterprise and industry.'

McQuaid was the enforcer of this right-wing dogma. People's welfare was the business of the Church, not the state. Birth control would follow the creation of a British-style welfare state. Even the Protestant Church of Ireland became alarmed, expressing the view that Browne's scheme represented 'a Communist interference in the family'.

McQuaid didn't just run the Church: he dominated the most powerful politicians and the mass media. Browne was quickly isolated and pilloried. He was a maverick (not good). He'd failed to turn up at cabinet meetings. He was arrogant in his discussions with colleagues and the bishops. He was temperamental, a prima donna. Much evidence was advanced to prove these allegations, including the revelation that he alone among cabinet colleagues had attended the Church of Ireland service to mark the death of Douglas Hyde, Ireland's first president. Hyde, a Protestant and Gaelic scholar, died in 1949. Browne's decision to enter St Patrick's Cathedral while other government ministers stood outside on the street was regarded as a betrayal, proof that he was not a man to trust.

In April 1951, Noël Browne was sacked by his party leader, Seán MacBride. McQuaid had won. As MacBride explained: 'Even if as Catholics we were prepared to take the responsibility of disregarding the bishops' views, which I do not think we can do, it would be politically impossible to do so. We are dealing with the considered views of the Catholic Church to which the vast majority of our people belong. Those views cannot be ignored.'

With republican socialists like MacBride, who needed a conservative right-wing Catholic cabal to do the dirty work? MacBride's craven capitulation to the reactionaries on the Mother and Child Scheme leads us once more to the unique Irish genius for myth-making. While Noël Browne was cast into the political wilderness, MacBride the capitulator became one of Ireland's most celebrated international crusaders for peace and justice. So potent did his myth become that he managed the extraordinary feat of winning both the Nobel and Lenin Prizes.

The citation for his Nobel award described 'a man who mobilized the conscience of the world in the fight against injustice'. Of course, to elevate MacBride, Official Ireland needed to denigrate Noël Browne. As the winners write the history, that was easily achieved, though not in our small living room where he remained for my father a hero, an honourable casualty in the war against injustice. The Communist tyrants who presented MacBride with the Lenin Prize doubtless thought him a useful idiot.

Not long before this great Irishman died, the journalist Mary Holland went to interview him in his Dublin home. He asked for £100, a princely sum in the 1980s. Mary later told me he was the most unpleasant individual she had ever encountered.

The inter-party government fell apart soon after Browne's dismissal. He stood successfully as an independent in the subsequent election but his time had passed. Later there would be a brief flirtation with Fianna Fáil, for whom he was a candidate in the 1957 general election. This time the electorate rejected him and his adopted party returned John A. Costello to power.

I was too young to understand the realpolitik of the Mother and Child Scheme saga. But the newspaper photographs of the forlorn Browne, pain etched on his drawn face, told their own story. 'He was a decent man,' my father remarked, as we sat at dinner that night. His despair was almost palpable.

4. Dessie

Our lives took a turn for the better when we had electricity installed and we acquired a radio, a huge rather mysterious piece of furniture manufactured by Pye. This magic box was bought by hire purchase, or HP, as the arrangement was commonly known. My mother disliked the notion of buying things you couldn't afford. In her mind there was something dubious about HP, which involved weekly repayments after an initial down-payment. But her reservations dissolved as time passed.

For me, street life was dominated by football: the impoverished games between classes at St Pat's and the epic after-school clashes in the Dump. At St Pat's, Ray Redmond and I were the organizers as well as the best players. The Dump was another story. The kids were older, stronger, more accomplished. I was way down the pecking order, lucky to get a game on bad days. I hung around awaiting my chance.

Dump football was organized by Dessie Toal, who was five years older than me. Dessie was the local gang leader. He was an outstanding footballer, a midfield general who controlled the tempo and the direction of any game he played in. Like all the best street footballers, Dessie had a mesmerizing array of tricks, feints and dummies that got opponents off balance. His passes were astutely accurate. In even the most chaotic game he pulled the strings effortlessly. When disputes arose, as they inevitably did in the street games, Dessie was the man who had the final say. He had about him a quiet authority that seemed to derive from something other than his playing skills.

His gang consisted of half a dozen lads, the youngest of whom was two years older than me. They smoked and kept pigeons in a shed in the back garden of his house in Clonturk Park, a posh location on the opposite side of the Dump from our house. After our matches, Dessie and his gang would saunter off to his pigeon loft. I was intrigued and envious. I can still recall the feeling of acute loneliness that consumed me after our games, watching Dessie's cheerful gang head off in the opposite direction.

Summer was the loneliest time. With school closed, the days were long and empty. Football was out of season, the Dump deserted by Dessie and his pals in favour of the seaside at Dollymount or Portmarnock. The lack of money to buy a bike or even an ice-cream left me isolated with only my ball, if I had one, for company. On wet summer days, going to the 'pictures' was the preferred alternative to beach life for the guys I played football with during the season. The Drumcondra cinema, the Drummer, was opposite St Pat's but the eightpence ticket was way beyond my means. Distraction came at a price I couldn't afford.

On one of those endless solitary afternoons when I was banging my ball against the Dump wall, I became conscious that I wasn't alone. A man whom I knew from the neighbourhood stood about ten yards away, watching my twists and dummies as I dribbled past my imaginary opponents. He approached with a compliment about my skill. He was carrying a bottle of lemonade and an apple, both of which he offered me. Though sensing something was not quite right, I accepted. He moved closer and reached for my waist. Confused and frightened, I backed away towards the wall. He closed in and pulled down my short trousers. He then attempted to perform oral sex on me, though I had no idea what that was then.

My screams must have scared him away. We were only thirty yards from the house. He left quickly. I stood in shock for a moment before racing home. 'What's wrong, boy, what happened?' my mother asked. I'm not sure how coherent my explanation was. Peg got her coat and we went to the police station in Whitehall. Details were given, forms filled in. The guards' calm demeanour was striking. They assured my mother they would look into it.

A couple of weeks passed. When nothing happened my mother went back to the guards. They had nothing to report. The neighbour had denied that any incident had taken place. File closed. This experience left no mark on my innocent mind. As I would discover, sexual deviancy was not uncommon in Drumcondra. Young boys would learn to work around it.

Encouraged by my teacher, Mr Hayden, I joined Drumcondra public library when I became eligible, aged seven. After complimenting me on an English essay I'd written, he'd asked about the books I read. I told him that I had never read a book, just my father's newspapers. Off I went to fill in my application forms. A week later my tickets arrived by post. Two tickets — one for fiction, one for non-fiction. Without

Mr Hayden's prompting, I would never have discovered Drumcondra's library at so young an age. For the next seven or eight years, I haunted the place. On my first visit I was struck by the silence and the kindness of the staff who directed me to the children's section.

My non-fiction choice was relatively easy. From the many sports books available, I chose one about Stanley Matthews, the legendary Blackpool and England winger, who had just won his first FA Cup winners' medal in the 1953 Wembley final that was already part of soccer folklore. Losing 3–1 to their opponents, Bolton Wanderers, Matthews's Blackpool seemed destined for disappointment until the hero who'd previously suffered two Cup Final defeats inspired his team to one of the great Wembley comebacks. The final score was 4–3, an epic victory on what was English football's greatest occasion.

As I stood perplexed, studying the fiction on offer, the lady librarian approached to inform me that they were about to close. I'd been there for ages, reading the dust jackets. She knew it was my first visit. She plucked a book from the shelf. 'Try this,' she suggested. It was from the *Just William* series by Richmal Crompton.

Forty-eight hours later I'd finished both books. Hungry for more, I returned to the library. I handed back my books and headed for the shelves. The librarian stopped me in my tracks. Bad news: I would have to wait two weeks before taking out more books, she explained.

'Why?' I asked.

'The rules,' she replied. I was baffled. I felt foolish, disappointed and angry. Two weeks can seem for ever when you're seven. I looked longingly at the mountain of books behind the librarian, trying to figure out a way to beat the system, but there was none. Crushed, I retreated.

The rules in the Dump remained the same. Status was achieved by performing. One evening after an epic contest in which I scored the winner, Dessie Toal invited me back to his shed with the other guys, the inner sanctum where he held court. He was a droll character. He smoked Player's Navy Cut. Although it wouldn't be long before I succumbed, I refused the proffered cigarette that first evening. Cards were another vice on offer. Hence the tables around which we sat. The others started playing poker – for money, which ruled me out.

Like Mr Hayden, Dessie Toal had a seminal influence on my life. Although I didn't have the means to participate fully – without a bike or money for the pictures that was impossible – Dessie made sure I was included when circumstances permitted. He introduced me to cigarettes and gave me my first big break in football. Outwardly, he was a cool cat, sardonically dismissive of conventional wisdom on subjects as various as football, films or girls. He was equally contemptuous of authority: the Church, the school and the guards who sought to enforce the laws governing the petty bourgeois world we inhabited. 'Fuck them' was his attitude, uttered not with venom but softly, with a conspiratorial smile on his face. He was *the* man.

And his shed was *the* place to hang out, so much so that I was reluctant to go home for my dinner. One dark winter night my mother appeared at the door of the smoke-filled shed. Worried and angry, she ordered me out. Worried and embarrassed, I jumped off my perch. As my mother and I made our way home across the Dump, Dessie caught up with us. He apologized to my mother. 'It was my fault, Mrs Dunphy,' he volunteered. She was a formidable force when roused but somehow Dessie calmed her. What might have been a heavy-duty incident was averted by his respectful approach. 'He wasn't smoking,' Dessie lied. 'I wouldn't let him. Don't worry about Eamon, Mrs Dunphy, I'll look after him.'

Something about his manner persuaded her. 'You will, won't you?' she enquired.

'He'll be okay with us,' Dessie assured her.

From that day on all time-keeping or other breaches of my mother's norms were settled by the simple expedient of explaining that 'I was with Dessie.'

Quite apart from his charismatic personality, Dessie Toal was respected for his footballing skills. He was acknowledged to be one of the best players on the northside of the city. He was playing for Stella Maris, then one of two big northside schoolboy clubs, Home Farm being the other.

Among Dessie's team-mates at Stella was a boy called John Giles. In terms of soccer folklore, Dublin was a small town. The name Giles resonated before any of us saw him play. Paddy Mulvey, Tony Dunne, Frank O'Neill, Billy Dixon and Ben Hannigan were other boys deemed certain to 'make it'. Making it meant going to England to play as a professional. Liam Whelan from Home Farm, long talked about as a 'prospect', left for Manchester United in 1953. Whelan's name was known to every northside street kid. But, of them all, John Giles was said to be the best. According to legend, Giles possessed all the gifts. He could beat opponents with ease, score and make goals, and was equally accomplished with both feet. He was also said to be tough, small but fearless.

Most reputations were made on the streets and parks across the city. Organized schoolboy football was run by the Dublin and District Schoolboy League, the DDSL. The quest for cups began in their under-14 competitions. The really outstanding players could start aged eleven or twelve, giving away just a couple of years to the majority of players. Part of the Giles legend was that he started playing in schoolboy leagues aged eight.

When he was ten he was the most renowned young footballer in the city. It was rumoured that Manchester United were already chasing him. They were, in the person of another Dublin football legend, United scout Billy Behan. Behan had been a Manchester United player before the war. Returning to Dublin when he retired, he got a job in the glass-bottle company in Ringsend. He also stood as a bookie at the dog stadiums in Harold's Cross and Shelbourne Park.

Behan was a close personal friend of Matt Busby. They shared a love of soccer and gambling. Busby was in the process of revolutionizing English soccer. Change, as Busby envisaged it, meant finding the best young players in the British Isles and persuading them to join United, where they would learn not just how to play the game – with flair – but how to live their lives as professional sportsmen ideally should.

Character was a concept Busby referred to in almost every interview he ever gave. There were lots of gifted footballers, he pronounced, but character was the decisive factor. He knew this from his own playing days. The war over in 1945, Busby applied for and got the job as manager of Manchester United. He was no overnight success. The squad he inherited at Old Trafford was no better than average. United had never been a top club. Manchester City, for whom Busby had played, was Manchester's favoured team.

Busby's first decision when he took over at Old Trafford was to appoint Johnny Carey captain. During the war, Carey had joined the British Army and served in Italy and the Middle East. The fact that he was widely admired for this by Irish people offers a clue to the yawning gap between Official neutral Ireland and many ordinary citizens. The close and enduring affinity between Manchester United and Ireland began with Carey.

To the Irish soccer community of the forties and fifties, Johnny Carey was more than a sporting hero. He was an iconic figure for reasons that had as much to do with national identity as sport. A form of sporting apartheid existed. In the Ireland de Valera dreamed of, the Gaelic games, hurling and football, were deemed superior to what were officially regarded as foreign games. Because they were played by the middle and upper classes, rugby and hockey were tolerated. Still, any member of the Gaelic Athletic Association found playing or even attending a foreign game was banned *for life* from the Association. The Ban was ruthlessly enforced.

Douglas Hyde, the Protestant first president of Ireland, was banned from the GAA for life for attending a soccer international. Soccer was the English game. Those who played were scorned, derided as 'shoneens', English lovers, working-class gurriers, the lowest of the low. This was, of course, a caricature invented by Real Irishmen.

For many in places high and low, a passion for soccer was regarded as treachery. For those bigots, true Gaels as they saw themselves, Johnny Carey posed a challenge. He didn't fit the caricature of national identity in which they cloaked themselves. There was no place in the national identity parade for a gentleman soccer player from Dublin who had served the British Army in the struggle against European Fascism, to which, in truth, many worthies of the Irish Church and state were in thrall. But on the streets of Dublin Carey was held in the highest esteem.

He had long been one of the most respected sportsmen in Europe. In 1947 Carey captained the Europe XI that played Great Britain at Hampden Park. In 1948 he captained Manchester United to win the FA Cup, Matt Busby's first trophy. The following year he led Ireland to a famous victory over England at Goodison Park. No foreign team had previously beaten England on their own soil. Later in 1949 he was honoured by the English soccer writers, who named him 'Footballer of the Year'. Gentleman Johnny, as he was known in England and at home, was clearly no gurrier. A magnificent footballer, he was a man of exceptional character, as were a number of his contemporaries, including Peter Farrell, captain of Everton, Tommy Eglinton, 'Eggo' as he was fondly known, a brilliant winger, and Con Martin. Martin had begun his career playing Gaelic football. Representing the Dublin Minor team, he won a Leinster Minor Championship. When he switched games to play soccer, the GAA withheld his winner's medal.

The public celebration of men such as Carey, Farrell, Eglinton and Martin was more than an irritation. True Gaels had a capacity to hate that was at once risible and scary. Their visceral contempt for our foreign game extended to schools where pupils preferring soccer to Gaelic games were ritually beaten by Christian Brothers.

All of this is far from ancient history. In 1970 Liam Brady was expelled from St Aidan's CBS. The Christian Brothers were angry. Liam had been selected to play soccer for Ireland against Wales in a schoolboy international. He was fourteen. The head brother summoned him to the office. Liam was told that the school had a friendly Gaelic football match on the same day that he was due to represent his country against Wales. If he chose his country and soccer before his school and Gaelic football, he needn't bother coming back.

Liam chose soccer and his country. He was expelled. This punishment meant that he could not sit the vital Intermediate Certificate exam at St Aidan's. How Christian were the brothers? Little wonder then that many in the soccer community regarded the Gaels as fanatics.

The True Gaels were in denial. They couldn't admit that Ireland was culturally diverse. Nor could they countenance a world in which the natives they were supposed to be ruling didn't buy into their caricature of Irish identity. Anyone who wasn't God-fearing, English-hating, pure plastic Paddy was deemed deviant. Getting pissed, picking fights and kissing foreign arse, the stereotypical Irish character of Hollywood movies, caused fewer problems to Official Ireland than the shoneen soccer crowd who looked to England for work and play.

Jack Doyle, the piss-artist boxer, a world-renowned womanizer and 'friend' of Hollywood stars, was adored absolutely by those who ran the show, and show it was, on the basis that Jack was 'one of our own'. Carey, a fastidious man and a devout Catholic, was damned as a delinquent soccer-playing shoneen. The Gaels loved Hollywood and John Wayne. America was a grand place, England the home of heathens. The Gaels dealt in caricatures, which they bought and sold. Carey didn't fit.

Billy Behan was a quietly spoken, modest man, a far cry from the flash, rapacious 'bookie' of popular myth. Dickie Giles, John's father and a close friend of Behan, was similarly elusive for those obsessed with Irish identity. Behan and Giles were old-style football men, steeped in the rich folklore of Irish soccer. Dickie coached successfully at junior and senior level. For a few years he managed Drumcondra, or Drums as we affectionately knew them. Drums were our local team, playing out of Tolka Park, which stood twenty yards from the Dump and my front door.

John Giles arrived to play for Stella Maris when he was thirteen. His signing was a big coup for the club and the priest who ran it, Father James McNamee, a curate from the inner-city parish of Arran Quay where the Giles family hailed from. Decades later, Father Mac would be exposed as one of Ireland's most notorious paedophiles, something that wasn't entirely surprising to many around Stella.

John had been playing for a schoolboy club founded by Dickie called the Leprechauns. The 'Leps' were not among the blue bloods of school-boy soccer in the city, but they became known as the club Giles played for. For years stories of his deeds radiated across Dublin. I went to see him play his first game for Stella. Dessie Toal was his midfield partner. This was a massive occasion in the locality. That Stella team were already the best in Dublin. Apart from Dessie, other noted names were Mick Millington and Davy Malone. Also Ray Martin, one of the most feared full-backs in the city.

Billy Behan showed up. Whenever Behan turned up at a schoolboy game a buzz went round the ground. Who was he scouting? On this occasion we knew it was John Giles and it wasn't difficult to see why. Even at thirteen years of age, he had an aura about him. Very calm, very focused, he controlled the tempo of the play from his first touch. He was small, well built, beautifully balanced. While all around him were stretching every sinew, lunging and panting, John played at his own pace. He made the game look easy.

He passed the ball with immaculate precision with both feet. Shim-mying and dummying, he drifted by opponents with ease. For those of us present that day, John Giles set a standard of midfield generalship the like of which we'd never seen before. All the talk had been right. It was wonderful to behold.

Talking to Dessie Toal afterwards, I marvelled at John's skills. Wise as ever, Dessie pointed to one feature of this master class that I had failed to appreciate: 'His attitude is great,' Dessie remarked. 'Most guys that good would do a little showboating but Johnny doesn't. He's all discip-line. It's business for him. He's a pro already.'

5.   Game Changer

On the night of 8 December 1954, the banks of the Tolka river burst, creating the worst flood in living memory. Richmond Road became a river. We woke up to the fearful sight of water all around us. It was like being marooned on a lake with water still rising to lap at our front steps just a few feet from our first-floor front room. With daylight came the fire brigade and other rescuers, some in canoes. The family living below us in the basement had escaped, but the flood in the house was over three feet high. The rain had stopped, but we were still trapped.

Things soon returned to normal. We didn't starve or drown. Living one up, we were fortunate compared to neighbours whose homes were very badly damaged by the water. Long term, though, our situation was more serious. The basement was uninhabitable. The family living down there never returned. The landlord was unwilling to clear up the post-flood mess and, as private tenants, we had no recourse to Dublin City Council's relief services.

Alfie Byrne, Dublin's lord mayor, set up a fund for flood victims. Byrne was on his tenth stint as mayor. He was a popular figure in the inner city where he owned a pub. When he wasn't occupying the Mansion House, he was to be found in Dáil Éireann serving as a TD. Nominally independent, his vote was usually cast for Fine Gael.

Before and after elections he cut a remarkable figure. A small man dressed in Edwardian clothes, he doled out sweets and pennies to the children of 'Jackeens' who consistently returned him to the Dáil. My mother and father despised him. In their view the sweets and the pennies were no substitute for proper representation, which this Blueshirt publican never provided.

One day in the week following the flood Kevin and I were sitting in our room when Peg spotted Alfie Byrne at the front gate. As he began to make his way up the steps she opened the front door. 'Get out,' she calmly ordered him. 'There's nothing for you here.' Byrne wisely retreated. No money from the lord mayor's fund ever reached us.

Life after the flood was much tougher for my mother. We were now living in a semi-derelict house. The basement was a ruin, backing onto the Dump, where rats and mice were never far away. She did her best to scrub it clean, but the damp, dark squalor became a permanent feature of our lives.

Something much more ominous also appeared on the horizon: the landlord seeking to move us out. I could sense my parents' fear, even share it up to a point. Bleak though it was in material terms, our life was essentially happy. From my own childish perspective I had friends, thanks to Dessie Toal, a contented school life, thanks to Mr Hayden, the pleasure of the local library and the ever-deepening immersion in sport. The idea that these things could be taken away terrified me.

Since I'd made my First Communion the year before, I went to mass with my mother every morning: seven o'clock mass at St Alphonsus Church, a fifteen-minute walk away. We prayed fervently, taking Holy Communion every morning. During what was now a threatening moment for our family, the daily ritual provided profound solace. Peg believed that God would guide us and take care of us: 'O angel of God, my guardian dear, to whom God's love commits me here, ever this day be at my side to light and guard, to rule and guide, Amen.' This simple prayer offered a reassuring start to each day.

The fear of eviction was not the only shadow lingering over our generally contented existence. Ireland in the fifties was a poor country, blighted by unemployment and emigration. Reading my father's papers, I became familiar with talk of recession, an economic catastrophe that appeared to be permanently imminent. A loss of employment in the building trade would, I read, be an early sign of an economic downturn. Builders' labourers would be the first to lose their jobs if the economy took a turn for the worse. My parents rarely discussed politics, but I would hear them talk about men being 'laid off' as building projects were cancelled, or speculating about my father's own prospects in the immediate future. Paddy was an optimist, a cheerful man for whom the glass was always half full. 'Don't worry' was his mantra.

But I did, not just about him losing his job or us losing our home. I also developed a morbid fear that something might happen to him at work. Life on a building site was dirty, hard and dangerous. Around this time I fell into a habit of waiting at the top of Richmond Road between half past five and six o'clock for my father to return from work. I felt something bad was going to happen to him. Happiness was the sight of him getting off the bus on Drumcondra Road. If he was late I would feel sick with fear.

This seemingly irrational fear that something bad was coming lasted for months. Then the bad thing happened. I'd met my father off the bus and walked home with him. When my mother opened the door I knew something was seriously wrong. Normally she would embrace him as if he'd been gone for years. The warmth of their enduring love, the deep affinity between them, is the most vivid of my memories. But now Peg had a letter in her hand and a look of fear on her face. The letter was a notice of eviction. We had twenty-eight days to vacate our room, or court proceedings would begin. What could we do, where could we go, what would become of us, who would help us? For once my father seemed stunned. This time we had to worry.

My mother had received the letter, hand-delivered, that morning. She'd said nothing to Kevin and me. But the room was too small to keep secrets. Or to hide fear – fear that now possessed the four of us.

My father came up with the idea of going to see Peadar Cowan. A solicitor who until recently had been a TD in the area, Cowan had been a member of Clann na Poblachta along with Noël Browne. When others deserted Browne over the Mother and Child Scheme controversy, Cowan had stood by the minister for health. When the Clann imploded, both stood for the ensuing election as independents. Both had been re-elected. Cowan lost his seat in the 1954 election and was now practising as a solicitor. He was our only hope.

The couple across the landing from us had received the same letter. As the only other occupants of the house and with no children to worry about, they were inclined to vacate their room. They hinted that the landlord, or rather his agent who collected the rent each week, might be prepared to 'make it worth our while' to move on. My parents decided they'd fight.

My mother's initial horror was now replaced by grim determination. Paddy had no time to engage with our landlord, whose identity remained a mystery. Peg made an appointment to see Mr Cowan. With Kevin and me at her sides, she set off to Dame Street in the city where Cowan had an office.

I was a watchful child. I gauged people by the way they reacted to my parents. That was the measure of the person, be they neighbours, shop-keepers, pawnbrokers or Dessie Toal. The responses varied from respect to indifference to annoyance or contempt. Peadar Cowan was courteous, respectfully gentle. Dressed in an Aran sweater, with sandals and baggy trousers, he cut an eccentric figure. He read the eviction notice carefully.

Were we up to date with our rent?

'Yes,' my mother replied. 'We've never missed a payment.'

Did we have any alternative accommodation to go to?

'No,' my mother said.

'Part of your house is derelict. Is it safe?' he enquired.

'Yes,' she insisted.

Peg then outlined her principal concerns: Kevin and I were going to a good school, St Pat's; she wanted to rear her family in a decent neighbourhood; she couldn't bear the idea of the flats in the inner city or the new housing schemes in Dublin's outer suburbs where the former inhabitants of inner-city slumland were now creating equally unappealing ghettos.

'You're settled and happy, Mrs Dunphy?' Cowan asked.

'Yes, we are.'

The landlord would have to be challenged in court, Cowan informed us. 'Are you prepared for that?'

Uncharacteristically, Peg hesitated, almost certainly reflecting on, well, a number of things: respectable people didn't find themselves in courtrooms; the idea of court didn't chime with justice, rather with wrongdoing; and the cost. 'Yes, we are.'

Sensing those concerns, Cowan broke the silence. 'You are entitled to keep your home, Mrs Dunphy, and the justice system is there to protect you and your family. I will represent you. That's what I do. Don't worry about money. It won't cost you a penny.'

Facing the first real crisis of our life, we had a champion. Shortly afterwards we received notice of the court case, upon which our future depended. Short of illness, the stakes could not have been higher. It's only when you face the prospect of losing the seemingly ordinary that you realize how precious what you've taken for granted truly is. The prospect of being cast out of our room filled me with dread. That feeling I will never forget. Waiting for the court hearing was a terrible ordeal for my parents and Kevin.

I don't remember much talk about what would become of us if judgment went against us. I do remember the bus journey down to the Four

Courts on the morning of the case. I remember feeling sick with fear, clutching my mother's hand, Kevin on her other side. We met Peadar Cowan outside the courtroom. He was spruced up with a suit and tie and a proper pair of shoes.

We sat at the back of the courtroom while other cases were heard. I remember the winners smiling jubilantly, the losers shuffling pitifully out the door. I remember the decade of the rosary we'd said the night before. I remember the look on my mother's face when the name Dunphy was mentioned. It was the image of pain.

The landlord's advocate sent a chill down my spine. In essence his argument was that the Dunphys were being unreasonable. There was plenty of accommodation for people like us. His client was entitled to his property. The other tenant was amenable to relocation. The judge remained impassive, impossible to read. Was that face hard or kind? It was neither, just indifferent it seemed to me.

Cowan outlined my mother's case as made to him. Decent people. Hard-working father. Pay their rent. Boys at good local school. Living at this address for more than ten years. Entitled to the protection of the court. He spoke quietly with real conviction.

'Application refused,' the judge declared, nodding reassuringly towards my mother. The nightmare was over.

'You won't be bothered again,' Cowan told us, as we left the court. 'If you are, come and see me.' Peg, tears in her eyes, reached into her purse for a five-pound note. Cowan gently demurred. 'You don't have to pay. Say a prayer for me.' We did that night and every night for years to come. On the way home we went to the building site where my father was working to share the good news.

Cowan had saved more than a home. He had preserved for us a way of life that, though materially modest, was in many other ways immensely rich. Living in Drumcondra was the key. Unlike the inner-city ghettos or the slightly tarted-up local-authority housing schemes that ringed the city, Drumcondra was respectable. Among the poor, whether huddled in the city or in the suburbs, delinquency was common. Drinking, thieving, violence and tolerance of fecklessness were the evils my parents feared. It was, I suppose, a prejudice, a view of urban life that many rural people shared; a culture clash that had a bearing on their lives and, more importantly they believed, on Kevin's and mine.

Compared to the concrete jungles or the crowded inner-city slums that the bleak suburban estates were designed to replace, Drumcondra was a tranquil village. Though we were undoubtedly the least materially advantaged family in the area we could, money permitting, access all of the local amenities: the school, the churches, the picture house, the library and, for Paddy, a choice of local pubs, Fagan's (his preferred drinking shop), the Cat and Cage or Kennedy's. The Dump was an ideal playground for Kevin and me. Tolka Park lay just across the road. Croke Park, the great cathedral of Gaelic sport, was a ten-minute walk away, the city centre a ten-minute bus ride.

Sometimes Peg would go into town to see a film or a variety show. Paddy would bring home a bag of sweets for Kevin and me and a bottle of stout for himself and settle in for an evening babysitting. Going out together wasn't an option. The idea of paying someone to mind their children never occurred to them.

Peg loved the musicals: Fred Astaire and Ginger Rogers, Bing Crosby and Doris Day. She adored variety shows at the Theatre Royal featuring Jimmy O'Dea and Maureen Potter. Charlie Chaplin and the English comic Norman Wisdom were particular favourites. Kevin and I were allowed to stay up until she came home so that she could tell us all she'd seen. Despite the often stern face presented to the world my mother had a great sense of humour. As she put us to bed Peg would tell us the story of the film she'd seen or reprise the jokes of O'Dea and Potter.

Din Joe Fitzgibbon, then a rising star on Radio Éireann, was another favourite. Din Joe brought dancing to radio, a feat that might seem uniquely Irish. His show, *Take the Floor*, was a huge hit in fifties Ireland. Between calling the steps the dancers were taking, so vividly you could see them in your mind's eye, Din Joe told jokes and stories that mocked the prevailing pieties. His cheerful irreverence greatly appealed to Peg, whose faith in the Almighty did not extend to his representatives on earth.

Apart from his abiding interest in politics, sport was my father's great passion. Despite living across the road from Tolka Park he had little interest in soccer. He was a GAA man. With his Kilkenny roots, hurling mattered most to him. Because Kilkenny football was a joke, he followed Dublin in that discipline. St Vincent's was the dominant club in both codes, so when we weren't in Croke Park for the big inter-county matches, my father, Kevin and I were in Parnell Park supporting Vincent's.

Sundays began with mass, followed by a cooked breakfast and a read of the Sunday papers. Then off to the match, the highlight of our week-end. Kilkenny and Dublin were powerful counties in their respective championships but in the fifties both underachieved, so we walked the short distance to Croke Park prepared for disappointment. We were usually joined by Larry Gaynor, the foreman in Macken's builders, a good pal of Paddy's.

Larry was a leading member of a local Fianna Fáil *cumann*, but their opposing political views had no bearing on his friendship with Paddy. As invariably became apparent during the championship games, Larry was a much cooler dude than my father.

The buzz around Croke Park was amazing. The streets were full of supporters up from the country for the match. In those days men gathered outside the many pubs along our route sporting their county colours. Tomorrow morning fifties Ireland would return, a barren landscape of poverty, oppression and high unemployment, but for these precious few Sunday-afternoon hours the bleak, everyday reality gave way to good-humoured optimism. This day would deliver hope and heroes. And big matches in Croke Park rarely disappointed.

We always stood on the terrace at the Railway End. From that vantage point we saw some of Ireland's greatest sporting men: the hurlers, Christy Ring from Cork, the Rackards from Wexford, John Doyle, the legendary Tipperary hard man my father hated with a passion. And great footballers like Mick O'Connell from Kerry, Seán Purcell from Galway and Dublin's silky Kevin Heffernan, 'Heffo' in folklore.

Long before I learned of Stanley Matthews, Johnny Carey or Wembley, I was beguiled by the giants of Gaelic sport in Croke Park. If religion was the opiate of people like my mother, sport as played by its greatest practitioners was a purer, more divine addiction. We didn't know if God existed, but Christy Ring and the others were real for sure. And fleetingly of a Sunday afternoon their deeds transformed our ordinary lives in joyful application.

Nobody was more transformed than Paddy Dunphy, the easy-going cheerful builder's labourer. Kilkenny hurlers and Dublin footballers were afflicted by the same disease: a lack of 'bottle'. Seán Clohessy and Eddie Keher were great Kilkenny hurlers, but in those years they always gave way to the hard men of Tipperary and Wexford. John Doyle and Nicky Rackard were meaner, more ruthless.

In football, all Kevin Heffernan's guile counted for nothing against the macho men of Kerry and Meath. Paddy's expletive-riddled rants seem funny in retrospect. At the time they were a source of aching embarrassment to Kevin and me. Larry Gaynor seemed quietly amused as his gentle work companion became consumed by rage.

After the game there was a weary walk back past the ominously dark hulk of Archbishop McQuaid's palace to Fagan's for the consolation pint of Guinness. Kevin and I would be parked outside, appeased with a bottle of orange and a bag of crisps.

Paddy wasn't a big drinker. He'd have a few pints on a Friday night and after the match on Sunday. In an age when the public house was a second home for many working men he was a moderate social drinker. As Kevin and I nursed our orange squash outside Fagan's we knew that the man who emerged after a couple of pints would not be the lunatic we'd been embarrassed by on the Railway End.

Having listened to the match on the radio, Peg, a Limerick woman, would be waiting to rub salt in Paddy's wounds. As she teased him he would laugh ruefully and admit that, yes, he'd lost the plot. Again. He the dreamer and she the realist would exchange a glance of pure love. Monday beckoned.

Every summer Father Mac ran trials to find new recruits for Stella Maris. In 1955 he came up with a new way of attracting the best of Dublin's schoolboy talent to his club: the Road League was a tournament that thirty-two neighbourhood teams could enter. Dessie Toal decided to field a team. He asked me to play. I bit his hand off. Aged ten I was very young to be mixing it with the cream of Dublin's street footballers but if it didn't bother Dessie I was up for it, big-time. I had no football boots and no settled position. I kept quiet about the boots. Dessie could decide my position in his team.

He picked me at outside-right. Most of my first game on a real pitch with markings, real goals with nets, an official referee and proper leather ball laced up is a blur. What I remember is a mixture of elation and bewilderment that I experienced crossing the whitewash into the arena. Nearly all schoolboy football in Dublin was played in public parks. Stella and Home Farm were unique for having proper facilities, enclosed grounds with dressing rooms and showers. Supporters lined the touchlines and crowded behind the goals. Appreciation and derision were meted out in raucous terms. A skilful manoeuvre drew a murmur of approval from the knowledgeable audience.

I can't really remember how I played. Emotionally, I was way out of my depth, overwhelmed by the authenticity of this fantasy come true. I'd been reading a new English comic, the *Tiger*, which featured Roy Race, a brilliant young footballer who played for Melchester. Roy of the Rovers was a match-winning forward renowned for his ability to lead his team to victory, usually with a stunning late goal. His opponents were invariably burly, tough and menacing. An avid fan, I was now in similar circumstances. I was the youngest and smallest kid on the pitch. Without proper football boots, I wore runners. The winning goal I scored was far from the heroic Roy Race style. After a desperate scramble in our opponents' eighteen-yard box the ball ricocheted in my direction. One deft touch later I was one-on-one with their keeper. I slotted it into the back of the net.

In that moment I glimpsed Paradise. Roy Dunphy scores winner. Player/manager Toal expresses delight. Fans acclaim a new star. Stella was a mere hundred yards from home, the Dump and Dessie's garden shed. We floated back to base for a celebratory cigarette.

6. Culture Clash

My trips to Croke Park to support Kilkenny or Dublin, worse still my support for St Vincent's hurlers and footballers, were rarely mentioned in Dessie Toal's presence. Like John Giles and many others in the soccer community, Dessie regarded Gaelic sport as primitive. The ban and the idea that theirs was a foreign game was a source of bitter amusement to soccer people. Country people were dismissed as 'culchies' or bogtrotters, and their sport was accordingly derided as unsophisticated.

For many Dubliners, rural Ireland was a strange, backward place inhabited by gobshites. 'Culchies' didn't get it. Their music, *céilidh* dancing, patriotic ballads and keening love songs placed our country cousins in the cultural slot reserved for stage Irishmen and -women. The Irish actor Barry Fitzgerald won fame and fortune as the quintessential Irish character (wasting his talents on such gems as *Top o' the Morning* and *Easy Come, Easy Go*). The Yanks loved it. In the foreign-game Dublin, Fitzgerald was a figure of fun, a gombeen man, a caricature for export only. Born in Dublin, Fitzgerald found fame playing culchie priests. My mother detested Fitzgerald's fey depiction of Irishness for many of the same reasons as Giles and Toal. He was a fake.

In the parts of Dublin where Gaelic Irishness and all its cultural reference points were scorned, the preference was for foreign films and music. Rock 'n' roll had arrived, thanks to Bill Haley and the Comets. American crooners Frank Sinatra, Bing Crosby and Tony Bennett were still popular favourites, their records coveted by smart urbanites, young and old. English music-hall stars like Flanagan and Allen were also favoured, particularly by Dubliners who dismissed as parody rural Ireland's fondness for *céilidh* dancing and men in Aran sweaters, whose stock-in-musical-trade was songs about the IRA, emigration and lost love. The soccer people had no time for what they termed paddywhackery, a peculiar form of Irish self-pity that lay at the core of many of the ballads sung at closing time in rural Ireland's pubs.

'The Mountains of Mourne, my arse,' would be Dubliners' response if anyone offered a rendition of this classic in the average Dublin bar. Native Irish music was like native Irish sport: strictly for the birds and the culchies.

As far as sport was concerned I had a foot in both camps. I loved Croke Park as much as Tolka Park. Both offered escape from the mundane, or worse: the pawnshop, eviction, the empty cupboard, the low-level fears of everyday existence.

Reading, of course, was my other great passion. I consumed *Just William* with undiluted pleasure. In my imagination I was a member of the Outlaws, William's gang. I continued to read sports biographies of all kinds. A book about Len Hutton turned me on to cricket. A Yorkshireman, Hutton was captain of England. Like Billy Wright, then captain of the English soccer team, and Stanley Matthews, Hutton seemed to me the perfect hero: tough, decent, dedicated, undemonstrative. These men and their stories provided an impression of Englishness I warmed to.

Biggles was another important discovery in the library. A daring pilot, Biggles fought heroically in the Battle of Britain. Influenced by the books I was reading, I became increasingly sceptical of the notion, embedded in Irish folklore, of the English as Godless oppressors.

Of course, there were many good reasons to believe the folklore, even in my own family. My grandfather was in Croke Park on Bloody Sunday in 1920 when the notorious British auxiliaries, the Black and Tans, murdered fourteen innocent people attending a Dublin–Tipperary football match. Earlier that day an IRA murder squad directed by Michael Collins had executed fourteen people, thirteen of them English intelligence agents, one a local informer. A number of them were murdered in their own beds.

People feared reprisal, and many felt that revenge might be sought in Croke Park. Michael Hogan, a Tipperary footballer, was believed to be an Irish Volunteer. For that reason my grandfather refused to take his son Paddy to the match. The tragedy that ensued was the work of the hated Tans, at least in the shorthand story of that day, etched in Irish folk memory, which omitted the morning murders ordered by Collins.

I remember my mother shuddering at the mention of the Black and Tans. My father felt the same, but in his version of Bloody Sunday the role of Michael Collins and his IRA assassins was not omitted. Like his father before him, Paddy had no time for the IRA, who were, he insisted, as likely to turn on 'their own' as the English.

Anti-English sentiment was out there somewhere in the ether, but few gave any meaningful expression to what was essentially an Establishment fetish. The rump of the IRA still in existence were regarded as headbangers commanding virtually no public support. There were hundreds of thousands of Irish people in England for work they were grateful to have. We read English newspapers, followed English soccer, spoke the English language and listened to the BBC. Soon those who could afford it would be watching English television. English films were popular. The idea that you could prove you were a patriot by hating England was frankly ridiculous in the Ireland I grew up in.

This was particularly true of the soccer community. When Hungary thrashed England 6–3 at Wembley in 1953 we were astonished. When I watched snapshots of the game on Pathé News on one of the rare occasions I went to the cinema, wonder at the brilliance of the Hungarians rather than pleasure at England's humiliation was my principal emotion.

In 1955 the Football Association of Ireland arranged a friendly international against Yugoslavia. The fixture was scheduled for Dalymount Park in October. The Yugoslavs were one of Europe's best teams. International games were rare in those days, so this was an occasion to look forward to.

A few weeks before the match Archbishop McQuaid got wind of it. As the Mother and Child Scheme controversy illustrated, McQuaid was a formidable adversary. Many believed him to be the most powerful man in Ireland. De Valera had consulted McQuaid when drafting the 1937 constitution. The FAI did not consult him before agreeing to host the Yugoslavs. This was a conscious decision.

In 1952 the FAI had extended the same invitation to Yugoslavia. Then they had informed McQuaid, who insisted the game be cancelled on the grounds that the Yugoslavs, led by Marshal Tito, were persecuting Catholics. On learning about the 1955 fixture, McQuaid summoned the FAI to explain. The Yugoslav footballers were puppets of a Godless regime, he argued. This time the Football Association stood firm: sport and politics could not be mixed.

An angry archbishop issued an edict: this match should not take place. A letter read out from the pulpit of every church on the Sunday before the Wednesday game ordered people not to attend on pain of mortal sin. The persecution of Catholic clergy was cited as the reason for this order; the house arrest of the Croatian Archbishop Stepinac who was facing criminal charges was highlighted. A bitter public controversy now raged.

The president, Seán T. O'Kelly, announced that he would not attend the match. Government ministers followed suit. The vast majority of the trade-union movement lined up behind McQuaid. The Army Band, who traditionally opened proceedings with the national anthems, pulled out. The radio commentator Philip Greene, the voice of Irish soccer, refused to work on the game. And RTÉ, the national broadcaster, declared that they would not supply coverage.

Official Ireland was on a roll. 'The soccer crowd', as they were dismissively known, were isolated. More or less. Oscar Traynor stood by the FAI, of which he was president. Traynor was a respected man. He'd fought bravely for the IRA before turning political to take de Valera's side as an anti-Treaty man. He served in Dev's cabinets as minister for justice and the longest-serving minister for defence.

Asked about their decision to defy Official Ireland – McQuaid being the Establishment's most threatening figure – FAI chairman Sam Prole remarked that he 'doubted that the Yugoslav Football Association had any more influence on the nation's politics' than he did on Ireland's.

The match, which Yugoslavia won 4–1, was attended by 22,000 spectators. Dalymount Park's capacity was 46,000. But the match was played on a midweek afternoon. They weren't seeking to rebuff McQuaid, rather to see one of the world's best soccer teams in action.

Something I didn't know then was well known to the educated blackguards who ran the country and backed McQuaid: Bishop Stepinac had collaborated with the pro-Nazi Catholic authorities in Croatia who were responsible for some of the most hideous atrocities during the Second World War. The bishop had written a letter to his flock urging support for a regime that had murdered 30,000 Jews, 29,000 gypsies and a couple of hundred thousand Serbs. Forced conversion to Catholicism was another Croatian policy. Godlessness seems harmless in comparison.

We now also know more about McQuaid, the most influential public figure in the Ireland I was growing up in. An alleged child molester himself, he'd turned a blind eye to complaints about child molestation by other clerics.

The Football Association of Ireland's brave decision to stand up to McQuaid is interesting for one other reason: Sam Prole, who led it, was a Presbyterian. His chief ally, FAI secretary Joe Wickham, was condemned from the pulpit of his local church on the Sunday after the game.

7.   Golden Age

Sam Prole bought Drumcondra Football Club in the early fifties from the Hunter family. League of Ireland football was entering its golden age. Grounds were packed with fans eager to watch their local heroes, which was as close as they would ever get to the great stars in England whose deeds they could only read about or glimpse on Pathé News.

The standard of play in the League was high. Drums was my team. They were the only League club on the city's northside, apart from the amateurs of Bohemians who didn't really count in this semi-pro game. Drums drew big crowds to Tolka Park, yet the club was always strapped for cash. Local folklore had it that old Mr Hunter, who was unpopular with fans and players alike, was stealing the money. Players were poorly paid and Drums generally underachieved under his regime. The arrival of Sam Prole was therefore welcomed. A wealthy man who'd made his money from the Great Northern Railway, Prole promised to invest to allow Drums to compete with the best.

Shamrock Rovers were the best. Based in Milltown, a leafy suburb on Dublin's southside, Rovers set the bar in terms of winning trophies. And they won in style, playing free-flowing, attacking soccer that was admired, however grudgingly, by rival fans.

Other powerful teams strove alongside Drums to match the leading club. When not disparaged as 'the foreign game', soccer was damned as the sport of 'the garrison towns', places where the English were based during the Occupation. In Waterford, Limerick, Galway, Dundalk, Sligo, Athlone and Cork, locals learned the alien sport from the enemy. In Dublin, Shelbourne and St Patrick's Athletic, both southside-based, also contended for glory. The League of Ireland thus provided a vibrant and slightly subversive alternative to the national sport administered with ruthless patriotism from Croke Park.

Drums' fortunes improved with the arrival of Sam Prole. In 1953 he installed Ireland's first floodlights in Tolka Park. We all went to the first floodlit game against the Scottish club St Mirren. It was an awesome, magical experience. From our room directly across Richmond Road,

I watched the new facility being tested on the nights before the game. The lights dazzled, casting a glow into our room.

I hung out with Dessie Toal and the gang, watching the players train on those dark winter nights. Among many outstanding footballers at the club, Kit Lawlor stood out. Kit was a beautiful player. An inside-forward, he'd played professional football in England for Doncaster Rovers, then managed by the great former Ireland player, Peter Doherty. Harry Gregg, later to join Manchester United, the hero of the Munich air crash, was on the same team.

Lawlor was the leader of this team. An elegant master of the football, he set the tempo and direction of every game. To the skills learned on the East Wall streets he'd grown up on, Kit added poise, guile and the vision to see a telling pass to 'make' the vital goal. The wit and imagination of his football were matched by his post-game persona. He was a character. He was good and he knew it. Kit liked a drink. He was said to be his own man, caring little for the bosses.

There were other marvellous players on that team. Dessie Glynn was a splendidly versatile centre-forward, a scorer and maker of goals. From a better-off Drumcondra family, he had no interest in turning pro and going to England. He had a good job in the civil service and wore a smart suit on match days.

Benny 'Rosie' Henderson also stood apart. A tall quick winger-cum-centre-forward, Rosie won one international cap for Ireland. On his day he was brilliant, on his bad days he was woefully inept. Rosie was a weather vane for the team. If he was on his game, Drums would generally win.

'Bunny' Fulham was another striking character in that team. He'd been a star in the League with Shelbourne. He had offers to play in England, but turned them down because the money, about fourteen pounds a week, wasn't good enough. Bunny was a bricklayer, building-site aristocracy. For a while he boosted his income by playing part-time for Holyhead Town, a boat trip across the Irish Sea, in Wales, over on Friday night, back on Saturday with tax-free sterling. Holyhead was a popular destination for many Irish players resentful of the pittance paid by League of Ireland clubs.

Bunny's signing was a big deal for Drums. As a right-back and dead-ball specialist, he'd won a League title with Shelbourne. Barrel-chested, never betraying any emotion, he was feared by tricky forwards.

He was hugely popular with the fans. Local legend had it that Bunny would never marry (though he did in his forties) because he'd never hand over his wages to a wife. His battles with Shamrock Rovers' brilliant left-winger Liam Tuohy were an eagerly anticipated highlight of every Drums–Rovers contest.

In that golden age Shamrock Rovers were the team to beat. Paddy Coad was their player/manager. When he took over in 1949, Coad set out to find the best young players in the city. Coad himself was the best player in Ireland by a mile. A quiet, shy man, he didn't yearn like others for the English dream.

John Giles, his father Dickie, and Dessie Toal – in fact everybody in and around football, regardless of club allegiance – were in awe of Paddy Coad. Much as John would later do for Manchester United, but especially at Leeds, Coad was the pivotal figure in every game he played. He was the quintessential midfield general. With perfect touch, beautifully balanced, great vision to pick out the telling pass and the immaculate technique to deliver it, Coad was a complete footballer. More than that: the young players he brought to Milltown proved that Coad was a great judge of talent and possessed the coaching gifts to nurture his youngsters to maturity. He built the greatest ever League of Ireland team.

It was watching Rovers that, more than any other single thing, made me want to be a footballer. Even the hurt of losing to them was assuaged by the lingering wonder of their football. Tuohy made it in England. Coad could have, easily. Several others played for Ireland alongside exiled stars: Ronnie Nolan, a powerful footballing wing-half; Gerry Mackay, their left full-back, as technically accomplished as most forwards; Liam Hennessy, the other wing-half, driving forward, his left foot spraying danger everywhere; Shay Keogh, the centre-half marshalling his defence with calm authority; right-back Mickey Burke, a rugged wall of resistance; 'Maxie' McCann, the dashing, perpetual-motion right-winger, a goal-scorer too. And centre-forward Paddy Ambrose, menacing and clinical in front of goal. All of them were Irish internationals, royalty in working-class Dublin in the 1950s. Rovers won the League three times and the FAI Cup twice. What's really puzzling, looking back, is how they ever lost.

Coad's vision of football as the beautiful game – long before that phrase was coined – bore more than a passing resemblance to the Busby project in Manchester: young men playing free-spirited, attacking football, winning in style. The Busby Babes were emerging as a phenomenon in England, the guile and impudence of United's game contrasting starkly with the power and fast-running strength of Stan Cullis's Wolverhampton Wanderers. Wolves were feared. United were loved.

It is fascinating to note that Coad's Colts, as Rovers were tagged by the media, pre-dated the Babes by several years. By the mid-fifties Rovers were a mature team and the more potent for that.

The northside/southside contests between Drums and Rovers in fifties Dublin are part of the city's folklore. We crossed town more in hope than expectation. I'd often travel to watch Rovers, but when Drums made the journey, my father would always take Kevin and me to see the game that captured even Paddy's Gaelic imagination. The bus to College Green. And then the special match buses bound for Milltown, which were lined along the walls of Trinity College. Long queues stretched back down Pearse Street, full of fans anxious to make kick-off. All week I'd worry about the outcome of the game. Now, standing in line, I'd worry about getting on the special bus; once on board I'd worry that we'd be late, that, as often happened, Milltown's gates would be locked, bearing the 'house full' sign.

We moved at snail's pace through the southside, along the tree-lined avenues, past the prosperous houses and the thousands making the pilgrimage on foot. They seemed to be moving faster than the specials, which backed up as far as the eye could see. Some Sundays it would take an hour to complete the three-mile journey. Then the queue at the turnstile, endless, it seemed, to my fearful mind. The delay was caused in part by the custom of the day, giving kids a lift over the stile.

Money was always an issue. Outside every football ground kids hovered, begging a lift over the stile. 'Give us a lift over, mister,' the urchins beseeched. I was usually among them. When my father took Kevin and me he would try to lift us over. Sometimes a friendly stile man would turn a blind eye. 'Go ahead' was the good news. 'Sorry, you have to pay for them' were the words you dreaded hearing. Between leaving our house and gaining entry to the arena, I had much to fret about. I was a world-class worrier.

The atmosphere inside the ground was wonderful. Milltown was special. Almost invincible during the game, Rovers looked the part as well. The green and white hooped shirts, the neat body-hugging white shorts, a contrast to the baggy drawers favoured by other teams. Coad's

Colts would dash onto the pitch like well-groomed movie stars. They looked fitter, moved more gracefully than any other team. They had presence, an aura about them that radiated confidence. In this theatre of dreams, Rovers were the leading men. For those of us who followed Drums, hope was represented by Kit Lawlor and Dessie Glynn, both match-winners in their day.

One other cause for optimism was Eamonn 'Sheila' Darcy, Rovers' eccentric goalkeeper. Unlike his team-mates, Sheila was not the athlete from Central Casting. Tall, slightly stooped, prematurely grey, taking dainty steps as if running on thin ice, Darcy had played as a pro in England with Oldham. He was a good shot-stopper, but prone to the occasional spectacular error.

A feature of every Drums–Rovers epic was the merciless, though affectionate, barracking Sheila was forced to endure from the northside hordes. He gave as good as he got, engaging with the fans behind the goal, a broad smile on his angular face. If Rovers were winning he'd hold up the appropriate number of fingers to remind his tormentors of the score. He was a gentleman post-game, much loved across Dublin's football community.

Sam Prole improved everything at Tolka Park. Being wealthy (and Presbyterian!) he didn't rob the gate money every week like the Hunters. He installed the floodlights, the players were better paid . . . and on time. The stands were painted, new dressing rooms built. A new manager, Frank Radford, was appointed.

Dickie Giles had been managing Drums but, for all his football nous, he was not temperamentally suited to management. Patience was not his strong suit. He was a very popular and respected character in soccer circles, more so now that John had left for Old Trafford. Dickie liked a drink. His work selling paraffin heating oil and football coupons to publicans and customers naturally took him to public houses, where he tended to linger, chewing the fat about the game. A genial, generous man, Dickie also had strong feelings about politics. Like many Dubliners he was pro-British, had no time for stage Irishmen or *céilidh*-hopping. He loved a singsong, his many party pieces being from the English music-hall tradition.

Radford played League of Ireland and knew his football. His brief at Tolka Park? Catch Rovers. It was a tall order. In 1956 when he took charge, Rovers still reigned supreme. Like all great teams they had any number of ways of winning games: a flash of Tuohy's left-wing brilliance; a Maxie McCann solo on the right leading to a bulging net; Paddy Ambrose rising high to head one home; Liam Hennessy bursting from midfield to unleash a rocket with his deadly left foot. With an army of supporters Rovers packed every ground they played in. What happened to their handsome gate receipts was not a mystery. The club was owned by the Cunningham family, whose core business was bookmaking. Paddy Coad was married to one of the Cunningham girls. That was why, many speculated, he'd never gone to play in England. As was customary with owners in League of Ireland football, the Cunninghams emptied the till after every match. Football was a cash business and the owner did the counting.

8.   Dreams Come True

When I was eleven I went for trials at Stella Maris. I was a year too young for their youngest team, the under-13s, but I thought it was worth a go. I was very small for my age, but a veteran of street games against grown men. Getting football boots was a problem. I played the trial match in runners. I did fine, more than that, really. Most of the kids were out for a laugh. I was deadly serious.

This was my long-cherished dream. After Home Farm and maybe St Finbar's on the southside, Stella Maris was Dublin's most renowned schoolboy club. Father Mac ensured Stella was properly run. An enclosed ground, showers, a pitch well manicured and marked. The goals had nets. The pavilion was well appointed, as was the recreation room, which featured a table-tennis table. Compared to the chilly wilds of public parks most schoolboy soccer was played in, Stella was Paradise.

Father Mac was a handsome, well-groomed young curate. He spoke in the well-modulated tone of the middle class. There was about him an air of natural authority. A man you wouldn't cross, yet approachable, with a kindly disposition. After my trial he approached me. 'Where are your boots?' he enquired.

'I don't have any at the moment,' I replied.

'Well, we want you to play for Stella, but you'll need proper boots.'

I went into town with my mother to get them. I sensed her anxiety about the money. Even the ordinary clothes and shoes she bought for Kevin and me stretched the family budget. But she knew how much this meant and somehow found the necessary.

Ciaran Martin was the star of the trial I played in. I'd seen him around Stella before, watching his older brother play; he was a couple of years older than us. Ciaran, known to everyone as 'Nipper', had a big street reputation. He came from the inner city, Mountjoy Square, where he lived in a tenement room. His mother had had twenty-two children, ten of whom had died at birth. Five of the kids had emigrated, five were still at home. Nipper was a brilliant player. A centre-forward, he was small but strong and fearless. He drifted past opponents with ease, and was cool as a breeze in front of goal. He scored for fun, usually with a cheeky flourish.

We got on famously from day one. Nipper was a leader, infinitely more streetwise than me. I was timid and shy, at least on the surface. Our bond was formed during games. Our first game for Stella was in Crumlin in a field on Clogher Road. This was a journey into the unknown, the housing schemes of my mother's fear and loathing. The team was to meet in town under the clock at the Ballast Office in Westmoreland Street, a landmark meeting point for Dubliners. The Ballast Office clock was, as one of James Joyce's characters put it, 'an item in the catalogue of Dublin street furniture'.

Some people remember their first kiss. I'll never forget that first match on a lovely autumn Saturday afternoon. To be at the Ballast Office for one o'clock I left Drumcondra, a ten-minute ride away, at midday. New boots in hand, I caught the bus. I was in some kind of blissful trance. I had dreamed about this day for so long, dreamed about its possibilities, good and bad. In the good scenario, we won; I played well. In the bad dream, we lost; I was hopelessly out of my depth. A third storyline had me turning up late at the Ballast Office to find that they'd gone to Crumlin without me.

So, I was on O'Connell Street at twelve twenty, forty minutes before our rendezvous. I hopped off the bus and strolled in the direction of the Ballast Office along what was then one of Europe's most magnificent boulevards. Nerves twitching, I stopped for a smoke on O'Connell Bridge, fifty yards from the meeting point. At twelve forty I spotted Mr Kennedy, our manager, arriving. I joined him. The others arrived more or less on time. I sat at the back of the bus with Nipper. We shared a quiet smoke on the upper deck on the way out to the Crumlin badlands. He seemed much more assured than me. The tobacco helped calm my nerves.

Silently we got changed on the touchline. Mr Kennedy distributed the jerseys. Number eight for me, inside-right. Nipper got the number nine; Liam Millington, number four; Rory McMahon, a Protestant who'd travelled from the salubrious southside suburb of Monkstown, got number five. Small, smart and tough, Rory was our centre-half. Liam Brady's brother, Eamonn, was our left-winger. There was no talk of tactics. Mr Kennedy's instructions were simple: go out and enjoy it . . . and remember you're playing for Stella Maris.

Street football was frenzied, with space at a premium. Close control, the ability to glide through tiny openings and an instinct for the killer pass were the gifts required. Today was different. The pitch was vast, the tempo slower. On the street everyone was drawn into the ball, the magnet. In this, the real game, players had positions they stuck to; the defenders patrolled their space like cops on duty, guarding the goal and all avenues towards it.

This was a new challenge, a steep learning curve. But we got it quickly enough. For all the difference between street improvisation and this more formal version of the game, the things that mattered most remained unchanged. Touch, the vision to pick out the right pass, determination and organization invariably determined the result. Thanks mainly to Nipper's deadly finishing, we won the game 2–0. He was our best player by a mile, getting stuck into guys twice his size, drifting past defenders as if they were statues, always threatening to score. Our Roy Race. I was content to play the supporting role of Blackie Gray, Roy's best friend.

This first victory was deeply satisfying. The bond within our team, which would endure for four very happy years, was forged that Crumlin afternoon. Mr Kennedy expressed his pleasure and told us to buy the evening paper on Tuesday, where our victory would be recorded. The big-time.

9. Blackmail

One night my father arrived home later than usual. His friend, the foreman Larry Gaynor, had invited him for a pint after work. The economy had stalled, nobody was building, Macken's would be laying men off in the next few weeks, Larry told Paddy. The foreman had a plan to save Paddy's job. If my father joined Fianna Fáil, Larry could remove him from the line of fire. If not, Larry speculated, Paddy was likely to find himself on the dole.

My father disliked Fianna Fáil and wasn't shy about letting it be known. Joining the Soldiers of Destiny meant more than token support. They were in opposition, but the Fine Gael-led coalition government, three years in office, was unpopular and an election looked imminent. As a member, Paddy would have to canvass for his party, but he would probably keep his job. That was the gist of their conversation.

That was how Fianna Fáil worked. Every job in the public service, from janitor to judge, was for one of their own. The building industry, dominated by Fianna Fáil donors, operated along similar lines, especially when times were hard.

With an election looming, Larry Gaynor was on a recruiting mission. He was trying to save my father from himself. The most ruthless and successful electoral machine in Western Europe was on our case. Paddy refused the offer: voting for the Soldiers of Destiny in the privacy of the polling booth, maybe, but knocking on doors urging neighbours to vote FF would be impossible.

He arrived home a shadow of the good-humoured man we were accustomed to greeting. Kevin and I listened as he told my mother the news. Short of illness or bereavement, unemployment was the most devastating fate that could befall a family in fifties Ireland; the most humiliating extinction of hope, a mortal blow to any man's pride. The dole was a pittance, the prospect of getting alternative employment virtually non-existent. Peg was, as always, defiant. 'You were right,' she assured my father. 'We'll manage.' A few weeks later Paddy was laid off. An election was called. Fianna Fáil gained an overall majority, which they maintained for another sixteen years.

Paddy signed on at the Labour Exchange in Gardiner Street. During school holidays I would go with him. The queue was long. Men desperate for work were condemned to this hell: seeking handouts to put scraps on the table. As the queue shuffled slowly forward, some men shared gallows humour; others, my father among them, bowed their heads in silent shame. They were the victims of failed politics.

And the perpetrators? De Valera, part thief, part Mafia don; Labour Party leader William Norton, a closet member of the Knights of Columbanus and a close collaborator with the Blueshirts, W. T. Cosgrave, Oliver J. Flanagan and John A. Costello; and the bastard in the Archbishop's Palace, John Charles McQuaid. These were the rulers in the Land of Saints and Scholars.

My father went out looking for work every day. But losing his job, he also lost the large chunk of a person's life that revolves around companionship, chat and banter about sport or life in general, the cheerful theatre of everyday existence you share with your workmates. In losing your job you shed an essential part of your identity. For my gregarious dad this loss was serious.

The money was another matter. We ate mince instead of sirloin steak, tinned vegetables in place of fresh. Socks were darned, trousers patched rather than replaced. Winter jumpers frayed until the holes appeared, then were darned with precious wool.

Returning home each evening Paddy looked wasted, diminished by rejection and the sense of failure and isolation that unemployment brings. Peg would embrace him gently. 'Don't worry, love, we're fine.' The love they shared through this ordeal was extraordinary.

Many memories of those months endure. One in particular: Christmas Eve, money all but gone, my father headed into town, to Moore Street, to try to get a bird. If you waited long enough, loitered outside the poultry shops, you might eventually get a cheap chicken at closing time. God knows what this exercise was like for Paddy.

10. Dessie Drifts

Several months after John Giles joined Manchester United he came home to help Stella win the Evans Cup. He was still eligible to play because he hadn't signed any forms at Old Trafford. In the Dublin regional final, Stella beat Finbar's 5–1. John scored four goals. The quality of that Finbar's team can be measured by the presence of two players: Eric Barber and Tony Dunne.

Barber enjoyed a very successful career playing for Shelbourne in the League of Ireland, winning one international cap for Ireland. Tony Dunne would eventually join Manchester United as a nineteen-year-old. He played left-back for United when they won the European Cup at Wembley in 1968. He is acknowledged as one of the greatest defenders ever to play in England.

The Evans Cup was an all-Ireland competition. In the final against Southend from Cork, Giles was sent off, but Stella still won comfortably. Dessie Toal played a major part in the victory, which confirmed Stella's status as one of Ireland's best schoolboy clubs. John Giles reckons that Dessie was robbed of his schoolboy cap that year. Stella already had three players on the international team and politics dictated that three caps for one club was enough. Dessie lost out. Fifteen was a defining age for the best schoolboy players. Failure to win your cap dramatically decreased your chance of 'getting away', as going to England was known. This was almost an iron law with few exceptions, Tony Dunne being one of them.

Perhaps it was disappointment or a certain disillusionment with the often vicious politics that determined so much in the parochial world of schoolboy football that caused Dessie to drift away from the Dump and indeed the game. He discovered girls, Elvis and fashion in the form of the Teddy Boys' uniform of drainpipe trousers, tight-fitting jackets and a DA haircut. DA stood for 'duck's arse', the shape in which the carefully coiffed hair was formed. Dessie was still a man to be reckoned with around Drumcondra, still unfailingly kind to me. 'You're doing well,' he assured me, when we met one day. 'I think you're going to make it.'

Coming from him this endorsement was a massive boost to my confidence.

Such a boost was timely. Without Dessie around I'd been spending too much time alone, becoming introspective in solitary moments, wondering about the future, worrying about my father, who was fighting a losing battle to find work. I was acutely conscious of my patched trousers, my darned socks and jumpers and my mother's desperate efforts to make the dole money last the week.

'How are you getting on with Father Mac?' Dessie asked me one day.

'Fine,' I replied.

'Well, be careful,' Dessie remarked. A wry smile accompanied the words. This was not the first time I'd heard a pointed reference to Father Mac. Nothing specific was ever mentioned, but by nods and winks the implication was that he was interested in more than our ability to play football.

Predatory sexual activity was not unknown to those of us growing up on the streets of Drumcondra. I'd already experienced that one incident with a neighbour which, though serious, left me unmarked. Another I found funny rather than threatening. Blind Matt lived at the top of Richmond Road. He was often spotted standing on the kerb, white stick in hand, waiting for assistance. We knew well enough to avoid him. If you helped Matt cross the road, he would ask your name – and age – as his hand caressed your bum.

Out shopping with my mother one day, we came across the blind man standing at the kerbside. 'Help him cross the road,' Peg ordered. An obedient child, I rarely refused my mother's commands. But on this occasion I demurred. 'Do as you're told,' she insisted.

'Is that Eamon?' Matt enquired.

'Yes, and I'm with my mammy,' I warned him. He gripped my hand but left my bum alone.

Mad Tom also featured on our list of adults to be avoided. He lived beside Griffith Park and the library. Seeing young boys, Tom would make his move. A huge man, Mad Tom's thing was to hunt his captive vigorously while you tried desperately to escape. Tom was mad and should have been in care. Threatening he wasn't. Sometimes, out of boredom, we would tease him, rather like a matador with a bull.

Paddy Church (not his real name: he's still around) was a layman, a prominent figure in a local church. He lived in Drumcondra with his bedridden mother. He paid for his kicks, which he got by spanking boys' bottoms. Short of the price of the picture house on rainy days, our best hope was an encounter with Paddy, or Mr Church as he was known.

Following an invitation to his house for a game of cards and some lemonade, the scam would begin. Poker was the card game, the deal being that he would stake us all, sixpence a hand. If we won, the money was ours; if we lost, our bottoms were spanked. Once we'd made the price of the pictures, we'd offer our excuses and were off.

Hints about Father Mac must be seen against that background. After Dessie's remark I became more conscious of Father Mac's presence in the showers after games. He would towel us down, there would be some touching and perhaps a hug. There was no sense of impropriety, much less of violation. I never felt threatened.

Ciaran Martin and I were best pals. Usually I would go down to Mountjoy Square to hang out with him and his pals. There was a fantastic tarmac football pitch in the public playground on the square. It was like Wembley compared to the Dump. The matches were amazing, open to all ages, but exclusively for guys who could play. The best players in the inner city turned up to test their mettle in that wonderful arena.

Special games would be arranged between competing gangs. The square was a world within a world, the best street football in the city, with the best players, many of them full-grown men on the dole without hope of employment. Coming from Drumcondra, I was treated with a certain caution, suspicion, even. Did I have notions about myself? Did I share the 'respectable' view of the inner-city working class to which my mother subscribed, the brutal, dismissive prejudice articulated by W. T. Cosgrave 'that people reared in workhouses are no great acquisition to human society, that their highest aim is to live at the expense of the ratepayers, that they didn't want to work'? Was I a prick or a prig? The question was never asked, but it was implicit in a certain wariness I could detect.

The fact that Ciaran and his brother Ray vouched for me mattered greatly. The Martins were a respected family. Tough? Yes. Well able to look after themselves when trouble brewed, but decent and generous. I felt far more comfortable with the guys on Mountjoy Square than the Drumcondra gang, most of whom, apart from Dessie Toal, shared my mother's views about respectability.

Most gratifying was the realization that I could more than mix it with the best street footballers in the city. I was soon accepted, ability to play my trump card. Everyone's clothes were patched, darned or merely scruffy; that I didn't stand out on that score was a significant bonus.

Occasionally Ciaran came up to Drumcondra, usually in the summer holidays when we were looking for a game in Griffith Park or some mischief to wile the day away, cost free. On one such day we encountered Father Mac on Richmond Road. He always drove a big car, the latest model with all the trimmings. He pulled up beside us. There were two other kids in the car. Would we like to go swimming? We hopped into this mansion on wheels and off we rode to Malahide, about ten miles out on the coast. The other kids were strangers from the poor parish Arran Quay, where Father Mac was curate.

He didn't take us to the beach. Instead we arrived at a secluded spot on private land with its own natural water pool. He parked his car beside the pool. Opening the car boot he took out an inflatable Lilo which he pumped up. He bade us take our clothes off. Ciaran and I told him we had no swimming togs.

'No matter,' he replied, 'that's no problem.' Father Mac was already stripping off. The two boys from Arran Quay had togs. Ciaran and I exchanged glances. What's the story? we wondered. It was Ciaran's call. He started to take his clothes off. I followed.

Father Mac was in the pool with the city boys. Ciaran, fearless as usual, dived in head first. I couldn't swim. I hovered around the water's edge, typically cautious. Father Mac offered to teach me to swim. We spent about half an hour cavorting around in the pool. Then Father Mac got out, produced towels from the car and dried us off. He reclined on the Lilo, inviting us to join him.

What followed might best be described as horseplay. There was much touching, hugging and wrestling as he challenged the four of us to take him prisoner and pin him down. At the time all of this seemed harmless, nothing more nor less than fun. After a couple of hours we headed for home. Father Mac bought us ice-creams on the way back to Richmond Road.

This was the summer of 1957. I was eleven, coming up for twelve. Three years later the first accusation of sexual molestation was levelled against Father Mac by a boy from Stella Maris football club. The suggestion was that he behaved 'inappropriately in the showers at the club, after a trip to the seaside'.

The Commission of Investigation into clerical child sex abuse, which reported in 2009, was chaired by Circuit Court Judge Yvonne Murphy. The Murphy Commission made serious findings against Father James McNamee. A total of twenty-one people had accused him of abuse. Remarkably, it allegedly took place either in his car or around swimming pools. The showers at Stella Maris were also cited as a crime scene.

One witness told the Commission: 'We would always be hovering around the late James McNamee when he arrived at the school because he had this very charismatic presence. I would say he was like St Francis of Assisi, you know.'

Media reports of the Murphy Commission referred to Father Mac as a 'monster'. My reading of the Commission's chapter on him, when placed in the context of my experience of being around him for three or four years, raises a serious question in my mind about the veracity of allegations he faced. And, critically, about the media's interpretation of the Commission's finding.

Various credible exposés have revealed profoundly shocking crimes committed against vulnerable young people by Irish clerics over decades. For its failure to investigate these crimes, to apprehend and punish those clerics responsible, Official Ireland is complicit in a scandal of unfathomable proportions. The Catholic hierarchy, led initially by Archbishop McQuaid, himself an alleged molester, conspired to protect many 'monsters'.

There is, however, a dimension to this story that prompts troubling questions about truth and justice. The depiction of Father Mac as a 'monster' is wrong, as far as I can judge. He undoubtedly enjoyed the company of young boys in what can be fairly deemed inappropriate circumstances. But if, as it does, justice requires each case to be judged on its merits, Father Mac should not be characterized as he has been. He should not be tarred with the same brush as serial rapists, such as Brendan Smyth and Seán Fortune.

11.   A Marked Man

Fianna Fáil's return to government after the 1957 general election was good news for their builder friends. The Soldiers promised prosperity in the form of work. None of this would trickle down to my father. His rejection of Larry Gaynor's offer, a job for his soul, made him a marked man around building sites. 'We always look after our own' was a core value for the Soldiers of Destiny. The corollary was that dissidents must be punished and be seen to be punished. The principle was ruthlessly enforced and applied to judges, janitors and builders' labourers.

Any business operator seeking government contracts or planning permission to build a factory or bicycle shed was subject to similar scrutiny. Every town and village had a Larry Gaynor serving the interest of the party. Loyalty was not so much a virtue as a licence to exist. If you were worldly and unprincipled, the game was easy to play. Paddy was neither. He stayed on the dole. The rent was a serious concern. The eviction nightmare was fresh in our memory.

Sam Prole continued to develop Tolka Park. One of his innovations was the provision of better stewarding on match days. Paddy applied for a place on the stewards' roster. The job was simple. You wore a white coat and ushered the fans to their seats in the stand, or an allotted place on the terraces.

Ray Ring was the head steward. Ray operated the reserved turnstile through which bigwigs and players' family and friends entered the ground. He'd often allowed Paddy to 'lift me over' just before kick-off on big match days. Ray gave my father a job. It paid five shillings per match, every fortnight. The money was no more than the price of a few pints but the symbolic importance of belonging to the match-day crew was massive. The brutal isolation of existence without work was in some small way ameliorated. A tiny light of purpose was lit. The camaraderie that came with being part of the match-day crew mattered greatly to Paddy's morale. And after matches he could go up to Fagan's for a couple of pints with Ray and the others, the five precious shillings in his pocket.

I never heard my father say a bad word about Larry Gaynor. He wasn't given to bitterness. Paddy knew how the system worked, which was why he despised it. But he was able to distinguish between the party and its operatives, for whom he felt pity rather than anger. That, at least, was how we believed the case to be. However, later in life, when his long spell without work was but a memory, I would learn how devastating the experience had been for my father.

Unemployment restricted our access to weekend sport. Croke Park was off the menu for a couple of years. Instead we'd listen to the matches on the radio. One awful memory endures to this day. St Vincent's were playing a must-win game in Parnell Park. Kevin and I pestered Paddy to take us, thinking he had the money. On Sunday morning he gave in. It was a thirty-minute walk to Marino. We set off in good time.

Paddy seemed apprehensive. When we reached Clontarf Golf Club, which bordered Parnell Park, he ushered us through the gates. 'Operation Bunk In' was under way. Walking quickly along the out-of-bounds markers, we reached the six-foot-high wall at the back of Parnell Park. Somehow we negotiated this obstacle. We were in. Vincent's won.

12.   European Dream

In 1957 Shamrock Rovers entered the European Cup as League of Ireland champions. Rovers were drawn against Manchester United in the preliminary round. The brilliant young United team had just won back-to-back championships in England, the latest by eight points. With an average age of twenty-two, they were known as Busby's Babes, a soubriquet Matt Busby disliked. Their other media tag, the Red Devils, was more appropriate.

Young and brash, playing daring attacking football, the Red Devils captured the public imagination in a manner unprecedented in English sport, certainly in soccer, where the indentured slaves were supposed to know their place. Encouraged by Busby, the Devils were cocky, their football a beguiling blend of power and elegance. Denounced as 'Teddy Boys' by Football League president Bob Lord, the Butcher from Burnley, they wore the badge with honour.

A decade after the war England was changing: deference was on the run, pursued by rebellion. The playwright John Osborne had famously 'damned England' for its stultifying post-war conservatism. Writer and jazz musician George Melly depicted the fifties as a time of 'austerity, of punitive convention, of a grey uniformity'. Busby's team bucked that trend and, worse from the football Establishment's point of view, they backed their irreverence with spectacular results. It is difficult now to convey the offence they caused to the likes of Bob Lord and his equivalent at the Football Association, Stanley Rous. For rival clubs they were a source of fear and loathing. The Red Devils sought to be the masters, not the slaves. The English expected their sporting icons to be modest, self-effacing, grateful for everything they'd been blessed with; Billy Wright, rather than Little Richard. United were rock 'n' roll and we loved them all the more for that.

Looming even larger than his team stood Matt Busby. In both persona and vision, Busby was unlike any football manager the game had known. The day he took over at Old Trafford he began to redefine the role. United would be his club, run on his terms, promoting his idea of what a football club should be and how the game should be played. It took him ten years to create the team he'd dreamed of. Proud, young and fearless, the Red Devils were that team. They would, Busby believed, conquer not just England but Europe, where English football's stock was at an all-time low, the 6–3 drubbing at Wembley in 1953 having been followed by an even more humiliating 7–1 defeat in Budapest twelve months later.

In 1955 Chelsea won the League Championship but the Football League refused the Londoners the opportunity to contest the inaugural European Cup in 1956. Real Madrid, led by the Hungarian Puskás, won that first pan-European trophy.

Champions in 1956, United resisted Establishment pressure and became England's first European Cup contenders. They lost narrowly to Real in the semi-final, a remarkable outcome considering the disparity in age and experience between the two teams.

Watching all of this unfold from Dublin, we fell in love with Busby and his team. There was, of course, an Irish connection through Gentleman Johnny Carey, Busby's first captain, and Liam Whelan, the Devil from Cabra. But more alluring than anything was the dream-like fantasy football United played, and the rock 'n' roll, fuck-you vibe they symbolized. Irish football people, lovers of 'the foreign game', could easily identify with Busby nonconformists.

When Rovers were drawn against United, a wave of divine anticipation flowed through the city streets. Then thoughts turned to a more practical question: how to get into Dalymount Park to witness the great occasion. The match was set for September. The previous May Ireland had faced England in a World Cup qualifier at the same venue.

I'd tried and failed to get a 'lift over' in May. Heart aching, I hung around the turnstiles that day until the crowd's roar, greeting the teams on the field, brought my quest to an end. Running as fast as I could, I made it home to Drumcondra in ten minutes. We listened to the match on the radio. Ireland led until the final minute. Then Tom Finney dribbled to the end line to deliver an inch-perfect cross that Bristol City's John Atyeo dispatched to the net. This is one of the most famous moments in Irish sporting history. A stunned silence greeted this equalizing goal, a header that, with all its ruthless finality, seemed a here-and-now reminder of all the cruelties the English had inflicted on our Land of Saints and Scholars.

The anguish was poignantly captured in Philip Greene's baleful radio response: 'They've scored. England have scored. Ireland are out of the World Cup.'

The Rovers–United game was a sell-out. I got to Dalymount early that Wednesday evening. Looking for a 'lift over the stile' was an interesting way to assess the human condition. Half of those canvassed walked straight past, refusing to make eye contact: 10 per cent looked at you as if you had crawled out of a sewer; another cohort smiled weakly, indicating that they'd like to get you in but, well, it was against the law. You were left with somewhere between 10 and 15 per cent who were willing to help you beat the system.

I got lucky for the United game and joined the crowd, which was officially estimated at 46,000. Dalymount Park was famous for the 'Dalymount roar' but that night was different. Rovers' fans were a minority among the crowd. Most simply wanted to be there to see the English champions we had read and heard so much about. Duncan Edwards, Liam Whelan, Tommy Taylor, captain Roger Byrne, Dennis Viollet, Eddie Colman, David Pegg were the names we knew; their deeds we'd never seen until that mesmerizing evening.

They burst with graceful purpose onto the Dalymount pitch to a welcoming roar of acclaim. Respectful, almost reverent, no sense of the partisanship that usually attended when visitors took the field. Most had come to pay homage. It was a strange atmosphere, which probably explains what unfolded over the ensuing ninety minutes.

In the return fixture a couple of weeks later, Rovers acquitted themselves well, losing a hard-fought contest 3–2. But they were destroyed at Dalymount. United scored six goals, conceding none. Liam Whelan, born a five-minute walk from Dalymount, scored two. So often the assassins, Rovers were now the victims, the bull to United's matador. The performance was at once clinical and beautiful. In the middle of everything stood Duncan Edwards. He roamed the pitch with menacing intent. His was the dominant physical – and psychological – presence in any space he occupied.

That Dalymount night, he demonstrated other gifts as well. Fleet of foot, he brushed nonchalantly past opponents, ball at his feet, delivering laser passes to others in red shirts. Edwards was the hit-man surrounded by elusive conjurors.

At twenty-one, Edwards was already a veteran. He was the youngest person ever to play in the Football League, making his debut aged sixteen in 1955. Aged eighteen he was capped by England. He would become, many including Matt Busby believed, English football's greatest ever player. None of us who saw him in Dalymount Park that night were inclined to dispute that claim.

Rovers lost nothing in defeat. For they, too, were football lovers, gifted exponents of the game, reduced to spectators for one night only. Afterwards, exhausted, we dispersed in the chill, late-evening air to wonder at the spectacle we'd witnessed. We talked of little else for days. We would remember it for ever.

Five months later, on Thursday, 6 February 1958, Matt Busby's glorious adventure ended in tragedy at Munich airport. The chartered BEA plane taking the team home after their European Cup quarter-final victory over Red Star Belgrade crashed on take-off from Munich's Riem airport.

The flight was delayed because of inclement weather. Ice on the aircraft's wings and slush on the airport runway were the problems identified. Joining the players in the United party were a number of supporters and the journalists who'd covered the game. The players relaxed with cards while waiting for the all-clear for take-off. Matt Busby sat brooding. When he had defied the Football League to play in Europe, United were warned that failure to fulfil their domestic commitments would be severely punished.

Due to play Wolves on Saturday, Busby was under pressure. United were six points behind Wolves in the League. The likely sanction, a points deduction, would hand the League title to Wolves. There would also be the 'Little Englanders' to contend with, those who had warned him about this European folly. As far as Busby was concerned, BEA Flight 609 had to take off. Some still speculate that Busby's concerns were conveyed to those making the call on take-off. Maybe not explicitly. Who knows?

What we do know is that take-off was attempted and abandoned twice before Flight 609 crashed at the end of the runway, having failed to rise from the slush-coated ground. We know, too, that those aboard were fearful as the plane sped up the runway for the fatal third attempt to reach home. 'If this is death, I am ready,' Liam Whelan said.

With the aircraft's smouldering hulk threatening to explode, the plane's pilot, Captain James Thain, urged those who could to flee the scene. Harry Gregg ignored Thain's plea. Hearing moans from inside the stricken plane, he plunged inside to rescue those he could. Gregg had been barely two months at the club. He'd signed from Doncaster Rovers for £23,000, then a world record for a goalkeeper. Among those he carried to safety that day were team-mates Dennis Viollet, Jackie Blanchflower and Bobby Charlton. He went back inside the plane to rescue a badly injured Matt Busby, returning to assist Vera Lukić, the pregnant wife of a Yugoslav diplomat, and her daughter Venona, to exit the carnage.

I was in Paddy Fallon's barber shop in Drumcondra when news of an air crash at Munich first broke. Paddy, a popular local character, always had his radio tuned to the BBC. He was an accomplished musician, a *bodhrán* player, and a Fianna Fáil operative in Drumcondra. A Soldier of Destiny, Paddy loved the BBC: 'Great music,' he'd explain.

The reception was lousy. But the urgency in the Home Counties voice that interrupted the music caused Paddy to turn up the volume. 'A chartered plane carrying the Manchester United team has crashed at Munich airport. Ambulances and firemen are at the scene. There is no news yet of any casualties.' News travelled slowly in those days.

RTÉ's six o'clock radio news provided more information, but little detail. Many injured, some fatalities, RTÉ reported, but no names were mentioned. Thursday was a training night for Drums, so I went across to Tolka Park, where people were beginning to gather, attempting to sift fact from rumour.

The players had survived. Busby was dead. Liam Whelan also. What about Duncan Edwards? Three players were dead. Nobody knew. Rumour thrived.

The novelist H. E. Bates reflected the mood of early evening when he later wrote:

Late on a cold February afternoon, I was driving home from London when I suddenly saw, under the first lighted street lamps, one of those blue and yellow news placards that are designed so often to shock you into buying a newspaper you don't particularly want and that, nine times out of ten, you would be just as well off without. MANCHESTER UNITED AIR CRASH, it said. My immediate reaction was, I confess, a mildly cynical one. The announcement seemed to me to belong to precisely the same category as WINSTON CHURCHILL IN CAR CRASH – the car crash almost invariably turning out to be nothing more than a tender argument between the starting handle of an ancient Austin Seven and the great man's Rolls somewhere in the region of Parliament Square. I am getting too old, I thought, to be caught by newspaper screamers.

At six o'clock, out of pure curiosity, I turned on my television set. As the news came on, the screen seemed to go black. The normally urbane voice of the announcer seemed to turn into a sledgehammer. My eyes went deathly cold and I sat listening with a frozen brain to that cruel and shocking list of casualties that was now to give the despised word Munich an even sadder meaning than it had acquired on a day before the war when a Prime Minister had come home to London, waving a pitiful piece of paper, and most of us knew that new calamities of war were inevitable.

Few in Dublin had television, none that I knew of in the soccer community. But the sense of impending calamity that Bates alludes to spread through the city that night. The scale of what the headlines now described as the Munich Air Disaster became clear when we read the following morning's newspapers. Liam Whelan was dead. Busby and Duncan Edwards were fighting for their lives. After a fifteen-day battle, the magnificent Duncan Edwards died. In all twenty-three passengers died, including eight players, United's coach Bert Whalley, trainer Tom Curry, club secretary Walter Crickmer and journalist Frank Swift, the former England and Manchester City goalkeeper.

The pall of despair that spread across the city touched even those who knew nothing of sport, 'foreign' or otherwise. As would subsequently happen with the killings of the Kennedy brothers, Martin Luther King and later still John Lennon, our spirits sank as the realization dawned that something rare and inspiring had been lost to the world.

13. Doors Closing and Opening

Drums won the League of Ireland in 1958. Kit Lawlor, returned from a four-year stint as a full-time pro with Doncaster Rovers, was their outstanding player. Much of the credit for the title victory was attributed to Sam Prole. In their undemonstrative Presbyterian way, the Proles had changed the culture at the club: the gate money no longer ended up in the owner's bank account; the players were paid and otherwise treated with respect, as were those like my father who laboured in the background.

A couple of months earlier Sam had approached my father, who he'd heard was on the dole. He had offered Paddy part-time work doing odd jobs around the stadium. Paddy would be paid cash-in-hand so he could still draw his dole. After almost two years of enforced austerity this offer provided a huge boost to Paddy's morale. And to our family's.

The rent would be paid and sirloin steak restored to the menu. When we did the sums, my father's income had doubled as a result of this arrangement. In fact, he was earning slightly more than he would have on a building site. He hadn't had to join Fianna Fáil. Or the Presbyterian Church.

I was in my last year of primary school. Although I remained in the top three pupils in class without having to work too hard, I was acutely aware that this was a defining moment in my life. The post-primary options were an academic education lasting five years in a fee-paying school, or a two-year stint in Technical College, where you learned a trade.

Along with my mother and father I went to Mr Hayden to discuss my future. My parents explained that we didn't have the money for fees, much less the uniform, books and other accessories required to attend the second-level colleges.

'Eamon should go to college,' Mr Hayden argued, adding that of course he understood our financial circumstances. He also understood, as did Paddy and Peg, that Tech could be a waste of time. Even if you were lucky enough to become an apprentice carpenter, plumber or electrician, those occupations, often closely aligned to the building industry, were vulnerable in recessionary times.

'He's one of the best students I've ever taught,' Mr Hayden insisted. 'Eamon should go to college and on to university.' This endorsement meant a lot to me. Thanks to Mr Hayden's encouragement, I'd never lacked confidence in the classroom. But now my time in his care was ending. As his conversation with my parents explored the options available, I felt a frisson of apprehension, bordering on fear, that I would end up working as an electrician for the builder Macken, with a Larry Gaynor ordering me to join the Soldiers of Destiny and handing me my cards if I refused. Fuck that for a game of cowboys. I'm not going there, I silently vowed.

At the end of our meeting, Mr Hayden offered a glimmer of hope: the government ran a scholarship scheme that awarded free second-level college education to seven students every year. He offered to sponsor me to get the application forms and fill them in. He also referred to a scholarship available from a fee-paying school on the southside, Sandymount High School. Thus, plans A and B were conceived.

The government scholarship exam took place in a huge room at the Department of Education in Marlborough Street. The room was packed with kids from all over the city. All present were in the same boat: deemed worthy by their teachers of the college education they couldn't afford.

Knowing how high the stakes were, I was extremely nervous. The exam papers were distributed by hard-faced men who made no eye contact. At nine o'clock the bell rang to signal the start of this ordeal. As I turned my paper over, I felt the kind of dread that I had experienced only once before: waiting for the judge's verdict at the eviction hearing.

I stared at the paper. My mind went blank. I couldn't understand question one or question two. I sat for a moment looking around the room. Everyone else was motoring. I returned to the exam paper. Nothing. It might as well have been written in Chinese. I got up and left the room. I was home at ten o'clock.

The following week I sat the Sandymount High School exam. The nerves had passed. I thought I'd done OK. This was confirmed when a letter arrived informing me that I had finished seventh in the exam. The school were pleased to offer me a one-year scholarship.

Having failed to read the terms and conditions before sitting the exam, I'd mistakenly believed that the top seven applicants would be offered a full scholarship. In fact, only the top two received the five-year deal. The remaining five places were accommodated on a sliding scale, four years, three years, two years and finally a couple of consolation prizes consisting of a solitary year.

Whoever sanctioned this arrangement obviously had a sense of humour. The one- and two-year scholarships were less than worthless. To acquire the first second-level qualification required three years' study before sitting your Intermediate exam. After one or two years you'd leave with nothing.

My parents wanted me to go to Tech where I might get a qualification that would enable me to become an apprentice tradesman. I resisted, quietly but firmly. I wasn't going to work in the building trade for the Mackens and their ilk. Tech was, in my mind, for fools. I was coming up to my thirteenth birthday. You could leave school at fourteen. So the one-year deal at Sandymount High would, almost, get me over the line. Then we could reassess the situation.

Without telling anybody, I'd been preparing for this moment for quite a while. I knew the score. Paying fees was never an option, so I knew a college education was a non-runner, bar a miracle. Going to Tech to learn how to become building-site fodder was not going to happen. I was left with two choices: the slender hope that I would get a chance to go to England to play football; or, more realistically, that I would go to England to join the British Army. The latter seemed more probable than the former. The prospect of joining the army became attractive when I ran into a neighbour known as Soldier McNally. He was three or four years older than me.

Soldier had signed up for the British Army aged sixteen. When he came home for holidays, he cut an impressive figure. He had money, loads of it, a healthy tan, and a certain swaggering confidence that made him stand out. When I asked him about army life he told me it was great. You learn a trade, see the world and get out of this 'fucking kip'. The money's good. And, he confided, you can save a lot because your food and board are free.

Curious, I checked out the British Army recruitment ads in the newspapers. You could join at sixteen, but you had to commit for a minimum nine years. Weighing everything up in the light of Sandymount High School's offer, the British Army seemed an attractive option. I didn't mention this plan to my parents.

There was another possibility lurking at the back of my mind, something that might have encouraged me to go to Tech. One of our neighbours was a printer. Maybe it was my fascination with newspapers, books and comics that drew me to the notion of printing as an attractive trade. When I mentioned this to my father he took me round to see the printer. What if I did well in the Tech, would there be any chance of a job in the printing works? 'No chance, Paddy,' our friend replied. 'You have to be family or related to get into this game.' I was becoming familiar with the sound of doors slamming in my face.

While all of this was going on, my football life was blossoming. We were now playing in the Under-14 League. Home Farm were winning everything in their section, but Stella Maris were their only serious opposition. The rivalry was fierce. There was something more than football at play in the contest. It was posh boys versus urchins, college boys against street kids.

Home Farm had two outstanding players, Jim Keogh and Paddy Mulligan. Jim was reckoned to be the best schoolboy in the country. A wing-half, he was an imposing physical presence with two good feet. He was the dominant character in every game we played. The word was that Billy Behan had already booked Jim for Old Trafford. He was a 'cert' for his schoolboy cap. Paddy Mulligan would in time play for Chelsea and West Bromwich Albion and win fifty full international caps. Like me, he was an inside-forward, but stronger, more physically combative than I was.

Ciaran and I were the main men for Stella. Both teams possessed good players, but the outcome of Home Farm–Stella contests was invariably decided by the respectable performances of Keogh/Mulligan–Martin/Dunphy. Physically they had the edge.

Home Farm won the League in 1959. Then we met in the final of the Paddy Thunder Cup. The game was played at Richmond Park, the home of League of Ireland club St Patrick's Athletic. After ninety minutes we were level. Towards the end of extra time we got a penalty. I took it and scored. For once we'd beaten them. Victory tasted sweet.

After the game the legendary broadcaster Jimmy Magee interviewed me for *Sports Stadium*, the country's marquee Saturday-afternoon radio sports show. 'We're not live,' Jimmy told me, 'so if you get home by five fifteen you'll hear yourself on the radio.'

I would like to report that I was unimpressed by the thought of hearing myself on the radio, that I stayed with Ciaran and my team-mates to savour the joy of our victory. Truth is, I grabbed my boots and my winner's medal and legged it to the bus stop, desperate to get home in time to listen to myself. By the time I got home, *Sports Stadium* was over.

Meanwhile, Sandymount High School was worse than a waste of time. The one-year scholarship could only lead me down an educational cul-de-sac. The lengthy book-list put an intolerable strain on the family budget. The cost of the school uniform made matters worse. Sandymount High was co-educational and non-denominational. The absence of God posed no problem. The presence of girls caused extreme anxiety.

I did OK academically, but after Mr Hayden the teachers seemed coolly indifferent. Rugby was the only game on offer. I won a place at scrum-half in the school team. That meant getting a jersey, which my mother somehow found the money to buy. In the first game of the season this expensive garment was ripped off my back by a rampant toff I was trying to outwit. That was the end of my rugby career. I also developed a crush on a girl who was at least a foot taller than me and oblivious to my existence. The only box I was ticking was the one marked 'pain'.

Plan A was still the British Army. As I couldn't sign up until I was sixteen, I started to scan the small ads in the newspapers for a job.

Plan B was a schoolboy cap, which now seemed a real possibility. Spurred by the absence of alternatives, I invested all my energy in football. The game provided refuge from the hurt and confusion of Sandymount High. On the pitch I was confident, in control, a leader. The Clark Kent of Sandymount High School transformed into the Superman of Stella Maris.

One of the highlights of the under-14s year was the annual game between Dublin and Belfast. North-South relations weren't exactly warm in 1959, but the vicious tribalism of the coming troubles lay dormant for the time being. Ciaran Martin and I were both picked for the Dublin team to travel to Belfast for the game, which was due to be played at Celtic Park. I learned of our selection when reading my father's newspaper the Tuesday after our Cup Final win.

Jim Keogh and Paddy Mulligan were also in the squad, as was Robbie

Cray, one of the best midfield players in the city, who played for Bolton Athletic out of Ringsend Park, a public facility known as Iodine Park. This was a big deal. Selection for the Dublin under-14 squad opened up the possibility of a schoolboy cap the following year.

Although only eighty miles up the road, Belfast was a foreign place, grey and forbidding to our young eyes. It was Protestant, British, many of its kerbstones painted in the colours of the Union flag. Flags in these alien colours flew from windows and lamp-posts. Celtic Park, the venue for the game, had its own shocking recent history. On St Stephen's Day 1948 the Belfast Celtic–Linfield derby, the equivalent of Glasgow's Celtic–Rangers fixture, had ended in horrific scenes of violence. A sectarian mob of Linfield supporters invaded the pitch to attack Jimmy Jones, Celtic's Protestant striker. Jones, Celtic's star player, was regarded as a traitor to his tribe. In the ensuing battle between rival fans, Jones was beaten to a pulp and his leg was broken, which shocked the whole island. Shortly afterwards, Belfast Celtic quit the Irish League and ceased to exist.

Our bus journey to the game took us down the Protestant Shankill Road. With its garish flags and painted pavements, the Shankill resembled a movie set, a strange, dark and sullen neighbourhood, the symbols of sectarianism, 'Fuck the Pope' among them, offering a chilling glimpse of hatred lurking in the shadows.

Celtic Park was now used only for greyhound racing. We played before a small crowd on a pitch that was perfectly manicured. A dull game ended 0–0. We were glad to get out of town and back to the Land of Saints and Scholars.

My year at Sandymount was up, and I needed a job. But jobs for thirteen-year-olds were thin on the ground. Messenger boy seemed the best bet: the ads usually ended with the comforting words 'no experience required'. My first application was successful. Kevin and Howlin was an upmarket draper's on Nassau Street at the bottom of Grafton Street, then and now Dublin's swankiest shopping boulevard. Two weeks after leaving Sandymount High, I answered their ad by turning up in person. After a brief interview I was hired for thirty shillings a week. My parents didn't approve. This seemed like a dead-end job on the road to Nowhere, which of course it was, if you discounted my plan to join the British Army. I said nothing about that.

Many of Kevin and Howlin's customers were American tourists who liked to spend their dollars on the shop's speciality, Donegal tweed. The local clients were mostly from the south Dublin professional class, the pinstriped bandits from law and accountancy, men in good suits behaving badly. My job was to deliver the goods. For this task I was given a bike with a large iron basket at the front.

My daily trips round the city took me to the best hotels where I would drop the order at the concierge's desk. On one memorable occasion I took a special delivery to the US ambassador's residence in the Phoenix Park. Received at the tradesmen's entrance, I delivered the Donegal tweed and was delighted to be handed a tip: twenty Marlboro cigarettes.

I enjoyed my work. Mr Foley, the shop manager, was a slyly genial character, a typical Dubliner, solicitous of his demanding clients, a model of deference as they prowled the floor plucking garments off the rails. Whatever it took to make the sale, was his motto. Patient diplomacy usually did the trick.

A lady in her thirties and a man in his twenties completed the sales team. Like Mr Foley, they treated me respectfully. I was shy and acutely conscious of my lowly status so their genuine warmth meant a lot to me, and left a lasting impression.

It is only now looking back that I realize the toll living in Drumcondra had taken on my self-esteem. There was something wonderful about life in our room on Richmond Road, principally the love lavished on Kevin and me by our parents. But there was also, for me, something very distressing about being the poorest kid in the locality. About sleeping on the floor, not having electricity, about the filth in the basement after the flood, the patched-up clothes, the empty pockets, the absence of money for schoolbooks, my father's unemployment, the threat of eviction, the long, lonely summer days when the other kids were biking to the seaside, or seeking shelter from the rain at the picture house I couldn't afford.

The merciless tyranny of poverty was redeemed by my parents' love, but not entirely. It was redeemed also by Mr Hayden and Dessie Toal, but not entirely. There was no escape from the hurt inflicted, the enduring sense of being different.

But now, as Kevin and Howlin's messenger boy, I had left Drumcondra behind. To those I worked for in the shop I was just Eamon. The fact that at thirteen I had a job while my forty-year-old father remained on the dole was perverse. That thought never occurred to me at the time. In my determination to avoid becoming a victim of circumstances, to escape from the box marked 'surplus to requirements' where my father languished, I thought only about myself.

One night at training in Stella, Father Mac enquired about my father. Was he still out of work? I confirmed he was. Later that night Father Mac knocked on our door. He brought good news. There was a job going at the Richmond Hospital, where he was the chaplain. The old Dublin saying 'It's not what you know, it's who you know' had never worked in our favour. For once it did.

Twenty-four hours later Paddy had a job as a ward orderly in Richmond Three, the hospital's trauma ward. The position was permanent and pensionable. And you could vote for any political party. Father Mac had used his influence, 'the bit of pull' as it was known, to trump the union boss *in situ* who'd earmarked the job for one of his buddies. In a corrupt society, where virtually every transaction was tainted in one form or another, this roll of the dice favoured a decent man.

He joined the union, kept his head down and remained in Richmond Three for twenty-five happy years. We were overjoyed, my mother most of all. 'Broken time' was a thing of the past.

14.   International

Billy Behan started coming to our games. Ciaran and I had been selected for the international trial match, the Probables versus the Possibles. Nobody was quite sure which was which, but everybody knew that Jim Keogh would be among the Probables. That was good news for me and my pal. We lined up alongside Jim.

Paddy Mulligan togged out for the Possibles. The scenario suggested that I was favourite to win my schoolboy cap, though there were a couple of negatives. Mulligan was playing for the better team, who were top of the League. And he was a Home Farm boy who'd forged an effective partnership with Keogh at club level.

Everyone who was anyone turned up to watch the international trial: the selectors, Billy Behan, friends, family and supporters of all the clubs represented. You got one shot at the coveted prize and this was it.

Ciaran was brilliant on the day. He scored, and more, leading the team, setting up chances, getting stuck into guys who were a foot taller. Over the years he and I had formed a deep bond, on and off the field. From endless hours on the street we'd learned to anticipate each other's moves, exchange perfectly weighted passes, suck opponents out of their comfort zone before leaving them flailing at thin air.

The alchemy was harder to work in the trial. Instead of the usual fodder we faced the best young footballers in the country. Mulligan was intent on roughing me up. But I was buzzing and hungrier than him. I lost nothing on the day. Afterwards Ciaran and I compared notes. I thought he was a certainty; he thought I was. He'd noted Mulligan's attempts at physical intimidation.

Two international games were due, one against Wales in Cork, the second against England in Tolka Park. The selectors operated on the basis of regular assessment. The most influential selector was said to be Jem Kennedy. Jem was one of the most respected characters on the city's schoolboy soccer scene. He worked for the Gas Board checking meters, but schoolboy football was his passion. He'd previously run Johnville, an inner-city club where Paddy Mulvey, the best-ever Dublin schoolboy footballer, had been the star. When Johnville collapsed for lack of funds, Jem became an administrator. You'd regularly see him riding around town on his rust-coloured Gas Board bike. He'd stop for a chat, always friendly, smiling, offering words of encouragement. Authority rendered human, Jem, gentle and streetwise, was the best kind of Dubliner. Knowing he was a selector gave Ciaran and me reason to hope.

A couple of weeks before the international team was due to be named we had an away fixture against Home Farm. Posh though they were, and thought themselves to be, their pitch was rough and narrow, appropriately known as the 'chicken run'. With points and international caps at stake, this was the big game of the season. With the scores level in the second half of what had become a war of attrition, Mulligan floored me with a ferocious tackle. Ciaran jumped in, fists and boots flying. I got up and piled in behind him. Within seconds a full-scale brawl was under way. Street boys against posh boys.

Mentors, among them Father Mac and Mr Kennedy, managed to separate the antagonists. The referee pulled Ciaran and me aside. We were booked and sent off. 'Gurriers, ye should be ashamed of yourselves, go back where you came from,' the hostile Farm supporters roared from their vantage point on the moral high ground.

Trudging disconsolately towards the dressing room, Ciaran and I ignored the noisy mob. Less easily ignored was the very unwelcome sight of Jem Kennedy and the chairman of the selectors, Jim Troy, witnessing our shame.

At training on Tuesday night Father Mac informed us that Home Farm had lodged a protest with the authorities. According to the letter he was holding, 'Dunphy and Martin were not fit to represent their country and we respectfully submit that they should not be considered for selection for forthcoming games.'

'Don't worry,' Father Mac assured us, 'we'll fight this.'

We worried, though. A hearing was arranged for the following Tuesday in Parnell Square. By coincidence, or not, I encountered Jem Kennedy on Richmond Road the day before the hearing. He pulled over. 'You're in big trouble,' he said, stern-faced. Then he smiled. 'Don't worry, I'll see what I can do.'

The Home Farm delegation was headed by Joey Tynan, a senior committee man. Tynan was well known for taking himself even more seriously than the average Home Farmer, who made much of the fact that they had nurtured Johnny Carey and the recently deceased Liam Whelan. They really meant business. Father Mac and Mr Kennedy were there to make the case for myself and Ciaran.

The hearing lasted a long forty-five minutes. We waited in the corridor outside the committee room. Eventually we were beckoned inside to hear the verdict. I tried to read Jem Kennedy's face. He made no eye contact. Jim Troy was equally poker-faced. We're fucked, I thought.

'This protest has no merit,' Jim Troy read from a piece of paper. 'Both players will be available for selection for the international team.'

When the team to play Wales was announced the following week Ciaran and I were both selected. Paddy Mulligan was on the bench. The failed protest had been launched to secure a cap for Mulligan. Like Fianna Fáil, Home Farm were ruthless when it came to looking after their own. The match in Cork was my first night away from home. The game, played on a bumpy end-of-season pitch, ended in a fairly uneventful draw.

Over the next few weeks my life would be defined. Things happened at bewildering speed. Billy Behan approached my father to offer a trial with Manchester United. My mother was alarmed by this development. Paddy tried to reassure her. It's only a trial, nothing may come of it. Why, Peg wondered, did I have to go to England to play football? Wasn't there plenty of football at home? Like John Giles's mother, and many other mothers before her, Peg took a dim view of Mr Behan, who'd come to take her first son away.

My focus was on the season's marquee game against England, due to be played across the road in Tolka Park. I retained my place in the Irish side, as did Ciaran. After all the years of fantasizing about the big-time, this was it: a big match, before a full house with no need to ask for 'a lift over'. Billy Behan told Paddy that Matt Busby's assistant, Jimmy Murphy, would be at the England game. In the meantime Bill Shankly had been in contact, offering me a contract with Liverpool. Shankly had been barely a year at Anfield, and Liverpool were in the Second Division. I wasn't too impressed by this offer.

England usually hammered Irish schoolboy teams. Their players were bigger, stronger, more experienced. They'd all been signed up by the top English clubs. We'd do well to avoid a hiding. The rain lashed down before the game. The wet pitch made for better football, the ball running true on the slippy surface. Lining up before the kick-off I felt a shiver of apprehension: they looked like muscled giants, radiating menacing intent. My instinct was that the task was impossible. Not Ciaran's. He winked at me. 'Come on, let's have a go.' And so we did.

It was what the papers described as 'a thrilling encounter', played at astonishing pace, with unbelievable intensity. Street wit and guile versus the power and graceful athleticism that typified the English game. Physically it was men against boys. The result, a 2–2 draw, moved the crowd to give us a standing ovation as we left the pitch.

Ducking and diving, passing and gliding past our burly opponents, I did OK. Ciaran scored a goal. He was, I thought, the outstanding player on the night, his have-a-go attitude inspiring the rest of us.

Sitting in our room across the road, Peg heard the commotion and wondered at its cause. I'd slipped in to see her before the game. 'Take care,' she said, sprinkling some holy water on my head.

Afterwards I met Jimmy Murphy, who confirmed United's offer of a two-week trial. My decision to blank Bill Shankly seems, in retrospect, bizarre.

15. To Manchester

On 1 August 1960, two days before my fifteenth birthday, I took an Aer Lingus flight to Manchester. Billy Behan arrived at the house to drive me to the airport. The room I was leaving was draped in sadness. My mother was distressed. She couldn't really come to terms with what was happening. Where was I going? Why? Who'd look after me? My father, subdued, could not supply the answers to Peg's questions. Billy Behan's soothing blather sounded unconvincing, even to me.

'Matt Busby is a Catholic,' Behan assured Peg. 'United is a Catholic club. The boys are well looked after, given the best of everything. And, anyway, it's only two weeks and he'll probably be home.' Hurt and bewilderment shadowing her face, my mother embraced me, blessed me with holy water, and bade us farewell.

On the way to the airport I asked Billy Behan about Ciaran. Why hadn't he been offered a trial? The answer was straight and to the sickening point: 'He's not the right type for Manchester United,' Behan declared. 'Character is everything at Old Trafford.' As vivid today as when it was voiced, that slur — based solely on Ciaran being from the wrong part of town — would often spring to mind in the years to come.

At Dublin airport I met my two travelling companions. Jim Keogh had signed as an apprentice professional for United. He was a made man, for two years at least. The other boy, Hughie Curran, was also from Home Farm. Hughie was two years older than us. He was Scottish, a late developer who'd had a great goal-scoring season for Farm under-17s. Like me, he was on a two-week trial.

On arrival at Manchester airport, we were met by Joe Armstrong. Joe was United's chief scout, renowned for his ability to persuade the best young footballers — and, more importantly, their parents, especially the mothers — that Manchester United was the place to be, with Matt Busby the man to turn promise into achievement. It was Joe who had signed many of the Busby Babes, Bobby Charlton, Eddie Colman and Duncan Edwards among them. This tiny, cherubic, ostensibly cheerful character was an indispensable figure in the Busby project. White-haired and wily, Joe made us feel welcome.

The feel-good factor lasted about an hour. He drove us to Old Trafford, gave us a tour of the famous ground, the highlight of which was a poignant look at the clock high on the stadium wall, recording the time and date of the Munich air crash. 'Now, boys, let's fix you up with your digs,' Joe announced. After a five-minute walk we arrived at a tall, terraced house. Bonhomie was Joe's stock-in-trade. As he ushered us into the narrow hallway, our landlady appeared from the kitchen further down the corridor. Like her house, she looked unprepossessing. All smiles and wisecracks, the chief scout entrusted us to her charge. 'Look after them and make sure they behave,' he chided. Before slipping away, he gave each of us a fiver. 'See you at training in the morning. Herself will tell you how to get there.'

After showing us to our rooms, Hughie and I sharing, Jim in a single on his tod, our carer took us down to the kitchen. It was lunchtime. The kitchen was an eye-opener. Long and narrow, an extension of the hallway, it featured a large rectangular table with benches on either side. Packed tightly round it, a group of working men were tucking into their grub. 'Move along there, lads,' the landlady urged. 'We've got some guests from Ireland.' A wave of indifference descended on the room. They moved along, but grudgingly.

Out of the back window I could see a number of large trucks. Our companions were truck drivers munching the traditional Lancashire working man's dish: pie and mash, covered with thick brown gravy. I wanted to go home to my mammy. Lunch arrived: a plate with two slices of Spam, one tomato and two boiled potatoes, with a cup of foul-tasting tea on the side. Real Manchester United fare. No prawn sandwiches here.

The training ground was a ten-minute bus ride from the city centre. It was crowded. Twenty pounds a week was the maximum wage, the average earnings much less than that. There were between forty and fifty players on United's books in 1960.

We were supplied with some training kit before joining the ranks of aspiring Babes. The First Team, tragically depleted at Munich, trained separately. The atmosphere was relaxed. There was no sign of Matt Busby, but we did glimpse Bobby Charlton, Harry Gregg and Bill Foulkes, and John Giles came over to say hello.

There were plenty of footballs around, a signal that Manchester United was a progressive club. A debate had been raging for years in English football, ever since the Hungarian débâcle at Wembley. The traditionalists, Stan Cullis the successful manager of Wolves among them, argued that access to the football should be restricted during the week. If denied balls during the week, players would be hungrier to get at the one they played with on Saturday. Absurd though that argument now seems, it was an article of faith at many clubs. Busby rejected this nonsense, pointing out that the more ball players enjoyed during training sessions, the more comfortable they would be on Saturday afternoon.

No distinction was made between trialists and those who were already signed as apprentice pros. Training sessions lasted a couple of hours, the first hour spent doing physical work, the second with the ball. The physical stuff was hard, and no allowance was made for newcomers. It was every man for himself. You stayed with the pack or looked stupid. We managed. The work with the ball consisted of passing and dribbling exercises followed by an improvised game. This was the Dump, except with much better players. It was an opportunity to test yourself against the best young players in the British Isles.

Post-Munich, United had the pick of the crop from England, Scotland, Wales and both parts of Ireland. In one way or another all these youngsters had something special to offer. There were gifted ball players, exceptional defenders, guys with burning pace and tough-talking perpetual-motion machines putting it up to boys like me who could play a bit. Hunger was the common denominator. Everyone wanted to impress. In every training session.

All had been exceptional in their home place, but this was the most famed academy in the world, a step up into the unknown. As the week passed I got into it in a big way. Concentration was the key. Playing for Stella I could sometimes coast through games, confident I could step up a gear when and if required. There was no coasting here: the matches were full on from the off.

At the beginning of our second week, Hughie and I began to wonder about the nature of our trial. Were we being assessed? If so, by whom? We still hadn't seen Busby. Jimmy Murphy was in another corner of the training ground with the First Team. Jack Crompton, a former United goalkeeper, was with Murphy.

Johnny Aston, who'd played right full-back in the 1945 FA Cup-winning team, took charge of our sessions. Would he decide our fate? Aston, a dour character, was hard to read. On the Wednesday, two days before our trial was due to end, we got what appeared to be our answer. As we sorted out the teams for the end-of-training game, Matt Busby appeared pitch-side. Jimmy Murphy and Joe Armstrong were with him. 'This is it,' Hughie whispered.

Busby was a tall, imposing figure. There was something unearthly about him, a calm assurance that exuded wisdom and authority. If you were casting a legend for a movie he would be your man. It's known as presence; Matt Busby possessed it in spades. This was it. And everyone knew it.

From the moment the game kicked off I was on fire. Some days you just know you're in control. This, for me, was one of them. Every time I got possession of the ball, I saw the right pass. I rode tackles with ease. My passes were precise to the inch. I was inspired, by what, I simply do not know. Maybe fear of failure, maybe the god of destiny. I'd never played as well before, and rarely would in future. But for that fateful thirty minutes I summoned up from the depths of my being everything I'd learned on the streets and parks of Dublin.

At half-time I was substituted. I'd given it my best shot, so I didn't mind. Joe Armstrong walked me back to the dressing room. 'You did well, son. The Boss was impressed,' he explained. After training the following day, Joe drove me to Old Trafford. He took me to Jimmy Murphy's office. Jimmy explained that he'd been in touch with Billy Behan who'd got my parents' permission to allow me to sign for United as an apprentice pro.

Forms were produced. I signed. I was a professional footballer. 'Go home and see your family and come back next week,' they told me.

The few days at home were strange. My mother was quiet. She couldn't come to terms with what was happening, something she had not foreseen and couldn't alter. She bought me a small suitcase and a few bits and pieces of clothes.

Everyone in Drumcondra seemed to know that I'd signed for United. I'd won the lottery that all street footballers dreamed of. I went to see Ciaran and Dessie to say goodbye. In different ways both had been hugely important to me, far more than they knew of, or than I did at the time. Father Mac called in to console my mother. He brought a gift for me: a set of rosary beads.

Kevin and I had always been close. Although the two-year gap between us meant we hung out in different circles, we'd spent many hours together in the room playing card games and snakes and ladders, swapping comics and listening to the matches on the radio. Over all the years together, going to Croke Park, Milltown or across the road to Tolka with our dad, or to mass with Peg, there had formed between us a deep, unspoken bond of shared experience. He was an outstanding footballer who would, two years on, win a schoolboy cap for Ireland. He was a defender, bigger and stronger than me, more dependable, more content with the hand he was dealt. Kevin signed up for Tech. He wanted to learn a trade. When I talked about joining the British Army, he thought I was mad.

Billy Behan arrived at the door the night before I was due to return to Manchester. He was the last person Peg wanted to see. Full of bonhomie as usual, Billy assured my parents that I'd be all right. Matt and Jimmy had been very impressed by my trial. I'd be well looked after; he would keep them in touch with my progress. As he was leaving, Billy slipped my dad an envelope. There was fifty quid inside. Deal done. Paddy was subdued. He knew the woman he loved was heartbroken. He knew that she felt he was mainly responsible for her pain.

The day I left was long and sad. I was going by boat to Liverpool and on to Manchester by train. My mother packed my small brown case, two shirts neatly folded, a spare pair of shoes, a change of underwear and socks, a toothbrush, some toothpaste and the rosary beads Father Mac had given to me. Kevin and my dad came with me to the North Wall to get the boat. My mother was too distressed to make that journey. I couldn't wait to go. She couldn't bear to see me go.

Unlike me, Peg knew what was happening. As a young girl she'd left home herself to find work and a better life. She'd never really returned. Now that better way of life she'd found was threatened. Her family, which was her life, was diminished, almost certainly for ever. In my callous adolescent mind I was off on a great liberating adventure. I uttered hollow words about return and regret. But Peg feared, and she was right, that this was the end of our story.

Joe Armstrong met me at Central Station in Manchester. He'd found me my digs where he assured me I'd be 'well looked after'. Mrs Cropper lived a ten-minute walk from Old Trafford. She was a bingo-playing widow. The bingo-playing would turn out to be important. Out of my seven-pounds-a-week wage, four went to Mrs C, as she was known to everyone, including Joe. From the remaining three, Joe advised me to send thirty shillings home. The rest was mine.

Mrs C was brisk and business-like. 'My, you're a little lad,' she exclaimed, when Joe delivered me. 'I'm going to have to feed you plenty to build you up for Matt.' As I would in time discover, other landladies ran tighter ships: set times for meals, no access to the parlour where the telly was, no girls in your room – a restriction that, given my experience with girls, seemed amusingly irrelevant. Mrs C was more easy-going. After showing me my bedroom, she gave me a tour of her neat semi-detached house, telling me, 'It's all yours, love. Treat it like your own home.'

At six o'clock that evening I presented myself in the kitchen for dinner. Mrs C was dressed to the nines and in a hurry. 'I'm off to bingo,' she declared, hastily placing the dish of the day on the table. 'There's some jelly and ice-cream in the fridge!' were the last words I heard before the front door slammed shut.

Meat of uncertain provenance, watery potatoes and peas lay on the plate in front of me. Smelling the meat I suddenly lost my appetite. I tried a taste. What the fuck was this? I wondered. The spuds were similarly unappealing, nothing like the tasty balls of flour my mother dished up at home. I couldn't eat this shit. The question was what to do with it. If I left it, Mrs C would be offended.

I wandered into the kitchen to get the jelly and ice-cream. Two tins inside the fridge solved the mystery of my dinner. Alongside the half-empty tin of peas stood a half-empty tin of 'prime beef' covered with 'rich gravy'. Eating my jelly and ice-cream, I made plans to dispose of my uneaten dinner. I tipped the 'prime beef', the potatoes and the peas into a plastic bag, then went in search of the nearest dustbin. On the way back I bought some fish 'n' chips.

Mrs C returned from bingo around ten o'clock. 'Everything all right, love?' she asked.

'Yes, thanks,' I lied.

'I see you've cleaned your plate.' She smiled. 'I knew you would – my boys always do. You need your food with all that training.'

I met Barry Fry on my first day as a United player. He'd played inside-forward for England schoolboys against us at Tolka Park. He was one of England's big schoolboy stars, regarded as a certainty to 'make it'.

Scorer of four goals in his five schoolboy international games, Barry was wanted by all the big English clubs. He had chosen Manchester United for many reasons, the main one, according to him, being the money.

When Matt Busby had first embarked on his youth-development project he had been a pioneer. It was relatively easy to persuade the best young footballers to join United. Of course, every club wanted the best young players, but no one pursued them as ruthlessly as Busby's United. He had built a network of scouts across the British Isles, all reporting to Joe Armstrong.

While other clubs, like Wolves, Spurs and Arsenal, would take notice only when talent appeared on the radar in schoolboy internationals, United would get interested much earlier. Duncan Edwards came from Dudley, near Wolverhampton, home of England's most renowned club in the early fifties. He was a Wolves fan. But United got to him first. Joe Armstrong courted Duncan's parents long before other clubs were aware of his existence. Busby's growing reputation as a nurturer of young footballers helped. So did the promise that Duncan would get his chance early. But the key was the personal touch, the relationship Armstrong built with his parents. Their boy would be looked after. And Armstrong invited Duncan and his parents, Gladstone and Sarah Ann, to Manchester. They were given a tour of Old Trafford, shown the digs Duncan would live in and generally encouraged to believe that they – and their son – were special. The wooing worked. Edwards was snatched from under the nose of his home-town club. Bobby Charlton, nephew of the great Newcastle United centre-forward Jackie Milburn, was subjected to the same intensive courtship.

By 1960, the spectacular success of the Busby Babes had alerted other clubs to the importance of harvesting young talent. Busby now had competition, some of it unscrupulous. Money was changing hands. It was no longer sufficient to promise opportunity and that your son would be 'looked after'. So, when United came knocking on Barry Fry's door, the question of money arose.

It was illegal to pay signing-on fees to parents. Acting for Busby, Joe Armstrong came up with a solution. Barry's father was appointed United's scout for the south of England. A lump sum also changed hands. Barry's father never scored any talent.

Barry came from Bedford. He would become, and indeed remains, one of English football's legendary characters. On that first morning, when most of us newcomers were shy, diffident, Barry breezed around the place as if he owned it. Barry was charming, funny and very confident. He remembered me and Jim Keogh from the Tolka game. When Barry met Hughie Curran, no introduction was needed. They had much in common. Hughie wasn't short of personality or confidence. When the four of us compared notes, we found a common grievance: our digs. I aired my concerns about Mrs C's idea of a good feed. Barry told us a lurid story about his landlady, who had, he claimed, tried to seduce him by bringing him a cup of Ovaltine, in his bedroom, as he was nodding off to sleep. Jim and Hughie were sharing a small room in a terraced house close to Old Trafford. It was cramped and the food was shit, Hughie declared.

I was as prone to bitching as the next man, at least on the surface, but in truth my reservations about Mrs C's hospitality amounted to nothing more than a talking point. I was a glass-half-full man, a Manchester United player, living the life so many other kids would die for. Although it served as a means of bonding with the lads, whingeing was a waste of time. Living the life, not the dream. The dream was for comics.

If moaning was your game there was plenty to complain about at Manchester United's dream factory. Nobody nurtured you. We trained at the Cliff every day except Friday, which was spent at Old Trafford. Overlooking the river Irwell and the old Manchester racecourse, the Cliff stood on high ground in one of the few posh neighbourhoods in the borough of Salford, made famous by Ewan MacColl's folk song 'Dirty Old Town'.

The First Team squad of roughly sixteen trained at one end of the pitch, the rest of us at the other. From a distance we could see Bobby Charlton, Harry Gregg, John Giles, Nobby Stiles and Bill Foulkes, the made men we wanted to be. Training was straightforward to the point of being primitive. We spent the first hour running round the pitch, the second hour with the ball.

There was no coaching. There were no coaches. Matt Busby and Jimmy Murphy were rarely present. Jack Crompton and Johnny Aston were coaches in name only. Both former United players, they had returned to the club after the crash to replace Bert Whalley and Tom Curry, who'd perished at Munich.

Jack, goalkeeper in the '48 FA Cup-winning team, took charge of the First Team. He supervised the running and refereed the improvised game afterwards. Johnny Aston looked after the rest of us. Like Jack, Johnny had played in the '48 Cup Final and seventeen times for England at left-back. Like Jack, he was more supervisor than coach. His son, John Junior, signed as an apprentice pro on the same day as I did.

The only coaching tip Johnny ever offered was the simple observation that 'The more you put in, the more you'll get out' of the game. Strictly speaking, this wasn't accurate. Some guys worked like dogs on the training ground, but simply didn't possess the talent to become Manchester United players.

Harold Bratt was by far the hardest-working player at the Cliff. A wing-half who was two or three years older than us, Harold was always first onto the training ground, last off. He ran harder and longer than anyone else. He did extra weight training. The more cynical players would mock him, remarking that if he didn't take it easy he'd be bol-loxed by Saturday. He played a couple of First Team games before disappearing to the lower leagues. In the end, talent mattered most. Which didn't mean that Johnny Aston's maxim was entirely redundant.

I bought into the concept, although in an amended form. Sizing up the opposition over the first few weeks at the Cliff, I did my own audit. I was smaller and physically weaker than any of the others. I lacked strength, but I had stamina in abundance. And I could play, control the ball, see and deliver a telling pass. Perhaps most important, I could con-centrate for the full two hours we trained. And more: I was hungry, very hungry.

I knew I needed to 'put more in' because most of the others were stronger than I was and could play as well. One player in particular caught my eye. Barry Grayson was the most gifted footballer of our year. Barry had played for Manchester Boys, one of England's best schoolboy teams, narrowly missing out on an England cap. Like me, he was an inside-forward. Well built, beautifully balanced, he waltzed past opponents with ease. He could score a goal, deliver the killer pass. Barry seemed to have the lot. In our improvised end-of-session games, I watched him carefully.

The training-ground matches were brutal, fiercely contested affairs, like the Dump in terms of intensity. Only at the Cliff there were no dummies to glide past. Everyone brought something special to the party. Your opponents were among the best young players in the British

Isles. Outstanding defenders, clinical finishers, hard bastards whose tackles would rattle every bone in your body. This was a hard school with nowhere to hide. We'd all been big deals back home, in Dublin, Manchester, Scotland, Wales or Belfast, accustomed to being top dog in almost every game we'd played in for years. That was why we were Manchester United players.

Psychologically and emotionally, this new situation was infinitely more demanding than anything we'd ever faced. Any weakness would be exposed. Those with dodgy temperaments would be exposed. What had been a game, recreation, was now work for which you were paid, and for which you would be judged very harshly.

After a few weeks I got it: the more you put in – every session – the more you got out, and the feelgood factor kicked in immediately after every session. This wasn't about raw ability, although that took you some of the way. It was about concentration, resilience, mental and spiritual hardness, a certain kind of inner resolve that had to be summoned up every day, on demand, regardless of your mood. Some days were good, some days bad, but every day mattered. After a good day, or week, you'd feel great, at ease with yourself. After a bad day, or week, you'd feel like shit.

I was happy. For the first time in my life I felt I had an equal chance. It didn't matter what I wore or where I lived. What my father did was as irrelevant as where I'd gone to school. After a few weeks I had almost forgotten about Ireland. I was preoccupied with the challenge of my new world. The football was obviously priority number one. I had two years to prove myself. When I was seventeen the club would either let me go or ask me to sign professional forms. In the back of my mind the British Army option still lurked: plan B.

I liked the English people, especially Mancunians. They were cheerful, tolerant, self-deprecating. The monster caricature of England and Englishness peddled by the True Gaels at home seemed ridiculous. Far from hating the Irish, most English people I met seemed well disposed towards me when I told them where I was from. 'I hear Ireland's beautiful,' they would say, or tell me about an Irish friend they had who was 'lovely'. I encountered absolutely no animosity. The English were utterly free of cant. They could laugh at themselves and the world. There were no Union flags painted on the kerbstones of Manchester. It struck me as the supreme irony that the Brit-loving Irish in Belfast would wave them, bang their drums for King Billy or the Queen, while the English themselves were generally dismissive of their own ruling class.

Sunday, though, was a bad day. It was the only day when I wished I was at home. The English Sunday took some getting used to. Nothing happened. In Ireland, Sunday was the big day for sport, the air alive with speculation about the matches at Croke Park, Tolka or Milltown. I missed that. A Manchester Sunday was strangely, troublingly quiet. The streets were empty. There was no training. Instead there was a national lie-in, as people read their *News of the World*, the paper banned in Ireland. I read it too, intrigued by the tales of adultery, dodgy vicars and errant big-shots who'd fallen by the wayside.

The English Sunday was melancholy, and time passed slowly. I thought of home – Peg, Kevin and my dad bustling through the rituals of an Irish Sunday: mass, the roast-beef lunch, the match and the late-evening comfort of the radio – Philip Greene, Michael O'Hehir, Seán Óg Ó Ceallacháin bringing us up to date with the day's results. Then the nightly comfort of the rosary.

I went to mass every Sunday morning. My faith remained intact, although I was less inclined to take the sacraments. There was nothing to confess, unless reading the *News of the World* was a sin. I was still addicted to newspapers. Only the variety and quality of the English Sunday newspapers relieved the boredom of the day. After scanning the *News of the World*, I buried myself in the *Observer* and the *Sunday Times*.

16. A New World

John F. Kennedy's bid to become the first Catholic president of the United States was the big international story of 1960. His family links to Ireland ensured the passionate support of the Irish. He had won the Democratic nomination in July, just before I arrived in Manchester. Being firmly in the camp, I was surprised at English scepticism about Kennedy.

British reservations about Kennedy were not rooted in his religion: rather, they had to do with his father, Joe, who'd been US ambassador to the United Kingdom from 1938 to 1940. Kennedy Sr was associated with appeasement, had sought meetings with Hitler, and forcefully resisted United States involvement in the war. He had been, like many Irish, on the wrong side of history, and that caused many in England to regard his son with suspicion, in some cases contempt.

For me and tens of millions of others around the world, Kennedy represented youth, vigour and hope for a better future, in which peace and justice would prevail over the darker forces his shifty opponent, Nixon, seemed to represent. Immersed in all of this, I was struck not only by the scepticism of the English chattering class but by the indifference of the people I was mixing with. They were watching a different movie.

Barry Fry was the person I spent most time with as I settled into my new life. Together we found new digs with Mrs Scott, a widow who shared a house with her sister in Sale, one of Manchester's more salubrious suburbs. Mrs Scott's spacious semi-detached house, on a tree-lined road, was a world away from the narrow, terraced streets in the shadow of Old Trafford where most digs were located. Nice though she was, Mrs Cropper had spent more money on bingo than on food. I'd felt my digs money was subsidizing her bingo habit. At Mrs Scott's, the money stayed in the project: the food was first class, the television was state-of-the-art, and Barry and I had our own rooms.

Our accommodation sorted, we could concentrate on our football and our social lives. The latter mattered more to Barry than to me.

Although no movie star, Barry was a ladies' man. With his extrovert personality, his sharp sense of humour and his Cockney accent, he cut quite a swagger on the Manchester scene. He was actually a country bumpkin from Bedford, but when quizzed about his accent he would claim to be 'from London, dahlin''. The fact that we were Manchester United players, regardless of how low-ranked, did no harm to our chances with the girls. On this issue Barry believed in full and early disclosure.

Our initial forays onto the city's social scene took us to the Plaza ballroom on Oxford Road. Jimmy Savile was the manager. He had yet to become a national figure but, with his colourful gear and black Rolls-Royce, Jimmy was the Main Man in Manchester's emerging scene. He had a club, the Three Coins, on Fountain Street around the corner from the Plaza. Rumours were already swirling around him, decades before his predilections became common knowledge. One day my girlfriend was lured back to his penthouse flat, which appeared to have only a bed as furniture, but she was canny enough to escape.

There was a carefree vibe around the Manchester scene. Britain was emerging from its years of post-war austerity.

One of Savile's early innovations at the Plaza was a lunchtime gig, which featured dancing to live pop music. With lots of girls from city-centre shops and offices, music types and young men who described themselves as company directors, the Plaza at lunchtime became our favourite after-training haunt. Jim Keogh and Hughie Curran often joined Barry and me there.

Jim and Hughie were in digs together. They were unlikely allies. Jim was a quiet, rather gentle fellow; too gentle, time would prove, for the hard world of professional soccer. Hughie, like Barry, was full of it. He had passed his trial and signed full-time pro. A Manchester United blazer with gold braid badge was one of the perks awarded to full-time pros. You were supposed to wear the blazer on match days. Hughie wore his every other day.

Deeming the presence of United players good for business, Savile made us feel at home at the Plaza. Complimentary tickets and the best table in the house were ours for the asking. If Hughie's blazer didn't catch the eyes of the assembled lunchtime ravers, Savile would let it be known from the stage that 'We have the United lads in today,' at which point Jim and I would duck . . . while Barry and Hughie stood up to take a bow.

Having time off to go dancing at lunchtime was hardly the reason the Professional Footballers Association had agitated for a reform, of which our 1960 intake of promising young players were the first beneficiaries. Under the old discredited system, youngsters in our position were categorized as ground-staff boys. That meant football training in the morning was followed in the afternoon by the kind of menial tasks now regarded as inappropriate by the PFA. Our immediate predecessors spent their afternoons labouring at Old Trafford or the Cliff, sweeping the terraces, cleaning baths, polishing the boots of the senior pros or otherwise making themselves useful around the United complex. You worked a full, demanding day until you turned pro at seventeen.

The new enlightened regime, designed to liberate young footballers, was not quite the Paradise its advocates imagined. In fact, one of the curiosities that struck me in my early days at United was that I was playing less football now than I had in the days of the Dump. Training began at ten o'clock. By twelve thirty we were finished, having spent maybe forty-five minutes to an hour actually working with the ball. On the odd occasion there would be an afternoon session, but more often than not, the working day ended at lunchtime.

At first, this seemed great. But as time passed, the unintended consequence of this reform would prove damaging for me and worse for some. With so much time to kill each day, boredom was never far away. Mischief, or something more destructive, was inevitable. Around the time we were becoming acquainted with Jimmy Savile and the delights of lunchtime dancing, John Giles was having his collar felt by the police.

John was by now a United First Team player, one of the rising stars of the English game. His legend in Ireland was already secure for the astonishingly brilliant goal he had scored against Sweden on his international debut in 1959. This was a famous Irish victory over opponents who had beaten England at Wembley the previous Wednesday.

Even as a twenty-year-old, John had a reputation as a serious thinker about the game. But behind the serious façade, he possessed a wicked sense of humour, shared by his constant companion and digs-mate Jimmy Sheils, a typically wily Derry man. Jimmy's promising career was to be blighted by injury. He'd been a popular member of the First

Team squad in 1959, when the training ground injury that would ultimately finish him occurred.

When I arrived in Manchester, John and Jimmy were very good to me. Although five years older than me, they let me hang out with them, taking me to the pictures in town (free passes for United players) and dancing on a Saturday night at the Locarno Ballroom in Sale. Compared to Barry Fry (whom they didn't approve of) and Hughie Curran, John and Jimmy were steady types. No flash behaviour, no Plaza, no town, except for the pictures.

So when I bought my *Daily Express* one morning and found the pair of them in an off-lead headline I was shocked. 'United stars arrested,' the story revealed, noting that they were due in the magistrate's court later that day. Along with them, two other United stars, Shay Brennan and Wilf McGuinness, were due to face charges of breaching the peace. The early editions of that day's *Manchester Evening News* led with the story, which was extraordinary for a number of reasons.

First, the players involved were not kids. Wilf McGuinness had been a member of the team that perished at Munich, only missing the tragic journey because he was injured. He was twenty-three. Shay Brennan, also twenty-three, scored the two goals that enabled United to beat Sheffield Wednesday in the first post-Munich match, an FA Cup-tie at Old Trafford. Like John Giles, they were current First Team regulars.

Their offence? Driving around Manchester in the early afternoon assaulting people at bus stops with water pistols. The gang would pull up at a bus stop in Brennan's car, pretending to look for directions. Lowering their voices to encourage their victims to bend down to the car window, they proceeded to spray their would-be guides with a well-aimed shot from the water pistol.

Matt Busby was angry. For once, the newspapers did not have to manufacture outrage. The prank was cruel and childish. Perhaps because they were United players, the magistrate, while taking a dim view, was lenient. The four lads were bound over for a year to keep the peace.

In 1960 the water-pistol gang escaped with a bollocking from Matt Busby. Were it to happen today, such an incident involving idle young footballers would doubtless induce a fit of outrage among the standing army of media moralizers who draw the direst conclusions about national character from the delinquent behaviour of a minority of Premier League footballers. The sight of young men behaving badly often leads the media preachers to call for the return of character-building National Service. In fact, Shay Brennan had just completed his two-year stint in the forces.

John Giles would go on to become one of the most respected players of his generation, and was a successful manager of West Brom and Ireland. After his playing career was curtailed by injury, Wilf McGuinness joined United's coaching staff and was Busby's anointed successor when the Boss retired in 1969. When Jimmy Sheils quit football, also due to injury, he returned to Ireland to become a successful businessman. It was hard to argue that these guys were delinquents.

Anyone seeking to draw conclusions from the affair might reflect not on the character of the men involved, rather at a way of life that induced boredom in people like them, with too much time to kill. After a couple of hours' training each morning professional footballers faced long, empty days with very little to do. The sensible, mature and married went home. But for the unattached, or those of even a slightly wayward disposition, there were many temptations. For the truly feckless or those with hyperactive tendencies, temptation lurked in the form of gambling, women or drink.

There is a tragic cast of victims whose downfall serves to illustrate the perils of idleness: Paul McGrath, Paul Gascoigne, George Best, Jim Baxter, Jimmy Greaves and Tony Adams are among the best-known modern casualties. The alcoholics are most easily identified. Less easily detected are those who squandered their money at racetracks or in betting shops, although in this regard, names such as Paul Merson and Stan Bowles spring to mind. As I would soon discover, it wasn't difficult to drift into the danger zone.

17. Two Captains

The 1960/61 season will always be remembered as the one in which a magnificent Spurs team won the League/FA Cup double. This was a feat no club had achieved in the modern game – the footballing equivalent of Roger Bannister's four-minute mile. Last accomplished by Aston Villa in 1897, the Double was believed to be beyond reach in the ultra-competitive modern era. Even Busby's Red Devils had failed to secure this elusive prize, although they came close in 1957 when, after winning the League, they lost to Aston Villa in the Cup Final.

It wasn't just the achievement, but the manner of it that added some magic to Spurs' historic triumph. Long renowned for their passing game, the push-and-run football advocated by the club's visionary early fifties coach Arthur Rowe, Spurs had rarely translated this purist philosophy into trophies. Rowe's Spurs did win the First Division in 1951, but his convictions about a game based on passing and movement were mocked as a continental fad by the reactionary forces still dominant in the English game.

After their championship win, Rowe stuck with his beliefs, but Spurs won nothing. He thought soccer was about guile and technical skills, brain rather than brawn. And even as the Hungarians and Real Madrid emerged from the despised 'continent' in the fifties to prove that brawn was a lesser virtue, Rowe remained a prophet without honour – or respect – in his own land. In 1954 he suffered a nervous breakdown, forcing him to quit the game for several years.

Although he was dismissed as a dreamer, Arthur Rowe's values endured at Spurs. Bill Nicholson had played in Rowe's 1951 title-winning team, before joining the club's coaching staff. Nicholson shared Rowe's beliefs, and when he was appointed manager in 1958, he remained faithful to the passing game. But Nicholson was more pragmatist than dreamer. In 1959 he signed two players who would define his Double-winning team.

Dave Mackay was potentially the complete footballer, a fierce competitor, hard as nails. He could see a pass and deliver as accurately as any forward. John White, another Scot, was a wonderful playmaker; slight, a gloriously perceptive passer of the ball, capable also of drifting cunningly into the opposition's penalty area to score telling goals. Known affectionately as 'the Ghost', White was a joy to watch, the ultimate street footballer.

Nicholson's Spurs would possess brains and, in Mackay and their rampaging centre-forward Bobby Smith, more than enough brawn to get by. And at the heart of this great team was one of the most remarkable men ever to grace the English game, Danny Blanchflower.

Blanchflower was born in Belfast. Football was part of his DNA. His mother played centre-forward in a women's football team. His brother Jackie was a Red Devil forced to retire after the trauma of the Munich air crash. Danny was a scholarship boy who left college to join the RAF in 1943, lying about his age to do so. He came to professional football late in life, aged twenty-three. An adult with a good mind of his own, he was not afraid to speak out. After two seasons with Barnsley, Danny was transferred to Aston Villa in 1951.

As captain of Villa he began to rail against the myriad idiocies of English soccer. He was not the only footballer to resent the notion that the less players saw of the ball during the week the hungrier they'd be to get on it come Saturday. But he was the first to articulate that resentment and in the most sardonic terms.

Danny was a leader, on and off the field. As a wing-half – a midfield player in today's terms – he possessed no particular technical gift. He rarely tackled. He moved the ball with precision, yet to no dramatic effect. He didn't give the ball away, but his passes wouldn't kill opponents swiftly in the manner of John White's. What did distinguish him was his grasp of what was happening around him at any given moment in a game. Danny was a very good player, and a great captain. Arthur Rowe paid Villa £30,000, a vast sum in 1954, for Blanchflower's services. Villa's board were glad to be rid of their intemperate rebel.

Nicholson and Blanchflower would prove to be perfect partners. The dour, wise Yorkshireman and the flamboyant Irishman between them conspired to produce one of England's great football teams. This fusion of English sturdiness and Celtic wit was a feature of many great football projects. The virtues were complementary, something I believe is true in life as well as sport. The footballer had at last found a manager he could respect, the manager a player he could trust.

As the season unfolded and the press began to consider the prospect of the Double, Nicholson remained taciturn, a one-game-at-a-time man. Danny was less inhibited. 'Yes, we can do it and I think we will,' was his response. None of the familiar false modesty characteristic of Britain's best sportsmen of that age.

Like John F. Kennedy, whose inaugural presidential address in January 1961 inspired a generation with hope of a better future, Danny dared to dream of things not as they were but of things that had never been. Watching from a distance, I was as beguiled by him as I was by the new young president of the United States. Both made the world seem a better, more optimistic place. They were singular men emerging to challenge the prevailing orthodoxies.

My childhood had left me haunted by a feeling that the good guys only won in the movies. In real life, my heroes generally lost, be it Noël Browne or my beloved Drums or, indeed, my adored parents. In my experience the underdog never triumphed. Now that seemed to be changing, Kennedy surviving prejudice and even hatred to claim the White House, Blanchflower, English football's tormented dissident, flourishing now with the great prize of the Double within his grasp.

One night in February 1961 I was watching *This Is Your Life* on BBC television. In its original version, presented by Eamonn Andrews, the show was a very big deal. To be ambushed live on TV by Andrews with his red book containing the details of your life was considered an honour. Not by Danny Blanchflower.

Having been lured to the BBC studios under false pretences, Danny was confronted by Andrews bearing his red book. Live on prime time, Danny responded angrily. 'I consider this programme to be an invasion of privacy,' he told the bemused television star, more accustomed to fawning acceptance by those upon whom this great honour was about to be bestowed. Amid the ensuing consternation, Danny could be heard protesting, 'Nobody is going to press-gang me into anything.'

In that moment, Danny Blanchflower seemed to me to be quite magnificently iconoclastic. I think I cheered as Andrews beat a hasty retreat. Next morning Danny featured on all the front pages. Some acclaimed his defiance; others damned this turbulent footballer for curmudgeonly arrogance. 'Who does Blanchflower think he is?' one critic ventured. Of course, another question begged to be answered: what right had the BBC to invade someone's privacy for the purpose of light entertainment?

With the First Division championship already secured, Spurs' great season ended at Wembley when they beat Burnley 3–1 in the Cup Final to claim the Double. The sight of Nicholson, Blanchflower and their team wandering dreamily around the hallowed Wembley turf was glorious – an unimaginable triumph for the good guys. And for many of us an unforgettable valedictory moment for the rebel Danny Blanchflower.

By contrast, Manchester United's season had been disappointing, at times grimly so. They finished seventh in the First Division, a berth many thought flattering. Having drawn away to Sheffield Wednesday in the FA Cup, United were thrashed 7–2 before their own fans in the replay. The following week Leicester beat them 6–0 at Filbert Street.

After the latter humiliation, Matt Busby uncharacteristically lost his cool. Sitting in his usual seat at the front of the team coach the manager grew increasingly irritated by the noise emanating from the card school at the back of the bus. In a gesture that shocked those present, the Boss left his seat, walked slowly towards the card players, picked up the deck and threw it out of the window. Behind the mask that rarely slipped, Busby's deep frustration and profound anger were revealed for all to see.

Things got worse at Old Trafford. United finished fifteenth in the First Division in 1962. A semblance of pride was maintained by a good run in the FA Cup, which ended in defeat against Spurs in the semi-final. But, in truth, Busby hadn't yet figured out a way to rebuild the club post-Munich. He blooded several talented young players, Mark Pearson, Alex Dawson and Ian Moir among them, but, although gifted, they were unable to meet the expectations that came with wearing a United shirt. The Red Devils had set the bar impossibly high. Every home game was attended by 63,000 passionate fans. Media scrutiny was intense. Every young player was measured against those who'd so recently worn the famous red shirts.

Jimmy Nicholson was typically a victim of such comparisons. An accomplished young wing-half, he burst into the first team in 1961 aged seventeen. Jimmy was a good player, powerful, an incisive passer of the ball. After some brilliant performances, he was tagged 'the new Duncan Edwards'. Mark Pearson, a mazy dribbler, was briefly compared to Eddie Colman. Alex Dawson, a powerful young centre-forward, might be the new Tommy Taylor, some speculated. Such talk was costly nonsense.

Busby moved into the transfer market to try to buy ready-to-go pros with the experience to handle such pressures. He broke the British transfer record to acquire Albert Quixall from Sheffield Wednesday for £45,000. 'Quickie', a dazzling wonder boy at Wednesday, could never come to terms with his price-tag, or the pressure that came with being The Man at Old Trafford. A cheerful Yorkshireman, who always had time for a smile and a kindly word of encouragement for us kids, Quickie was popular as a person, but not respected in United's First Team dressing room. It was believed that he didn't have the 'bottle' for the big games. And, of course, every game United played was a big game.

Albert Quixall died a slow death. He lasted five years at the club, playing one of his final competitive games in the 1963 FA Cup Final, which United won. After a humiliating 4–0 defeat to Everton in the Charity Shield in August 1963, Busby dropped Quixall, John Giles and David Herd, another expensive transfer failure. Quickie had a nervous breakdown shortly afterwards.

Noel Cantwell cost £30,000 when Busby bought him from West Ham in November 1960. Cantwell ticked a number of boxes for Busby. The big Cork man was the kind of footballing full-back Busby favoured. Like Johnny Carey and Roger Byrne, he was creative with the ball, as good a passer as most forwards. And, like Byrne and Carey, Cantwell was a man of exceptional character, a leader of men, with a distinct personality. Busby gave him the captaincy. The big man had captained West Ham and Ireland.

With his family still in London, Noel occasionally stayed on for training sessions with the kids. One day he was chatting to me in the bath after training. We talked about home, how I was settling in at Old Trafford and getting on with English girls. Noel was likeable, shrewd as any Cork man, funny, highly intelligent and more aware of the world outside football than most professional players.

We discussed John F. Kennedy and the horrors of life at home, the willingness of English girls to, as Noel put it, 'do the biz'. He teased me about still going to mass and listening to those 'fucking sky-pilots' (priests) and 'fucking mickey-dodgers' (nuns). I was flattered, big-time. Growing up, I'd watched Noel play for Ireland from the terraces at Dalymount. He was a hugely admired stalwart of the Irish team.

Suddenly he switched the focus of the conversation. There were just the two of us left in the bath. Looking over his shoulder to make sure nobody could overhear, Noel leaned closer and asked, 'What gives with this fucking place?' I didn't know what he meant. 'Well, the fucking training for a start, a few laps of the Cliff, a game of head-tennis, and the fucking five-a-sides are a free-for-all. Is that it?' he queried. 'Do you ever see Busby? Where is Jimmy Murphy? Does anyone ever talk about the game? Think about the fucking game?'

When I confirmed that, yes, that was it, Noel shook his head in disbelief. 'Look at the training kit,' he went on. 'It's fucking filthy. I've got sweat rash from wearing someone else's shorts.'

He was right about the gear we wore for training. Every Monday morning, a pile of freshly laundered kit was placed on the dressing-room table. You grabbed what you could from the pile of worn, sometimes torn shirts, tracksuit tops and bottoms. As the week progressed, the kit got dirtier, the muck and sweat accumulating day by day. By Thursday socks and shirts would be caked with dry mud. Sweat rash was contagious, one of the hazards of training at United, especially in summer. It was the same for everyone, from Bobby Charlton to those of us near the bottom of the pyramid.

The FA Youth Cup was an important competition for Manchester United. Beginning in 1953, United had won the first five Youth Cups. It was at this level that great players like Bobby Charlton, Eddie Colman, Duncan Edwards, John Giles and Liam Whelan provided Matt Busby with evidence that his pioneering youth policy was working.

The scorelines from the early finals were spectacular. In 1953, the inaugural FA Youth Cup Final, United hammered Wolves 9–3 over two legs. West Brom were demolished 7–1 in 1955, West Ham were humbled 8–2 in 1957. Large crowds attended the games at Old Trafford. Jimmy Murphy managed the Youth Team; Matt Busby sat impassively in the stand.

For us youngsters, getting into the Youth Cup team was a must, second only to signing full-time pro at seventeen. United fielded four teams every week: First Team, Reserves, the A Team and the B Team. The most promising kids went straight to the A Team. From our intake, Jim Keogh, Barry Fry and Barry Grayson bypassed the B Team. It took me six months to make the breakthrough.

The B Team was a mix of the less-promising apprentices and local amateurs hoping for a contract. This team played in one of the local Manchester Leagues against older guys out to make a name for themselves by stuffing the Busby Babes. At every level, from First Team to B Team, opponents took immense satisfaction from beating United. That was why there were no easy games for United teams. Even in the B Team, you sensed that the opposition were geed up to fight for their lives. If football was just about ability, they had no chance. So most set out to kick the shit out of us.

Our instructions were simple: match them for effort and your superior ability will see you through. It usually worked out that way. As a frail little playmaker, I would be one of the first targeted by the opposition's hatchet men. My pain threshold was low to non-existent so I didn't – and never would – relish the muck-and-bullets aspect of the game. My six months in the B Team were a lesson in self-preservation. Through guile and the cunning you acquire in street football, I found a way to make my skill count. The enemy would run out of steam before I ran out of determination. And, crucially, concentration.

The A Team experience was different. You played against young pros from other Lancashire clubs: Bolton, Everton, Liverpool, Burnley and Manchester City. At this level the game was more sophisticated, though no less intense. When it came to the physical side, the hard-men pros were more dangerous. In the B Team you faced accountants and welders with attitude; the pros were trained assassins. It was the difference between Dad's Army and the SAS.

In the A Team, skill alone was virtually worthless. If you wanted to succeed, you had to understand that, and quickly. Every game was a battle between creativity – my game – and physical aggression – emphatically not my game. So much in a football match is determined in the first phase, the fifteen or twenty minutes after kick-off. Who wants it most? Who's got chinks in their armour, and where?

Intimidation begins with the first tackle. If you evade the initial lunge, well and good, but there will be a second attempt to soften you up, to find out if you possess the resilience to match your technical ability. Evasion, the ability to create time and space to make your skill count, won't always work. If you're not hard outside, which I wasn't, you need an inner core of determination to cope with the war of attrition that is ninety minutes of pro soccer. Nourished by a desperate hunger to succeed, I found within me the necessary determination. I flinched when the studs raked my shin, but I rarely buckled.

I learned a lot in my first twelve months as a pro. The young pros I played against were hard bastards; not all of them, but in every opposing team, enough to give pause for thought. I'd never encountered such raw aggression in the Dublin Schoolboy League. With my wit and skill I'd been running past trees, playing for Stella. In the Lancashire League, the trees moved fast, and they were fucking oak trees with size-twelve boots and steel studs.

I survived and, by year's end, began to flourish. Not all of my peers could say the same. Jim Keogh and Barry Grayson were both visibly struggling. The physical presence that had made Jim a star of the Irish schoolboy game now counted for nothing. He was an extremely laid-back guy, pleasant, good company, popular. But the old cliché about nice guys finishing second could have been scripted for Jim. For all his talent, Barry Grayson tended to wilt in the games where you had to dig deep. He was a very good footballer, but being a pro was about other things, which tend to fall under the catch-all word 'character'.

Some of the players you'd want beside you in battle could be extremely unattractive characters: greedy, stubborn, self-centred and, in some cases, nasty bullies. You wouldn't be offering character references for many of the guys you would be happy to line out beside. What you needed was someone who would be focused for ninety minutes, who couldn't bear the thought of losing, who would be prepared to drown his children's kittens for two points. Or one, if that was all you could get.

In my second season I made it to the Youth Team. Things were going well.

18.   Gone to the Dogs

Away from football, I led a double life. One night when we were at a loose end, Barry Fry suggested we go to the dogs. Greyhound racing had been a very popular sport in England before and immediately after the war. By the early sixties it was in decline. The big crowds no longer came. The tracks were mostly dingy, home to compulsive gamblers, inveterate thrill seekers and a hard core of aficionados who loved the game.

White City Stadium around the corner from Old Trafford was our first port of call. On a wet Monday night with nothing better to do, Barry and I headed off to make some money. According to Barry, we couldn't fail. He'd owned a greyhound at home in Bedford, which had raced at the local 'flapping' track. These were unlicensed venues, dens of iniquity where all kinds of strokes were pulled. Barry was a stroker familiar with all the tricks of the game.

Matt Busby, though ironically a big punter himself, didn't approve of gambling. Hence the anger that prompted him to chuck the deck of playing cards out of the coach window. With the senior pros, he might tolerate a trip to the races at Haydock Park or Manchester racecourse. But for the youngsters, an interest in gambling was deemed a character flaw. From his own experience, Busby knew that heavy losses incurred – and heavy losses were inevitably incurred – could be a tormenting distraction for young footballers.

My gambling career got off to the worst possible start: I won a tenner and thought the game was easy. 'I told you, mate,' Barry crowed triumphantly as we strolled, contented, into the damp night air.

Shay Brennan was at White City that night. He was the quintessential Mancunian: mischievous, savvy about street life, funny, especially about the frailties of the human condition. He looked like a movie star and talked like a street bookmaker. Everybody at United loved Shay. Bobby Charlton, serious and straight, was one of Shay's closest friends. Shay was a wonderful footballer and a lovable rogue, but gambling was his Achilles heel.

Shay went to the dogs every night and the racetrack any time he could. Busby knew but, like everyone else, the Boss was inordinately fond of Shay. Manchester was full of rogues, most of them, like Shay, doing harm to no one but themselves. In United's dressing room, his nickname was 'the Bomber'. This was an ironic reference to his languid disposition and to the fact that he possessed none of the weapons traditionally deployed by top-class defenders. He couldn't tackle. He rarely headed the ball. He was slim. Dainty might be the most accurate description of his gait.

Despite those perceived deficiencies, Shay was an outstanding defender. He was fleet of foot and mind. Where other full-backs were forced into lunging tackles, Shay's gift was to read the game, see the danger early and defuse it with a timely interception. He was cool under pressure – a great, and greatly underrated, attribute for defenders. And, like nearly all of Busby's full-backs, he was a good passer of the ball. A Shay Brennan performance was a study of applied intelligence, wit, guile and perception, more than compensating for the rugged aggression absent from his nature.

Shay liked to keep a low profile at the dogs. He generally shunned the restaurant, preferring instead to loiter in the shadows on the terrace opposite the winning line with a couple of mates. That was where Barry and I spotted him on our first trip to White City.

Even with someone as easy-going and approachable as Shay, a certain protocol had to be observed between First Team players and young pros. Seeing us, he acknowledged our presence with a smile. But further intimacy was not encouraged. While I hung back, Barry bounced up the steps to press the flesh. He was looking for information, which, he told me, was the secret of the dog game. Being a United star, Shay would know what was 'off' and what was not. No tip was offered, though, and not much warmth. Eventually Barry got the message and left Shay in peace. Between us we managed to find a few winners and left the track in good spirits.

As we left White City on that fateful first night, all we remembered was the adrenalin rush as the hare sped towards the traps, and the euphoria as the dog you'd backed moved into the lead around the final bend. 'Go on, my son!' Barry roared, as our winner flashed by the finishing line. And on we went, four nights a week, most weeks, for the following two years. Mondays and Thursdays at White City, Tuesdays and Fridays at Salford; two mugs to the slaughter.

One outing to White City ended particularly badly. Shay had a 'tip' for a dog that was running in the second-last race. It was Thursday, pay day, and Barry and I were flush, with almost twenty pounds between us. We decided to be patient, betting tiny sums on the early races, until Race Seven arrived, by which time we were a fiver down. We prowled along the bookies' pitches, seeking the best price, which turned out to be five to one. Barry placed our bet: fifteen pounds to win seventy-five. The feeling of being on the inside track, knowing something the other mug punters didn't know, was intoxicating. I felt sorry for people betting against our dog.

It got knocked over in the scrimmaging on the first bend. Fuck! We looked across at Shay. He shrugged his shoulders and turned away.

I was screwed. Barry always had an extra few quid but I'd gambled almost everything. Worst of all, I'd put Mrs Cropper's money on the dog and I couldn't go home unable to pay my landlady. I had just five shillings in my pocket. We went into town for a Coke at the Plaza. I couldn't bring myself to ask Barry for my four pounds' rent. He pulled a girl, leaving me to make my own way home.

I hung around the Plaza until closing time at midnight, then went for a cup of coffee in an all-night café in Piccadilly. It was a cold winter's night, the temperature below zero. I decided to try the Salvation Army hostel. Freezing, shame oozing from every pore, I approached Reception. Did they have a bed for the night? Yes. The bed with breakfast cost thirty shillings. Jesus! I'd thought Salvation Army hostels were free. 'Sorry,' the stone-faced clerk said, 'you'll have to leave now.' He ushered me out into the cold night air. I had enough money for one more coffee. Back in the all-night café I was consumed by shame and fear. I smoked my last cigarette. Would morning ever come? How would I train without food and sleep? What would I tell Mrs C?

At two a.m. I hit the streets. I walked around the city centre, pretending to be going somewhere, until I ended up back where I'd started in Piccadilly. Roadworks were under way along the side of Manchester's most famous square, with men working under lights laying asphalt. There was a watchman's hut with a burning brazier at the entrance. The watchman was busy inside making tea for the men. I went to warm myself by the brazier. The watchman asked if I was OK. He was Irish. I told him I was homeless. He invited me into his refuge and gave me a cup of tea and a fag. I didn't tell him my story but concocted some fiction about travelling over from Ireland looking for work. 'You can stay here for the night if you want,' my compatriot told me. He was a large, warm country man. We talked all night about home and stuff, and then at dawn he made me a bacon buttie. He gave me five shillings and said, 'Take care of yourself,' when I left.

I was early for training next morning. God knows what I looked like. I told Barry my story. 'Fuck me, mate, why didn't you ask me for the money?' He doshed me up from the Barry Fry Perpetual Emergency Fund and Mrs C never asked where I'd been.

In August 1962, on my seventeenth birthday, I signed full professional forms for Manchester United. I had made the cut. The failure rate was high: about two-thirds of the apprentices were released at this stage. I felt relieved rather than jubilant. My contract was for two years at twelve pounds a week. I was also measured for a club blazer, a neat navy-blue garment with United's famous badge prominently displayed. I was still closer to the bottom of the pyramid than the top, but moving in the right direction.

The extra money was welcome. Indeed, it was vital to feed my growing gambling habit. The buzz of the dog-track was addictive. I wanted more, which was readily available, thanks to Harold Macmillan's Tory government: it had recently legalized betting shops. As a consequence of my infatuation with the greyhounds, I was permanently strapped for cash. I'd stopped sending money home to my family.

Now and again I felt guilty. For ten minutes or so. I was largely preoccupied with urgent matters: football, gambling and the world of politics and current affairs. Every morning I bought three newspapers: the *Daily Express*, the *Guardian* and the *Sporting Life* – the punters' Bible. I read the *Express* on the bus to the Cliff. I kept the *Guardian* for evening reading at Mrs Scott's. The *Sporting Life* was essential for studying the form in preparation for an afternoon in the betting shop.

For Barry and me, the big decision of every day was whether to go to the Plaza for lunch and some music or straight to Gus Demmy's betting shop around the corner from Old Trafford. The music scene in Manchester was really taking off. Herman's Hermits played the lunchtime gig at the Plaza, which was now more popular than ever. We were pally with Peter Noone, the Hermits' lead singer, a Manchester lad and United fan. The Plaza was also packed every weekend night, hopping with amazing new music from bands like the Hollies and Freddie and the Dreamers. In the Three Coins nearby on Fountain Street we saw the Beatles and Gerry and the Pacemakers.

Saturday night was music night. Gambling was a constant preoccupation. What had been for most ordinary people an illicit pleasure, involving illegal bookies in pubs and on street corners, was now coming to a high street near you. The Tories decided that the state could not stop people having a punt on their equine fancies. Barry Fry and I thoroughly approved.

So did Gus Demmy, Manchester's most popular bookie. He opened a chain of betting offices, one of them a two-minute walk from Old Trafford. By today's standards the first betting shops were pretty basic. Race commentary, along with prices and results, came via the 'blower' – a radio signal transmitted to the shop from the racecourse. Prices were chalked on a blackboard. When you placed your bet you received a docket recording the transaction. It was a male and generally working-class environment, though not exclusively: women worked behind the counter and the odd dodgy bank manager, solicitor or small-time businessman would slip in self-consciously to feed his habit.

Gamblers tended to smoke, especially during the race commentary when nerves were taut and the shop fell silent. Displays of emotion, elation or despair, were rare. The punters suffered in silence. Celebration, for which there was mostly little cause, was equally low-key. The more accomplished actors affected a look of insouciance, their fast-beating pulse masked by an air of indifference. Photo finishes were agony, taking as long as five minutes to be decided, testing the mettle of even the hardest punter.

As the afternoon progressed and the losses mounted, the stress of it all began to take its toll. By twilight on a winter day, the façade of indifference was beginning to dissolve. A pall of quiet despair lingered in the air, the optimism of early afternoon a distant memory. Poorer but no wiser, we shuffled out onto the street, guilty but unbowed. Tomorrow was another day.

Other than my unhealthy tendency to hang around dog-tracks and betting offices, I was a relatively vice-free zone. Unlike Barry, I didn't chase girls. Neither of us drank alcohol. Apart from Saturday nights and our lunchtime trips to the Plaza, we steered clear of the city's burgeoning music scene. Lunchtime at the Plaza proved a fertile hunting ground for Barry the skirt-chaser, though.

His opening pitch never varied. 'Where do you work?' Barry would ask. He would then reveal where we worked. Game on. My role invariably involved talking to his target's best friend. Small-talk was not my game. Apart from football and gambling, my only area of expertise was politics and current affairs. Knowing that an in-depth analysis of the Cuban Missile Crisis, the Lady Chatterley trial or the Profumo scandal would go down like a lead balloon with the teenage girls we were attempting to impress, I usually kept quiet. I couldn't dance either. Life as Barry's wingman was hard going.

While he was dating, I spent much of my time staying in at Mrs Scott's. I read a lot; a book a week, at least. For anyone interested in public affairs, England in the early sixties was fascinating. When compared to the drab and essentially bogus posturing of Irish politics, public discourse in England seemed vital, infused with energy and deep convictions. There was no Archbishop McQuaid determining a final outcome. A free and diverse press enabled ideas to flow, and with programmes such as *Panorama*, *That Was the Week That Was* and *World in Action*, television was central to the debate about England's future.

Every weekday evening at six o'clock, Granada Television transmitted a magazine programme presented by Gay Byrne, Michael Parkinson and Bill Grundy. And this was just a regional TV programme. On the BBC, Richard Dimbleby and David Frost were starring: Dimbleby presenting *Panorama*; Frost the irreverent satire *That Was the Week That Was*. On any given night, you might see Robin Day or Malcolm Muggeridge arguing the toss about the issues of the day. For a kid full of curiosity, the robust exchange of competing ideas was compelling. Coming from the oppressive conformity of a society mediated by a foul archbishop, the scepticism and derision aimed at the English ruling class by free-thinking, articulate commentators seemed extraordinary.

I felt I had escaped from a pantomime prison, from a village where thought was proscribed, to a free world where you could believe what you wanted and act accordingly. I felt liberated, vindicated too, for never buying into the myth that the English were inherently bad, the enemy you had to hate to prove your Irishness. Forced to choose between the Land of Saints and Scholars and my new home, I had no doubt where I would rather be.

Gus Demmy's sons Selwyn and Harvey ran his betting-shop operation. Barry and I were acquainted with Harvey, the more amiable of the brothers, who was often in the Demmy shop we patronized. Harvey was an avid United fan. As part of our cash-flow policy, Barry had an arrangement with Harvey. Each United apprentice was entitled to two complimentary tickets for home games. Even though the team was struggling, every Old Trafford fixture was a 63,000 sell-out. Tickets were hard to get. So on Fridays before home matches, we sold our 'comps' to Harvey. He got the coveted tickets. And usually the money was back in his till an hour later. As useful idiots go, Barry and I were up there with the greats.

One afternoon Harvey came up with a proposition. He offered us a job in the betting shop, chalking up the prices before each race – he'd pay us a pound per day. We enthusiastically accepted the offer. 'Wear your United blazers on Monday, we'll get a photo, and you can start straight away,' Harvey suggested.

When we turned up on Monday, a number of press photographers were on the premises. Dumb and Dumber gladly posed for the pictures with our new boss Harvey. Betting shops had been condemned as dens of iniquity by bishops and the more conservative media commentators. For Gus Demmy, Inc., this was PR gold, price a pound per day.

The pictures featured in the next day's papers. 'Babes in the Betting Shop' was the headline. Dumb and Dumber were in big trouble. We were famous, but not in a good way. Wilf McGuinness was now on the coaching staff after a career-ending injury. 'What the fuck are you two at?' he scowled when we arrived at the Cliff. The other players took the piss mercilessly all morning.

After training we were ordered back to Old Trafford. The Boss wanted to see us. For once, Barry looked fearful. 'We're fucked, mate,' he speculated, on the bus to the ground.

I disagreed. 'No,' I argued, 'we're entitled to do what we want in our own spare time.' I'd been watching too much *Panorama* – human rights and all that!

Matt Busby's office was large and comfortably furnished. He sat behind his desk, which was slightly raised, leaving the visitor looking up and feeling small. I'd volunteered to go first. The morning newspapers were spread across the desk. 'What's this all about?' he asked, pointing to the 'Babes in the Betting Shop' headlines. He seemed more puzzled than angry.

'We were offered a job. We decided to take it. We needed the money,' I replied, as firmly as I could.

He outlined his objection without a hint of rancour: 'Look, son, you're a Manchester United player. You have an obligation to the club and to yourself. Working on your feet for four hours in a smoke-filled betting shop every afternoon will do you no good.' He spoke calmly.

God knows what he thought of this young pup insisting on his right to serve Manchester United and Gus Demmy in equal measure. In the circumstances, Busby was extremely patient. 'I've only got your best interests at heart,' he reminded me. 'Think about what I've said.'

On my way downstairs I met Barry on his way up to Busby's office. 'What happened?' Barry whispered.

'I told him he had no right to stop us,' I lied. I was back chalking the board that afternoon. Barry never showed. I was on my own. Babe in the Betting Shop.

My career in bookmaking ended abruptly a few days later. At the close of business, Harvey Demmy sat me down for a chat. Matt was unhappy, he told me. It would be best if I returned to the other side of the counter. 'No hard feelings,' he assured me, handing over a couple of crisp five-pound notes. I wasn't sure who was supposed to feel hard done by.

When Harvey talked of 'Matt', he spoke reverently. But in the First Team dressing room, the likes of Noel Cantwell, Maurice Setters, Harry Gregg and Albert Quixall were increasingly inclined to believe that the emperor who'd created the club wore no clothes. These non-believers, bought expensively to restore the club's fortunes, thought Busby hadn't a clue what he was doing.

Outside the club, ordinary Mancunians, be they bookies, landladies or football fans, knew Busby as 'Matt' – the word uttered softly with a fondness notably absent within the confines of the club, where he was referred to as the Boss. Among the people, his legend still pulsed as powerfully as ever. The glorious adventure that had ended so tragically at Munich, the pride the Red Devils had bestowed on the city and the grief of 6 February 1958 were emotions still keenly felt.

There was a certain intimacy in that simple word 'Matt', as indeed there was when Mancunians spoke of 'Duncan', 'Tommy', 'Roger', or 'Jimmy' (Murphy), who'd kept the club going in the months after the crash. Duncan Edwards, Tommy Taylor and Roger Byrne were not stars, or mere deliverers of trophies: they were family to Mancunians, hence no need for the family name. Manchester was more village than city; hardly a day passed without an encounter with someone who'd known 'the lads' who'd lost their lives at Munich.

All things considered, Busby treated me gently over the Babes in the Betting Shop affair. There were no threats or harsh words, just a discreet phone call to Gus Demmy. The incident was soon forgotten.

19. Best Foot Forward

I broke into the Youth Team in the autumn of 1962. Like signing full-time pro, this was a significant step forward. That year the First Team was struggling. Busby's visits to the transfer market had yielded little. In August of that year he'd broken the British transfer record yet again, to sign Denis Law from Torino for a stunning £115,000. But despite Law's undoubted brilliance, the team continued to labour.

Youth Cup games were played at Old Trafford under lights. Up to 20,000 spectators attended the matches. The atmosphere was loaded with possibility; most of all, the chance to impress Busby, to prove that you had what it took to make it. Warm, passionate, voluble, Busby's assistant, Jimmy Murphy, was a remarkable man in his own right. He'd taken Wales to the World Cup quarter-finals in 1958. Many clubs had tried to lure him from Old Trafford but Jimmy stayed loyal to the Boss. Even the senior players who doubted Busby at that time regarded Jimmy with respect and affection.

His pre-match instructions were simple: pass it to a red shirt; match them physically and your ability will make the difference; enjoy it. That was it. There was no magic formula, no tactical complexity. The simplicity of Jimmy's approach was reassuring.

We won our first two games, both at Old Trafford. I played really well, inspired by the amazing floodlit stage, the crowd and the realization that I was good enough to make an impact on a match at this level. After a couple more victories we had a Cup run going. FA Youth Cup games featured prominently in the two local papers, the *Manchester Evening News* and the *Chronicle*. The northern editions of the national dailies also carried reports of our exploits. Writing in the *Chronicle* after one game, Peter Slingsby, the paper's dedicated United correspondent, ventured that 'Dunphy, the young Irish inside-forward, could well be the new Denis Law.' Things were looking up.

Just as our Cup campaign was gathering momentum, the Big Freeze descended on Britain. Arctic weather caused the country to grind to a halt. Part of the Thames froze over. Six inches of snow fell in Manchester city centre. Temperatures dipped to −16°C. The Big Freeze began at Christmas; it was the first week in March before the thaw set in.

We trained as usual at the Cliff. The ground staff rolled the pitch to flat perfection. Our Cup run had focused attention on the Youth Team. Jimmy Murphy set up a series of practice matches against the Reserves, some of whom were in the First Team squad. The treacherous conditions suited me, others less so. I was nimble, well balanced, able to keep my feet where bigger, stronger guys floundered.

We were drawn to play Sheffield Wednesday away in the next round of the Youth Cup. This was a tough draw. Wednesday were never easy. If Manchester United were renowned for their fluent passing style, Wednesday were known for the more traditional English virtues of physical strength, pace and getting stuck into opponents.

Eventually the game was fixed for the first week in March. We'd been flying in the practice matches at the Cliff, no one more than John Aston, our outside-left. John was a pacy, direct winger, an excellent crosser of the ball who worked hard to win it back when we needed to defend. A week before the Wednesday match, John got injured. That was a blow. George Best was selected to replace him.

George was a very different kind of player: sometimes brilliant, sometimes infuriating. With John you knew what you were going to get; with George it was either feast or famine. In five-a-sides on the car park, he could be unbelievable: riding tackles, leaving people on their arse, taunting, teasing and on good days finishing all his dazzling fore-play with a clinical strike on goal. But for every astonishing goal there were five or six occasions when he'd run into a dead end, falling to a crunching tackle while team-mates waited for a pass that should have been delivered. He was a genius in embryo, but we didn't know that. I suspected he might be like Barry Grayson: brilliant, but ultimately frustrating.

George was a year younger than me. He arrived at Old Trafford in the summer of 1961. He came with another Belfast lad, Eric McMordie. After two days they bolted back home. Remembering my own feelings from the first few days in Manchester, I wasn't particularly surprised. Lunch with the truckers, the shite food, the strangeness of it all, the sense of being abandoned by Joe Armstrong after all those promises about being well looked after. Bolting seemed a reasonable response if you had the courage.

After a couple of weeks George was persuaded to come back. We didn't see much of him in his first year at United. He signed as an amateur, working as a clerk in an office at Trafford Park industrial estate. He trained two nights a week with the other amateurs at the Cliff. Mostly he played in the B Team. The following summer he signed as an apprentice pro.

There was something different about George. He was quiet, shy, yet self-assured in certain ways. He enjoyed the coarse banter of the dressing room without ever contributing very much to it. He was fastidious about his appearance. After training every day, he produced shampoo and talcum powder from a washbag and groomed himself as if he were going dancing. Jimmy Ryan, a dour Scot with a droll sense of humour, was his buddy. They shared digs together, and were inseparable. Barry Fry would wonder sarcastically if they ever spoke to each other.

Some days after training, George would come into town with Barry and me to the Plaza. While Barry did his thing with the girls, George and I would sit quietly surveying the scene. During the Big Freeze horseracing ceased, leaving a hole in our daily routine. It was then that George and I discovered a shared passion: snooker. One day after the Plaza, the three of us headed off to the Temperance Snooker Hall in Chorlton.

Before the days of colour television and Alex Higgins, snooker was a form of low-life recreation. Not exactly a vice, but being good at snooker was deemed a sign of 'wasted youth'. George was very good. We wasted many happy, harmless afternoons in the Temperance Snooker Hall while waiting for the Big Freeze to end.

At this stage Barry had a girlfriend. He was going steady with a girl whose father, Barry boasted, was 'loaded'. And it turned out Jimmy Ryan was also courting. With no Saturday game to play, there was an opportunity to go out on Friday night, a rare treat if you had somewhere to go, or someone to go with. One Friday George and I decided to hit the town. The Plaza was packed: the Hollies, then the hot Manchester band, were playing.

Neither of us drank alcohol. Two woefully shy Irish kids, we sipped our Cokes while waiting for something to happen. We eyed the girls, but we didn't know how to make a move. Then I got lucky. One of Barry's cast-offs recognized me and joined us at our table. I introduced George. After some hesitant conversation she asked me to dance. I'd never danced. I couldn't dance. But there was no option short of being rude. The ordeal over, we returned to the table. I suggested she dance with George. She declined. Her preference was clear. So was mine. I was staying with George.

When the Sheffield game was finally played, they knocked us out of the Youth Cup. George was poor on the night. We all were, but on the coach travelling back across the Pennines, the mutterings of the disappointed at the back of the bus focused on him and how badly we missed John Aston. We'd peaked at the Cliff during the Big Freeze, leaving our form on the training ground. Although I didn't know it at the time, those few months in the autumn and winter of 1962/63 would prove to be as good as it got for my career at United. I would be too old for next season's Youth Team, and the prospect of First Team football was at best remote.

Over the following two months I played several games for the Reserves. In theory, this was a promotion. The reality was rather grim. Picking me for the Reserves left space in the A Team for the emerging young players who would form the nucleus of next season's FA Youth Cup team. The Reserves was limbo. The team consisted of older players who'd failed to secure a First Team place, First Team regulars coming back from injury and those such as me, who'd been promising but were failing to fulfil that early promise.

The Reserve Team vibe was, to put it mildly, uninspiring. In this void, the malcontents held sway. The team changed every week. Guys dropped from the First Team were pissed off. Others heading for the exit on free transfers, or for sale with low price tags, were similarly demoralized. Hardly anybody wanted to be in the Reserves, much less play with passion and resolve. The 'New Denis Law' felt like the old Harold Bratt. Limbo was no fun.

The First Team was also struggling, at least in the League, and for a while that spring, relegation looked on the cards. But in the FA Cup, United were on a roll that would lead to the final at Wembley. The relegation scare passed and, after beating Southampton 1–0 in the semi-final, United progressed to meet Leicester City in the final. The real Denis Law made a major contribution to this Cup run. Even in a poor side, he scored vital goals and injected energy and belief into a group of players who were far from united.

Paddy Crerand, signed from Celtic in February '63, was the latest

1. My parents, Paddy and Peg, on their wedding day.

2. Team photo in the Dump: myself and my brother Kevin (*sitting*), Dessie Toal (*standing left*) and Frank O'Neill (*standing centre*).

3. Bunny Fulham (*left*) and Tommy Rowe (*right*), two of my childhood idols at Tolka Park. Our house was right behind the stand, and we could see the glow from the first set of modern floodlights at any Irish ground. (*Sportsfile*)

4. Paddy Coad's Invincibles. Watching that Shamrock Rovers team was what, more than anything else, made me want to be a footballer. (*Sportsfile*)

5. The Stella Maris 1956 Evans Cup winning team, with John Giles (*kneeling extreme right*) and Dessie Toal (*kneeling next to John*), at Turner's Cross in Cork.

6. The complete staff of Manchester United before the 1961/62 season. The first team, in the centre, included John Giles (*far left*), Bobby Charlton (*seventh from left*) and Shay Brennan (*sixth from right*); the Boss, Matt Busby, was next to Shay. The reserves were on the left; the youths, on the right, included Barry Fry (*fourth player from left*), myself (*to the right of Barry*) and George Best (*to the right of me*). Joe Armstrong is at the extreme right; the photo also includes the tea and laundry ladies, the groundsmen and the secretaries.

INTRODUCING...

A SERIES OF PEN PICTURES BY DAVID MEEK AND PETER SLINGSBY

Eamon Dunphy is one of Manchester United's young reserves waiting one day for his big chance. In his time he has been likened to Denis Law, with his natural ability on the ball, his fair hair, lean build, and willingness to tackle hard.

Certainly he has showed all the promise of a successful career. Back home in Dublin he played for the Eire schoolboy team and he quickly made his mark at Old Trafford.

He played in the youth team for two seasons, 1961-62 and 1962-63. He also showed his versatility because he was a key figure in both sides, one year at wing-half and the other at inside-forward.

He arrived in Manchester straight from school at 15 after playing for Stella Maris, the Dublin youth team that provided United with John Giles among other players.

Eamon was a regular in the reserve team last season, but lost ground at the beginning of this with another spell in the "A" team. Now he is back in the Central League and was 12th man with the senior side at West Bromwich.

Football is in the family. His young brother played for Eire schoolboys last season. Eamon does not claim to have any hobbies, it's football all the time he says.

Perhaps that is not strictly true, for we hear an engagement was rumoured for this Christmas!

A Manchester Evening News Photo

EAMON DUNPHY

KETS, 1965/66

the Club. The remaining season tickets will be issued **through the Programme Token Scheme**. Applications will be invited during the close season, and full details of the number of tokens required will be given at that time. **No applications can be considered until the announcement is made next year.**

The Programme Token Scheme
In order to protect the interests of supporters who do not wish to purchase a season ticket the Programme token scheme will continue. Tickets for special matches and cup-ties when in short supply will be allocated through this scheme as in previous years.

MANCHESTER UNITED v. SHEFFIELD UNITED — 28th DECEMBER, 1964
David Herd heads the ball over Hodgkinson to score United's goal, while Richardson and Badger try unsuccessfully to stop it going in the net. Sheffield scored later in the second half to force a 1-1 draw and stop United winning the Christmas double.
Photo by courtesy of the Daily Express

7. and 8. The programme for Manchester United's FA Cup third-round match against Chester, on 9 January 1965, included a note on me: 'He has been likened to Denis Law, with his natural ability on the ball, his fair hair, lean build, and willingness to tackle hard.'

9. Looking for a way past Matt Busby in training, with Willie Anderson (*left*) and John Aston looking on.

10. 'Welcome on board': with George Teasdale, secretary of York City, after my transfer from Manchester United in 1965.

11. A collector's item: the author heading the ball.

12. Behind enemy lines: further evidence that I was useful in the air during my Millwall days.

13. Celebrating the Lions' promotion in 1966. (*Front row left to right*): Ken Jones, Tommy Wilson, Harry Cripps, myself, Joey Broadfoot; (*back row left to right*): Mickey Purser, Len Julians, Benny Fenton, Hunt, McCullough, skipper Brian Snowden, Lawrie Leslie, John Gilchrist, Billy Neil.

14. On the pitch with Bryan King (*left*) and Terry Venables (*right*) before our FA Cup tie against Spurs in 1967.

15. With skipper Noel Cantwell (*ball at feet*) at an Irish training session. (*Sportsfile*)

16. The Old Thief shakes hands with John Giles before John's first senior international match, against Sweden at Dalymount, in 1959.

expensive addition to the team. As the flirtation with relegation demonstrated, Busby was still struggling to restore the club to its former glory. United finished nineteenth in the League while Everton claimed the title. The Cup Final was a huge bonus. In 1963 the FA Cup Final was one of the game's marquee events, not just in England, but across the world. Wembley in all its early-summer glory was the ultimate aspiration for fans and players alike.

Quite apart from the glory, reaching the Cup Final gave the players an opportunity to cash in by selling their tickets on the black market. For Manchester United players the carrot was particularly tasty. The maximum wage of twenty pounds a week had been abolished after the players threatened to strike in 1961. This was a seminal moment in the English game. Faced with revolt on a grand scale, the butchers, bakers and local worthies who ruled football with Stalinist fervour caved in. Up to a point. The slaves were still indentured for life, but with the abolition of the twenty-pounds-a-week cap, footballers were free to command whatever wage they could negotiate. The new law worked better in theory than in practice.

Johnny Haynes, Fulham's great England inside-forward, was the most spectacular beneficiary of the new deal. Tommy Trinder, the impresario owner of Fulham, promised to pay Haynes a hundred pounds per week, if permitted. Trinder honoured his promise. Matt Busby had made no promise, just hinted that he would reward his players handsomely if allowed. Two years after abolition, United players were on twenty-five pounds a week, with an additional fiver for a First Team appearance.

One of the reasons for discontent in the dressing room at Old Trafford was the realization that its inhabitants were among the lowest paid in the country. There were no exceptions to Busby's Law; not Bobby Charlton, Denis Law or Noel Cantwell. When the maximum wage was done away with, John Giles rang Charlie Hurley at Sunderland, then in the Second Division. He asked Charlie what he'd been offered. The answer was sixty pounds a week. And Charlie was brassed off, thinking he was worth more.

On the question of Cup Final tickets, Busby was more pragmatic. FA rules restricted the players to an allocation of twelve tickets each. Busby was happy to circumvent the law by allowing every member of the First Team squad 100 tickets. After taking care of family and friends, players could flog the remaining tickets on the black market. This was a demeaning perk, but welcome all the same. At the going rate in 1963, the profit accruing from this transaction was roughly £1,000 – the bones of one year's salary, or the price of a new family saloon from the local car dealer. In the weeks leading up to the final, a number of brand-new cars appeared in the players' car park at Old Trafford.

John Giles wasn't comfortable with the black-market option. In the three years I'd been in Manchester, he had been very good to me. He and Jimmy Sheils were like brothers, looking out for me, pointing out the perils of betting shops and the lunchtime Plaza crowd. When Barry was off courting, John and Jimmy often took me dancing on a Saturday night at the Locarno Ballroom in Sale, a bastion of suburban respectability. Both of them were in serious relationships at home, so pulling girls was not on their menu. Knowing my ineptitude in that department, they fixed me up a blind date with a very pretty girl of their acquaintance. We went to the pictures. It was a disaster. They laughed, gently mocking my assertion that I didn't fancy her anyway.

Permanently strapped for cash due to my gambling habit, I couldn't afford a decent suit of clothes. Mrs Scott's sister had a Littlewoods catalogue. One night she suggested I peruse its glossy pages, where clothes could be purchased on the never-never. I picked a nice blue suit, which looked smart. When it arrived, the clobber wasn't quite what I expected. The cut was fine, the colour was the problem: turquoise. I looked like a bingo-caller. When I turned up at the Locarno one night, the two lads wet themselves laughing. 'You should have warned us, we'd have worn our sunglasses,' said Jimmy.

'Ask for your deposit back,' was John's contribution to my humiliation.

'You're bound to pull in that, Eamon,' they jeered. The suit never again saw the light of day. Nor was it ever forgotten. Not to this day.

On hearing that John had no plans for his spare Cup Final tickets, Barry came up with a proposal: we would sell the tickets for him on a commission basis. 'We'll give you a grand if you let us keep anything extra we make.' I was the silent partner in the deal. John agreed. Barry and I headed off to town to find a buyer.

In an account of his life and times subsequently published, Barry claimed that his first encounter with Stan Flashman, the notorious ticket tout, involved a deal to sell John's tickets. That was fiction. In truth, we were flying blind when we hit the city centre with our precious cache of tickets. In the Plaza at lunchtime the following day, Barry let it be known that he had tickets for sale. A lot of tickets. A smartly dressed young guy soon appeared. Some bartering ensued before a deal was struck at a price of £1,500. The client offered to pay by cheque.

'No problem,' said Dumb, as Dumber nodded in agreement. The cheque bounced. The client disappeared. We were fucked. John was down the best part of £1,000, a year's wages.

This was without doubt the worst moment of my life till then. John was unbelievably gracious. 'Don't worry,' he told us, when we broke the news to him. We were the talk of the town and Old Trafford for months. Jimmy Sheils christened us the 'Ticket Twins', adding derisively that we were 'a pair of gobshites'. We would have been better off if we had met Stan Flashman: at least we would have got paid.

20. Happy Families

Despite its glamorous image and international renown for stylish football, Manchester United remained at heart a homely club. Everybody mattered. There was no 'them and us' divide between the famous stars and those occupying humbler roles – the ground staff, the laundry ladies and the catering staff who served the tea, sandwiches and drinks in the boardroom after First Team matches. Busby had fostered a sense of solidarity and belonging at Old Trafford from day one. Challenged by big-name players, he would face them down, insisting that no one was bigger than Manchester United; neither, in his eyes, was anybody smaller than someone better known or better paid. The club's arrangements for FA Cup Finals reflected this core value. United hired a special train for the great day out in London. Everybody employed by the club was invited – not just to the game but to the post-game banquet at the Savoy Hotel.

Leicester were favourites to win the Cup in 1965. They'd finished fourth in the Championship. Frank McLintock was captain of a solid, well-organized team. Gordon Banks was in goal. But United, led by Noel Cantwell, were by far the better team on the day. Denis Law was outstanding. Paddy Crerand controlled the tempo of the game from midfield. Wembley, with its pristine turf and wide-open spaces, was made for United's expansive style. The final 3–1 scoreline accurately reflected United's superiority.

The Savoy laid on a splendid feast to celebrate the victory. The disappointment of the Championship season was history now. Bonhomie was the order of the night. From our table at the back of the banqueting hall we listened to the speeches, raised our glasses to the toasts, and wondered what it was like to be the stars in this movie rather than extras on the fringe.

Across the room I could see Dickie Giles. I wondered if he knew about the tickets. After the evening's formalities, as people began to mingle, I went over to say hello to him. John's mother was with him. John had been outstanding that afternoon, playing outside-right.

Dickie, animated as always, was less than happy, though. John was an inside-forward, not a winger, he insisted. The euphoria of an FA Cup victory had not clouded his rigorous football brain. This family trait would soon assert itself and lead to John's departure from Old Trafford. We were a long way from Tolka Park and Fagan's pub, at least in terms of our surroundings. But in his passionate convictions about the game, Dickie yielded to nobody in this or any other room. 'Are you doing OK?' he asked me, a hint of scepticism in his voice.

'I'm fine,' I replied, rather unconvincingly.

'Don't worry, son, you can play,' he said. Coming from Dickie, the compliment was welcome.

Later I met George Best's mother and father, Ann and Dickie. They were lovely people. Anxious, though, as all parents were, to know how we were doing. George got his good looks from his mother. The close-ness between them was evident. The memory of her drawn, pale face and troubled eyes that night stayed with me through the many years of strife and glory that George was fated to endure. Ann died of alcohol-ism in 1978, long before the worst of George's nightmare final years. But she lived long enough to witness the beginning of his downward spiral into the hell of tabloid notoriety.

Dickie Best lived to see the horror show to its dreadful end. In the Savoy that night, there was no inkling of the future, no trace of or rea-son to suspect the tragedy that lay waiting for the boyish son, the anxious mother and the quiet, stoical father from the Belfast shipyards.

Dickie Best was a member of the Orange Order. George marched with his father's Lodge on 12 July every year. In one of many tawdry books churned out in his name in latter years, George conceded that the Order was an important aspect of his family's life. The Bests were Free Presbyterians, members of Ian Paisley's church. Just as de Valera and McQuaid had promoted hate-filled bigotry in Dublin, Paisley com-pared the Pope to Satan when rousing his followers in Belfast.

Free of the sectarian vice that infected our respective tribes back home, the Bests and I enjoyed a pleasant half-hour together in the Savoy. Like my mother and father, they were decent working people, beguiled by clerics and politicians for whom they were merely fodder for bogus tribal warfare. Despite my devout, rosary-chanting Dublin background, I had more in common with the Bests than with the vile sectarian leaders of my tribe. I would meet Dickie Best often in the years to come. He was an unassuming, decent man, traits he shared with Sam Prole, another Presbyterian I had reason to admire.

Years later, when George was in his prime, the prospect of an all-Ireland soccer team was mooted. He was an enthusiastic supporter of the proposal. His public endorsement elicited a vicious response from his loyalist tribe in the form of death threats, which the authorities took seriously.

Shortly after the Cup Final, I travelled to Zürich with the Youth Team for the Blue Stars international tournament, a prestigious event that United had won for the previous four years. Many of Europe's top clubs, such as AC Milan and Bayern Munich, regularly competed in Zürich. Like the FA Youth Cup, Busby took the Zürich engagement seriously. He was there with Jimmy Murphy. For Barry Fry and me, Zürich would be the end of Youth Team football. We'd both played in the winning team the previous year, now we struggled to get a game.

George and a number of other young players who arrived at Old Trafford in his year were moving up through the ranks. John Fitzpatrick, Willie Anderson, Bobby Noble and David Sadler were all emerging stars. We failed to retain the trophy, but George played brilliantly in every game. Any doubt we might have had about him was settled that early summer week in Zürich.

After our final game, a third-place play-off, we were granted a night on the town. Zürich didn't exactly rock. We found a bar and decided to sample the local beer. Bored by eleven o'clock, most of us returned to the hotel, a modest enough three-star place fronted by a pleasant terrace where Busby, Jimmy Murphy and Youth Team coach Wilf McGuinness sat enjoying a nightcap. George stayed out with John Fitzpatrick, Jimmy Ryan and Bobby Noble, his closest pals.

The four *amigos* eventually appeared on the street outside the hotel. They were moving slowly, George in the middle being propped up by the others. He was so drunk he could barely walk. Wilf McGuinness was up like a shot to shepherd the boys past Busby and Jimmy, who watched impassively. As far as I know, this was George's first encounter with alcohol.

For most of us, getting pissed was a rite of passage, and the end-of-season Zürich tournament was frequently the crime scene. After winning the trophy the previous year, Barry and I had set out to get drunk. I had a bizarre notion that it was impossible to get so drunk that you would lose your senses. Setting out to prove my point, I started downing rum and blackcurrant. I felt great. Until the alcohol kicked in. Soon I was in the toilet of the bar being violently sick. We managed to evade Busby on the way to our hotel bedroom.

Laying my head on the pillow, I experienced that terrible head-spinning disorientation that alcohol consumed in industrial quantities induces. 'Please, God, let this pass and I'll never drink again,' I prayed. God gave me a break and I never over-indulged again until I'd finished playing.

Apart from some piss-taking the following day, George suffered nothing more than a sore head. Three months later he made his First Team debut.

21.   Falling Stars

In August 1963, FA Cup winners Manchester United faced League champions Everton for the Charity Shield. The Charity Shield meant nothing; only pride was at stake. Everton humiliated United, the 4–1 scoreline flattering Busby's team. He was stung. John Giles, David Herd and Albert Quixall were dropped for the season's opening League game.

The relationship between John and Busby had been tense for some time. In the FA Cup semi-final of 1962, Spurs beat United 5–1. John, then twenty-one, played inside-forward in that game. He performed poorly against a great Spurs team. By his own admission, he was out of his depth against a Spurs midfield consisting of Danny Blanchflower, John White and Dave Mackay. After that débâcle Busby was cool with him. When selected, John played as a winger. It was clear to him that Busby didn't believe he could cut it as a midfield player. In the Wembley victory over Leicester City, John played outside-right. He played well. But he knew what his best position was and outside-right wasn't it.

After the Everton defeat, John asked for a transfer. Ostensibly, money was the issue, John rejecting Busby's offer of twenty-five pounds a week and refusing to sign a new contract. Money was not really the bone of contention, though. The dispute was about football. Although quiet, John was single-minded and very determined when it came to business. He stood up to Busby, insisting that he wanted to leave Old Trafford.

Within a week he was gone, to Leeds United, then a Second Division club managed by Don Revie, one of the game's new, innovative coaches. The fee was £32,500. As speculation about the transfer made headlines in the press, Wilf McGuinness, who was friendly with John, approached him after training one morning. 'Don't worry,' Wilf told him. 'The Boss might change his mind.'

'He might,' John replied, 'but I won't.'

Years later, when John was generally acclaimed as the greatest midfield player of his era, Busby conceded that he'd been wrong: 'Selling him to Leeds, not seeing his potential as a midfield player, was my greatest mistake in football.' When he was England manager, Alf Ramsey, rarely guilty of overstatement, remarked, 'As I look at all the talent and character at my disposal, my one regret is that John Giles wasn't born an Englishman.'

I, meanwhile, was going nowhere. Reserve Team limbo was as good as season 1963/64 would get. Too old for the Youth Team, not even close to First Team football.

I was at Salford dog-track on 22 November 1963 when news filtered through that John F. Kennedy had been shot. We were sitting in the restaurant just before the first race. In those days, communication was slow. The only screen we could see was the one showing the Tote odds for the next race. Initially the word was that Kennedy was wounded, but still alive. By the fifth race the rumour was that he had died. By the time we got home his assassination was confirmed.

This was an unforgettable moment. As with the news that Manchester United's plane had crashed in Munich, there was a profound sense of loss that was personal, sorrow that this tragedy left the world a darker, more threatening place. Like the Red Devils (and later John Lennon), Kennedy was young, daring, brave, one of us, part of us; a hero it was possible to believe in.

He'd visited Dublin five months before, in June 1963. I was home on holiday. Everyone in the city turned out to greet the first Catholic president of the United States of America. I stood in the crowd on Tolka Bridge on the airport road, fifty yards from St Pat's, my old school, as Kennedy passed slowly in an open-top car. It was like a scene from a movie. Bronzed, wearing a blue suit, a white shirt and flashing a boyish smile, he waved at the throng. The leader of the Free World looked the part. It was Camelot in Drumcondra.

It is difficult now, in this more cynical age, to convey the sense in which our deepest longing for a better world was vested in Kennedy and America. He was, of course, standing up for liberty, facing down the Soviet Union, then deemed a moral threat. The day before his arrival in Dublin, Kennedy had delivered his famous Berlin speech in which he assured besieged West Berliners that the Free World would defend their liberty.

The Berlin speech was important. For those of us in Britain and Ireland, the so-called Communist threat could be regarded as an abstraction, a figment of the fevered imagination of America's vocal Cold Warriors. But the Soviets had erected the Berlin Wall in 1961, dividing the city overnight and imprisoning 16 million Germans in the East.

Much more easily understood on a human level was the struggle for civil rights, led by Martin Luther King in the southern states of America. Thanks to King's personal courage and stirring oratory, the eyes of the world were focused on the struggle between black Americans and white supremacists. Television pictures transmitted this story across the world. The images of brutal oppression were shocking.

In August 1963, King led the March on Washington to urge the federal government to hasten the pace of reform. His 'I have a dream' speech was televised across the world. It made the most profound impression on all who witnessed this defining moment in US history. King ended his moving invocation with a vision of the world that would be as threatening to the white supremacists and to de Valera, Archbishop McQuaid and Oliver J. Flanagan, now a minister in the Irish government, as it was inspiring to all who longed for justice wherever they were:

> And when this happens, when we allow freedom to ring, when we let it ring from every village and every hamlet, from every state and every city, we will be able to speed up that day when all God's children, black men and white men, Jews and Gentiles, Protestants and Catholics, will be able to join hands and sing in the words of the old Negro spiritual: 'Free at last! Free at last! Thank God Almighty, we are free at last.'

When visiting Ireland, Kennedy was lionized by those who held sway in the Land of Saints and Scholars. They wouldn't have known, much less cared, what King was on about. They clung to their own shabby narrative, the Roman Catholic pieties about Jewboys, heathen Prods and the undeserving poor. To Official Ireland, Kennedy was a rock star, Elvis with gravitas, his visit to their Emerald Isle a cause for self-congratulation, for the president was, after all, 'one of our own'. At a reception in the grounds of the American embassy, Kennedy was mobbed by a gaggle of Dublin matrons, being forced to retreat to the Residence to change the shirt almost ripped from his back.

My childhood hobby of reading everything I could get my hands on about the world outside our room was now a passion I indulged with much richer sources. Through newspapers, books and television I followed the great stories of the day, forming opinions, taking sides, discovering heroes. I derived little real satisfaction from my football. I knew the 'Grand Dream' of making it with United was out of reach.

My addiction to dog-tracks and betting shops was the cause of much misery.

My passion for politics and current affairs was endlessly stimulating. I was moved by King, his civil-rights campaign, his nobility and stoicism in the face of hatred. I consumed the Kennedy saga like a drug, reading everything I could about his battle for the White House and the various dramas that ensued, such as the Cuban Missile Crisis. *The Making of a President*, Theodore A. White's gripping account of Kennedy's presidential campaign, informed my view, not just of the now-dead leader but of Nixon, Bobby Kennedy and Hubert Humphrey, his rival for the Democratic nomination.

The assassination of Kennedy caused little comment in the dressing room. The real world was regarded as a distraction from the vital business of winning games. Politicians were a pain in the arse, even the best of them like JFK. Banter about birds, betting coups or the inhabitants' character traits – vanity, being tight-fisted or stupid – was the order of every day. The dressing room was an extension of the playground, grown men clinging to adolescence. On being asked after retiring from the game what they miss most, players invariably refer to the banter.

As any reference to civil rights in America or the terrible consequences of Kennedy's assassination would have been regarded as an affectation, I kept quiet. I could banter with the cruellest of the lads, yet in terms of my deepest beliefs and passions, my life was solitary.

Even when directly affected, footballers seemed indifferent to injustice. Happy slaves, most endured the tyranny governing their lives without complaint: the low wages paid by Busby; the absurd retain-and-transfer system, which allowed the club to bind you to a contract, renewed every two years, for life, yet enabled the bosses to dump you when, through injury or loss of form, you were deemed surplus to requirements; the endemic exploitation of youngsters signed at fifteen and consigned to the scrap-heap two, three years later – fit for nothing except unskilled labour.

The major players at United were far from stupid. Noel Cantwell, Denis Law, Bobby Charlton and Harry Gregg were smart, proud men. But even they seemed obsessed by the next game, the last result and soldiering on despite their serf-like conditions of employment. I admired them greatly, but was puzzled by their passivity. Danny Blanchflower, then just retired from Spurs, was an exception to all rules. He'd started writing a weekly column for the *Sunday Express*. Full of wit and whimsy, Danny's writing also mocked the idiots who ran the game, the little men in high office who called the shots and never called them right.

As a player, Danny won everything, did everything, and did it his way. His rejection of Eamonn Andrews and *This Is Your Life* was, to my mind, heroic. Strangely, or maybe not, Danny was unpopular among his peers. An original thinker, a courageous exception to the rules of serfdom, not even his great achievements as a player could insulate him from the dressing-room charge of attention-seeking. I thought he was magnificent.

22.   Reality Dawns

United offered me a new contract in the summer of 1964. Apart from John Aston, I was the last survivor of the class of 1960. It had turned out to be a non-vintage year. Barry Fry was given a free transfer, Barry Grayson had disappeared. Jim Keogh was working in a factory somewhere in Manchester. Hughie Curran did go on to have a decent career after leaving Old Trafford in 1962: after a spell in Scotland, he played for Wolves, Oxford, Norwich and Millwall, scoring consistently, surviving as much on self-belief as ability. John Aston was the biggest success of the class of 1960, his career peaking in 1968 with the European Cup victory over Benfica at Wembley.

Season 1963/64 saw United begin to restore its reputation. The First Team finished second to Liverpool in the First Division. George Best nailed down a First Team place during the second half of the season, Bobby Charlton moved into midfield from the wing and Denis Law was on fire, justifying the spectacular transfer fee Busby had paid for him. Busby's patience was paying off. Particularly with George. Had he heeded the dissidents led by Noel Cantwell, Busby might have ruined George's career before it took off. Instead of curbing his natural instincts, some of which, while dazzling, were self-indulgent, Busby left him alone.

George was never coached, tutored in the basics of team play or tactics, as Cantwell would have wished. Filling George's head with stuff he didn't need to know could have done for him. The same was true of Denis Law and Bobby Charlton. Like George, they were naturals, great instinctive attacking players. Busby had the courage to believe in them. That was now paying off.

Inspired by George, the Youth Team won the FA Youth Cup. John Fitzpatrick, Bobby Noble and Willie Anderson featured prominently. They would progress to the First Team in time. I watched enviously. I was a regular in the Reserves, good enough to survive, but nowhere near good enough to make further progress. I knew the score. I signed my new contract and worked out my plan. I'd give it six months before asking for a transfer. Although it was obvious I couldn't make it at

United, I felt I could elsewhere. At nineteen, with no skills outside football, I was definitely scrap-heap material.

My options were unattractive. I could go home with my tail between my legs or get a labouring job in a Manchester factory, playing part-time in non-League football for a few extra quid. Those were paths well trodden by other cast-offs. And I wasn't going there. The best I could hope for was to shine in the Reserves and impress another League club. That was the plan.

I knew my faults, gambling and smoking too many cigarettes. The smokes hindered my physical development. I lacked the strength to be a United player. The skill, I had. Every time I played I worked like a dog. Every morning I grafted hard in training. When your career is on the slide you can be your own worst enemy: feeling sorry for yourself, whingeing about imagined slights, or guys who were getting chances that should have been yours by right. I resisted those morale-sapping vices, remembering Johnny Aston's injunction: 'The more you put in, the more you get out.'

In those early months of season 1964/65, I learned the virtue of grafting for grafting's sake. I was an ordinary player at football's biggest club; the plan was to become a First Team player at an ordinary club. Liberated from the illusion that I could break into the First Team at Old Trafford, I began to enjoy my football in the Reserves. Before every game I convinced myself that I was auditioning for a scout sitting somewhere in the stand. I was playing mind games with myself.

The First Team was mounting a serious challenge for the Championship. George was becoming the hottest young player in the country. Scoring and making goals, he tormented opponents, especially the tough guys who set out to 'do' him. Despite his extraordinary swift transformation, he still changed in the Reserve Team dressing room. He still hung out with the lads who'd carried him to bed in Zürich. He moved out of the digs he'd shared with Jimmy Ryan to move in with David Sadler.

After a stellar career with the English amateur international team, Sadler signed for United, aged seventeen. He was a grammar-school boy with a languid disposition, a cut above the rest of us with his polished Home Counties accent. He played a few First Team games and seemed set to make it. He and George hit it off. Despite his growing fame,

George remained unaffected, becoming more confident and increasingly audacious on the training ground.

One Monday morning, Jimmy Ryan arrived for training grim-faced. He still stripped next to George. Now he took his gear and moved across to another corner of the room. George was equally subdued when he showed up. Nothing was said, but there was tension in the air. During the course of the morning the news broke: at a party on the Saturday night, George had disappeared with Jimmy's girlfriend.

The tension didn't ease. It was obvious that Jimmy was badly hurt. He was a popular lad, quiet, with a droll sense of humour. One morning when Jimmy was out of the room, George reached into his little beauty bag, where he kept his shampoo and talcum powder, and produced a bundle of love letters Jimmy had written to his girlfriend. He started to read the letters out loud. We were stunned. It was bad form, seemingly out of character for George. 'Fuck off, George,' I told him. 'That's not on.' Strangely he didn't seem to get it. Everyone else did. Rather sheepishly he put the letters back in his bag. Often in the years to come I would reflect on that moment of gratuitous cruelty, which provided the first hint that George was different, and not in a good way.

In March 1965 I went to see Jimmy Murphy. He'd always been kind to me. Jimmy rarely appeared on the training ground. Nobody was sure exactly what his duties were any more. There were rumours that his relationship with Busby had cooled. I knew from John Giles that the rumours were true. The popular belief that Jimmy had saved the club after the Munich Air Crash pissed Busby off. When Busby returned to work, his first move was to get rid of Stan Crowther and Ernie Taylor, the two players Jimmy had brought in to steady the ship. Crowther was trouble and Taylor was over the hill, Busby insisted.

Shipping them out, he asserted his authority at Old Trafford. Giles and other senior players believed that Busby resented the media depiction of Jimmy as the man who'd rescued the club in its hour of greatest need. There was only one 'Boss'. *Uno Duce, una voce.*

Jimmy took me up to the back of the main stand at Old Trafford. I told him I wanted a transfer. I wasn't going to make it and I wanted to try somewhere else. He was warm and honest. I was doing OK, he replied, but he understood. He'd have a word with the Boss. The next day, after training, I was summoned to Busby's office. Jimmy was warm, passion flickering behind his bulging eyes. Busby was cool, poker-faced, eyes betraying nothing.

'Jimmy tells me you're not happy,' he said, the quiet Scots burr indicating some surprise. I explained that I had no complaints about the club, I simply felt I was going nowhere, and would be better off trying somewhere else. 'You mean you want a transfer?'

'Yes.'

'Well, son, players never want to leave this club.' The emphasis was on the word 'this'. I outlined my reasoning, pointing out that the club was doing very well, though it wasn't working for me.

'Do you think you should be doing better?' he prompted, inviting me to have a whinge, the reason most players found themselves sitting where I was. I insisted that I had no complaints, that I was simply doing what I felt was best for me.

'Nobody asks for a transfer from Manchester United,' he repeated, a hint of exasperation in his tone. I was tempted to refer him to John Giles, now starring for Leeds United, who were challenging Busby's team for the League title, which they eventually won on goal difference. 'I want to get on, improve myself, play First Team football, and I think I need to leave,' I said matter-of-factly.

'OK.' He sighed. 'Put your request in writing and I'll put it to the board.' He was the board. I thanked him and left the office.

Downstairs I met Noel Cantwell. Noel was having a hard time himself. Billy Behan had discovered another great Irish player – Tony Dunne, a left-back who cost £6,000 when bought from Shelbourne in the League of Ireland. Tony was keeping Noel out of the First Team. I told Noel about my encounter with Busby. 'Fuck him.' Noel laughed.

I wrote my letter requesting a transfer. I heard nothing for a couple of weeks. Then one morning Noel approached me after training. He told me he'd fixed me up. A friend of his, Joe Mallet, was managing Birmingham City, who were struggling to avoid relegation from the First Division. Joe fancied me and would pay £8,000. Birmingham had made Busby an offer. I was thrilled. Birmingham was a big club in waiting, a sleeping giant, with a huge fan base. 'Don't accept any other offer,' Noel cautioned.

I waited. And waited. Nothing happened for several weeks. Then Noel told me Busby had refused Birmingham's offer. Birmingham were relegated to the Second Division. I went to see Busby. He told me they'd received no offers, even though the board had circulated other clubs about my availability. I didn't mention Birmingham. I wasn't supposed to know.

'He's a bastard,' Noel explained grimly, when I told him there had been no offers. A week later Busby sent for me. York City were offering £5,000 to sign me. York had just gained promotion to Division Three. I agreed to talk to York. York were *not* sleeping giants. Their fan base was tiny. They yo-yoed between the Third and Fourth Divisions. 'He's going to bury you,' Cantwell fumed, when I told him my news. 'And he's probably taken a bung,' the big Cork man explained. Noel did the sums. His read on the situation was chillingly cynical. Busby wouldn't want me at Birmingham, a big club where I might do well and embarrass him, as John Giles had done at Leeds. Busby would have told York City of the £8,000 Birmingham offer, adding that United would accept five grand if he was 'taken care of'. York got an £8,000 player, cut price, and Busby would split the difference, taking £1,500 for himself. Everyone was a winner. Except me.

A lesson learned, I packed my bags and headed for York.

23. Journeyman

I travelled to York by train. The club secretary, George Teasdale, met me at the station. George was a smoothie. His welcome was effusive: 'Welcome on board. Great to have you. Matt tells me we've stolen you for the fee.' Matt was right. Still, it was nice to feel wanted. I negotiated my deal with George. I was entitled to a £500 signing-on fee. My wages were the only outstanding matter. After some token haggling I settled for eighteen pounds a week, plus a fiver for a First Team appearance. A bonus of four pounds for a win and two for a draw meant I could earn twenty-seven pounds on a good week.

I signed the forms in George's office underneath the main stand at Bootham Crescent, City's intimate little stadium. The Crescent reminded me of Tolka Park. We were a world away from the grandeur of Old Trafford and the other great cathedrals of the English game. York City had just been promoted from the Fourth Division. Optimism was in the air on that summer's day. Workmen were painting the terrace railings. A tall man with a lawnmower was manicuring the pitch. The tall man was club manager Tom Lockie. George introduced me to my new boss before returning to his office – more important matters awaited his attention. The master/slave vibe was clear. While the club manager cut the grass, the man in the suit ran the club.

Tom Lockie was a Scot. He'd played for Rangers before plying his trade in the lower divisions of the Football League. He'd been at York for thirty years, most of them as First Team trainer. In 1960, they had promoted him to manager. The recent promotion was the highlight of his career. But he still had to mow the lawn. I liked him from day one. 'We've got some good players here,' he told me. 'We like to play our football the way it should be played. That's why I'm delighted we got you and Dave.'

Dave Dunmore was returning home after an eleven-year spell in London, where he'd played with some distinction for Spurs, West Ham and Leyton Orient. York had received £10,500 for him when he had left for Spurs in 1954, a record fee for the club at that time. He'd scored a lot of goals in the First Division, but was also admired for his lovely touch and the intelligence of his movement.

Standing by his souped-up lawnmower, Tom talked about the coming season with cautious optimism. He spoke warmly of Dave, Billy Rudd, his clever midfield player who had played a key role in their promotion year, and club captain Barry Jackson, a local lad, loved by City fans for his derring-do performances at centre-half. Around us, as we chatted, Bootham Crescent was neat and tidy, the grass green and lush, the paint fresh; a measure of pre-season optimism filled the air.

I was content. The prospect of playing First Team football excited me. Every game, every point would matter. I hadn't played in a game that really mattered since the Youth Cup team at Old Trafford.

I lodged with Mrs Dunne, a widow who lived in a cosy semi-detached house five minutes' walk from Bootham Crescent. Despite the name, Mrs Dunne had no Irish ancestry. She was sixty-something, recently widowed, trying to come to terms with living alone since the passing of her husband. Warm and chatty, Mrs Dunne was happy, as she put it, 'to have some company'. The food was excellent, and when she urged me to make myself at home she really meant it.

When Mrs Dunne discovered I liked to bet on the horses she was intrigued. She thought she'd like to have a bet herself. Whenever there was midweek racing on the telly we'd study form over breakfast, she would pick her fancies and I would place the bets after training. After lunch we'd settle down to watch the racing.

York was a beautiful city, full of history, but quiet at night – no dog-track or dancing to distract an idle mind. Evenings were peaceful. I watched a lot of television and read much more than I'd ever done before. A Yorkshireman, Harold Wilson, was the Labour prime minister. Despite their county kinship, Mrs Dunne didn't like Wilson or 'the Labour crowd'. She was a monarchist and a small-c conservative. England was changing and Mrs Dunne did not approve. The Beatles and the Rolling Stones, the loosening sexual morality, *Top of the Pops*, all these manifestations of the Swinging Sixties were, Mrs Dunne believed, a sign of a country losing its way. 'Did we fight a war for this?' she wondered. I teased her mercilessly, promising that the England she knew and loved, the world of Harold Macmillan, the Queen, Joe Loss and his orchestra, was a relic of the past. The revolution, I argued, was taking place and couldn't be stopped. Our disagreements were light-hearted, nothing more than banter. She was fond of me and I of her.

I admired her sturdy, decent Englishness, her allegiance to Queen and country, her evident belief in fair play and moderation in all things. In her kindness and quiet acceptance of my different points of view, Mrs Dunne embodied the virtues that, after five years in England, I now most associated with its people, tolerance being principal among them.

After an evening's television, she would make me some hot chocolate, with milk, before I went to bed. One night as we sipped our bedtime drinks, Mrs Dunne began to talk about her husband. He'd fought in 'the war against Hitler', as she described it. She reminisced about their courtship and happy marriage. His death was sudden, just after he'd retired from Rowntree's, the Quaker sweet manufacturer based in York. In keeping with the social-justice ethos for which Quakers were known, Rowntree's had ensured that Mrs Dunne received a handsome endowment upon becoming a widow. That, together with her life-insurance policy, left her comfortably off. So she'd decided to fulfil her dream of a world cruise with the Cunard line. This trip of a lifetime had not disappointed. Cairo was the highlight, she recalled.

Afternoon tea in the Cairo Hilton was a special treat. In those days, Hilton Hotels epitomized luxury and exclusivity. As Mrs Dunne remarked, 'No foreigners were allowed' inside the hallowed Cairo Hilton. Just tourists, most of them English. The crazy idea that Egyptians could be depicted as 'foreigners' in Cairo was distinctly English, a residue of empire and all that. Grist to the mill of the English-haters I'd grown up among. When I smiled and gently made the obvious point, Mrs Dunne relented: 'Well, you know what I mean.' I did.

By the end of September it was becoming clear that the team was in for a long, hard winter. The step up from the Fourth to the Third Division was too much for too many in the team. There was very little fight in this squad. The guys with talent wouldn't graft; the grafters didn't have enough talent. Sloppy goals were conceded. Fingers were pointed, angry words exchanged; instead of digging deep, the weaker spirits drifted out of games, offering nothing more than token resistance.

The home games were worse than those played on the road. Away from Bootham Crescent, the 'Frankie Howerds' could simply pack it in, jumping out of physical challenges, hiding when we had the ball. In home games, where the fans were more demanding, hiding developed into an art form. Nobody wanted the ball because nobody wanted to make a mistake, to take responsibility.

I was playing well. I scored a couple of goals, the first away to Brentford in the second game of the season proving to be the winner. For all my faults I never quit. With my low pain threshold I didn't relish the physical side of the game. But I worked for ninety minutes and possessed more than enough ability to stand out at this level. My press reviews were good. The *Sunday People* would mark each player out of ten after every game. Every Sunday morning I grabbed my copy to see how I'd done. The news was usually good. Still, the pleasure of being the top man in a poor team was limited. I needed a break.

And I got a big one in early October when I was named in the Irish squad for a World Cup qualifying game against Spain. No York City player had ever been capped, so my selection caused a stir around Bootham Crescent. Proud as Punch, Mrs Dunne baked a special cake. I met up with the other Irish players at Heathrow as arranged. I wasn't in the team, but it was still a move in the right direction. This was a big game for Ireland. Having beaten Spain in Dublin, we needed only a draw to qualify for the 1966 World Cup Finals. Syria, the other country in the three-nation group, had withdrawn for political reasons. Spain chose to host the match in Seville, where they played all their must-win games.

Johnny Carey was Ireland's manager. Noel Cantwell was captain. John Giles, now acknowledged as one of the English game's major stars, was Ireland's main man in midfield. Though he seemed to have forgotten the Cup Final ticket business, I certainly hadn't. I was, to put it mildly, a little self-conscious in his company. Noel and John were old acquaintances, Tony Dunne and Eric Barber I knew from Dublin. They were all nice, welcoming, expressing no surprise at my elevation. Johnny Carey blanked me, more or less. There was a reason for that. The manager hadn't a clue who I was.

In those days the Irish team and the squad were selected by the 'Big Five'. The gents concerned were members of a special FAI committee whose task was to pick the team and present their chosen XI to the manager. Hence my presence in Seville. In his role as FAI president, Sam Prole automatically chaired the selection committee. My suspicion was that Sam had read some favourable newspaper accounts of my endeavours at York and decided to bestow a favour on a neighbour's son.

Another feature of Irish teams in the good old days was the mandatory presence in them of at least one player from the semi-pro League of Ireland. In Seville, that lucky individual was Shelbourne's centre-forward, Eric Barber. Eric was a prolific goal-scorer in the League of Ireland. But the step up to international football was massive. The pace of the game, fitness levels and sheer technical ability meant the gap between international footballers and League of Ireland heroes was unbridgeable. This didn't deter the Big Five. They had their own imperatives: currying favour with the fellow committee men was one of the rules of their game and, of course, the age-old Irish trait of cronyism, which demanded the promotion of mediocrity in the form of 'helping a neighbour's child'.

The small-place mentality ensured my presence in Seville, and Eric Barber's. At least I was on the bench. Eric was starting, as was Frank O'Neill, then rated the best player in the League of Ireland. Frank, a winger, was outstanding for Shamrock Rovers against limited opposition. Much less effective against top-class international full-backs, he still won twenty caps for Ireland.

Frank and Eric were local heroes. Frank had played schoolboy soccer for my club, Stella Maris. Eric had starred alongside Tony Dunne in the Finbar's team trounced by John Giles's Stella in the Evans Cup in 1955. Both were respected Dublin football people. But their presence in the national team meant that Ireland were effectively down to ten men before kick-off.

Giving his team talk before the crucial game in Seville, Johnny Carey betrayed no passion. He delivered instructions, cursory in nature, to a number of players. Moving around the dressing room, his gaze fell on Eric. There was a moment's pause. Carey gestured towards Eric, snapping his fingers impatiently, 'Eh, eh, I'm sorry I've forgotten your name,' he stuttered. 'We'll call you Paddy,' he blundered. A wave of embarrassment swept through the room. Shay Brennan smirked; Noel Cantwell raised his eyes towards heaven; John Giles maintained his poker-face. Eric was visibly wounded. This was his first (and only) cap for his country and the iconic manager didn't know his name. Ireland took a 1–0 lead early on. The final score was 4–1 in Spain's favour. A play-off would decide who was going to the World Cup Final.

Back at Bootham Crescent, the mood was grim. October seemed a bit early to be speculating about a relegation battle, but that was what was happening. Guys were going through the motions in training and increasingly in matches. I felt sorry for Tom Lockie. He wasn't a cup-thrower. He didn't lose his temper or raise his voice. His tone was reasonable when he urged us to keep trying to do the right things. But few were listening.

After training one morning, George Teasdale called me into his office to tell me I'd been selected to play for Ireland against Spain in the World Cup play-off game in Paris. I was astonished. 'This is a great honour for the club.' George beamed. I resisted the temptation to tell him that he should write a thank-you note to the Big Five.

In the back of my mind I'd been trying to figure out a way to escape from the good ship York City, which was slowly but inexorably sinking. A speculative piece of transfer gossip in my favourite newspaper, the *Sunday People*, had recently suggested that Millwall were keen to buy me. My good form for York and my extreme good fortune in being selected to travel to Seville had raised my profile. An international debut could only help.

Ireland came tantalizingly close to qualifying for the 1958 World Cup Finals only to be denied by John Atyeo's last-minute equalizer for England at Dalymount Park. Now the game against Spain held out the prospect of redemption. Winner takes all. We'd beaten them 1–0 in Dublin and led briefly in Seville, so it was hardly an impossible task.

It was while waiting at Heathrow to board our flight to Paris that we were told by the travelling journalists that the Football Association of Ireland had done a treacherous deal with the Spanish FA. FIFA had originally scheduled the play-off match for London. Highbury, the home of Arsenal, was the governing body's preferred venue. This would have given us a significant advantage. We played our football in England, and London was home to tens of thousands of exiled Irish. Realizing this, the Spanish had dangled a carrot: if the FAI agreed to play in Paris, they could keep the gate receipts. Every man has his price: £25,000 was the FAI's.

'Fuck them,' Noel Cantwell angrily exclaimed. Nobody disagreed. The bastards in blazers seemed impervious to our agitation. They were too preoccupied loading up with duty-free to detect the anger all around them.

In this travelling party of players, journalists and assorted blazers, Johnny Carey cut a rather solitary figure. With his tweed jacket, pipe and copy of the *Daily Telegraph*, Gentleman Johnny might have been taken for a businessman on an export mission. He kept his distance, in the manner of Matt Busby, whom he had served so well as captain. He had been a successful manager, gaining promotion with Blackburn in '58 and leading Everton to fifth place in the First Division in '61 – their highest finish since the war. Shortly after their fifth-place finish, Everton sacked Carey.

It was the manner of his dismissal that scandalized football people and led to a savage media campaign against John Moores, the football-pools millionaire who was the club's owner. Moores conveyed the news of his sacking to Carey in the back of a taxi as they were on their way to a post-season function. For the media and Everton fans, the moral of this tawdry story was clear: if they were offered a taxi ride by John Moores, future Everton managers should take alternative transport. Had the very public humiliation terminally wounded Carey? I wondered.

No player had ever been as respected as him. Having proved himself a great player and an outstanding leader of men, Carey still remained vulnerable to the whim of his millionaire chairman and, in an Irish context, the often surreal team selection of the Big Five. Not to mention the betrayal that had us en route to Paris.

After dinner at our hotel on Monday night, we were free for the evening. Some of the lads stayed in the hotel, John Giles, the world's early-night champion among them. Led by skipper Noel Cantwell, a group of around ten of us decided to go for a stroll. We were bored. Forty-eight hours before the game we couldn't drink. We couldn't chase girls or go dancing. The Louvre was closed for the night. Standing in Place Vendôme, someone suggested a visit to Pigalle to see what was going on. Sex was off the menu, but we could have a look at the scene. On a November Monday night with business far from brisk, the arrival of ten Irish idiots did not go unnoticed by the Parisian ladies of the night.

Some exotic creatures approached, offering to show us a good time. I'm not sure who proposed the idea of an 'exhibition', but it was Captain Cantwell who opened negotiations with a pair of good-looking hookers. The price agreed, we had a whip-round and headed for the brothel. A lesbian sex show was the exhibition on offer. In the high-ceilinged apartment we gathered round a large bed while the girls got down to business. Two of the lads took their clothes off and joined the action. It was as erotic as playing in Darlington on a wet night. The thought occurred to me that we should ask for our money back. Instead we made our excuses and left before the allotted hour was up. Our night of shame remained a secret for more than twenty years. We were back in the hotel well before the eleven-thirty curfew.

Parc des Princes was packed with Spanish fans on match night. Paris was home to multitudes of Spanish exiles who'd fled the Franco regime. As our goalkeeper Pat Dunne bitterly observed, the only Irish flag in sight was the one flying on the stadium roof. Theo Foley, a hard-tackling full-back with his club, Northampton, was selected in midfield to man-mark the great Luis Suárez, then playing for Inter Milan. Suárez was the reigning European Footballer of the Year. Spain had won the 1964 European Championship. In the circumstances, we played well. John Giles was magnificent alongside Foley and me in midfield. Foley stuck like a limpet to Suárez, putting the boot in at every opportunity. I did OK, without having any real influence on the game.

In his Paris commentary, which I heard about later, Philip Greene insisted that I was playing 'a blinder'. I wasn't. Crucially, Theo Foley injured himself trying to kick Suárez and had to be carried off in the second half. Andy McEvoy missed a very good chance to put us ahead. Spain wore us down in the closing stages of the contest. With eleven minutes to go, Roberto Ufarte scored the decisive goal with a slightly mis-hit shot that crept in at the far post. Had the game been played in London, we might well have won and qualified for the 1966 World Cup Finals. In defeat, it was not unreasonable to argue that we'd been the victims of the FAI's friendly fire. Ireland did eventually make it to the World Cup Finals. Twenty-five years later.

After the game, I tried to clear up some unfinished business with John Giles. Our match fee was fifty pounds, an FAI cheque for forty-five and a crisp fiver. I offered it to John in lieu of the £1,000 we had lost on the Cup Final tickets. He laughed and told me not to worry.

Exaggerated accounts of my performance in Paris raised my profile still further back in England. According to the *People*, Millwall had upped their bid for my services. Things at York were going from bad to worse. Loyalty, particularly to Tom Lockie, was not an option. I liked Tom and didn't want to add to his woes, but I was determined to get out of the now looming relegation battle. When I broached the subject of Millwall's interest with him, he said he knew nothing. I believed him.

Teasdale, smoothie George, was the man to see. The transfer speculation mentioned a fee of £10,000, more than double what York had paid for me.

When I spoke to Teasdale, he hummed and hawed without denying the newspaper reports. When pressed, he made matters more explicit: we can't be seen to sell you; the fans will be angry; on the other hand, if you make trouble, ask for a transfer and insist you can't settle here, that will put a different gloss on things. 'If you want to go, put it in writing,' he said, ending the conversation.

Even though it meant shafting Tom, and by implication Mrs Dunne, I wrote a letter saying that I was unhappy in York and wanted to leave. Mrs Dunne took it badly, the local papers even worse. The City fans vented their spleen on me rather than the club. After a few difficult weeks, the posse arrived. Millwall, aiming for promotion, wanted to sign me. I took the next train to London.

24.   The Lions' Den

Millwall looked set for their second promotion in a row when I arrived in January. Back-to-back promotions would see them in the Second Division. They were vying for League leadership with their main rivals, big-spending Hull City. The gap to the chasing pack suggested that Division Three was a two-club race, both likely to claim promotion. I made my debut away to Workington. A coastal town in the far north-west of England, it was no holiday destination. They had a useful side in the top half of the table.

Like other northern outposts in the Football League, places like Hartlepool, Darlington and Barrow, Workington was believed to be a formidable test of character for the brittle visitors from the south. According to folklore, those soft fuckers from London wouldn't fancy the cold winds and the sturdy-studded challenges of their rugged northern opponents. 'They don't like it up 'em,' the locals would mockingly declare of their visitors from the south.

There was more than a grain of truth in this generalization. Many southerners didn't fancy it when they headed up the M1 north of Watford Gap. Even the great London clubs Arsenal, Spurs and West Ham approached their northern trips with a degree of trepidation. Visiting Anfield, Elland Road or Old Trafford, the big London clubs were frequently less than resolute opponents. History bears this out. In Cockney slang the north was Karsie Country, a bleak, distant place, foreign almost, where coal was mined, steel was forged and ships built. And the natives were thick and hostile. The long coach journey could take meek spirits way out of their comfort zones.

Millwall were different. There was nothing soft about the team I joined. They were a group of tough, experienced pros who'd been together for three or four seasons and were now poised to claim a place in the Second Division. Workington was just another step along the way. In training the week before our journey north, I was struck by their determination and maturity. And their indifference to the newly capped Irish international who'd joined the ranks. They weren't impressed. 'Prove yourself' was the unspoken but unmistakable message.

In a squad of strong characters, John Gilchrist stood out. A canny, hard-tackling right-back, 'Gilly' was a Scot with attitude. In one of our early training-ground five-a-sides he introduced himself to me with a heavy challenge. Later Gilly would scorn my selection for another international fixture by informing the dressing room that anybody who could do ten keepie-uppies with the ball got an Irish cap. He came from Wishaw, fifteen miles from Glasgow, where anti-Catholic sentiment was not unknown. But he was a good man to have on your side on a dark, cold winter night in Workington.

Millwall's successful season saw an innovation introduced for this game. For the first time in Football League history, the match was relayed back to the Den, where our fans watched on closed-circuit television. The famous BBC DJ Pete Murray hosted the event. Nine thousand Millwall fans turned out to view the game on four giant TV screens. Before 4,000 hardy locals we drew 0–0 with Workington. It was a typically dour, on-the-road Millwall performance. Unlike the York team I'd left, these guys didn't expect to lose. Nobody went missing when the going got tough. The load was shared. We defended as a team and attacked as a team. I did my bit in what was deemed a satisfactory debut. Happiness is a 0–0 draw at Workington.

Billy Gray, the manager who'd built this team, was content as well. Billy had played in the Nottingham Forest side that won the FA Cup in '59. Roy Dwight, Elton John's uncle, played alongside Billy in that Forest team. Billy joined Millwall as player-manager in 1963, when the club was in the Fourth Division. Alex Stepney, our goalkeeper that night in Workington, was one of his first signings. Stepney came straight from non-League football. Len Julians was another inspired buy from Forest where he'd played with Billy. Like Dave Dunmore, Len was a technically gifted centre-forward whose intelligent movement and deadly finishing were key to Millwall's success. While Len scored goals, Stepney and a mean, resilient back four gave nothing away. Gilly at right-back, Brian Snowden at centre-half, Tommy Wilson alongside Snowden, and at left-back a Millwall legend, Harry Cripps.

Snowden was skipper in more than name. Quiet off the field, he was a leader when the muck and bullets were flying. When he said, 'Well done, son', you knew he meant it. When he stared you out with a look of withering contempt, of unvoiced anger, it cut right to the bone. Brian was Gilly's mate and I knew from day one he shared the Scot's doubts about my 'bottle'. Would I go missing in action was the question on their minds. Good teams, winning teams, are built on that kind of unrelenting scepticism. Prove yourself to us. Not to the fans or the sportswriters, deemed to know fuck all, but to the guys you go to work with.

I understood the ethic within this team and I relished the challenge of earning respect. Viewed from a certain perspective, men like Snowden and Gilly were journeymen, Third Division labourers of no particular distinction. I quickly came to see them differently, as good pros, men of real character who gave everything, playing every game to the limits of their ability and beyond. Even as I endured their disdain I respected them greatly.

Tommy Wilson, another Scot, was a lovely footballing centre-back. Elegant on the ball, quick to see danger and smother it with a timely intervention, Tommy was gentle and witty. Harry Cripps was something else. Even today, after so many outstanding footballers have found a place in Millwall's hall of fame, 'Arry Boy is the player most associated with the club. The iconic figure Millwall fans most *want* to be associated with, Harry was our left full-back.

He was an East End boy. Harry played in the West Ham team that reached the FA Youth Cup Final in 1959. Bobby Moore captained that team. Harry didn't make it at West Ham. He joined Millwall on a free transfer. Burly and barrel-chested, he looked awkward on first inspection. This impression was compounded by the inconvenient fact, for a left-back, that he was right-footed. His left foot was his swinger. He didn't run, he shuffled, and not very quickly.

According to legend, Harry was a hard man who terrified opposing forwards. Harry wasn't hard. In the eight seasons I played with him I can't recall a single bad, bone-threatening Cripps tackle. John Gilchrist was hard. Harry, by comparison, was soft; not quite as soft as me, but a lot closer to me than to Gilly.

What made Harry special was the depth of his desire. We all wanted to be professional players. In one way or another many of us had been destined for the scrap-heap, knew the feeling of failure and feared its consequence: a life spent working in an office or a factory, answering to some prick in a suit. Harry was acutely aware that we were playing for high stakes in the last-chance saloon. The word in our dressing room was that Billy Gray's predecessor, Ron Gray, had given Harry a free transfer at the end of his first Millwall season. Harry begged for a reprieve, which Gray granted. A free transfer from Millwall, then in the Fourth Division, would have been the end: the ignominious drift into non-League football and a proper job among civilians for 'Arry Boy, who'd once played alongside Bobby Moore. Harry played as if his life depended on it, because his life did depend on it. He was clever. A good defender, calm under pressure, always focused for every minute of the game. Despite his lack of pace, few wingers got past Harry. He held them up, slowed their gallop and deftly flicked the ball into touch. It was for his heart that Harry was the fans' favourite Lion. And it was at the Den that his legend was secured.

The Den was like no other football ground in England, or elsewhere. When I joined, the team were on an eighteen-month unbeaten home run, which would stretch to three years and a Football League record of fifty-nine games before it ended. To reach the Den, visiting teams would turn off the Old Kent Road and wend their way through a maze of narrow streets before reaching Cold Blow Lane, then pulling up outside what looked like a derelict factory. The Den. Here, grey was the primary colour. What wasn't grey needed a coat of paint. The away-team dressing room was dark and small, about as welcoming as a British Rail loo. The pitch they ritually inspected was tight and bumpy.

Only good teams and brave players felt comfortable after looking round the Den. And most of them exited their comfort zone when the game kicked off. At that stage, visiting teams discovered that the fans were as hostile as the décor. Even small Millwall crowds made a fearsome noise, which chilled the bones of many a northern hard man who'd come to London believing that southerners were soft. This was the wrong part of London, a long way from Buckingham Palace, Mayfair and The Mall. This was Dockland. Badland.

To us, the Den was home, its wit always good for a laugh, its passion often worth a goal or two. If the game was boring, the crowd would amuse itself by picking on some unfortunate player – one of us, sometimes me, or one of them – whose every desperate lunge would draw roars of derision. Sometimes this unique gathering would parody itself. If the home team's efforts weren't delivering on the day, yielding nothing of real consequence, mock passion could be conjured up on the terraces.

In this raucous Dockland music hall, 'Arry Boy was king. If we were chasing the game, needing to switch up a gear or two, Harry would lead the charge, provide the required injection of pace and passion. As he monstered forward from his left-back station, Harry would gesture to the fans, urging them to raise the roof, which they invariably did. This happens elsewhere, at the Kop End at Anfield or the Stretford End at Old Trafford, for example, but there was something primitive, almost violent about the noise that engulfed the Den when the Lions' supporters roared. In the ensuing frenzied tempo we would grow, our opponents wilt and the desperately needed goal would come, often scored by Harry, latching onto a loose ball that had eluded the panic-stricken opposition defenders. Bliss would descend on the Den, swiftly followed by taunts directed at the visitors.

'Nobody loves us and we don't care' is the infamous slogan that contemporary Millwall fans have adopted. It hadn't been coined in our day, but the defiance implicit in it was an essential element of being a Lion, fan or player. For Millwall fans, 'Arry Boy embodied defiance. They knew he wasn't really hard, they knew his limitations, they knew he was slow and fell some way short of being the perfect physical specimen. Lions fans didn't care about those things. They loved him *for* his imperfections, for his ceaseless endeavour, his hunger, and the wide-boy smile that lit his face as he trundled back to his defensive duties after scoring the goal that made their weekend.

This cauldron of rowdy passion was quite a change from the sullen gentility of Bootham Crescent. Millwall was not so much a club as a cause, its fans, like me, distinctly working class. We were the only club in London never to have made it to the First Division; the city's poor relations.

Lions fans were conveniently identified as dockers, hence the raucous passion. But the Den was more complicated than that. Though some supporters were dockers, most were ordinary South-east Londoners who'd grown up in the narrow streets of Bermondsey, New Cross, Peckham or Elephant and Castle. They and their families had known hard times, the rigours of unemployment, the rationing of basic foods in wartime and later on into the mid-fifties. They or their parents had lived through the horror of the Blitz when on fifty-seven consecutive days and nights Hitler's bombs rained down upon them, killing 20,000 and damaging a million homes. Some had moved on, left Bermondsey or Peckham for leafy suburbs with neat semi-detached houses.

Millwall was their club, their dad's club, the fortnightly pilgrimage to the Den a return to their roots, a chance to show their kids where they came from, who they really were. Families scattered to the suburbs reunited at the Den, remembering the past, the good old, bad old days of deprivation and fear. The fans that flocked down Cold Blow Lane were wonderful hardy people, much like those I'd known at Tolka Park or Milltown growing up. Now that we were poised to claim promotion to the Second Division, the atmosphere at the Den was loaded with expectation.

But as our triumphant march towards the big-time proceeded, tensions were building inside the club. Our manager, Billy Gray, was visibly pissed off with the board of directors. Millwall's board was notoriously tight-fisted. Even now, with one promotion behind them and another looming, they were loath to invest in their team. In order to buy me for £8,000, Billy Gray was forced to sell my old pal Hughie Curran to Norwich for £12,500. To secure promotion, Billy wanted to sign Rodney Marsh from Fulham for £15,000. As time proved, this would have been good business, but the board refused to sanction the deal.

When Queens Park Rangers moved in to sign Marsh, Billy's frustration turned to anger. QPR lay third in the League table, several points behind ourselves and Hull, but still a danger – the only one – in the promotion race. We had to go to Loftus Road for a crunch game in March. A good result away to Rangers and we felt we'd be home and hosed.

Loftus Road was packed for the most important fixture of the season, theirs and ours. They slaughtered us, and predictably Rodney Marsh was our principal tormentor. Mark Lazarus, their flying right-winger, gave Harry a right chasing too. The final score was 6–1. As the goals poured in, the mood in the ground turned ugly. There was no love lost between East and West London fans. Someone threw a coin that struck Len Julians on the forehead. Len angrily threw the coin back into the crowd. A hundred or more Lions fans invaded the pitch. There was danger in the air.

A small cohort of cops and a few QPR stewards couldn't cope with this. A voice on the stadium Tannoy pleaded with the mob, urging them to get off the pitch or the game would be abandoned. We were 4–1 down: 'match abandoned' seemed more promise than threat to the invaders. Somehow the pitch was cleared, only for QPR's fifth goal to prompt a second incursion. Things were rapidly getting out of hand. Len, blood seeping from his wound, stood grimly still. There were angry exchanges on the terraces.

QPR players moved fearfully towards the safety of the touchline in front of the main stand. The next voice on the Tannoy was Billy Gray's. He appealed to Millwall fans to get off the pitch in the interests of the club's good name. 'And we do not want the game abandoned,' Billy insisted. 'We are losing fair and square.' Billy's heartfelt intervention calmed things down. QPR scored a sixth goal, and our humiliation was complete.

In the boardroom after the game, a couple of Millwall directors took Billy Gray to task. He should have kept quiet. If the game had been abandoned we could have got a replay. One of our players had been hit by a missile thrown by a QPR fan. Security was the home club's responsibility; they should suffer, not us. After pointing out that the hooligans on the pitch were Millwall fans and therefore our responsibility, Billy left the directors with their gin and tonic to join his players on the coach.

Loftus Road was the beginning of the end for Billy and Millwall. He'd done the right thing in the interests of fair play, football and the genuine Lions supporters at risk in any potential riot. The directors had wanted him to connive in a shabby little plot to rescue two lost points. Decency, an imperative for Billy, was not an option for the men who counted: the directors.

'Millwall Shame,' the papers screamed the following day. In the years to come, the name of Millwall Football Club would become synonymous with the spreading plague of football hooliganism. In his programme notes before our next home game, Billy Gray defended the decision he'd made at Loftus Road. 'Some people at this club didn't agree with what I did last week. But if we're going to give in to hooligans, we might as well pack it in.'

In fact, a few weeks later, Billy announced that he was leaving Millwall. He'd had enough of the little men in the boardroom, enough of their penny-pinching ways, their unwillingness to acknowledge what he and his team had achieved, their hubris, which seemed to suggest that they, rather than us, had done the business. What they withheld – apart from money – was respect. Back-to-back promotions they took for granted, an endorsement of their stewardship of their club.

Billy was very popular with the players. We tried hard to make him change his mind, but he wouldn't budge. He was a proud man, old school, a Geordie from Ashington, the mining village that was also home to Bobby and Jack Charlton. He loved the game, but was not prepared to doff his cap to those who wielded power within it. He went on to manage Brentford for a season, then Notts County for another. And that was it for Billy. He ended up back at Forest, working as a groundsman.

We recovered from the crushing defeat to secure promotion. York City were relegated. Tom Lockie was sacked.

Mickey Purser was chairman of Millwall Football Club. He had a Volkswagen dealership on the Old Kent Road. It was said that the Germans rewarded Purser with the franchise for his pre-war support of the English Fascist Oswald Mosley. I don't know if this was true, but it was believed.

He was not a popular man with the fans. When things were going badly for Millwall, stingy Mickey was blamed. It was said that he sold the club's best players, that he refused to invest in new talent. On occasions, after a disappointing result at the Den, Millwall fans would vandalize Mickey's car showroom on the way home from matches.

He was a shy man, quietly spoken. Before every game, home and away, Mickey came into the dressing room to wish us luck. He wore a brown trilby hat. Behind a wispy moustache, his hare lip was visible. Every player received a limp handshake. He never really made eye contact. It was hard to imagine this mild-mannered character wearing a black shirt and giving the Fascist salute.

On his dressing-room visits, Mickey was usually accompanied by the only other director who counted, Bill Nelan. Bill owned a fleet of barges on the Thames, some of them named after Millwall stalwarts. He was a Cockney boy made good. One of Us rather than one of Them, he would have us believe. In winter, he sported an ankle-length camel-hair coat, and brown suede shoes. Bill was chatty. He had opinions about the game, liked to hang out in the Players' Lounge shooting the breeze. Over a beer, he would convey the impression that he didn't like Mickey, that if he had his way Bobby Charlton and Bobby Moore would be playing for Millwall. Bill thought we should be thinking big. That was his line. But keep it between ourselves, he would wink, after post-game indiscretions had been swapped. Bill was a bullshitter.

John Rickard completed the boardroom troika. Import–export was his game. Like Mickey and Bill, John was a self-made man. Unlike Mickey, he was popular with the lads – he seemed genuine. Every Christmas he would press an envelope containing a crisp five-pound note into each player's hand. At the time we were on twenty-five or thirty pounds a week so a fiver came in handy. But it was the thought that counted, even if we weren't entirely certain what the thought actually was.

After Billy Gray left, the board sold Alex Stepney to Chelsea for £50,000. They then appointed Benny Fenton manager. Many names were linked to the post but Benny's was not on the radar. 'Benny who?' was our reaction and the fans'. The mood in the dressing room was sullen. The troika had pocketed £50,000 and appointed a yes-man. Benny got a cool reception. He'd managed Colchester and Leyton Orient without any real distinction. He'd been out of work for a couple of years. Why him?

25. Glorious Controversy

In the early summer of 1966 a major controversy raged around the England team preparing for the World Cup Finals. At the centre of it was England manager Alf Ramsey. Much was expected of England attempting to win the Jules Rimet Trophy for the first time. When he was appointed England manager in 1965, Ramsey had promised that England would win the World Cup in '66. The tournament was on home soil and England had the advantage of playing all their games at Wembley. But a multitude of critics in the media and within the game argued that Alf Ramsey himself was the major obstacle standing between England and an historic victory. They argued that victory was possible but not the way Ramsey was setting out his stall.

The difference between Ramsey and his detractors was about style and indeed substance. Ramsey favoured a team that would function as a unit. A team that would be hard to beat rather than entertaining. Most provocatively, Alf Ramsey did not believe that managing England was merely a matter of selecting the best eleven players in the country and letting them get on with the job. In the context, 'best' meant most technically accomplished. A team, he believed, must have shape and purpose, something that would not necessarily be achieved by the most gifted individuals.

Another source of controversy was Ramsey's inclination to dispense with wingers, who in his view often flattered only to deceive. He'd proved this point when winning the First Division championship with unfashionable Ipswich in 1962. This team was largely composed of journeymen who set out to win rather than play the Beautiful Game.

But his critics raged: 'Do we want to win the World Cup playing like Ipswich? With no wingers, with Nobby Stiles and without Jimmy Greaves? With Geoff Hurst, a burly former West Ham midfield player operating as a powerful centre-forward in place of Greaves, an elusive, graceful and clinical goal-scoring machine?' Preferring power over class, a dour functionalism over beguiling imagination, Ramsey was killing the game, his critics argued.

Brian Glanville, the *Times'* football correspondent, was among Ramsey's fiercest critics. Many of the best and brightest within the game disparaged Ramsey as a dangerous reactionary, a man of narrow vision. Malcolm Allison, Danny Blanchflower and Ron Greenwood, manager of West Ham, were openly sceptical of Ramsey's unapologetic pragmatism. I was passionately with the naysayers.

In all of this, Ramsey did nothing to help himself. From a public-relations point of view he was a disaster. He never cared for winning hearts and minds, except the hearts and minds of his players. He never hid his contempt for the media. He wasn't interested in popularity. Ramsey was a cool customer.

When it came to style, there was no little irony in the fact that he was accused of lacking vision. As a stylish full-back, Ramsey had played in the outstanding Spurs team coached by the idealist Arthur Rowe to win the championship in 1951. However, as a coach Ramsey was a realist. He'd concluded that there was no point in trying to emulate the great Spurs team he'd played in when his dressing room at Ipswich was populated by journeymen, and with England the same pragmatism applied.

The clamour for wingers was a case in point. Ramsey was not obdurate. He tried them. In the early World Cup Finals games John Connelly, Terry Paine and Ian Callaghan got their chances but didn't impress. Jimmy Greaves started in England's opening game against Uruguay, which ended scoreless. Greaves also played against France before falling victim to a bad tackle.

For the quarter-final game against Argentina Ramsey dispensed with wingers and with Greaves. Geoff Hurst scored the winning goal. Portugal were beaten in an epic semi-final. England would face West Germany in the World Cup Final. Jimmy Greaves was fit again. He had to play, Ramsey's critics argued. But Ramsey stuck with Hurst, who scored a hat-trick against the Germans and secured the trophy for England.

I went to the final, hoping England would lose. I wasn't anti-English but, blinded by anti-Ramsey prejudice, I thought he must lose and be seen to be wrong for the good of the game. I was in the market for 'progressive' ideas. Ramsey-hating was in vogue. And it didn't cease after the World Cup victory. Despite leading England to the World Cup semi-final four years later, Ramsey remained the focus of vitriolic criticism.

Yet it's clear that he was England's greatest manager, magnificently defiant, a man of enormous courage and integrity. He ended up as 'technical adviser' to Panathinaikos in Greece, and died in penury in a Suffolk nursing home.

It may seem strange, but we never debated the Ramsey controversy in the Millwall dressing room. We never really discussed anything of substance or talked about things personal. Life resembled an extended adolescence. We were the kids; the manager, coaches and trainers were the teachers enforcing discipline. We read the tabloids, played practical jokes and engaged in laddish banter of the crudest kind. Anybody who was timid, who showed the slightest sign of vulnerability, was targeted for special taunting. It was a hierarchy where the senior pros called the shots.

In this regard the men who mattered in my early days at the Den were led by John Gilchrist. He, Brian Snowden, Tommy Wilson, Ken Jones and Len Julians set the tone. Alex Stepney, now departed, was in their camp. They barely disguised their contempt for Benny Fenton from day one. They were Billy Gray's men. They suspected Benny was Mickey Purser's puppet. He'd sold Alex Stepney for £50,000. Would he spend the money?

They weren't mad about me either. Gilly kept banging on about the Irish, 'the peasants', as he called them. My habit of making the sign of the cross on leaving the dressing room before games drew a sarcastic reference to the 'fucking Pope'. The 'bar of soap', in Gilly's words. My *Guardian* reading was another issue for the Scot. One morning after training my paper was missing. As I searched the dressing room, a giggling Gilly suggested I try the toilet. 'I wiped my arse with your fucking *Guardian* this morning,' he sneered.

'That's all right. I've still got the [Sporting] *Life*.' I laughed.

Benny witnessed this incident, betraying no emotion. Later he called me up to his office. 'Don't let them get to you, son,' he advised. 'I'll sort them out.' It took him a year or two, but eventually Benny did change the culture at the club for the better.

I was no shrinking violet. Nor was I any longer the shy youngster of the Dump. I could banter with the best of them, played in the card school, liked a bet and was as keen as anyone to talk trash about girls and what we might do to them. Gilly's suspicion that I was nothing more than a *Guardian*-reading 'poof' was prompted by my inability to get 'stuck in' when games got physical.

I began to flourish in the Second Division, playing the best football of my life. But I didn't relish the muck-and-bullets dimension of the game. However hard I tried to compensate, with hard work and neat, occasionally visionary football, my low pain threshold could not be denied, or disguised. Virility was the issue.

26.   Mickey's Boy

Benny Fenton was an interesting man. A *Guardian* obituary after he died, aged eighty-one, in August 2000, described him as 'the quintessence of Cockneyism'. That was fair enough. He was born in West Ham and, like his older brother Ted, started his career with the Hammers. He played for Millwall and later Charlton in the First Division. A cultured player at wing-half, Benny was quite a cultured person in other respects as well. He was a dapper dresser, with suits and shirts from Savile Row, cuff-links and tie-pin on match days. Though he was caricatured within the game (and in the *Guardian*) as a wheeler-dealer, ducker and diver, a typecast Cockney spiv, I never found him to be like that. He was smart. Benny was also sensitive.

When he first arrived he got the negative dressing-room vibes from Gilly and Co. As a long-time people-watcher, I could sense his hurt at the gibes he knew were somewhere in the ether about him being 'a fucking conman'. Initially he was no more popular with Lions fans than with the dressing-room hard cases. He affected indifference but I knew otherwise. We got on very well. As a coach Benny knew his stuff. He belonged in the West Ham tradition, believing in the passing game, in guile more than brawn. Acquainting the denizens of the Den with his sophisticated tastes would be quite a challenge. But Benny was up for it.

It took him a couple of seasons to transform Millwall Football Club. He used the £50,000 from Stepney's transfer superbly. He bought Bryan King cheaply from non-League Chelmsford to replace Stepney in goal. He paid big money, by Millwall standards, to buy Keith Weller and Derek Possee from Spurs Reserves. Both proved to be outstanding players. Possee was a prolific goal-scorer, and when Weller moved on to Chelsea in 1970 he fetched £100,000, a handsome profit for Mickey and the board.

Benny favoured youth and quality. Snowden, Wilson and Len Julians were moved on. Two young Reserve Team players, Barry Kitchener and Alan Dorney, formed a new partnership in central defence. We got Gordon Bolland cheaply from Charlton. Gordon had been around, starting under Tommy Docherty at Chelsea before moving to Norwich, Orient and Charlton. A delightfully gifted footballer, tall, thin, a regular goal-scorer, Gordon thrived at the Den.

Some deals didn't work out. Joey Broadfoot played in our promotion team before moving upmarket to Ipswich. Benny brought Joey back. A mistake. Second time around he didn't want to know. A tricky little winger, Joey had gone big-time. He drove a white E-Type Jag and hung out with some very dodgy characters. The last I heard he was in prison. Something to do with massage parlours, I believe. Nine months in Brixton. I liked Joey. He was a nice guy, fun.

Gilly and 'Arry survived Benny's cull. But in the new order Gilly was the odd man out. Without his cheerleaders, he kept a lower profile restricted to kicking the opposition. 'Arry was 'Arry. Off the pitch he was a pussy cat. He'd go along to get along. Benny understood his value to our cause.

One morning soon after Benny arrived, Harry stopped me in the car park before training. 'What d'you fink, Eamon?' he asked, about Benny. I told him I had no problem, let's suck it and see. Harry agreed. 'They don't like him,' he went on, talking about the hard men.

'Fuck them,' I responded.

'Yeah, fuck them.' He smiled. Then he beckoned me over to his car. 'Look at these, Eamon.' There was a stack of LPs. 'I'm selling them cheap,' he confided. I believed him. I bought two at a pound apiece. A week or two later I was browsing in WH Smith's record rack. Harry's LPs were for sale for 12/6. 'You're kidding me,' he pleaded when I confronted him. There were no hard feelings. 'Arry was 'Arry, always looking for an edge.

We drew Spurs in the FA Cup in January 1967. The Den was packed with 41,000 fans. The rain poured down all morning. The pitch drained well, and the usual bumpy surface was greasy. The ball ran true. Spurs' team was all quality. Dave Mackay, Jimmy Greaves, Cyril Knowles, Pat Jennings, Alan Gilzean and Terry Venables, class everywhere. Nobody expected much of us, we'd nothing to lose. I played really well, the best I'd ever played, and was named man of the match. We drew 0–0 but lost the replay 1–0 at White Hart Lane.

Spurs' manager Bill Nicolson was reportedly interested in signing me. A number of newspapers carried stories over the following weeks suggesting the same. A fee of £45,000 was mentioned. A journalist from the London *Evening Standard* called me to say that the speculation was true. I went to see Benny. He didn't deny the rumour, just told me I was going nowhere. He was building a team, he reminded me. He was not in the business of selling. Anyway, the board would block any move. He offered me a new contract with a five-pound rise. I signed. I was Mickey's boy. Bought and paid for. That was as close as I'd come to the big-time.

The hooliganism that would plague English football for the next three decades started on our train journeys. Fans and team travelled on the same train. Most Millwall fans were great. But there was a group of young thugs, no more than a dozen or so, who liked trouble.

On a trip back from the north one Saturday night, someone pulled the train's communication cord. The train stopped. We were in the dining-car. The delay of about thirty minutes was, at first, a minor irritation. The journey resumed. The cord was pulled again. This time the delay lasted more than an hour. British Rail staff called the police. We were stuck in the middle of nowhere. Passengers' irritation turned to anger. We arrived at Euston Station two hours behind schedule, with six policemen waiting on the platform.

The cord-pullers could not be identified. They simply mingled with the fans and drifted off into the night. The incident merited only a small story in the next day's papers: 'Trouble on Millwall Train'. But when we surrendered our proud unbeaten home record to Plymouth Argyle in January 1967, the result provoked a savage assault on the visitors' team coach. 'The Millwall Boys', as they were known, rained rocks and other missiles on the coach, breaking windows and terrifying all on board. This time the headlines were bigger, and the Millwall shame story made the evening's television news bulletins.

Now notorious, the young tearaways grew more brazen, and grew in number. Publicity and passive policing formed a deadly cocktail. On our next train journey, a gang that now numbered around thirty pulled the communication cord again. And again. And one more time for luck. As we sat in the dining-car the door burst open. Pale and shaking with fear, the two barmen from the buffet cowered in our carriage. The thugs were smashing glass, and screaming visceral roars of triumphant defiance. We were helpless. After destroying the buffet bar the hooligans raced through our carriage, wild-eyed, menacing, unstoppable.

Euston Station was full of police but no arrests were made, as far as we could see. Our next trip was away to Oxford United. We travelled by coach. As we made our way through the town the police were out in force. The Millwall problem had escalated to the point where trouble was now expected. Worse, when the Millwall Boys were due in town, their local equivalents were ready and waiting. The virus was spreading.

And in Oxford we witnessed an ominous new development: the Millwall Boys no longer felt obliged to hide among the genuine fans. From the railway station where the Millwall train was met by the police, and a group of local would-be football hooligans, the Millwall Boys fell into formation and began to swagger towards the Manor Ground. We passed them near the town centre. Shouting slogans, brimming with menace, they were granted a police escort. Bemused and fearful Saturday-afternoon shoppers were ushered off the pavement by the forces of law and order to allow the Millwall Boys free passage to our game.

Reflecting years later, when football hooliganism was known through-out the world as the English disease, I wrote:

On this day the hooligan was noticed, his presence felt, he grew a little in stature. He was allowed to breach the peace of a provincial English town, to do so with impunity, enabled by the guardians of the law. If England wants to understand its current national shame its leaders might do no better than reflect on that day in Oxford – what happened and what might have happened in another society or per-haps the England of another time. This was sixties England, the permissive age. Thus a small band of aggressive young men were not intercepted at Oxford railway station and sent back to where they'd come from. Rather they were permitted to go about their business: to seek gratification through the incitement of rage, disgust and fear in others.

Over the next few seasons, gangs of football hooligans formed all over England. The Millwall Boys had invented a new sport. In the beginning football hooliganism was about notoriety. The Millwall Boys found that by banding together, being uncouth, 'taking over' a town centre like Oxford, pulling a communication cord or two on the way home from matches and chanting a few slogans, they could make national headlines.

They discovered something else: that society at large was prepared to tolerate their behaviour – a tolerance that was reflected in the hands-off policing, the fact that football clubs were still prepared to accept their money at the turnstiles, and the derisory ten-pound fines imposed on those who found themselves before the magistrates. A tenner was a small price to pay to get your name in the papers.

The Millwall Boys were pioneers in a generation of comparatively affluent young men for whom there was no great war to fight and no national service. They roamed from the ugly shadows of urban ghettos, where alienation from the glossy materialism of the mid- to late sixties was a demoralizing fact of life, to take their place in the glamorous, then fashionable world of the glory game. It was Millwall's misfortune to be the first club infected. In the very year that England won the World Cup. By 1977, when mobs of Englishmen wrecked the centre of Luxembourg, football hooliganism had gone international. The route to the Heysel Stadium in Brussels, where thirty-four people died at the 1985 European Cup Final, had been mapped out.

As useless then as they are today, leader writers and politicians urged football to 'get its house in order'. The idea that society should get its house in order first was rarely broached.

27. Troublemaker

Although the Professional Footballers' Association had led the fight to get rid of the maximum wage, most players had little regard for their trade union. Footballers thought they were privileged. They'd escaped the dreaded nine-to-five existence of family, friends and neighbours. They were playing a game they loved. They were admired, celebrated for their skills, the envy of their mates who hadn't 'made it'. Footballers were being well paid to do what others they'd grown up with had only dreamed of doing. Comforted by this dangerous illusion, footballers focused on the things they felt really mattered: winning games; staying injury free; striving to win promotion or avoid relegation.

Even at Millwall level, life, on the surface, seemed good. You earned more than guys you'd gone to school with, drove a nicer car and, by and large, courted a prettier girl. You lived in a comfortable home. Match tickets for the bank manager or the car salesman meant that you got the best perks going on loans and cars. You were fit and healthy. You worked for a couple of hours each day, except Wednesday, your day off. Who needed a union?

When I arrived at Millwall John Gilchrist was the PFA rep. His only obligation was to collect our union dues – a tenner – and deliver the money at the AGM, which was traditionally held on a Monday in Manchester. Gilly invariably spent the forty-eight hours before his trip to Manchester begging the lads to cough up their dues. Saturday was D-Day. On thirty pounds a week we were never flush with cash. 'For fuck's sake, lads, we'll embarrass ourselves!' Gilly would plead, in a desperate attempt to fulfil his obligation to the PFA.

When Gilly left to join Fulham nobody volunteered to take over his PFA job. Nobody except me. I thought the players' union was important, a forum where the case for reform could be made. Influenced by what I'd seen and by Danny Blanchflower's eloquent polemics damning the buffoons who ran the game, I didn't share the prevailing dressing-room view that footballers were privileged.

Despite the hours, the pay and the illusory glamour, we were basically slaves. You couldn't leave the club until the bosses decided they didn't need you any more. A bad injury could end your career. There was no pension. The only certainty was that some time in your early to mid-thirties you would be disposed of. Parting would be swift and brutal. Just as most men were reaching their prime in their chosen walks of life, you would be finished. If you lived in a club house, a tied cottage, as many players did, you and your family could end up on the street, with just your scrapbook and memories of 'the best years' of your life.

For old footballers the options were few. Some would try coaching or management. Most of them would fail. There was the prospect of serving as a pub landlord for one of the big breweries, who tended to look favourably on former footballers for this line of work. You could spend your nights (and days) reminiscing about the 'good old days' with the regulars.

For professional footballers, journeymen *and* stars, the road to Nowhere was clearly mapped out. Sign your rights away aged fifteen, forget about training or educating yourself for any real job in the real world. Live the fantasy while it lasted. Think football, loyalty to your club, stay healthy and fit. Don't have sex after Wednesday. And then fuck off when your legs and lungs have had it in your early thirties. Or earlier, if afflicted by serious injury.

Defer to your superiors: members of the board, their wives, the club secretary, the gimlet-eyed suit who holds your contract in his files and can barely disguise his contempt whenever your paths might cross. Keep your opinions to yourself. You're paid to perform, not to think.

Most players bought into this deal. Most of the game's great men, Busby, Shankly, Bill Nicholson, Tom Finney, Stanley Matthews, virtually everyone who was anyone, accepted the status quo. In the mid- to late sixties, even Jimmy Hill, who'd led the revolt against the maximum wage in 1961, was managing Coventry City, enforcing the core principle of football slavery – the one-way contract that bound players to their clubs for their footballing life.

Anyone who questioned the system was deemed a troublemaker. Although respected for captaining Spurs' Double-winning team, Danny Blanchflower did not endear himself to the occupants of England's dressing rooms by using his *Sunday Express* column to argue for reform. Quoting John F. Kennedy, who in turn was quoting George Bernard

Shaw, Blanchflower wrote in the *Express*, 'Some men see things as they are and ask why . . . I dream of things that never were and ask why not?'

Why not freedom of contract, as in every other craft or profession? Why not allow former professionals to serve on the boards of football clubs? What other industry cast its best and brightest into the wilderness in their mid-thirties?

The Football Association had a particularly pernicious rule that decreed no member of a football club board could receive a salary. This made no sense, but it ensured that the game's great elder statesmen, the likes of Joe Mercer and Matt Busby, could wield no real influence in the corridors of power.

When Matt Busby retired as manager of Manchester United, the great club he'd built from a bomb-site, he was knighted by the Queen for services to football. Sir Matt, the modern game's great visionary, still had much to offer. The problem was that if he took a seat on the board – which he wanted to do – he couldn't receive the salary he needed to live on. A typically shabby compromise was reached. United opened a souvenir shop at Old Trafford and funnelled the profits – illegally – to Sir Matt by way of payment. He joined the board of directors, receiving his remuneration in the proverbial brown-paper bag.

Stripped bare, Busby's story reveals a savage irony. He had never been a troublemaker. On the contrary, he had ruthlessly enforced the oppressive wage and contract football laws for his own and United's benefit. In 1950 Manchester United went on a twelve-game tour of America where they played in front of massive sell-out crowds. The maximum wage in England was twelve pounds per week.

Charlie Mitten, an England international, was one of Busby's best players. But Charlie was a troublemaker. He wondered why men like him could sell out vast stadiums – at home and abroad – yet receive a pittance for their troubles. During the US tour, Mitten was approached by a wealthy Colombian businessman to play for Independiente Santa Fe in Bogotá. Charlie was offered £5,000, plus a weekly wage of forty pounds, plus bonuses. He jumped ship, took the money and was branded the Bogotá Bandit by the British press.

After a year, Santa Fe went bust. Charlie returned to England to face the music. The FA banned him for six months and imposed a hefty fine. Busby told Charlie he would never play for United again. He was sold to Fulham, who were fighting a (losing) relegation battle. For the game's rulers, and Busby, it was vital to punish troublemakers severely and publicly as a warning to others inclined to buck the system.

Busby played by football's twisted rules. His reward? Every Friday this giant of the game, revered wherever football was played, left Old Trafford with a bag full of cash. The elder statesman had been reduced to a common spiv.

Wilf Mannion was another troublemaker. His story was part of football folklore. Mannion was three years older than Charlie Mitten. Like the Bogotá Bandit, Mannion was an England international. The 'Golden Boy', they called him when he established himself as one of the outstanding post-war inside-forwards. Goalmaker as well as goal-scorer, Mannion was an idol in the north-east. Middlesbrough was his club. Seeking to better himself with one of the bigger clubs, Mannion posted a transfer request. 'Boro refused. In 1948 Mannion caused a sensation by going on strike.

Mannion felt he had nothing to lose. Football clubs operated as a cartel. They imposed an arbitrary ceiling on the earnings of their employees. In Mannion's day you were paid twelve pounds during the season, ten pounds in the summer. The cartel decided the maximum wage with no reference to ability, law or common justice. You were contracted to them for life; they, in return, were committed to you for twelve months. When the year was up they could sack you. They could decide to reduce your wage on the grounds that they couldn't afford to pay, or for any other reason they chose.

If, like Mannion, you refused to sign a new contract you were paid no wages. If you walked away you couldn't, like other workers, ply your trade elsewhere. The club held your registration, your licence to play football in *the* Football League. If you lived in a club house, as many players did, you could be evicted with two weeks' notice.

By any standards, professional footballers were at the mercy of a tyrant's charter written and enforced by brutes. Mannion hung tough for a while, but lack of income forced him to back down. The Golden Boy received no support from his comrades in England's dressing rooms.

After Middlesbrough let Mannion go, when he was thirty-six, he joined Hull City, in the Second Division. Still making trouble, he began contributing critical articles to newspapers, identifying football's many ills. The Football League took exception to this and Mannion was banned from playing in the League. The Golden Boy ended his career playing non-League football for Poole Town and Cambridge United. During his two-year spell in this wilderness, where there was no maximum wage, Mannion earned more per annum than he ever had as one of England's greatest players.

Len Shackleton was another celebrated rebel from the Mitten/Mannion era. 'Shack', as he was known, played five times for England. In an autobiography published after he retired he caused much amusement with a chapter titled 'The Average Director's Knowledge of Football', which consisted of one blank page.

When I became Millwall's PFA delegate in 1969 I'd been a pro for the best part of a decade. I knew about the exploitation and corruption that was endemic to the game. At the heart of all that was wrong was a fundamental truth there was no escaping from: those most committed and knowledgeable about football were the professionals who remained second-class citizens in a sport governed by the butchers and bakers for whom the game provided an opportunity to wield power and acquire prestige in their community. They devised the rules, policed the etiquette and enforced their petit-bourgeois values with brutal conviction.

This was primarily an English soccer thing. The rest of the world was changing in this and many other ways. Cricket's annual Gentlemen (amateurs) versus Players (professionals) contest had been abolished in 1962. In 1968 tennis binned the rule that denied professionals the right to compete at Wimbledon and other Grand Slam events. This reform ended the exclusion of pros such as Rod Laver, Roy Emerson and Tony Roche, all-time great exponents of the game, from the major championships.

Horseracing was arguably the most conservative sport of all. In 1966, racing's greatest professional, Lester Piggott, made a revolutionary move when he chose to ride the filly Valoris for Vincent O'Brien in the Epsom Oaks. Piggott was the stable jockey for champion trainer Noel Murless, who also had a filly in the race. On the grounds that the O'Brien-trained filly was the likeliest winner, Piggott spurned his boss, Murless. Valoris won the race. But in racing and in the national press, Piggott was the subject of vicious and prolonged vilification. He'd broken a sacred rule and the consensus was that he was finished in racing.

It was this world that offended Danny Blanchflower. He believed that the slaves should break free of the chains of convention by which all his peers were bound. Piggott survived and prospered. This was a hugely significant moment for professional sport in Britain. Watching from afar, I cheered at this display of quite awesome courage.

In the grander scheme of things, the sixties are remembered as swinging: sexual liberation, long hair, short skirts, the Beatles and the Stones. For professional sportsmen and -women, the sixties was the decade when freedom could be glimpsed, became more than a dream. But not, alas, in soccer. England won the World Cup in 1966. The nation stood to salute its heroes who would achieve immortality for their deeds. Each player received a £1,000 bonus. Before tax.

Travelling to my first PFA AGM in Manchester, I met the other London delegates at Euston Station, among them Terry Venables representing his club, Spurs. On the journey I sat with him. He was good company, smart, funny, much admired by his fellow pros. He'd been the leader of an exciting young Chelsea side, managed by Tommy Docherty, which narrowly failed to win the League and the FA Cup in the early sixties. That team broke up when Docherty sent Venables and seven of his team-mates home for breaking a curfew while preparing for a game in Blackpool.

In 1966 Bill Nicholson paid £80,000 to take Venables to Spurs. The idea was that Venables might replace Danny Blanchflower, who'd retired in 1964. Venables had brains and personality. One of his footballing distinctions was that he'd represented England at every level, the only pro at that time who'd done so. When we got talking on the Manchester train I mentioned my admiration for Blanchflower. The response surprised me: 'Danny's fucking mad,' Venables laughed, 'away with the fairies. He's a fucking dreamer,' he continued, warming to his theme, which had a cynical anti-Irish edge that I had rarely encountered in my time in England. 'Good with the words, you Paddies,' he sneered, ending what was becoming a bit of a rant with a disparaging reference to Danny's *Sunday Express* column.

When in response I began to make the case for reform, Venables intervened to enquire if I really believed 'all that bollocks'. When I confirmed that I did, citing the powerlessness of professionals, their serf-like conditions of employment and my growing disgust at the exploitation of uneducated kids coming into the game, his reply was a brutally effective putdown: 'It's a day out, Eamon. Give us a fucking break.'

The Manchester AGM proved to be more or less as Venables depicted it: a day out. The PFA executive board had prepared the agenda.

Motions were proposed, seconded and passed unanimously. Mention was made of the benevolent fund, which eked out subsistence money to old pros fallen on hard times. When it came to any other business, the top table informed the delegates about the annual golf outing and of various deals cut with businesses – travel agents, furniture and consumer-durable manufacturers – who offered discounts 'to our esteemed members'.

As the platitudes echoed round the posh room in the Grand Hotel, I briefly considered some intervention that might startle this smug assembly. But why spoil a good day out? While elsewhere in Britain the unions were said to be running the country, the Professional Footballers' Association was running golf outings.

The complacency of the PFA was depressing, especially when viewed in the context of events elsewhere in the 1960s. Muhammad Ali, the great American heavyweight champion, was being persecuted for refusing the draft to fight in Vietnam. A convert to Islam, Ali had shed his slave name, Cassius Clay, and pledged his allegiance to the radical black-power leader Malcolm X. 'I ain't got no quarrel with them Vietcong,' Ali declared, when challenged in 1966. He was charged with draft evasion, then stripped of his heavyweight title and his boxing licence. But Ali's resistance was the catalyst for the wave of popular protest that saw millions of people across the world take to the streets to oppose the Americans' war in south-east Asia.

The struggle for racial justice was a massive issue for sport throughout the sixties. South Africa was the problem. The evils of apartheid may seem apparent now, but many in sport chose to turn a blind eye when forced to confront this cancer head-on. The sports of rugby and cricket were particularly brazen in their willingness to play against racially segregated South African teams.

In 1968 the D'Oliveira affair erupted, a controversy that would prove to be a defining moment in the battle against apartheid. When one of the English cricketers originally selected to tour South Africa withdrew through injury, the MCC defied the South Africans by choosing Basil D'Oliveira, a South African who'd been designated 'coloured' by the apartheid system and had emigrated to England, as the replacement. The South Africans duly cancelled the tour, and in the process revealed themselves and their political system to be not only wicked but stupid. Even those English people disinclined to engage with politics – and that often seemed to be the majority – were appalled by 'the D'Oliveira affair', as it came to be known.

This feeling was compounded by Basil D'Oliveira's mild-mannered demeanour. Insisting he was just a cricketer, he refused to play victim or to express outrage at his treatment by his fellow countrymen. He was no rebel, no threat, yet the South Africans insisted on making him a martyr.

Then at the Olympics in Mexico City two black US athletes, Tommie Smith and John Carlos, raised black-gloved fists in a Black Power salute while receiving their medals on the victory podium. Smith, the 200-metres gold-medal winner, and Carlos, who took the bronze, also stood barefoot on the podium to protest against poverty. Their gesture caused outrage. They were pilloried for introducing politics into sport and banned from the US team. Smith and Carlos were heroes for many, but a majority in sport strongly disapproved of their actions.

These were for me intoxicating times. My fascination with politics and current affairs was not new. But, especially where politics and sport intersected, as with Ali, D'Oliveira, Smith and Carlos, and indeed the exploitative caste system prevailing in professional soccer, I was passionate about the issues at play.

Politics was a no-go area in the dressing room, which didn't bother me. I enjoyed the banter, piss-taking and bawdy exchanges as much as anyone. I was often the ringleader in practical jokes cruelly inflicted on those most vulnerable, frequently at the heart of politically incorrect stream-of-consciousness jokes that could run for days, a form of amusing drivel common in any all-male space. I was part of the card school, a backer of horses and, with Harry Cripps, Barry Kitchener and my best mate Alan Dorney, an occasional visitor to Hackney dog-track on idle afternoons.

In 1970 the South African rugby team provoked massive anti-apartheid protests when they arrived to tour England. One day I joined the protesters. We marched to Twickenham where there was a midweek game. At the same time I sent a telegram of support to the Irish anti-apartheid movement, who were protesting against the Springboks' game against Ireland at Lansdowne Road. The message of support made a minor news story in Dublin, along the lines of 'Millwall footballer offers support to anti-apartheid movement'. A number of English journalists picked up on the Irish news story. It seems bizarre now, but the fact that a journeyman footballer had joined tens of thousands of other people in a popular protest was news. 'Dunphy blasts rugby stars' was one tabloid take on what seemed to me to be a non-story.

Manager Benny Fenton wasn't happy. What was I playing at? he wanted to know. Was I looking for publicity? Benny was a decent man. He wasn't too troubled about what he clearly considered a breach of the rules. The problem, he explained, was the board of directors, specifically Bill Nelan, the know-it-all barge owner. One of Nelan's friends had called him to complain about 'the little Irish Commie' who was shooting his mouth off. This friend was a member of the MCC, cricket's governing body. Nelan had assured him he would 'take care' of the matter.

'You're a footballer, Eamon, not a politician' was Benny's final word on the matter. His heart wasn't in it, I could tell, but Benny himself had been put under pressure by my 'misdemeanour'. On Nelan's say-so, Benny's job was to shut me up, so that Nelan could 'take care' of his MCC mate's concerns. From that point on I was a marked man, a troublemaker, if not Muhammad Ali or Danny Blanchflower.

28. Bottler

By late 1970, early 1971, Benny had transformed the Millwall team for the better. He had basically inherited a tough, disciplined Third Division side, and we had evolved into one of the best footballing teams in the Second Division. Promotion to the First Division now seemed a realistic prospect. Benny had operated shrewdly in the transfer market, always making money while simultaneously acquiring more technically accomplished players.

After Keith Weller had been sold to Chelsea for a big profit in 1970, Benny replaced him with Barry Bridges, a former England international who was fit as a flea and still scoring goals at the age of twenty-nine. In another quite controversial break with Millwall tradition, Benny changed our playing kit from the traditional blue and white stripes to the all white sported by Real Madrid. At a time when caveman football was favoured by many emerging coaches – Graham Taylor was about to begin his crusade against football as manager of Lincoln City – Benny was determined to play the game stylishly. At a club renowned for its blood-and-thunder approach it took some guts to opt for something more sophisticated.

As Benny continued our upgrade, other new players arrived. Frank Saul had scored the winning goal for Spurs in the 1967 FA Cup Final. Derek Smethurst came from Chelsea, a gifted striker who, like Saul, could easily play in midfield. A regular in the first team since joining the club, I was now under pressure to stay in the side. Until Saul and Smethurst arrived, my main rival for a place was George Jacks, a dependable grafter who possessed the physical strength I lacked. George was brave, prepared to put his body on the line in a way that I quite simply wasn't. Physically, I was timid, a coward.

Mostly I made up for this sin by working hard, taking responsibility to get on the ball and pass it, especially at the Den when the going got tough and the fans were baying for action. This was 'bottle' of a different kind. But sometimes you have to be hurt, take the pain, be prepared to do it. I wasn't.

One night away to Derby County at the Baseball Ground my cowardice cost us a match. It was a League Cup game, midweek under lights. This was Brian Clough's team that had taken the Second Division title and automatic promotion in 1969. Now they were storming up the First Division table, soon to be crowned champions of England in 1972. Derby were a magnificent team, led by Dave Mackay, a great player from the Spurs Double team of '61.

It was a cold autumn night. The pitch was hard, a crust of ice coated what grass there was on the rough surface that was the norm before undersoil heating and the year-round carpets they play on today. Promoted in Mackay's first season, Derby were making big waves in the First Division, threatening big clubs like Leeds, Manchester United and Manchester City, the latter enjoying a renaissance under Joe Mercer and the flamboyant Malcolm Allison. Derby were no longer a soft touch. Their team was hard, skilful, fast, full of quality players: Willie Carlin, Alan Durban, Alan Hinton, Kevin Hector, Roy McFarland and John O'Hare.

That October night we played them off the pitch from the get-go. After half an hour we were 2–0 up. The crowd were restless, we were coasting. Mackay was prowling like an angry dog, steaming into tackles, bollocking his team-mates, hassling the ref, desperately trying to ignite some fire that might reverse the pattern of the game. I was playing really well, comfortable on the ball, controlling the tempo of the play, in cruise control, the way you are on good days.

Getting to half-time with the two-goal lead was critical: both sides knew that, nobody more than the old warrior Mackay. With a couple of minutes to go to the break, a high ball hoofed aimlessly from our defence was dropping over my head. As the ball fell towards my waiting chest I sensed a force of nature charging towards me. A quick glance told me it was Mackay driving forward full of menacing intent. His boot was raised and aiming straight at the waiting, puny chest. I hesitated for a split second. Then pulled back, avoiding the boot, which took the ball, pushed it forward and, from thirty-five yards volleyed it to the back of our net: 2–1, game on.

I'd bottled it. I felt sick, ashamed, engulfed by despair beyond all reason. I hated myself. I was past the point of redemption, for in that moment every instinct I possessed told me that in pulling out of that tackle I'd delivered a fatal blow to our chances of winning the game.

In the dressing room, Benny stood pale with anger. He didn't go in for histrionics, throwing cups at walls and ranting like many managers. 'Get in the bath, son,' he ordered me. I put my hands up to apologize to my mates.

As I began to unlace my boots, the silence in the room was broken by a hesitant voice: 'Boss, give him a break. Leave it, we're still ahead.'

As Gordon Bolland spoke there were murmurs of assent from all corners of the room. It was an extraordinary moment. Gordon was a quiet, droll character, immensely popular in the dressing room. An elegant goal-scoring forward, he'd started his career at Chelsea alongside Terry Venables, Ron Harris, Peter Bonetti and Bobby Tambling. He'd been a member of the Chelsea youth team that won the FA Youth Cup in '61 and '62.

As standing members of the back-of-the-bus card school, along with Harry Cripps, Barry Kitchener and Alan Dorney, Gordon and I were pals. But I was astonished to hear him plead with Benny. Even more so that the other lads were supporting him. Benny relented. If anything, I felt worse, even more guilt-ridden for my unforgivable weakness, just forgiven.

In the second half, Derby killed us. Urged on by a roaring crowd they won 4–2. It was a long coach journey back down the M1 to London. I passed on the card school, sitting alone with my shame. It took a long time to heal that particular wound.

After the Mackay incident I don't think Benny ever fully trusted me not to let him down again. I was still mostly a first-choice pick in midfield, but he left me out of the side on a few occasions before the end of that season. George Jacks or Derek Smethurst offered options that were, for one reason or another, more appealing. George was dependable and never likely to shirk a tackle. Derek provided a goal threat as well as being a classy footballer.

It didn't help my cause that the Derby 'bottle job' coincided with my anti-apartheid protest. I was talking the talk but failing to walk the walk. There was some media interest in the 'Millwall star', who'd joined a political protest. Asked for my views on apartheid, the Northern Irish civil-rights movement or the state of football, I was more than happy to mouth off about the issues. Before long I was a mini Danny Blanchflower, minus the footballing skills and the medals.

For some time I'd had an idea about writing a book on the life of a journeyman footballer. My traumatic experience at Derby's Baseball Ground prompted me to reflect on the difference between the reality of a Second Division footballer's life and the perception. Reading the papers the day after I'd lost my team the game, I was struck – and embarrassed – by the good notices I received. From the press-box, the view was that Millwall had lost despite my elegant contribution to the cause!

Football books of that time were notoriously banal. Tales of glory, dreams fulfilled, great victories and golden memories of sunny days when the heroes triumphed to universal acclaim. Nothing about the brutal reality of professional sport, the desperate insecurity, the cease-less exploitation of the caste system, the fear of failure or the poignant end when, past your sell-by date, you were dispatched to the scrap-heap in the prime of life.

The book I had in mind would be bleak, about real people rather than fictional heroes, about muddy pitches rather than sun-kissed meadows. About boyhood dreams that crashed on the jagged rocks of reality, rather than being fulfilled on Wembley's hallowed turf.

I'd become good friends with Peter Ball, the sports editor of the new left-leaning magazine *Time Out*. Peter encouraged me to write the book. In fact he offered to write it for me, if I agreed, to be my ghost. Every sports book was ghosted by a journalist. You told your story, the journalist put the words into serviceable prose. I didn't want that. In any case, who would publish the story of a Millwall journeyman with lots of opinions and little in the way of bottle? For now, the book remained no more than a notion.

Peter lived in the fashionable liberal enclave of North London. He often invited me to his dinner parties, 'supper', where *Time Out* types mingled with people from advertising. He had been a copywriter before following his passion for football and journalism. The guests were gen-erally pleasant, educated people. Wine was consumed in moderation; everyone behaved, save for the occasional token Tory, who tended to be a 'character', drinking Scotch and taunting the polite majority who tended to be liberals.

I enjoyed my Hampstead dinner parties. Passion was not generally on the 'supper' menu, a rule I occasionally broke, causing Peter some grief. Football would later become fashionable, but in the early seventies there was a touch of the *Guess Who's Coming to Dinner* about the presence of a Millwall footballer at a cosy Hampstead evening. What struck me most forcefully was the contrast between the career curves my fellow guests were on and the rather frightening prospect awaiting me in the not-too-distant future. The stark truth of a footballer's life was that the career curve was heading in the wrong direction, something I was becoming increasingly aware of. Socializing outside the dressing-room bubble could cause a panic attack. With other players, the question 'What happens next?' never arose, even when it stared us in the face, as it did at every season's end when those surplus to requirements were let go. Too old, not good enough any longer, goodbye.

When asked what they were going to do next, if they had any plans, players heading for the door marked 'exit' would put a brave face on things. 'I've got a few irons in the fire,' was a stock answer. Semi-pro non-League football was one of the options, but it could only be a short-term fix. A couple of former Millwall players, Pat Terry and Joey Broadfoot, were London taxi drivers. Liam Brady's brother Ray, a former Lion, was a pub landlord. The future was another country, a frightening one, at least for me.

What kept us going was the diminishing hope that we would make it to the big league, the First Division, the Promised Land where more money could be earned, where football really was the glory game played on the its hallowed grounds, Old Trafford, Goodison Park, Anfield, Highbury, White Hart Lane.

For Benny Fenton's Millwall, promotion to the First Division was a realistic ambition. And in season 1971/72 we seemed poised to fulfil the potential we'd been showing for years. We got off to a fast start, losing only two of our first twenty-one games. I was playing well. I needed to be at my best to stay in the team. Benny had converted Denis Burnett, a classy defender we'd signed from West Ham, into a holding midfield player. This left me and Derek Smethurst fighting for the other midfield jersey.

Birmingham and Norwich were the other teams in the promotion race. Any two of the three would make it to the First Division. Trevor Francis was Birmingham's main man, a prolific goal-scorer. Aged eighteen, he was on fire. He would go on to command Britain's first £1 million transfer fee.

We suffered a rare setback at Luton on New Year's Day losing 2–1. Eric Morecambe, one half of Britain's favourite comedy duo, was a Luton director. He stuck his head into our dressing room after the match, making one of his trademark funny faces. A flying boot struck him on the shoulder. 'Fuck off, you silly cunt!' someone roared. After this reverse we went on a twelve-game unbeaten League run.

29. Bloody Sunday

On Sunday, 30 January 1972, British paratroopers opened fire on a civil-rights march in Derry. Thirteen people, seven of them teenagers, were shot dead. Many more were wounded. News of this terrible incident broke on the evening television news bulletins. The usual calm objectivity of BBC and ITN reporters was noticeably absent from the coverage. Trouble in Northern Ireland was nothing new but it was apparent that something dreadful – and almost certainly criminal – had taken place. Innocent people lay dead. The local hospital, Altnagelvin, was full of wounded victims of indiscriminate shooting. This was a defining day in British–Irish relationships.

Sitting at home in South London, I watched, shocked and angry, as the story unfolded through the early evening and late into the night. The following morning's newspapers confirmed the death toll. Thirteen innocent lives taken on the streets of the Bogside. The horror of the day was captured poignantly by a photograph of a local priest, Father Edward Daly, waving a blood-stained handkerchief as he attempted to escort an already mortally wounded man – Jackie Duddy – to safety.

Like most people from the South of Ireland, I'd been indifferent to the plight of Northern nationalists. While marching against apartheid or for the emancipation of black Americans, I'd largely ignored the Northern troubles. Of course we supported civil rights, but not the embryonic Provisional IRA campaign of violence. Bloody Sunday changed many minds. The following Wednesday a mob of 30,000 Dubliners burned down the British embassy in Merrion Square. My father and my brother Kevin were part of the mob.

I was stunned, coldly angry. On Monday morning I wore a black armband to training. Nobody said a word. The story was all over the papers, even the redtops strewn around the dressing room. I wore the armband all week. I also hatched a plan that would enable other Irish players in England to express solidarity with the bereaved families and the people of Derry. A plan that would also make ordinary British people aware of what was being done in their name. We should all wear black armbands the following Saturday.

When I phoned around to rally support for this proposal there were no takers. The responses ranged from polite refusal to outright derision: 'For fuck's sake, Eamon, are you mad?' I planned to do it anyway. We were due to play Middlesbrough in the FA Cup at the Den. Benny left me out of the side! After a drawn game I was also left out for the replay.

Our next League game away to promotion rivals Norwich was massive. I was back in the side, thirteen days after Bloody Sunday. Thirty-four thousand fans packed Carrow Road. I wore the armband. More important, from Benny's point of view, I played well. We drew 2–2. Travelling back to London on the coach, the directors were frosty, except the old docker Mr Rickard. 'Well done, son. Stick up for what you believe.'

After a seven-match unbeaten run we lost 1–0 at Fulham on Easter Saturday. I was substituted, Smethurst back in the number-ten shirt. With five games left to go, everything depended on the away fixture at Birmingham. I was desperate to play in a game we couldn't afford to lose. I wasn't even on the bench. I sat in the stand at St Andrews, not knowing what to think. A good result meant I was out for the season. A loss and we'd probably blown promotion. It was lose-lose. We lost. I regained my place.

On the last day of the season we played Preston at the Den. This was the biggest day so far in Millwall's history. If we won and Birmingham lost away to Sheffield Wednesday we were promoted. Just under 20,000 packed the Den. With twenty minutes to go we were 2–0 up and coasting. Suddenly, for no apparent reason, the crowd began to roar. It was the sound of joy.

Spectators with transistor radios spread the news that Birmingham were losing at Sheffield. As the minutes ticked off the clock the Den became a heaving mass of unadulterated joy. The Lions were on the brink of history. Our lives would change on the glorious march to football's marble halls in Manchester, Liverpool and North London.

When the final whistle blew the fans invaded the pitch. We were hoisted on shoulders to be carried triumphantly to the dressing room beneath the terrace at the Cold Blow Lane end. *This* was what we had lived and worked for. What our wonderfully bawdy decent fans had dreamed. We'd fucking done it.

The dressing room was chaos. There was confusion, some doubt about the outcome in Sheffield. The transistor radio on the table announced results from across the country. Benny called for hush. 'And Birmingham remain on course for promotion after their victory at Sheffield.' Denis Burnett grabbed the radio and smashed it on the dressing-room floor. We were finished. Birmingham had a game left to play away to Leyton Orient. Needing one point, they got two to secure promotion.

Something died that day, at least for me and, I suspect, the other lads who'd been my friends and team-mates for half a dozen years. Maybe it was the cruel way it happened, a dream seemingly fulfilled, then crushed in an instant. Our Lions were never the same again. I stayed another eighteen months, in and out of the team. I was restless and more than a little bit afraid. The serious injury every player dreaded struck in the form of chronic back pain that was to remain undiagnosed for ten years.

30. Disrepute

My thirtieth birthday was looming. I was a fading journeyman living in a tied cottage with an overdraft. I was an international no longer. Three years earlier in 1969 I'd led a revolt against the Football Association of Ireland. We were sick of the Big Five picking the Irish team: everyone thought it was a joke but nobody was willing to do anything about it. I spoke to John Giles and Alan Kelly, the senior players in the squad. Let's put it up to them, I argued. We want a professional manager with the power to pick the team.

They agreed to my suggestion to go on strike if our demands weren't met. After a brief robust bout of negotiation, the FAI surrendered. Mick Meagan, a highly respected former Everton and Ireland wing-half, was our choice to become Ireland's first professional manager. He got the job. When I was omitted from Mick's first squad I didn't know whether to laugh or cry. 'Bring back the Big Five' seemed an unlikely campaign slogan. There was nothing to be done.

I needed a break and I got a big one when a local paper, the *South London Press*, asked me if I would contribute a weekly column that they wanted to call 'Dunphy's Diary'. The deal they proposed required me to do nothing except chat to one of their reporters, who would write up the copy for publication. I agreed. Then I began to reflect and decided that I didn't need a 'ghost'. I'd have a go at writing the column myself. Though dubious, the *South London Press* agreed. It took me three weeks to write the first 'Diary'. Seven hundred and fifty words was what the paper wanted and that, to the word, was exactly what they got.

Danny Blanchflower was working as assistant to Bill Nicholson at Spurs. I went to see him for some advice about the column and the book I had decided to write. He was wonderful. A warm, intelligent observer of football's warped culture, he encouraged me to be as radical and forthright as possible. 'Tell it as it is, Eamon, don't be afraid.' He advised me to read Orwell's essays (I already had). 'Keep it simple. You don't need big words.' This was 1974. Bill Nicholson was close to retirement. Danny hoped to succeed him. Terry Neill got the Spurs job. Blanchflower could not be trusted.

Peter Ball agreed to help me write my book. We had no publishing deal. I wasn't box-office. But we both believed that an unflinching look at the often harsh reality of life as an average pro might make for a good read. Every Sunday we sat down to record the day-to-day experiences of a struggling Second Division footballer. Millwall fans might buy it.

My weekly *South London Press* column, though, was bugging the board of directors. One day the club secretary called me into his office. On his desk he had my latest column, a copy of my contract and the club rule book. I was told I was in breach of contract. I couldn't write for a newspaper without permission, which had not been sought. I was to stop, otherwise there would be consequences. 'What consequences?' I enquired.

'That's up to the manager,' Gimlet-eye retorted.

I wasn't writing about the club or breaching any dressing-room confidences, I told him.

'You're bringing the game into disrepute,' he insisted. Our old friend 'bringing the game into disrepute' was a catch-all charge often levelled at any pro, player or coach, annoying his masters. Brian Clough was a regular offender.

I tried to reason with the prosecutor. 'Look, the column is work experience. I'm preparing for life after football. You can't stop me acquiring an alternative way of earning a living.'

'You're our employee,' he reminded me.

'Yes, but you don't own me.' He didn't say it, but it was clear that he did in fact believe that Millwall owned me. That was what the contract implied. And the rule book.

Benny got involved the following day. I felt sorry for him. I knew the column was causing him grief with the board. He told me I'd have to stop writing. I refused. At this stage, I was in and out of the side. He was playing some young players, planning to build another team. He'd sold Denis Burnett to Hull. Denis was a strong character, influential in the dressing room. His departure was the beginning of the end for our team, the nearly men of 1971/72.

He threatened to suspend me. I told him to go ahead. I wasn't bluffing and he knew it. I'd walked out for six weeks the previous season after a row over wages. He was sick of me, although he didn't put it that bluntly. 'Maybe it's best if I leave,' I suggested.

This was tricky. I couldn't formally ask for a transfer without losing my cut of the transfer fee. But if the club made the call, dispensed with your services at the time of their choosing, you got your few bob. 'Leave it with me,' Benny replied.

I was now in survival mode. I focused on doing my best in the Reserves, my weekly column for the *South London Press* and my book, whose working title was *The Diary of a Fading Star*. Here's an extract from the entry for 7 November.

ORIENT RESERVES 2 MILLWALL RESERVES 4

Back in the bloody Midweek League again. It's an unbelievable sensation going to play at Orient on a Wednesday afternoon in November. There is no one there, absolutely nothing at stake, except your own pride. You don't feel like it at all. And whereas for two hours before a First Team game you are beginning to get nervous, beginning to get geed up, feeling a bit of tension and atmosphere, here you go to a ground which is empty. It is like a grave-yard. You have to walk around a bit to find where to go in – especially at Orient.

When you do get in there, the dressing rooms are cold, because they don't bother switching on the heating for the Midweek League. They get no gate, of course, so they do it as cheaply as they can.

I never start getting changed until half an hour before the game anyway, but even then you feel absolutely empty. No tension at all. Not a glimmer of excitement. Today we had a decent side – Gordon, Harry, Brian Brown, Franky, all in the Reserves. All in the doghouse. All a bit sick. Made worse by the fact that the First Team won yesterday. Gordon went up as sub yesterday, but he didn't get on, so he came to play for us. He gave us all the bad news, told us how they had done . . .

We were all in the dressing room trying to build up some sort of feeling. Which is where Harry is so good. He would be the same on Hackney Marshes. He was still geed up, walking around saying, 'Come on, we've got to have a go. There's £2 at stake.'

You have got to think of a million different ways to motivate yourself.

Really it is down to personal pride. And the possibility that there might be a scout in the stand just having a look. And you might impress him. But it is all very intangible. It is very hard to get hold of something and say, 'Right, let's have a go.'...

We went two down, even though some of us were having a go. Harry was having a go, but there was this little right-winger who was giving him the biggest chasing of his life. Harry was kicking him all over the park. They were a good side with a lot of good young players.

At half-time we went into the dressing room and Benny was there. We hadn't seen him before the game. He didn't say anything. He just stood in the corner. They won last night, so really he doesn't give a damn how we do today. In fact he looked smug, as if he was pleased we were struggling. As if he was thinking, 'My young lads did it last night. Look at you lot.'

Billy Neill was in charge. And it was difficult for him to have a go at us, because we are his contemporaries. He is used to having a young side. He can have a go at them. But he knows how Gordon feels. And Benny was casting his shadow over things. Because he wouldn't say anything himself, but his presence stopped anyone else from saying anything.

So we went out again. And we were still getting a chasing, but after 15 minutes we pulled one back. Then we got a penalty. Then Gordon got this brilliant goal. He still wasn't bothering, but perhaps all the rucking he was taking was getting through to him, and he started doing a little bit more. And he picked up this ball about 35 yards out, took it past two men and hit it from 25 yards into the top corner. A brilliant goal. I was delighted. He is such a good player, and it is sickening to see a class player, who could have played at the very highest level, struggling.

Then we nicked another one before the end, so we won 4–2. We came off the park really pleased. It is meaningless. The Midweek League. They hardly even bother to print the result in the paper. But you come off with a little glow of satisfaction. Because you have got a little bit of self-respect back.

Benny came in afterwards. 'Well done, that was better. See you tomorrow.' And he was off. You haven't really shown him, but you feel as if you have.

A week later we played Peterborough, then being managed by Noel Cantwell.

MILLWALL RESERVES 4 PETERBOROUGH RESERVES 1

I geed myself up by thinking: 'Maybe Noel Cantwell is here. I'd like to play for Peterborough. I don't care what division they are in. And even if I don't go there I would like to think that he is sitting in the stand wondering, "What is a good player like that doing in the Midweek League?"'

I played great. I was doing things on the ball – magic. And I scored direct from a free kick. Curled it round the wall into the top corner from just outside the box. Which gave me enormous pleasure, as it did the three OAPS who were sitting in the stand.

I enjoyed the game aesthetically in a way that you never can in a League game. I enjoyed doing a little on the ball, flicking it over people's heads and half volleying it out to the wing, that sort of thing. Back to childhood again – just playing for personal enjoyment, for the sheer joy of doing something well. That is missing from League football. There your motives are much more base. The battle for points, League position and bonus is something which doesn't exist in the Reserves.

But I could never settle for reserve-team football. I left Manchester United, when they were the greatest club in the country, to go to York so I could get First Team football. I'd go down to a Third Division team now for First Team football. The thing that has always kept me out of the Midweek League and kept me in First Teams is my insatiable desire to be in them. Not ability. I've got no more ability than most people, it is just desire, desire, desire.

I went to see Benny again. I had decided to ask for a transfer. It would cost me money, but I couldn't go on treading water in the Reserves. Benny had been talking in glowing terms to the press about his 'new team', which he claimed would be Millwall's best ever. Gordon Hill was one of the rising stars. Hill was a former England amateur international. The cocky little fucker thought he was George Best. We'd been giving him a hard time in the dressing room but he was bulletproof, Benny's favourite son.

My meeting with Benny ended badly, raised voices and a slammed door. With nothing to do on Saturdays, I had agreed to cover a match for LBC, London's new commercial radio station. Non-League Walton & Hersham were playing Brian Clough's Brighton in the FA Cup. Having won the First Division with Derby, Clough got the sack after 'getting too big for his boots', as his club chairman, Sam Longsden, put it. Ambitious, with a newly self-made millionaire in the boardroom, Brighton hired Clough to do for them what he'd done for Derby! LBC wanted me to interview Clough. I promised to try. Hence the trip to Walton.

That week I'd written about Clough and Malcolm Allison, also in the boardroom wars, for the *South London Press*. The gist of my piece was the contrast between Clough and Allison and the grey little men wielding power in football.

After the Cup match I travelled back to LBC's studio. Their reporter from Millwall's home game against Leyton Orient had good news – Orient had won 1–0 – and bad news: the editorial in the match programme.

> *No doubt many Millwall supporters and not a few* South London Press *readers who know of Millwall but are not supporters, are puzzled by the weekly article which appears in that journal under the heading of 'Dunphy's Diary'. Of course, if you happen to know Eamon and his philosophy you will appreciate his attitude to the established order of life. Obviously, if you have not already recognized the fact, Eamon is opposed to the Establishment, football or otherwise. Deep down in all of us there resides this spirit of rebellion, but if we all rebelled, if we all took up the cudgels in support of a complete revolution of the present order of things, there would be only one result – CHAOS. The latest diatribe from Dunphy finds him supporting the ideas and ideals of those paramount rebels of soccer society, Malcolm Allison and Brian Clough. Fair enough, we are all entitled to our opinion and Eamon has frankly confessed his. He is opposed to what he calls 'the little men'. Now we have never doubted that people like Eamon suffer from a lack of intelligence, but when he begins to describe people who have given a life-time to the game, and provided brains and finance to ensure its continuance, as 'little', then it is about time he got his priorities right.*

Etc., etc.

The voice wasn't Benny's; neither were the sentiments expressed. I knew the faceless arsehole who'd written this diatribe. But I knew also that Benny must have sanctioned it for inclusion in the match-day programme.

A few days later I got a phone call from Theo Foley, my old Ireland team-mate who was now managing Charlton. 'What's the problem at Millwall?' I told him I wanted to get away. 'Well,' he said, 'I had a chat with Benny this morning and he's willing to let you go. I can't understand it, because when I came in for you last year he wouldn't hear of it. Do you want to play any more? Benny tells me he's sick of you.'

Technically, this conversation was a breach of the rules covering football. A prospective employer couldn't talk to a slave without permission from its owner. 'Don't say anything in the morning,' Theo cautioned. 'Benny will call you into his office and tell you, then come over and we can have a chat about terms.'

When I arrived at work the following morning Benny sent for me. 'I've fixed you up with a nice little move. Just down the road at Charlton.' I feigned surprise. I said I was up for it.

'I don't want you to leave,' Benny said quietly. 'There's a place for you here as long as I'm here. But you've put me where it's as easy for me to sell you as keep you.'

I said I'd go and talk to Theo. 'I'll order a taxi.'

'No,' Benny said, 'I'll run you over.'

I was scared, excited, nervous. Benny sensed my confusion. He stopped the car in Greenwich Park. 'Look,' he said, 'you know I've never done you any harm. I've only tried to do the best for you. We've had our differences, but as long as you want to stay at Millwall there's a place for you. I'll give you a testimonial. You've only got two years to do, so you should think about that. I can't guarantee you First Team football, nobody can, but I want you to stay. This could be a disastrous move for you and it could be disastrous for me.'

The first part of that observation was true. Charlton was a dead club, characterless compared to Millwall. 'Don't sign anything until you come back and see me' were his parting words as he dropped me off at the Valley, Charlton's home ground.

I liked Theo. He was a Dubliner: brash, extrovert, optimistic, intense, thin as a whippet, hard as nails when he played, full of sardonic humour around the dressing room. He'd captained Northampton Town in the sixties when that tiny club shot through the leagues from Fourth to First Division in successive seasons.

'What's the story, Dunphy? Do you still want to play . . . or are you looking for a rest home?' was Theo's opening gambit. I assured him

I was still hungry. 'I know.' He laughed. 'I saw you playing against Orient Reserves.' He explained what he was looking for. 'I need a bit of leadership, someone to gee my lot up. The attitude is wrong at the moment. It won't be easy, but we've got some good kids coming through. If you're up for it, this can work for both of us.'

The transfer was £15,000. As I hadn't given Benny a written transfer request I was entitled to a £1,500 signing-on fee. We quickly settled the wages, a fiver more than I was on at Millwall, forty pounds a week. The snag was accommodation. I was living in a Millwall club house. I wanted to buy it. Theo told me that Charlton had a house. He took me to see it. A kip.

Benny's offer of a testimonial for two years, worth maybe twelve or fifteen grand, gave me some leverage with Theo. In theory. Would Benny still be at Millwall in two years' time, Theo wondered. Actually, I wasn't so sure. We agreed I'd go back to Benny and try to get a deal on the house. Theo offered an extra £500 signing-on fee to help with the deposit.

At first Benny was not very amenable. 'Look, you're making a profit on the deal,' I argued. 'You've had eight years' service and you won't have to give me a testimonial.'

He relented. 'I'll have to clear it with the board. Leave it with me.' The board were glad to be rid of me. I could buy the house. Deal done. Not quite.

I went back to the Valley. 'What about that column you're writing in the *South London Press*? My guys won't like that,' Theo said.

'I'm not giving it up,' I told him.

'Okay, we're on,' he agreed.

I had to get my boots from the Den. Next morning I waited until the lads were out training before slipping in and collecting my tools. No goodbyes. After eight years I was out of the door with no regrets. Pro footballers don't do leaving parties.

31.   A Club in Decline

Charlton had been relegated to the Third Division the year Millwall nearly got promotion to the First. With a capacity of 70,000, the Valley was the biggest ground in the Football League. A vast natural amphitheatre, it felt like a graveyard with less than 10,000 spectators watching our games. The passion ever present at the Den was noticeably absent. The baying discontent of the sullen crowd echoed around the acres of empty terracing. This was a club in decline.

The squad was a mixture of bright youngsters and sour old pros. Peter Shreeves, who later went on to manage Spurs, was Theo's coach. A smart, reasonable guy, Peter knew his stuff. Everything was right. Except the players. I worked really hard but we were flogging a dead horse. The sense of purpose and absolute commitment that was the norm in the Millwall dressing room, especially when playing on the road, was missing. At home, these Charlton players were frightened to get on the ball, lest they make a mistake and incur the barely suppressed wrath of their fans, waiting like snipers to home in on their target of the day.

London lads hated travelling north. Brian Dear was in many ways the quintessential Londoner. Benny signed him for the Lions in 1970. Brian on song was a decent goal-scorer. At West Ham, where he started in the same team as Bobby Moore, Geoff Hurst and Martin Peters, he scored 33 goals in 69 League games. He played in the Hammers' 1964/65 European Cup Winners' Cup-winning team.

In April 1965 he scored the quickest five goals in the history of English football, against West Brom. Five goals in twenty minutes. But somewhere along the way he'd lost the plot. Benny took a punt, hoping for a miracle. When we reached Watford Gap on our first trip up north, Brian started singing his favourite ditty, 'Up Here in Karsie Country', to the melody of a popular Bird's Eye ad.

I was reminded of Brian, or 'the Stag' as he was known, when I travelled to Grimsby with Theo's Charlton team. It was Good Friday.

Grimsby were flying in the League; we were struggling. When we arrived at the ground, Blundell Park, a biting east wind was blowing. As we walked the pitch before the game you could tell the lads didn't fancy what lay ahead. Back in the dressing room, Charlie Hall the kit man had laid out the gear. 'Fucking hell,' someone roared, 'you've brought the short-sleeved shirts.'

'Come on, guys, get on with it,' Theo pleaded. But the players had their excuse. Apart from one or two, they didn't try a leg. We lost 5–0. Theo was fucked. A few weeks later he lost his job. And then Andy Nelson arrived.

Andy Nelson had played in Alf Ramsey's Championship-winning Ipswich team of 1962, the centre-half in that extraordinary side. In fact he was one of life's centre-halves – they used to call them 'stoppers'. A stopper took no prisoners. Among the legends of the modern game Ron 'Chopper' Harris, Norman Hunter and Tommy Smith are the most renowned stoppers. Nelson was of their ilk. He came to Charlton from Gillingham, where he'd enjoyed some modest success as a coach.

He was a good fit for a team of delinquents badly in need of discipline. Or, at least, that's how the board of directors at Charlton saw it. The chairman, Michael Glickstein, was an Old Etonian. He owned the club, his fellow board members simply there to do his bidding. Glickstein liked his slaves to address him as 'Mr Michael'. Early on I took to calling him Mr Glickstein, a major breach of protocol. 'It's Mr Michael,' he insisted.

He wasn't one of the little men, rather a big brazen toff with that unique sense of entitlement Eton confers on its pupils. 'How's my little Commie friend?' he would greet me, a broad smile lighting his face. I rather liked him. He had a twinkle in his eye, a sign of life rarely spotted on boardroom faces. 'Glicky' was a cut above the butchers, bakers and car salesmen, the usual directors of football clubs.

The board gave Nelson the money they had denied Theo to buy in some fresh blood. He was a bully. It was his way or the highway. Nelson was probably what Charlton needed in the short term. Two of our better players, Derek Hales and Mike Flanagan, had been sent off in an FA Cup-tie the previous season for fighting. With each other! Flanagan, talented but inconsistent, upped his game. Hales, known as 'Killer' for his lethal striking (and his generally menacing personality), began scoring prolifically.

I was in and out of the side. From day one Nelson made it clear that he was taking no bullshit from me. He rarely made eye contact. I wasn't his kind of player, or his kind of person. But in the Third Division I had my uses. As the season progressed we emerged as promotion contenders. Nelson signed Harry Cripps from Millwall to add experience to the squad.

Through the winter months I could no longer conceal my chronic back pain. I was throwing up before and during training. At half-time in games I'd be retching in the loos. Sleepless nights became the norm. Stress made matters worse, and stress was a constant for any number of reasons: Andy Nelson; my column; the sense that at thirty my career was in irreversible decline. And fear that after I'd vomited and the spasm passed it would return later in the day. Diagnosis was the key. I went to Harley Street. No joy. Bristol University Hospital had the latest X-ray technology, but that failed to locate the cause of my pain.

Laughs were few and far between. The relationship between Nelson and Mr Michael was, however, the source of much amusement at the back of the bus that ferried us up and down the M1 to exotic locations such as Rochdale, Darlington and Workington. Glicky liked to sit up front across the aisle from Nelson. Occasionally he would beckon the hard-faced stopper to his side. Never invited to sit down, Nelson would stand stooping, slightly off-balance, as his master pontificated on the day's events. The tyrant of the training ground and dressing room visibly wilted in the Old Etonian's presence.

'Yes, Mr Michael,' he would coo, bringing deference to a new Olympian level. 'Good night, Mr Michael,' he would grovel, as we got off the coach in the Valley car park. Andy was a suck-up, piss-down guy.

But 1975 was his year. We needed just one point from our last home game to secure promotion. Preston at home was not a daunting task. It was Charlton's biggest night for years. I'd been in the side for the final games of the promotion push. Nelson dropped me for the decisive game. He replaced me in midfield with Harry Cripps. I was disappointed, but not particularly surprised.

The real shock before the game was his decision to leave Keith Peacock out. Keith had played every game that season. He was a fantastic pro, respected by everyone at the club, fans and players. He'd been at Charlton since 1962. He had played almost 500 games, through good times and bad, mostly bad. A measure of the esteem in which Keith was held by all at the Valley is the plush Keith Peacock banqueting suite, which is a feature of the smart all-seater stadium the club now plays in.

When Nelson announced the team, Keith turned pale with shock. The other players were stunned. Nelson remained poker-faced. Not just dropped, Keith wasn't even on the bench. I took him outside to the players' car park, where we sat in my car. He was tearful, badly hurt, confused, shaken beyond anger. There was no rational explanation for Nelson's decision. It had nothing to do with form or character. Keith was a consistent performer and a model professional. Nelson's brutal dismissal of Keith Peacock that night was the most perverse act I ever witnessed in my football life.

Promotion achieved, Nelson swiftly began to plan for the future. I learned from a newspaper that I was to be given a free transfer. This was a deep, very public humiliation. Finished at thirty. In five weeks' time my contract was up. The weekly wage would stop on 30 June. I had a wife now and a newborn son, a bad back and a reputation as a trouble-maker. The phone didn't ring.

I was due to go to Lilleshall to try for my full FA coaching badge. I'd had my preliminary badge for a couple of years. If I considered journalism to be a back-up plan, coaching and ultimately management was what I really dreamed of. Getting my full FA badge was essential to that project. Morale at an all-time low, I set off for Lilleshall in leafy Shropshire. Getting the preliminary badge was a formality for a pro. The full FA badge was another story. The pass mark was 70 per cent. You took the exam at the end of an intensive two-week preparation in the Shropshire countryside.

Coaching, as defined by the Football Association, was a controversial topic in the seventies. Some pros, John Giles among them, thought it was a load of bollocks: you either knew the game or you didn't. You weren't going to learn about football from an FA course. I disagreed. You didn't take the FA badge to acquire knowledge, the point being that, no matter how much knowledge you possessed, you had to learn how to impart it.

More practically, from my perspective, the badge might help me get a job. Top players, like John Giles, could walk straight into management on the basis of their reputations as players. But a stellar playing career did not, in my view, prepare you for coaching or management.

Former World Cup heroes Nobby Stiles and Geoff Hurst were on my Lilleshall course. Nobby, a brother-in-law and close friend of John Giles, clearly felt the badge was worth the effort. While taking the course, I checked in at home each day to see if the telephone was ringing. There was no good news on that front.

I enjoyed Lilleshall. The challenge of learning to convey your ideas about how the game should be played was exhilarating. The work was taxing, the days long, the evenings full of football talk as well as gossip and slander about the slave trade and the slave traders who governed the game that was our life. For the purposes of the course we divided into groups of fifteen, with an FA staff coach assigned to each group. When it was your turn to take a session, to be the coach, your fellow pros became the pupils. If you didn't know your stuff and, crucially, how to put it across, you were toast.

In this test, reputation counted for nothing. Putting your international caps or medals on the table counted for nothing. Journeyman or World Cup winner, it didn't matter a damn. Coaching demanded knowledge, personality, preparation, the ability to articulate what you wanted. I was in my element.

During that fortnight I formed what proved to be a lasting friendship with another struggling journeyman, Ray Harford. Ray was with Colchester, who'd paid Port Vale £1,750 for his services. He'd played for Charlton, Exeter City, Lincoln City, Mansfield Town, places I knew well from my own journeyman travelling.

Quiet, thoughtful, funny, Ray was a good companion. The same anxiety stalked us both. Where to next? Would we ever get a job? Would we pass the most immediate test by getting the badge? Everything was decided on the last two days. The written test consisted of theory, and the mandatory exam on the laws of the game. Unless you were a dummy – and there were a few of them around – the written stuff was easy.

The big challenge, where the high marks on offer decided pass or fail, was a practical demonstration of your ability to coach a group of fellow pros. Like everyone else I was a bag of nerves. The FA staff coach stood on the touchline, clipboard in hand. You had forty-five minutes to complete the session. He had spent a fortnight teaching us how to teach straight from the textbook. I thought the handy hints, the dos and don'ts he passed on were largely irrelevant. What he'd handed down was a formula; lifeless, dry, unoriginal. I believed a coaching session should develop organically, allow scope for improvisation. Bottom line, I thought I should do it my way, which would be different from Ray Harford's, and from the Bible as written by the boffins from the Football Association.

I decided to go for it. Thirty minutes into the session the man with the clipboard intervened. He didn't like what he was seeing. 'You can't do it this way,' he told me.

'Why not?' I queried. 'It's not the means but the end that counts. We're having a good time.' It was true. The pupils/pros were animated, engaging with the ideas bubbling in the air.

'Your session is finished,' Clipboard insisted. Over.

'Fuck you,' I responded, as I walked away.

As I headed for the touchline I spotted Allen Wade, the FA's director of coaching, standing about fifteen yards away. He called me over. 'What was all that about?' he asked. I told him that I'd apparently breached the law as set out in the FA's coaching manual. His reply astonished me: 'That was a great session. I was impressed.' Nodding in the direction of the clipboard, Wade told me not to worry: 'I'll mark your paper myself.'

Wade had been director of coaching since 1964. An urbane intellectual, he was regarded with suspicion in the pro game. Like anyone advocating new ideas, he was seen as a threat by most if not all professionals. Many of his ideas about coaching had originated in Europe, which only rendered them less acceptable to those playing and coaching in 'the greatest League in the world'.

England's World Cup victory in 1966 had only reinforced the notion that it had nothing to learn from the rest of the world. Which was precisely what Alf Ramsey claimed when asked why he wasn't staying in Mexico to watch the concluding phase of the 1970 World Cup after West Germany had eliminated England in the quarter-final.

Wade did have some disciples in the pro game. Bobby Robson, Don Howe, Dave Sexton, Dario Gradi and, though he didn't shout too loudly about it, Malcolm Allison were all open to new ideas about how the game should be played and coached.

Distinguished and world-renowned though he was, Wade evangelized on the margins of the pro game. One of the great canards of those seventies years, a conviction shared by many of its best and brightest practitioners, including my friend John Giles, was that if, like Wade, you had never played the game for money, you didn't really know what you were talking about. That bigotry was copper-fastened by an even more absurd sub-clause: only top players were equipped to be top managers.

In one of the many books he published, Allen Wade addressed the insularity of the game's professionals by quoting the German philosopher Arthur Schopenhauer: 'There are two stages through which worthwhile ideas must pass before they are accepted,' he wrote. 'In the first stage they are ignored, in the second stage they are ridiculed. Coaching has passed through these stages and is now accepted as a necessary process.' That fateful day at Lilleshall, Allen Wade understood and appreciated what I was trying to do. Later he would make good on his promise that I would be OK.

By early June it seemed as if my Football League career was over. I'd been available free of charge for several weeks. The phone wasn't ringing. If something didn't happen quickly it would be cut off. Non-League Maidstone United were advertising for a player-coach. In desperation, I applied. I spent half a day in Kent trying to persuade the newly minted millionaire owner that I was the man to take United into the Football League. I was a world-class spieler, but Maidstone's Mr Big was looking for a 'safe pair of hands'. Someone like Andy Nelson.

Then Charlie Hurley rang. He was managing Reading. He'd been trying to get them promoted from the Fourth Division for a couple of years. He thought I might be the missing link.

32.   Where's the Beef?

I knew Charlie from our time on the road with the Ireland team. He was a popular character with a droll sense of humour. Born in Cork, reared in London, he'd started out at Millwall. He was a big-money signing for Sunderland where he became one of the best centre-halves of his day. Many great players graced Roker Park, Brian Clough and Len Shackleton among them, but when in 1979 Sunderland fans voted for their player of the century, Charlie was their choice.

As a kid I'd watched him play for Ireland. He was adored by Irish soccer fans, the media and the Blazers, who fawned in his presence. An imposing, handsome man, there was a touch of the movie star about Charlie. Apart from the fact that he was a tight bastard who never bought anyone a drink, nobody had a bad word to say about him.

Trying hard not to appear too eager, I agreed terms and signed a two-year contract. Reading had not been promoted for fifty years. But Charlie and his assistant, Maurice Evans, had assembled a good squad. Robin Friday was Reading's star player. One of Charlie's suggestions when I signed was that I might try to keep Robin on the straight and narrow. 'You're a fucking rebel, he's a fucking madman,' Charlie told me. 'You should get on well together.'

I liked Robin from day one. Everybody did. Everybody in the dressing room loved him because he was an amazing player, a centre-forward who scored and made goals. He had great feet, wonderful vision and was brave as a lion. With pace, which sadly he lacked, Robin could have played for England.

Off the field Robin was wild. He looked like a rock star, and lived like one. Girls found him irresistible. He smoked joints, dropped pills, uppers and downers, drank and partied most nights until dawn. His dress code was leather jacket, Cuban heels, blue jeans and T-shirt. His long hair stood in sharp contrast to footballers' traditional short-back-and-sides. George Best was one of his heroes. They had things in common. Both were beautiful, childlike, vulnerable and, behind all the bravado, shy.

Robin came late to professional football. He joined Reading from non-League Hayes a year before I arrived. He was twenty-two. He'd served fourteen months in Borstal for persistent petty thieving. When he was released, Robin met and married a local girl from Acton, West London, where he'd grown up. Maxine's parents were from the West Indies, and interracial relationships were uncommon in sixties England – Robin's father refused to attend the wedding. His daughter, Nicola, was born soon after. Although the marriage didn't last, the scars of its failure did.

After Robin died of a heart attack, aged thirty-eight, the Cardiff rock band Super Furry Animals wrote a song dedicated to him, titled 'The Man Don't Give A Fuck'. The problem was, he did. On the road late at night or on the piss, he'd talk about Nicola, eyes teary with sadness for what might have been. Then, uncomfortable with emotion in that distinctly English way, Robin would laugh and pop another amphetamine pill. ''Ere, Eamon, 'ave one of these,' he'd mock.

Some of his mates were Hell's Angels, Reading branch. I gave him Hunter S. Thompson's book *Hell's Angels: The Strange and Terrible Saga of the Outlaw Motorcycle Gangs*. I also got him a copy of Thompson's *Fear and Loathing in Las Vegas*. 'Fuck promotion, let's go to Vegas,' he said, laughing, one morning after what looked like a hell of a party the night before. We made a deal: promotion first, then we'd go to Vegas.

In our happy dressing room, Robin was the outlaw. Gordon Cumming, our captain, was a Scot. That rare creature, a winger with brains, Gordon was solid as a rock. John 'Minty' Murray operated up front alongside Robin and hung out down the back of the bus with Robin, myself and goalkeeper Steve Death, a pale-faced chain-smoker who didn't give a fuck about anyone or, if he did, he never let on.

As Fourth Division players we and the rest of the team were going nowhere. There were no cups, medals, money or glory. All of us were to some extent hurt, bruised, bearing scars of one kind or another. Living hand-to-mouth, week-to-week, our futures in the main behind us, we longed for one good season, just one win to make it all seem worthwhile.

Nineteen seventy-six was that year for our Reading team. After a good start we stayed in or around the promotion places all season. We recovered from a blip that saw us lose three games on the road at Watford, Swansea and Exeter to remain undefeated in ten of our last eleven games. Promotion was secured when we beat Crewe 3–1 before an ecstatic Elm Park crowd. I played in forty-five of the forty-six League games, scoring the decisive second goal in the game against Crewe. 'Hurley's Heroes' was the headline in the *Reading Evening Post*. After fifty barren years, Reading was finally promoted. Happy days, or so we thought.

For years a local farmer had promised to slaughter a bullock and give the meat to the players if Reading won promotion. A fortnight before the final game, when promotion seemed assured, we went to the local cattle-mart to select our bullock. It was a good photo opportunity for the *Post* as we posed contentedly beside our chosen beast.

After the victory over Crewe, the lap of honour, the champagne shower, the pictures taken of our brief encounter with glory, we drifted off to reflect on a wonderful season. A date was set ten days hence, when we would return to claim the promised beef, pick up our prized prime cuts and enjoy a celebration lunch in the local pub. That was the plan.

When we arrived at Elm Park the plastic bags containing our meat were neatly laid out in the home-team dressing room. The bags were suspiciously small. I opened mine. Inside, a small portion of mince and an even smaller chunk of stewing beef. No sirloin, no roast beef, no fillet steak. We looked at each other. Bemused at first. Then the penny dropped. They'd kept the good stuff for the board.

When challenged, Charlie was dismissive. 'It's only a bag of beef. What's all the fuss about?' He smirked. He claimed not to know who had got the roast, fillet and sirloin. We didn't believe him. He didn't get the significance of this shabby little stroke. We left the mince where we found it as a gesture of protest and went off for our celebration lunch.

Next item on our agenda, and the club's, was the issue of the new improved contracts following our successful season. If 'Beefgate' was anything to go by, another more grievous stroke might be in the offing. We agreed to keep in touch with each other during the post-season break.

In truth, we weren't crazy about King Charlie, even before the beef had gone missing. Behind the smart suits and the movie-star looks, we thought he was a bluffer. Living proof that you could look like a manager, talk like a manager, walk like John Wayne – and still know fuck all about the game. The only thing he brought to the training ground was a bag of balls.

Maurice Evans did the work. A nice man, Maurice made a massive contribution to our promotion. While Charlie spouted generalizations about attitude, Maurice understood the forensics of the game, how to identify what was going wrong. And know what to do to put it right. Maurice was the chef, Charlie the maître d'.

The old bonhomie that had made him a popular character in the Irish squad was still an aspect of King Charlie's persona. But behind it there wasn't much that might assist in winning football matches. He was, as we were about to discover, a bosses' man. The board of directors at Reading were a repulsive lot: big men in a small county town, the golf club bore meets that splendid chap from the Chamber of Commerce. They made Mickey Purser and Michael Glickstein look like heroes.

When Charlie strode among them they saw officer material. They thought Robin a useful idiot, me an uppity little pest. They knew we were laughing at them and the badly dressed wives they brought to the bigger home games. But, of course, they knew as well that, football being football, they would have the last laugh.

My book, *Only a Game?*, was published to acclaim while I was at Reading. The *Reading Evening Post* offered me a weekly column. This caused trouble, but we were on the promotion trail so, for the moment, there was nothing they could do.

When contract negotiations began in June, it was clear that Charlie and his boardroom pals intended to screw us. When we assembled for pre-season training and compared notes, it was clear that no wage rise was on the table. Robin, Gordon Cumming and I were offered a fiver more, but most of the other lads got nothing. If 'Beefgate' was cheap, this was insulting.

At a meeting we convened, we agreed to stick together. Nobody would sign a new contract. The atmosphere on the training ground was poisonous. News got out to the *Evening Post*. 'Players Revolt' was the headline. Hurley's bonhomie dissolved. 'The club is not for shifting' was his message, 'Take it or leave it' the slogan of the day.

He tried to pick us off, one by one. A few caved in. Nobody blamed them. But Robin, John Murray, Steve Death and I vowed to stay the course. Geoff Barker backed us up. In their own way, Robin and Geoff were the most significant figures in the dispute: Robin because he was our main man; Geoff because, of us rebels, he was the most vulnerable. Geoff had only played thirty games in the promotion season. But he'd been brilliant at key moments when our backs were to the wall in the tense end-of-season matches.

Robin was heroic. His legend was well established and, unlike Hurley's, well deserved. Fans loved him as did the media and his team-mates. Opponents feared him. If he relented, our struggle was lost. And as the stand-off played out it became clear that getting Robin onside was Hurley and the board's priority. 'Fuck them, Eamon,' he told me, when we reflected on the state of play. 'We're all in this together.'

In early August, with the first game of the new season fast approaching, the wage row cast a shadow over the club. One morning after training, Hurley called me into his office. We'd always got on well. He was unaware of my disdain for him: a promotion season can disguise a multitude of misgivings.

The conversation began pleasantly enough. We'd known each other a long time, he reminded me. 'Let's sort this out between us now,' he continued. He had a proposal to make. He wanted to sue for peace. On his terms. The deal was that I would get a handsome rise, along with Robin and John Murray. The others would fall into line, he argued.

'What about Geoff Barker?' I asked.

His eyes narrowed, his mouth pursed, the genial smile froze. 'Fuck Geoff.' The words echoed like gunshot round the office.

'What about Steve Death?' I looked him straight in the eye.

'For fuck's sake, Dunph.' He was beginning to lose it. 'What do you think you are, a fucking shop steward?'

'No, but we're in this together and we're sticking together,' I informed him, then elaborated: 'We got promotion and the new contract should reward the lads who did it for you. Instead you're fighting us when you should be fighting *for* us in the boardroom.'

At that he turned puce. Before I could react he was off his chair and rounding the desk in my direction. As I stood up he grabbed me by the throat and flung me to the wall. 'You little cunt, I've fucking had it with you. You're out of here, out of this fucking club. I'm giving you a free [transfer] as of now.' He was a big man in a serious rage.

'That's OK,' I told him, 'but I've a year left on my contract. Maybe you'll be on your bike before me.' He made to lunge again, but I was out of the door before he could intercept me.

The next day the club issued a press release announcing that I was available on a free transfer. For the second time in three months,

Reading FC was making history. Nobody had ever been given a 'free' before the season started. Unless somebody came in for me I'd be idle for a season. Nobody did.

Three months later Hurley resigned in equally bizarre circumstances. By sacking me the club quelled the revolt. But this proved to be a Pyrrhic victory. Robin effectively went on strike. Geoff Barker was dropped and placed on the blacklist, playing only six games that season. A sense of lingering resentment infected the mood in the dressing room and training ground. Ironically, the season began brightly enough, with decent results in the first few games. But we got a couple of 4–0 defeats, at Chesterfield and away to Mansfield Town.

After the Mansfield game, Hurley recalled me to the side for a home game against Preston. They destroyed us in the first forty-five minutes, leading 2–0 at half-time. It could have been six. The crowd booed us off the park. In the dressing room Hurley was raging.

'Get up,' he barked, as we made to sit down for our cup of tea. 'Get up, you bastards, and get back out there. I'm fucking out of here now. This is the last you'll see of me, you fucking useless twats. Call yourselves professionals? You're a fucking disgrace. Now fuck off back out there.' With that, he was gone. Another historic moment: the first time a Football League manager had resigned at half-time.

We were stunned, speechless, as we made our way back onto the pitch we'd vacated only three or four minutes earlier. Gathering in the centre circle we had a quick team talk. It was a freezing November afternoon. But we resolved to have a go to save some pride in the second half. 2–0 was the final score.

Maurice Evans was appointed manager. We had a chat. He wanted me back in the side. But he told me the board wanted to sell Robin to Cardiff, who'd offered £30,000. Without Robin, we'd struggle to stay up. Maurice assured me that I would be in any team he picked. However, he confirmed that the board wanted me out at the end of the season, so in that regard his hands were tied. Maurice was a straight shooter, a much respected man who went on to enjoy a successful career at Reading, and later with Oxford United.

At the time of writing, Reading are a Championship club playing out of the magnificent Madejski Stadium. A plaque on the stadium wall commemorates Maurice, who died aged sixty-three. The memorial reads: 'Maurice Evans, 1936–2000. Player, Manager, Gentleman'.

One morning shortly after Beefgate, I received a letter from the University of London Football Club. Would I be interested in coaching the university team for the coming season? I had been recommended for the position of head coach by Allen Wade, the Football Association's director of coaching. This prestigious post had previously been occupied by Bobby Robson and Jimmy Hill. My expenses would be covered, the letter assured me.

I was stunned and thrilled by this bolt from the blue. I asked Stewart Henderson, a team-mate at Reading, to come and work with me. The university soccer club was in bad shape. The logistics of running a football club in London were complicated by the fact that the university did not exist on a single campus. Different faculties occupied sites all across the capital. We found a small group of enthusiasts at the clubhouse in West London, out of touch with like-minded would-be footballers in other colleges.

So we organized a recruitment drive, ordering our hard-core students to spread the word across the city that university football was about to take off. Trials were arranged and eventually a squad of eighteen players was selected.

Stewart was cool, I was passionate. We both worked hard. University football provided the perfect antidote to the soap-opera at Elm Park. More importantly, it was a chance to prove our worth as coaches.

Compared to one-site universities, London was a Cinderella club. There was no single sense of identity because the players all hailed from different colleges. There was a traditional fixture list, the highlights of which were the matches against Oxford and Cambridge, the two annual outings against Football League clubs – West Ham and Millwall in our year – and the campaign's final assignment, the British Universities Championship.

Blessed with a terrific group of players, we set out on what would prove to be the most successful season in the history of the University of London Football Club. We did the double over Oxford and Cambridge, beat the two Football League clubs and finished third in the British Universities Championship, losing to Wales in the semi-final. This was the happiest, most fulfilling experience of my life to that point. More than anything, I wanted to coach and manage. The University of London experience encouraged me to believe that I could do so successfully. Stewart agreed to come with me if I got a job.

Back at Elm Park, Reading were fighting what would prove to be a losing relegation battle. Beefgate, the subsequent row over money and the departure of Robin Friday had all sapped morale. 'Hurley's Heroes' were now subject to taunts from disgruntled fans and sniping in the local media.

In the spring of 1977 I was only a matter of weeks away from the dole. With my wife and child, mortgage and overdraft, I was feeling desperate. Yes, I had shown some aptitude for writing and coaching, but nobody wanted to employ me. When Hartlepool United sacked their manager, I applied for the job. I included a glowing reference from Allen Wade, another from Maurice Evans. I got no reply.

Brentford were also looking for a manager. Their owner, Dan Tana, was an American entrepreneur with a number of fashionable restaurants in LA. I applied for that job as well. This time I decided on a more direct approach. I got Dan's phone number and called him, seeking a meeting. He invited me round to his West London mansion. I made my pitch. He listened politely. Then he told me to come back when I had some experience.

33. Going Home

Out of the blue I got a call from John Giles. How was I doing? I was tempted to tell him I had some 'irons in the fire'. Instead I told him the truth. He told me he was going home to Dublin to take a 50 per cent share in Shamrock Rovers, with a view to creating a top-class professional club in that football-crazy city.

Earlier that season, John shocked the football world by announcing that he was quitting management at the season's end. He had taken over as player/manager of West Brom after leaving Leeds in 1975, and had led the Midlands club to promotion in his first season, then topped that by finishing seventh in the First Division the following year.

John Giles had also been appointed player/manager of the Irish team in 1973. Under his leadership, the discredited 'Carry On Around Europe' culture associated with the international team ceased, at least as far as the players were concerned. 'The Blazers' still engaged in guerrilla raids on duty-free, brothels and bars. But the players behaved themselves. Giles's Ireland was a respected professional outfit. He introduced Liam Brady, Frank Stapleton and David O'Leary to international football. Hotels and training facilities were upgraded.

He offered me a job as player/coach with Shamrock Rovers. When I asked him why he was quitting the English game, when he seemed destined to manage one of the bigger clubs, he cited his experience at West Brom to argue that football management in England was undoable. As manager, you had responsibility for results without the power to influence the key decisions upon which results depended – the buying and selling of players and the wage structure. As an example, he noted that West Brom had decided to build an expensive new stand instead of investing money in players to consolidate their First Division status. Despite his success as team manager, nobody sought his opinion about where the club's priority should lie.

John earned respect as a great player. But among his peers and great football men, like Bill Nicholson, who'd wanted John to succeed him as Spurs manager, he was admired also as a highly perceptive student of the game. Throughout his career, he kept his distance from the media. Unlike his Leeds midfield partner Billy Bremner, John was no media darling. He was notably self-possessed, a cool, tough customer, with whom it didn't pay to mess, on or off the field.

He was acutely aware of the master/slave relationship that was professional football's defining vice. On road trips with the Irish team or on golf outings at home in Dublin in the summer, we would often reflect on the culture of the sport that was our life: the cruel, often petty, injustice of everyday transactions inflicted on players by the Gentlemen who ruled the roost, the likes of 'Mr Michael', Mickey Purser or Louis Edwards, the master at Manchester United who shafted his 'friend' Matt Busby in the end.

More than any other footballer I encountered, John Giles understood not just the game as it was played, but the anachronistic rules by which it was governed. And their consequences. Nothing, he argued, would protect you, least of all success. The pro would never be respected.

At West Brom he'd faced a choice: do his best for the players, or do the bidding of his masters. After winning promotion, John naïvely imagined the board would back his judgement when it came to strengthening his squad. The board's opening gambit was that money was tight. Among the list of players John wanted to bring in were Paul Mariner and Brian Kidd.

Mariner, a promising young striker, was playing for Plymouth Argyle. He would cost £200,000. Too expensive, the board thought. A couple of days later, John was privately approached by a director with deep pockets. He could make a bid for Mariner, his benefactor told him. 'I thought we didn't have that kind of money,' John remarked.

'For Mariner, we do' was the director's response.

The message was clear: if the suits fancied a player, money could be found. This meant in effect that the board had a veto on a matter they knew nothing about. Brian Kidd was finishing with Arsenal. He would cost £100,000 and £200 a week in wages. The board thought Kidd was too old. No deal.

Responsibility without power did not appeal to John Giles. Nor did he care for another feature of English club management: shafting your players after they had served the club's best interests. Tony Brown was a West Brom stalwart. He'd spent twelve years with 'the Baggies', as West Brom were nicknamed. A prolific goal-scoring centre-forward, Tony was a great pro, a huge crowd favourite. John was thinking of letting him go, but he wanted to repay the service Tony had given to the club.

The best way to do that was to give him a free transfer, even though a modest enough £30,000 fee could be raised from some other club. On a free transfer Tony would get the bulk of the thirty grand. When John proposed this deal to the board, it was rejected out of hand.

Some tangible recognition of the service this great clubman had rendered to West Brom was, from the masters' perspective, inconceivable. So John faced a choice: support Tony Brown or serve the venal interests of the ruling caste. John decided that if he couldn't do the job on his terms it wasn't worth doing. This was a courageous decision born of deep conviction.

Bert Millichip was chairman of West Brom. A solicitor by profession, he was a rising star in football politics. In 1981, he would be elected chairman of the Football Association. He had hired John. The day West Brom won promotion, away to Oldham, the players and directors boarded the coach to return to the Midlands to rousing cheers from their travelling supporters.

Standing beside John in the aisle of the coach, Bert basked in the applause, which he graciously acknowledged. Turning to John, Bert gestured towards the seated players and chummily remarked: 'We mustn't forget these boys. They've played their part as well'! That, John later recalled, was the moment he decided to quit. Some time in the eighties Bert became Sir Bert, knighted for services to football.

Before handing in his notice to West Brom, John talked to Bill Nicholson about the boardroom manoeuvres he'd witnessed. Bill, now retired from Spurs, was not surprised. 'That's the way the game is played, and always has been,' the great man confirmed.

Sadly, even for the greatest football men, it always ended in tears. Or penury. Nicholson lived in the same terraced house he'd occupied as a player before the war. He eked out an existence on a small pension from the great club he had created. Busby was in the same boat, living in a semi-detached house with dodgy money his only income. Bill Shankly, broken-hearted when Liverpool accepted his resignation, offered in a fit of pique, lived in a council house. He'd taken to turning up at Liverpool's training ground on weekday mornings. The man who had built Liverpool was now becoming a nuisance.

Wolves had shafted Stan Cullis in the early sixties. More recently, the great Jock Stein had been humiliated by Celtic. The first man to bring the European Cup to the British Isles, in 1967, Stein won a record nine successive Scottish titles with the same great team. When he retired in 1974, Stein hoped for a seat on Celtic's board. His directors refused that request. He was offered a sinecure in the club's pools office. Tears and bitterness.

John Giles's plans for Shamrock Rovers were very ambitious. With his football knowledge and investment from the wealthy Kilcoyne family, to whom he was related by marriage, the idea was to create a club capable of competing in Europe. Keeping the best young Irish players at home was essential to the project. League of Ireland football was part-time. The new Rovers would be a full-time professional club. Celtic and Rangers had proven that it was possible to be competitive in Europe despite a weak domestic league. Ajax had revolutionized Dutch football by creating an academy that produced great players from a country with no football tradition.

Now in the EEC, Ireland was more prosperous. There was no doubting the passion for soccer, or the existence of talented young footballers, who were obliged to emigrate to pursue their careers. John thought that trend could be reversed. With his option to buy 50 per cent of the club, there would be no masters – or slaves. I liked the concept. Yes, it would be challenging, but it was doable. I returned home filled with optimism.

34.   Soldiering On

After seventeen years away I had no fully formed idea about Ireland. Instead I had a number of impressions of the place, all of them to some extent contradictory. Seen from my adult perspective, the Ireland of my boyhood was a harsh bastion of bigotry. Outside the loving warmth of the room I had shared with Mammy, Daddy and Kevin, Ireland was a cold place for a kid seeking nothing more than an even break. In contrast, England had been liberating, a place where fairness mattered more, where you had a chance if you could grasp it.

I hadn't forgotten the Ireland of my youth. Indeed, every time I pulled on the green shirt to play for the international team I thought not of glory but of the cruel stupidity of the buffoons who ran the Football Association of Ireland. When I heard the national anthem 'Amhrán na bhFiann [The Soldier's Song]', I felt like laughing.

Joe Kinnear was my big pal on the Irish team. Born in Dublin, he moved to England with his family when he was seven. He played right-back in a good Spurs team alongside Pat Jennings, Jimmy Greaves, Alan Gilzean and Cyril Knowles. He was a witty character, Cockney through and through. Joe made his debut for Ireland away to Turkey in 1967.

The game was played in Ankara, a hostile kip we thought we'd never get out of alive. Joe and I roomed together. The pre-match playing of the national anthems began with 'The Soldier's Song', the long, long version. When it finished Joe, standing next to me, muttered, 'Fuck me, Eamon, is ours as long as theirs?'

'That was ours,' I told him. We both laughed.

I never felt that playing for my country was a great honour. For any number of reasons it clearly wasn't. In my case, I was mostly playing for the Big Five, who didn't know what they were doing. On another level altogether, I didn't think of Ireland as my country, or 'The Soldier's Song' as my song. It glorified violence and stank of anti-English sentiment. To paraphrase Muhammad Ali, I didn't have anything against the English.

None of us, on any Irish soccer team I played in, had any beef with the English. As professional players we were blessed that England existed to offer us a living. When Official Ireland scorned us, England embraced us. Our childhood imaginations feasted on the wonders of English football, its heroes and folklore. What the fuck were we supposed to be doing standing on a soccer pitch in a green shirt singing an anti-British dirge?

> *Soldiers are we*
> *whose lives are pledged to Ireland;*
> *Some have come*
> *from a land beyond the wave.*
> *Sworn to be free,*
> *No more our ancient sire land*
> *Shall shelter the despot or the slave.*
> *Tonight we man the gap of danger*
> *In Erin's cause, come woe or weal*
> *'Mid cannons' roar and rifles peal,*
> *We'll chant a soldier's song.*

The long version of the anthem was an expression of Gaelic fanaticism, its venom directed at England. The sentiment voiced was not shared by the majority of Irish people, certainly not those of us who loved soccer, or arguably the more thoughtful decent men and women who loved Gaelic games. It was, still is, a simplistic parody of our national identity and our relationship with our nearest neighbour.

When I was playing for Ireland in the sixties, the Ban was still in place. Rule 27 of the GAA handbook stated that 'Any member of the Association who plays or encourages in any way rugby, football, hockey or any imported game which is calculated to injuriously affect our national pastime is suspended from the Association.' After much bitter argument, that rule was repealed in 1971. Those Gaels in favour of retaining the Ban could cite Michael Collins, the great national hero who voted against its removal when the issue arose for the London branch of the GAA in 1912.

As a youngster living opposite Tolka Park, I often recognized great Dublin footballers and hurlers furtively watching big soccer matches. Years later, one of the most iconic Gaels, the great Kerry footballer Mick O'Connell, told me about going to see his hero, Danny Blanchflower, play for Spurs at White Hart Lane, wearing a cap and muffler over his face, lest anyone should spot him. In short, the Gaels were the tyrants forcing even their greatest men to become subversive. In 1963, the Waterford hurler Tom Cheasty was banned for six months for attending a dance organized by his local soccer club.

When I played for Ireland I was simply doing my job. And generally, results apart, having a good time. And earning fifty pounds, which was more than a week's wages for me. I played twenty-three games for Ireland. We won only two of those matches. John Giles would occasionally tease me with that statistic by suggesting some link between my presence in the side and the low success rate. He might have been right, but there were other factors in the equation. One of those being that our best players, John, Tony Dunne and Noel Cantwell, the latter two playing for Manchester United, didn't turn up for some of our Lost Cause trips to Europe.

For the trip to Ankara, all our main men did show up. The game against Turkey was a European Championship qualifier. We'd beaten them at home before losing away to Spain, who were favoured along with Czechoslovakia to win the group. There was something more than pride – and the match fee – to play for.

When we arrived to train at the stadium the day before the game we got a shock. The pitch was a bumpy bog. None of us had ever seen anything like it. It was our trainer, Billy Lord, who first alerted us to the state of it. The other unwelcome surprise was the presence of 15,000 frenzied Turks, who turned up to watch us train. They were passionate, but not in a good way. The vibes were bad, the intention to intimidate us. Giles and Cantwell were not easily intimidated. But the vicious sounds and angry gestures emanating from the terraces as we trained certainly gave us something to think about. What would this kip be like when the serious business got under way the following day?

After training, Cantwell was in great form. A large character in every way, he laughed at the prospect of facing up to 'these mad bastards' the next day. His amused resilience raised our spirits. 'Fuck them, we'll be all right. But that fucking noise makes the Dalymount Roar seem like a whisper,' he joked. John Giles was equally reassuring. Nothing fazed him. Like the notoriously attritional Leeds team he played for – in many ways led – John realized the kind of challenge the next day seemed certain to pose. The pitch, a bog full of sand-filled holes, was his main concern. It was unplayable.

Thirty-one thousand passionate Turks packed the stadium the following day. We lost 2–1. By and large we gave as good as we got. Giles and Cantwell led the resistance to opponents inspired by the fervour of their supporters. Turkey scored after thirty-five minutes, and sealed victory with another score twelve minutes from the end. Cantwell, brave to the very end, scored a consolation goal in the ninetieth minute. Our chances of qualification for the Euro Finals evaporated with this defeat. But, as was always the case in my experience, the Irish team gave all we had.

Victory did not assuage the hostility of our hosts. An angry mob gathered as we made our way to the team coach after the game. They bellowed threateningly and spat at us as we wove our way through a tunnel of heaving flesh towards the bus. I happened to be last in line. I'd almost made it to safety when I felt a boot across the back of my legs. It was a scary moment, causing us to wonder what might have happened if we'd won.

Although we lost that game it was an honourable defeat. But our leaders were unhappy. The boys in blazers had high standards. Turkey was barely on the international football map. To lose in Ankara was disappointing. The post-match atmosphere was frosty. The murmured commiserations rang hollow. Backs were turned on us in the hotel lobby and dining room. Backs remained unslapped.

Any rational analysis of Ireland's loss to Turkey in this important match would have to take into account team selection. In 1967 the Big Five were still calling the shots. They liked to include at least one League of Ireland star in every Irish team. This boosted the domestic game. The inclusion of a local hero would sometimes be the result of lobbying by other Blazers seeking to wield some influence – help a neighbour's son – a virtuous act in Irish culture.

Thus the team that lined out to face Turkey contained two League of Ireland players, Al Finucane and Frank O'Neill. Both were outstanding players in the part-time professional game. But the step up to international football was too big an ask, especially in the late sixties when the League of Ireland was beginning to lose the lustre of earlier decades. Charlie Gallagher, a squad player with Glasgow Celtic, also played in the game, another questionable selection. And then there was me!

So, Giles, Cantwell, Charlie Hurley, Mick Meagan, Mick McGrath and Alan Kelly, all top players, were obliged to shoulder an unwanted, unnecessary burden. The power vested in the Big Five was a peculiar form of Irish madness. A destructive compound of misguided faith in League of Ireland players and cronyism that hurt the national team.

If I had any serious reservation when John Giles asked me to participate in his Shamrock Rovers project, it concerned the fools and blackguards who ran the game in Ireland. The term 'Blazers', used to disparage the men from Merrion Square, is too vague to properly describe the gents concerned. To flesh out the portrait, imagine the big man in the small Irish town, the local accountant, hotelier, estate agent. Kicking in a few bob for his local soccer club, taking a seat on the board, eventually becoming chairman or, when another tranche of cash was needed, President for Life. His profile raised, his business prospered and he was respected for 'giving something back' to his community. Next stop, Merrion Square.

For the little man in the big city – Dublin, Cork or Galway – the junior football leagues offered opportunity for advancement. Every affiliated league was entitled to representation at the Football Association of Ireland's parliament in Merrion Square. Volunteerism is a hugely important feature of all Irish sports. Ironically, while the genuine volunteers are catering for players' needs, putting in the hours on pitches and in gyms, winter and summer, there is among them a parasitic breed eyeing a bigger prize. Power.

A seat on the board of the management committee. An ear for every complaint. An eye for the main chance. And before long our hero is chosen to represent 'the grass roots' of 'this great game of ours' in Merrion Square.

Many of the city men worked for the state in one form or another. The semi-state man had time on his hands. Some of the most appalling blazered creatures we encountered worked for the government (local or national) and emerged from 'the grass roots' of the game. Big men in small towns, small men in big cities, they ran our show.

To a man, they knew nothing about football. Power and patronage was their game. The Blazers grabbed tickets for international games to be distributed among their friends. They formed alliances with each other as they climbed the greasy pole in Merrion Square. Like politics everywhere, theirs was a dirty business. When not being slapped, backs were stabbed.

In this sordid world, becoming a member of the Big Five was one of the most coveted prizes. Everyone with any interest in football had an opinion about who should be in the team. The Big Five were in the enviable position of actually making the call. For the small-town Titan, this was a wet dream. Ditto for the big-city functionary or the man who'd made his money in scrap metal. In the golf club, Rotary Club, local shop or bar, our hero would lend an ear to colleague and neighbour on the pressing football matter of the hour: who should get to wear that coveted green shirt?

Being one of the Big Five conferred another privilege: foreign travel. They loved their trips. We never saw them for home games at Daly-mount Park apart from a fleeting glimpse, perhaps, in the dressing room before the game, designed to boost our morale. It was on the road that our rulers were up close and visible. Rampaging through duty-free, running in packs through hotel lobbies, making speeches at the post-game banquet, proposing toasts to enduring friendship between 'our two great countries that have so much in common'.

Ankara put paid to Ireland's chances of qualifying for the 1968 European Championships. Our final game in the group stages was against Czechoslovakia in Prague. Most of our top players abandoned ship for this engagement on a freezing November day. No Giles, Cantwell or Tony Dunne. No manager. Johnny Carey had surrendered. Charlie Hurley was player/manager for a game the Czechs only had to draw to qualify for the finals. Czechoslovakia were a force in the game in 1967. Captained by their great centre-half Ján Popluhár, they had got the better of Spain, the other seeded nation in our group.

The stadium was empty for what was regarded as the formality of a Czech victory. The pitch was icy, barely playable. We might have been the worst Irish team ever. In midfield I was alongside Eamonn Rogers, Jimmy Conway and Oliver Conmy, then starring with Peterborough. Ray Treacy joined Turlough O'Connor up front. O'Connor was the designated League of Ireland player on this occasion.

Alan Kelly played in goal behind a decent back-four: Joe Kinnear, Charlie Hurley, John Dempsey and Mick Meagan, a wing-half converted to left-back for the day. When the Czechs took the lead, our goose seemed cooked. Needing only a draw, they stopped pushing forward. Given more time and space, we began to play with that degree of fortitude which, however desperate things appeared to be, was a given for Irish teams. Treacy equalized. Turlough O'Connor got the winner. Spain qualified for the Euro Finals.

Back at the Prague Hilton, the Blazers were euphoric. Backs were slapped, hands shaken. Big Charlie held court in the lobby explaining to the eager members of the Fourth Estate how he'd done it. Joe Kinnear and yours truly hit the town. Champagne cocktails was our tipple for a delightful evening.

Euphoria was not confined to the Irish camp. The Prague Spring was beginning to blossom. Optimism was tangible in this beautiful city that night. In clubs, bars and restaurants people laughed, glasses tinkled, strangers chatted to each other – and to two Irish drunks they encountered. There was a spring in the Prague step – and in ours. We nearly missed the plane the following morning.

35. Blazers in Dreamland

It was five years before Ireland won another game. Victory over the mighty Czechs gave the Blazers notions. On the journey home some crazed consensus seemed to form: commitment to the shirt (the green one) was what mattered. Did Ireland really need Giles, Cantwell and Dunne, who turned up for duty when it suited them? Maybe not.

Elated by the stroke of good fortune that enabled them to take their place at the Euro Finals, the Spanish Federation sent a message of congratulations to the FAI and twenty-four cases of good Rioja for the heroes of Prague. Our next international match was a friendly against Poland in Dublin the following May. Before the game, each Prague hero was presented with a bottle of Rioja. Like the beef at Reading, the rest of the Spanish wine remains unaccounted for.

The FAI had a special relationship with their Polish counterparts. Ireland played Poland six times between 1964 and 1970. All the games were friendlies. The remarkable frequency of our trips to Poland did not go unnoticed in the soccer community. In their post-match speeches, the Blazers invariably referred to the special relationship between the two countries. Both Catholic, both oppressed by larger neighbours. There was, it was claimed, a special bond between our peoples.

The players, though, weren't mad about trips to Poland. Life was bleak behind the Iron Curtain. The food was lousy; the people were sullen. The misery of a Communist existence was tangible. Poles went about their work as if they were in some kind of living nightmare. Which, of course, they were. The optimism of Prague was notably absent. A whiff of desperation was always in the air.

On our after-dinner strolls around town, young people would approach us looking for denim jeans or English cigarettes. In the hotel, young women stalked the bars and lobby, seeking dollars from the visitors from the West. A currency black-market flourished. Every hotel housed a black marketeer offering multiples of the local currency, the zloty, for sterling or dollars. Players and Blazers took advantage of this get-rich-quick arrangement. This grubby trading was like a scene from a bad movie. The whispered bartering in quiet corners might have been a metaphor for life under Communist tyranny. Anxious glances over shoulders, fear and greed the cocktail of the moment.

For some of the Blazers, this was Dreamland. The man with the hundred-dollar bill was king. Some shopped for the best local goods. Others bought local girls. One arsehole from rural Ireland boasted of buying a young woman, a student, he claimed, for 200 Marlboro cigarettes. Good man, Paddy.

But some Blazers were decent men, notably Sam Prole, Jim Younger, the Big Fiver whom I believed favoured me, and the Association's general secretary Joe Wickham, a lovely man, who signed our match-fee cheques. But Poland, with its opportunities for extra-curricular behaviour, brought out the worst in some of the other 'mentors'. Mentors! Yes, that's how the Blazers would sometimes be described in newspaper accounts of FAI affairs.

In October 1968 we played Poland in Chorzów. We lost 1–0. In the dressing room after the game, we learned that Joe Wickham had had a heart attack at half-time. The stunned silence was broken after a couple of minutes when one of the lads enquired if Joe had 'signed the message', as the match-fee cheque was known. He had.

In the subdued atmosphere at our hotel afterwards, our mentors began to squabble among themselves. The next morning we discovered the cause of the row. Mr Wickham was in intensive care at Katowice hospital. Some members of the FAI delegation would have to stay behind to monitor the situation. The dispute among the Blazers was about which of them would remain in Katowice to attend to Joe Wickham's tragic situation. None of them wanted to go home. After bitter recriminations, the matter was settled. Joe Wickham died three days later.

In May 1969, the Big Five made headlines when they decided to drop John Giles, not just from the Irish team but from the sixteen-man squad to play Denmark in a qualifying game for the 1970 World Cup Finals. The match in Copenhagen would, in effect, be our second qualifier. The home game against the Danes the previous December was abandoned five minutes into the second half because of fog. We were drawing 1–1 at the time. Giles had scored our goal from the penalty spot.

Czechoslovakia beat us 2–1 in Dalymount Park on 4 May. In a group with Hungary, Denmark and ourselves, the Czechs were clear favourites. But second place was a reasonable possibility. The away game against Denmark was critical to our hopes.

Leaving John out of the team was crazy. Omitting our greatest player from the squad reeked of malice. Leeds United had just won the English First Division, losing only two of forty-two games. Don Revie's champions had broken the League record for points won in a season. In a team full of magnificent footballers, John Giles and his midfield partner Billy Bremner were the driving forces. In May 1969, the names Giles and Bremner would feature in any list of Europe's great players.

Like everyone else, I was shocked by John's omission. I was to partner his replacement, Billy Newman, in midfield. Billy played for Shelbourne in the League of Ireland. When the team was announced I briefly thought of refusing to play. Some protest was surely necessary in the face of this madness. I did nothing. Maybe I needed the fifty-pound match fee.

When journalists apprised Don Revie of the Big Five decision, he smiled in disbelief. 'This Billy Newman must be some player. Perhaps I should sign him.' Billy was a smashing lad. In Copenhagen he was embarrassed to the point where, as he wryly put it, 'I am getting two caps tonight: my first and my last.' He was right. We lost 2–0. Billy was subbed after fifty-five minutes.

When John and I met that summer we agreed to confront the FAI about the Big Five. There was speculation about a new manager. Mick Meagan's name was in the frame. Mick was a popular and respected colleague who had just ended his career in England. John and I concluded that if Mick was to have any chance of succeeding in the job he would have to have the power to select the squad and pick the team.

Mick was appointed, but on the old terms: the Big Five were part of the deal. His first match in charge was a friendly against Scotland in Dublin. John called a meeting of the senior players, Tony Dunne, Alan Kelly, with Frank O'Neill representing the League of Ireland players. Our proposition was simple: if we didn't dump the Big Five we were going nowhere. We had to stick together and present the Blazers with an ultimatum. If they refused to reform the system, we would refuse to play.

I drafted the manifesto with a simple demand: the manager is in complete charge of selecting the squad and the team. But I didn't have the clout in the dressing room to lead a rebellion. 'Here comes trouble,'

Shay Brennan would sometimes say, smirking, when I appeared. Fellow gamblers and card players, we were good pals, but Shay was allergic to aggro or anything else that distracted him from the *Sporting Life* and the card school at the back of the bus.

Even though he was respected, John struggled to rouse the other players. By nature, footballers were passive when it came to standing up for themselves. Sure, they despised the Blazers and thought the Big Five were a joke, but going on strike, refusing to play for Ireland, was a big call, too big for some. (When Liam Tuohy succeeded Mick Meagan as Irish team manager eighteen months later he impressed the players by making his position on the FAI crystal clear: 'I fucking hate them.')

John pushed the right buttons and won a mandate to put our demands to the Association. At the subsequent meeting with an FAI delegation led by Sam Prole, the masters played for time. This was a problem for us. We were in Dublin for just a couple of days. And they knew it. Politicking was their game. In twenty-four hours we'd be out of town, things would settle down, the status quo would prevail. They asked for time to consider the issues involved. We gave them two weeks.

The next meeting would be in Manchester. John was on duty for Leeds. I went to Manchester with Alan Kelly, Tony Dunne and Frank O'Neill. Sam Prole proposed a compromise: the selection committee, the Big Five, would stay in place. They would pick the sixteen-man squad from which Mick Meagan could select his team. A week later, after talking to John and a few other players, we accepted the deal. Mick Meagan was happy.

The Blazers were also happy. Retaining the selection committee meant the coveted trips abroad would continue. The following summer we embarked on a road trip to Poland and West Germany. The night before the game in Poznań we were sitting in the hotel lobby after dinner when we spotted a fat little Blazer with a young Polish girl. They weren't discussing the local culture. They were negotiating. As they headed for the lift, it was clear a deal had been struck. I was with Joe Kinnear and John. This Blazer was one of the worst of his type, a big-shot in a small Irish town who thought players should know their place, should be proud to wear the green shirt. He was a great man for the duty-free, the black-market zlotys and young girls desperate for a few quid.

'Come on, lads, let's fuck him up,' I suggested to Joe and John. They were up for it. We got his room number. I rang the room and, in broken English, asked to speak to my girlfriend. He panicked and put the girl on the line. 'Whatever he's giving you, we'll pay you more, and you won't have to do anything,' I told her. We arranged to meet her at the lift on the fifth floor, along the corridor from his room.

His door opened and the girl emerged carrying her 'wages': a bottle of duty-free Scotch and 200 Marlboro. As she hastened towards us, your man appeared naked except for his open shirt. As he began to chase the girl down the corridor, looking to retrieve his swag, the little bastard spotted us laughing at him. We gave the girl fifty dollars and saw her safely into the night.

In the *Irish Times*, that man would be described as one of Irish football's leading 'mentors'. We thought he was a little shit. But you couldn't put that in the paper of record. We lost 2–1 to Poland the next day.

We travelled by train from Poland to Berlin for the game against West Germany. About an hour into the journey, the train stopped in the middle of nowhere. There was some kind of cock-up. Some carriages were removed, including the one we were sitting in. The Irish party waited trackside while new arrangements were put in place. Finally we were ushered back on board. The mentors and the gentlemen of the press were seated in a comfortable carriage. We were shunted into the wagon containing passengers' luggage.

And that was where we stayed for the lengthy journey to Berlin. Sitting on suitcases or on the floor, we fell about the place, like drunks at closing time. It was a nightmare journey for players due to face Franz Beckenbauer and his powerful West German team two days later. The Blazers had taken humiliation to a new level.

As the train rumbled on through the black East German night, we longed for that hellish journey to end. We were tired and, as always after a couple of days behind the Iron Curtain, hungry. West Berlin was a startling blaze of light and colour when glimpsed from the gloom of the eastern half of the divided city. You didn't have to be a political scientist to reflect on the obscenity of Soviet Communism as you crossed the border from prison camp to Liberty Land.

It was around nine thirty when we checked into our plush Berlin hotel. As if knowing the ordeal we had endured in Poland, the West Germans laid on a grand buffet with every imaginable culinary delight. If 'welcome to freedom' was the message, it was received loud and clear.

We enjoyed our food. We enjoyed with equal relish the uncouth face-filling of our mentors, who attacked the buffet as if engaged in an eat-as-much-as-you-can competition. The journalists, we observed, weren't much better. Plates piled high with all kinds of food, Blazers and hacks moved carefully from buffet counter to table. And back. And back again.

Three days was usually the maximum amount of time we spent in their company. On this two-game trip, we were on our fifth day. The more we saw, the less we liked our mentors. Some of them got it and kept out of the way, shopping, drinking, seeing the sights. Some attempted manly banter with the troops. Bart Cummings was in the manly banter camp. When he'd finished stuffing his face with prawns, he stopped by our table. He was a scrap-metal dealer. A hearty, hail-fellow-well-met type of guy. A flashy dresser, blue mohair suits, brown shoes, loud ties. He was the main man at St Patrick's Athletic. Funder-in-chief, he wasn't shy to let you know.

Anyway, Bart had a story to tell us. He had bought the Berlin Wall. Not the real Berlin Wall we'd crossed that night, but the prop used in the film *The Spy Who Came In From the Cold*. The film, starring Richard Burton, had been shot in Dublin. When the Cold War thriller was in the can he had bought the wall for scrap from the producers. 'Wow!' we humoured him. 'Well done, Bart.'

'I was wondering,' he mused, 'if the local media would be interested in my story.'

Ray Treacy encouraged him on his ego trip. 'Definitely, Bart.' Ray spotted an opportunity for some badly needed fun.

'The German journalists at training tomorrow would love that story,' John Giles chipped in.

'Do you think so?' he asked, eyes alight at the thought of some self-aggrandizement.

'Yes,' we chorused. 'They'll lap it up.'

Sure enough, Bart gave his fellow mentors the slip the next morning. While they went shopping, Bart came to training at Berlin's Olympic Stadium. We watched him stalking the German hacks. We noted their shrugging shoulders, observed the so-what look on those Teutonic faces. And sniggered as Bart proceeded to make a fool of himself. 'How'd it go, Bart?' Joe Kinnear enquired later.

'Great, they want me to go on television later,' he further gilded the lily.

John Giles was a merciless piss-taker. The persona he presented in public – cool, tough and, if you were a journalist who'd criticized Leeds United, intimidating – was a disguise. He loved a sing-song, hated affectation of any kind. He was the ring-leader in a plot we now hatched to torment Bart Cummings. John put a call in to Bart's hotel room.

'Mr Bummings,' John began in German English, 'Mr Fart Bummings?'

'No,' Bart replied, 'it's Cummings, Bart Cummings.'

'You are ze man who bought ze Berlin Wall, no?'

'Yes, I bought the Berlin Wall.'

'You say you bought ze Berlin Wall, but I saw it zis morning. It's still here. I'm from German television, we'd like to interview you, Fart.'

'It's Bart. B-A-R-T,' he roared.

Bart then launched into his story about Richard Burton, whom he now claimed to have met at the film, and suggested a fee of £500 for the interview. 'Hold on a minute, Fart. I'll have to ask my boss.'

We were now helpless with laughter, rolling around John's bedroom, knowing we had the greedy bastard on the hook. 'We can only offer a hundred pounds,' John told him curtly.

'OK, that's good,' Bart responded. He wasn't going to haggle over money once his opening gambit was knocked back.

The trick now was to arrange the interview at a time of maximum inconvenience to our prey. On the night before an international match the Blazers always attended a dinner, as guests of the host Association. 'We can send a film crew at nine thirty this evening. Does zat suit?'

There was a long pause before Bart chose his precious TV interview over the usually sumptuous dinner.

At nine thirty, Bart is pacing the hotel lobby. His buddies have gone to dinner. A group of players, all in on the prank, stroll over to him. 'What's the story, Bart?' Ray Treacy enquires.

'I'm waiting for German television,' he crows.

Herr Giles is upstairs putting a call in to Reception. 'Would Mr Fart Bummings please come to Reception?' Off he scuttles. The interview is cancelled. Rearranged for tomorrow morning. No dinner, no TV interview. Big loss of face. As we head for the lift to get an early night before the game, a disconsolate Bart trudges to the bar for a stiff drink.

The dénouement to Bart's Berlin story still warmed the cockles of our hearts when John and I recalled it recently. Tormenting Bart offered a measure of revenge for our humiliation on the train journey from Poland. We kept the torment simmering for two more days. Another interview was arranged for the morning of our departure after the match, which we lost 2–1.

John was back on the phone to Reception one last time. The German TV crew were running late. But, not to worry, they'd booked the VIP lounge at the airport to conduct the interview. On the *Autobahn* to Berlin's Tegel airport, Bart urged the coach driver to put his foot down. Anxiety was getting the better of this TV star in waiting.

At the terminal he was first off the bus. First in the queue at Passport Control and first on the escalator steps, which he took two at a time as he hastened to the VIP lounge. Joe Kinnear and I kept close tabs on Bart, which wasn't easy, for he was moving at speed. Normally the king of duty-free, Bart gave his favourite airport destination a miss on this occasion.

Now another problem loomed: the Germans couldn't speak English. 'Where's the VIP lounge?' he asked bemused passers-by. Their puzzled looks caused him to become more agitated. 'VIP lounge?' His voice rose as if talking louder would better help the Germans comprehend. Tracking him discreetly, Joe and I almost began to feel sorry for him. But that notion soon passed.

Then Bart found what he was looking for. An attractive blonde lady guarded the entrance to the VIP lounge. Bart told her that German television was waiting for him inside. Shaking her head, she told him that there must be some mistake. There was no TV crew.

Bart visibly wilted. Something, he didn't know what, had gone wrong. On the bus taking us from terminal to plane, a deadpan John Giles enquired how the TV interview had gone. Bart began a long explanation containing various theories about how and why German TV had screwed up and missed a great story. 'These Germans have a reputation for efficiency,' he concluded. 'I'm not so sure they deserve it.'

36.   Treachery

Florence, 8 December 1970: Mick Meagan's tenth game in charge. Ten games played, zero victories. Player-power in disrepute. The media are trigger-happy. The Big Five are itching to make a comeback. Our big players, Giles, Tony Dunne, Steve Heighway, are missing. Shay Brennan captains the side. Italy, the reigning European champions, cruise to a 3–0 victory. Our scheduled flight home is cancelled due to fog at Florence airport. We are diverted to Pisa for an early flight the following morning.

On the way to Pisa airport Shay, Don Givens, Terry Conroy and I are involved in a heavy card school that had begun the previous night. Shay is losing, his match fee on the line. The Blazers want to detour to see the Leaning Tower of Pisa. As the bus pulls up alongside the great tourist attraction I pause, deck of cards in hand, to take a peek. Shay's back is to the tower: 'Look, Shay,' I urge.

'Deal,' he drily instructs.

Steve Heighway made his debut for Ireland a few months before our trip to Florence. His first game was a friendly against Poland in Dalymount Park. It didn't take him long to figure out how playing for Ireland worked for top players. Travelling to Italy in the middle of winter for a European Championship game you were unlikely to win was a no-no. He had just broken into the Liverpool side Bill Shankly was rebuilding to challenge Leeds and Arsenal, the dominant clubs in England.

Chasing a lost cause against the European champions in Florence would have been as discouraged by Shankly as by Don Revie or Matt Busby, who had returned to manage Manchester United that very month after the club had sacked his successor, Wilf McGuinness. Hence no Heighway, Giles or Tony Dunne for this daunting trip to Italy.

Mick Meagan was in trouble. In place of the missing stars he was forced to field a team containing two League of Ireland players against Italy: Al Finucane from Limerick and Paddy Dunning, a part-timer from Shelbourne. When I got injured just before half-time, my replacement was another part-timer, Mick Lawlor of Shamrock Rovers. No wonder Mick was in trouble. In fact, he was doomed.

Steve Heighway's emergence in English football was regarded as a landmark. He was twenty-three when he turned pro. And he was a university graduate. The back-page headlines implied that some kind of miracle had occurred. 'Man with Degree Plays Professional Football' the story ran, like one of those *National Enquirer* splashes informing us that Elvis is alive and well and living on the moon.

He was an outstanding player: a swift left-winger, a great crosser of the ball and a regular goal-scorer too. When Steve declared for Ireland it was a rare good news story. Within weeks of signing for Liverpool, he won his first Irish cap. His arrival in Dublin caused great excitement. The Irish custom of fawning over distinguished visitors was much in evidence as the media circled Steve at our first training session. Deference was the order of the day. Here at last was a footballer the scribes could relate to, an educated chap who, like themselves, could string a few words together.

While welcoming Steve as a colleague who would significantly improve the team, I was sceptical about the idea that a genius had arrived in the camp. I'd met too many dopey university graduates at Hampstead suppers and in *Time Out*'s office to get carried away. In fact, Steve turned out to be a pleasant enough guy, a touch mannered in an English kind of way, not given to strong expressions of emotion. That his debut game was in Dublin was a mixed blessing. The good news was that he wouldn't be shocked by encountering the 'Blazers on Tour'; the bad, that he would be billeted with the rest of us in the Four Courts Hotel on Ormond Quay.

The Four Courts was cheap and not at all cheerful. The rooms were furnished with two narrow single beds and a washbasin. The bathroom was down the corridor, close to the top of the main staircase. The food was awful, served by pleasant staff whose body language hinted at a desire to offer something nicer than was on your plate. The bump you might hear in the middle of the night was a drunk falling down in the corridor. The noise of squabbling couples might be from the street outside, or the room across the landing. Think the motel in Alfred Hitchcock's *Psycho* and take away the shower scene. The Four Courts was alive with possibilities, none of them appealing.

Shay Brennan was Mick Meagan's choice to share a room with Steve

Heighway. Except for being top players with illustrious clubs, they had little in common. But with his gently humorous disposition Shay was deemed most likely to make our new team-mate feel at ease in the less than salubrious surroundings.

At breakfast next morning, Shay emerged from behind the *Sporting Life* to respond to those asking what the new man was like with a telling observation: 'He's not one of us.' Shay laughed. 'He doesn't piss in the sink.'

After almost two years in charge, Ireland's first manager with the power to pick the team was under pressure when we arrived in Dublin for three back-to-back games in May 1971. The players still believed in Mick. We respected him and understood the difficult circumstances he worked under. The Big Five still picked the sixteen-man squad. Our best players were frequently unavailable. We were in a tough group with Italy, Hungary and Austria. But the natives in Merrion Square were restless, and elements in the media were beginning to question Mick's integrity.

Between two European Championship matches against Italy and Austria we were due to face an England XI in a game to mark the FAI Golden Jubilee. After a very good Italian side beat us 2–1 in the opening fixture at Lansdowne Road, the sniping started in earnest. An anonymous former member of the Big Five told a journalist: 'I don't agree with Mr Meagan's appointment as manager, and I'm sick of all the favourable comments I read about him.'

Sam Prole's son Roy, an FAI Council member, also put the boot in, accusing Mick of operating 'the old pals' act' with his team selection. 'Who picks the team?' Prole wondered, implying that senior players like Giles and Alan Kelly were wielding undue influence. The most dangerous malcontent was John Farrell, a rising star in Merrion Square, who accused the manager of selecting 'unfit players'. 'The Pig' Farrell, as he was unaffectionately known, told the press, 'When I asked Mr Meagan if Eamonn Rogers was fit on Monday night [against Italy], the manager replied, "He is 99 per cent fit."'

One narrow defeat by the reigning European champions had turned the atmosphere poisonous. Treachery was abroad. As one of the more respected journalists, Seamus Devlin, wrote in the *Irish Times*, 'The little men obviously want their share of the limelight, even if it does mean reverting to the outdated system of selection by the self-selected

Big Five and a possible breach in relations between players and head-quarters.'

'The Pig' Farrell was a serving member of the Big Five. A product of the Leinster Junior Leagues, he worked for Dublin Corporation. He claimed to represent the game's grass roots. In the not-too-distant future Pig would assume the office of FAI president. Blackguarding Mick Meagan was part of his campaign.

After the various full-frontal attacks on his competence and integrity, Mick tendered his resignation. He was badly hurt. His players were deeply offended on his behalf. In any fight between Mick Meagan and the Pig we were going to get involved. John Giles played against Italy but he was returning to Leeds to prepare for their Inter-Cities Fairs Cup Final game against Juventus. Before he left we held a team meeting, which decided to back Mick Meagan and resist any restoration of power to the Big Five.

We contacted the FAI to arrange a meeting after the game against the England XI. The Football Association sent a Mickey Mouse team to Dublin, causing great offence to Pig and Co. The players were conscious that the best service we could render to Mick was to win a couple of games, but the absence of Giles for our two remaining matches didn't help. The melodramatic politicking that was sapping our energy was another negative. Our dull 1–1 draw with England charmed nobody.

Next day I joined Tony Dunne and Alan Kelly for the showdown in Merrion Square. The case we made was blunt. While accepting that, like any other manager, Mick Meagan must be judged by results – and hired or fired accordingly – there could be no return to the bad old days of Big Five team selection. Short of a public commitment to the latter we would refuse to play the following Sunday's Championship game against Austria.

Although we made our argument forcefully, we knew in our hearts that there was no way we would refuse to play. As ever, Sam Prole across the table was emollient. We were assured that the Big Five were not going to be picking teams in the future. Prole went on to express his personal view that the selection committee should be scrapped altogether. As for Mick, well, he'd have to be judged by results. We couldn't and didn't argue when Sam Prole ended the meeting by reminding us that the best way to get what we wanted would be to beat Austria on Sunday.

The game was played at Dalymount Park. It was a rare hot Dublin day. No breeze. No air. No Giles. I was drained of all emotion. My legs were rubber. My head in a jam jar. It was time to put up or shut up. At half-time Austria led 4–0. I was having a nightmare. Waves of contempt and hostility burst onto the pitch from the terraces. Crossing the touchline to retrieve the ball for a throw-in I saw the contorted face of an angry fan. 'Go back to England, you fucking chancer,' he screamed. I asked Mick to take me off at half-time. He was reluctant to do it, but I insisted. That was my last game for Ireland. Sadly, it was Mick's last game as well.

Writing in the *Irish Times* the following morning, football correspondent Peter Byrne reflected the view of the more reactionary occupants of Merrion Square: 'Pathetic, pedestrian, puerile,' Byrne thundered. 'If we must find out the price of international success the hard way, far better to do it with a team built around home-based players.'

That rather surreal notion was quickly tested and found wanting. Liam Tuohy was appointed to replace Mick Meagan. For his first game in charge, Tuohy fielded a team with ten League of Ireland players in it. Away to Austria, Ireland lost 6–0. Tuohy lasted two largely barren years before being sacked. The Big Five were stood down.

Another reform we'd argued for was an end to Sunday matches. The FAI rejected this on the grounds that Sunday was the big sports day in Ireland. Maybe, we reasoned, but as English League games were played on Saturday, the deal as it stood meant our players turning out twice in twenty-four hours. Each game was preceded by an overnight trip, often via the Holyhead–Dublin ferry. There was another vital consideration: it would be much easier to obtain the release of key players from their clubs if we harmonized our fixtures with those of the English national team who played theirs on Wednesdays. We got no joy.

John Giles was appointed player/coach in 1973. He picked me in the squad for his first game in charge against our old friends Poland. Deep and lasting bonds had been forged with the Polish people throughout the previous decade. The Polish link was cherished in Merrion Square. Benny Fenton refused to release me for this Sunday fixture.

John's next assignment was a three-game tour of South America in the summer of '74. Brazil, Uruguay and Chile were the hosts. I was one of eighteen players selected. As soon as the tour was announced a question arose about the game against Chile, which was to be played in the National Stadium in Santiago.

The previous September, Salvador Allende's democratically elected socialist government had been overthrown in a US-backed *coup d'état*. A military dictatorship led by Augusto Pinochet now ruled. Chile was a *cause célèbre* for the left across the globe. Pinochet's counter-revolution was murderous. Death squads targeted leftists, democrats and trade-union activists. The coup was a crime against the Chilean people and their democratic institutions. An example, also, of US power at its most malevolent. Much of the bloody drama was played out in the National Stadium. Approximately 40,000 to 50,000 people were detained by Pinochet's forces in the stadium. Many were tortured, some murdered.

I was contacted by a number of journalists who wanted to know if I was prepared to comply with demands that Ireland boycott Chile and, in particular, refuse to play in the National Stadium, where so much blood had been spilled. As the Irish football team would be the first international sports group to visit Pinochet's Chile, the symbolism was important.

I decided to reflect on the situation before making any decision. I hadn't been shy after Bloody Sunday, or in voicing my anti-apartheid views. And I'd recently attended a public meeting calling for the Old Bailey bombers to be repatriated to Northern Ireland to serve their sentences. Journalists Eamonn McCann and Mary Holland solicited my support for the Price sisters and the other IRA bombers. With some misgivings, for I did not support urban terrorism, I went along to a meeting at the Conway Hall in London's Red Lion Square. For someone with aspirations to coach and manage in English football this probably wasn't the smartest move.

After weighing up the pros and cons, I decided to go to Chile. Yes, for sure the game in Santiago's National Stadium was a real issue. But eight months after Pinochet's coup there was no sign of any sporting or cultural boycott of Chile, despite the opprobrium attaching to the junta. Unlike apartheid, which specifically discriminated against black people in sport, Chile was, in the final analysis, just politics. If we were going to boycott countries whose politics we didn't like, the Soviet Union and our old friends Poland might be near the top of the list.

Pinochet's sponsors, the United States of America, would also feature on many people's list in 1974.

John Giles's regime was more professional than any we had previously experienced as Irish players. When we assembled in London for our pre-tour training camp, there was an almost palpable sense of purpose. The best players would play. The days when politics and other forms of cronyism influenced team affairs were over. Brothel creeping was out. Any partying would have to wait until after the game.

We trained at Crystal Palace in South London. As our team bus pulled up outside the ground on the first morning, we were greeted by a small band of protesters urging us not to go to Chile. I stopped to talk to them, explaining why I felt it was OK to travel, despite the sympathy I felt for their anti-junta views. I accepted the pamphlets they offered, which outlined the reasons why we should boycott the match, and promised to distribute them among my team-mates. I put the pamphlets on the dressing-room table and urged the lads to read them. 'At least you'll know what we're heading into,' I remarked. Nobody seemed very interested.

My occasional public advocacy of this or that political cause was never a problem at the various clubs I played for. There, the lads knew that I was prepared to take on our own bosses when necessary, so when I went public, it wasn't just for show or publicity. At Millwall and Reading, where I'd been the unofficial shop steward, my bona fides were never doubted.

The Irish squad was different. And that morning at Crystal Palace the difference was evident. Those who weren't indifferent to my plea that they acquaint themselves with the situation in Santiago were vocally hostile. I was asked explicitly why I was travelling if I felt that the protesters had a legitimate case to make. There was no angry scene, rather the frosty suspicion that by choosing to distribute the pamphlets *and* take my seat on the flight to South America I was having my cake and eating it. And, of course, getting my name in the papers.

Although John stayed out of it I suspected he shared the view that I was engaged in self-serving posturing, a bit of a media tart, and that was a hanging offence in every dressing room.

After dinner at our hotel that night, John introduced us to Mandrax, the powerful sleeping tablet favoured by Leeds United under Don

Revie. Anyone who wanted a good night's sleep was welcome to swallow a 'happy pill'. 'It will take about forty-five minutes to kick in,' John advised. Fifteen minutes later, those of us who'd indulged were high as kites. Buzzing with euphoria, all inhibitions dissolved, we were ready to fly, baby. With a wicked grin, John presided over the free-flowing banter, much of it directed at 'Eamon, the People's Hero', the joke *du jour*. No offence was intended or taken. Instead, encouraged by John, I popped another Mandie. Aching from laughter, Joe Kinnear and I floated up to bed, where I slept for fifteen hours, missing the following morning's training session. I was still unsteady on my feet for our evening session, which ended with a five-a-side where I tried hard to focus on one of the two balls I thought were in play. Next morning I was, as John now gleefully recounts, first on the plane for our glamorous trip to South America.

I was on the bench for all three matches. Our first game was against a strong Brazilian team, which included their iconic midfielder Rivelino. There was no disgrace in a 2–1 defeat. The game was played in the historic Maracanã Stadium, a vast open-air arena that could accommodate 200,000 people. Sadly the Maracanã was semi-derelict and devoid of atmosphere, with a mere 10,000 spectators present.

After losing 2–0 to Uruguay in Montevideo, we took a scarily turbulent flight across the Andes to Santiago. The city was still tense eight months after the *coup d'état*. A curfew was in place. Evidence of the brutal conflict lay in burned-out buildings, blackened shells once home to people now dead or on the run. Many of those houses were marked with a painted white cross. That was how the junta identified the dwellings of political activists and trade unionists loyal to Allende for the death squads hunting them down. There was a heavy military presence throughout the city.

We trained at the notorious National Stadium on the evening before the game. The walls of the dressing room, where people had been tortured and murdered, were freshly painted, but that could not disguise the scent of fear that lingered in the air. In a sombre moment I experienced a frisson of shame, the guilt of a hollow man. I should have stayed at home.

The match itself took place in extraordinary circumstances. The stadium was packed. It was the first time a free gathering of people had been permitted in a public space since the coup and Allende's subsequent suicide. Hundreds of armed troops, each restraining a hungry-looking German shepherd dog, lined the touchlines. Facing the crowd, eyes empty of emotion.

The night before, some young Irish priests and nuns had visited us in our high-rise hotel. They hadn't come to scold us, but to explain the significance of this moment for the Chilean people, among whose dispossessed they had chosen to live. Dressed in civilian clothes, exuding the sense of pastoral purpose central to the liberation theology they had embraced, these young men and women eschewed the clerical pieties associated with Mother Church. They were radiant, with a disarming gaiety and playfulness about them.

We were invited to join them at a party after the match. When we told them about Ray Treacy's banjo they insisted we bring it along. As our visitors hurried to beat the midnight curfew, Joe and I went upstairs to bed. Sitting on our balcony we watched enthralled as the city's lights dimmed. The clock ticked slowly towards the curfew hour.

Soon after twelve, a saloon car raced along a stretch of motorway leading to the city centre, close to our hotel. We were about seventy-five yards away. Armoured cars crawled idly along the hard shoulders. A volley of shots split the darkness. The car slewed crazily off the road, ending up on its roof, smoke billowing from the smouldering wreck. Guns cocked, the soldiers moved cautiously towards their prey.

After beating Chile 2–1, John's second victory in four games since he'd taken charge of the team, we went to the party with the young people we'd met the night before. The venue was a house in one of Santiago's poorest districts. The furniture was basic, the house lit by candles. Our hosts, Irish, Spanish, Chilean, offered us wine, beer and tapas. They played guitars, Ray starred on the banjo. In a city under siege from Pinochet's murder squads, where death was the price you paid for bad time-keeping, these young people were serene. And fearless. They ordered a mini-bus to ferry us to their house and back before the curfew fell.

Just before we said goodnight, a young Irish nun took a guitar to sing a deeply moving version of the Woody Guthrie song 'Deportees'. It is a lament for twenty-eight migrant Mexican fruit-pickers who died in an air crash while being deported from California. Guthrie was prompted to write it by anger triggered when the *New York Times* report of the tragedy failed to name the fruit-pickers who had died, recording only the identities of the aircraft's crew and the security guard. 'All they will call you will be "deportees".'

I arrived back in Dublin to be met by Sam Smyth, a newshound from the *Sunday World*. I told him the story of our visit to Chile, mentioning in passing the misgivings I'd felt about travelling when showering in the freshly painted torture chamber at the National Stadium. With characteristic bonhomie, Sam milked gullible Eamon dry. He was looking for a tabloid 'splash', not the nuanced anguish of a journeyman. 'We Should Never Have Gone to Chile,' the *Sunday World* screamed a few days later on its front page. It must have been a quiet week for news.

John was summoned to Merrion Square to account for my sin. He knew nothing about the Sam Smyth exclusive. When informed that I had brought football and the Association into disrepute, there was nothing he could say to save my skin. Even if he was inclined to, which I doubt. My mouth was the problem. The punishment, though severe, was unlikely to damage Irish soccer. I was suspended from playing for Ireland. For life. The letter informing me of the ban must have been lost in the post.

37. Welcome Home

We arrived home in the summer of 1977 full of hope. The idea that John Giles, the most respected young football manager in England, had walked away from the Football League to restore Shamrock Rovers to its former glory intrigued even the most hardened cynic. In fact, the project as outlined by John and his backers, the Kilcoyne family, was even more ambitious: the new Rovers would become a force in Europe. We would keep our best young players at home, reversing the decades-old trend for our most gifted footballers to seek fulfilment in England.

Naturally there were sceptics who argued that this was an impossible dream. Ireland was too small. How could we compete with Manchester United, Liverpool and the other great English clubs then plundering the best young Irish players? It was a reasonable question, but not impossible to answer. Up to 85 per cent of the youngsters seduced by promises of English glory failed. Another 10 per cent ended up plying their trade as I had in the lower leagues, a dismal, insecure existence. What appeared to be a great adventure when you were fifteen or sixteen years of age too often ended badly. Why should you have to emigrate to become a professional footballer? Why leave your family and friends, give up all hope of a decent education, and in doing that all hope of a decent job, should your football dream evaporate?

As practised by the powerful English clubs, the trade in promising young Irish footballers was profoundly cynical. They regarded each youngster they signed as a ticket for the lottery. If it was a winner, great. If it was a loser, you tossed the ticket into the bin.

When John initially approached me about the Rovers project, we talked about the youth academy that we both agreed was essential to our plan. Ray Treacy had also agreed to join as player/coach. He and John would look after the First Team, while I ran the academy. Within weeks, we had recruited half a dozen of the best youngsters in the country, Pierce O'Leary, David's very promising younger brother, among them. More importantly, I thought, we had put in place a structure that would ensure, win or lose, that every boy leaving the club would be better equipped for life than he was when he'd signed for Rovers.

After training every morning, our young footballers would go to college to study for a qualification that would enable them to secure employment if football didn't work out. A local college agreed to assess each player and design a course suited to his individual gifts and temperament. We also committed to doing everything we could to find suitable work for any young lad who failed to make it as a footballer. You couldn't avoid the hurt that comes with failure, but limiting the collateral damage was eminently achievable.

We recruited John Wilkes, a respected veteran of the Dublin schoolboy soccer scene, to be our chief scout. John was attached to Cherry Orchard, one of Dublin's great schoolboy soccer clubs. Based in Ballyfermot, the Orchard was a superb example of volunteerism in action. Without a penny of government subsidy, the club catered for hundreds of boys in a part of the city that had been synonymous with crime, deprivation and delinquency when I was growing up.

In the city I grew up in, there had been only a handful of big schoolboy soccer clubs. By 1977 a couple of dozen existed, run by extraordinary people doing incredible work on a voluntary basis. All were affiliated to the Dublin and District Schoolboys League. Establishing strong links with this movement was vital to our project. I approached that task with missionary zeal.

Dublin is a wonderful city. The people are warm and witty, especially with strangers. There's a gaiety about the place that distinguishes it from other capital cities. People are helpful and, compared to their counterparts in London or Paris, they seem content with their lot, optimistic about what any given day might have to offer. On the surface all is tranquil. But below ground the beast begrudgery lurks. A distinctly Irish brew, a mixture of envy and suspicion, it's an ever-present fact of Dublin life, from which, of course, the visitor is insulated.

From the day John Giles arrived back in Dublin begrudgery stalked the Shamrock Rovers dream. By 1977 the Golden Boy of fifties and sixties legend was no more. Not, at least, for a small cohort of Dublin journalists who'd long been on John's case.

John's association with Leeds United and Don Revie was an obvious starting point for anyone seeking to cast aspersions on his character. Revie's Leeds was a mean-spirited team, masters of football's darker arts, especially in their formative years. The football they favoured was negative, win at all costs and quite nasty at times. They had many detractors, including me. Giles was arguably their most influential character. Leeds changed for the better over the years, and Giles was influential in this as well, but the opprobrium of those early 'Dirty Harry' years stuck. Even when they began to blossom in the early seventies their critics did not relent. Brian Clough spoke for many when describing them as 'dirty cheats'.

Quite apart from the football played by his team, Revie was notorious for other reasons. He quit as manager of England to take over the United Arab Emirates' team. No England manager had ever resigned. The decision to step down for a job in football's third (or fourth) world was motivated solely by money. The Football Association learned of his departure when they opened their *Daily Mail* one morning. He sold the exclusive to the *Mail* before sending his letter of resignation. Great scandal ensued. And, unfortunately for us, Revie's shabby behaviour coincided with John's arrival in Dublin. For those inclined to find John guilty by association with the notorious 'Don Readies', the coincidence was too tempting to resist. Both on the move, both on the take.

There were other more tangible bonds between Don Revie and John Giles. For example, it was an open secret that Revie had nominated John to succeed him as Leeds manager when he left to take on the onerous England job. There was also the controversial Giles testimonial match of 1976, twelve months previously. Revie obliged his former player by fielding a full England team for the game at Lansdowne Road. The stadium was packed, the game a 0–0 bore. The crowd booed both teams off the field. Giles/Revie/money: more grist to the begrudgers' mill.

Con Houlihan, a columnist with the *Evening Press*, was the most enthusiastic and persistent advocate of the view that, in coming home to Shamrock Rovers, John, son of Don, was pursuing a hidden agenda. The *Press* was an innovative paper with a large circulation. Houlihan, a Kerryman whose specialist subjects were rugby and Gaelic games, knew nothing about soccer. But he had his followers, for whom he was the fount of wisdom on all matters to do with sport.

He tended not to mix with other sportswriters, preferring to stand among the fans on the terraces and later in the pub. A man of the people. But a man who'd read books and let you know that he had, by dropping literary allusions into his copy, referencing anyone from Virgil to Yeats or Shakespeare. Houlihan occupied a special place in the pantheon of great Irish characters. It was a position he worked hard to maintain. Crucially, his readers trusted him.

When my own small book about life at Millwall was published in 1976, it was generally well received. Houlihan begged to differ. Reviewing *Only a Game?* he alluded to Samuel Johnson's remark about dancing dogs: 'It wasn't so much that the book was good,' he wrote in his review, 'what was amazing was that it was done at all.'

That cheap shot betrayed a vicious snobbery, prejudice to do with class and culture that would have been laughable in England, where you were judged on merit rather than where you came from or which sport you played. But we were back in the small town where the little man was king and big ideas were subject to the begrudgers' favourite put-down: 'Who do you think you are?'

As far as John was concerned, there was a certain antipathy that attached to him, which wasn't easy to explain. He was our greatest ever footballer. In England he was held in the highest regard, not just for his talent but for his unique knowledge of the game. Men like Danny Blanchflower, Alf Ramsey, Bill Nicholson, Matt Busby and Jock Stein admired him greatly. Brian Clough, with whom he had clashed bitterly at Leeds, would later say of John: 'Giles could grab hold of a match, tuck it in his back pocket, and carry it around with him. He didn't need to find space, it was as if space found him.'

Yet in his home town, for Houlihan and others like him, respect, if it existed at all, was heavily qualified. Genuine soccer fans – most of them – appreciated John and were proud of him. But media types – most of them – and others beyond the Pale didn't get him. Or, if they thought they did, they didn't like him. This was the gallery Houlihan played to.

John was cool, cerebral and self-assured. A great player, he was comfortable in his own skin. Outside family and a tight circle of friends, he was reserved. He didn't smoke. He wasn't a bevvy merchant. He didn't like a bet. In the Ireland that Houlihan belonged to, and played for, the greats of sport were expected to be flawed, losers in the game of life. Flawed or humble or lucky – the archetypal Irish sporting great should tick one or other of those caricatures.

The boxers, the Gaelic stars, the jockeys, the footballers who couldn't cope with life's vicissitudes were strangely comforting for some who had once celebrated their wondrous deeds. For hacks like Houlihan, the rags-to-riches-back-to-rags story made for good copy. The fallen giant was easy to embrace. There were many George Bests before George Best.

Giles was circumspect in his dealings with the media. He looked them straight in the eye and kept his answers short and not so sweet. Dumb questions were treated with undisguised disdain. There was no attempt to please, no juicy quote. Sometimes, standing close by, I would wince at the awkward silence that descended on an embarrassed press conference as a consequence of John's indifference to proceedings. He didn't like the hacks and it showed. His was a slightly intimidating presence for guys who needed copy from a man unwilling to play the game. 'Judge us by deeds not words' was the unvoiced message.

I thought John was wrong. He should have been selling the Rovers project, getting the message out to the public, insisting that what we were aiming for was achievable, and countering suspicion that he had some hidden agenda. Why not articulate our belief that an Irish club could be a force in Europe? Why not talk in public as we did in private, about Celtic, who'd won the European Cup just ten years before with a team of local players, all of them born within thirty miles of Glasgow? Or Ajax, who'd emerged from the Netherlands, a country with no football tradition hitherto, to win Europe's greatest prize three years in a row between 1971 and 1973.

John refused to go there. This left a void to be filled by the begrudgers, Houlihan being the most vocal and credible. According to Houlihan, our stated objective, the creation of a powerful Irish club, was bogus. Giles was in Dublin to make money by stealth: to poach the best young Irish players, groom them for a couple of years, then sell them on to the big English clubs. His option to buy a 50 per cent stake in Rovers was the means by which he would trouser a small fortune if things worked out. The Giles–Rovers thing was, Houlihan argued, all about money.

In an attempt to rebut these lies I persuaded John to do an interview with Vincent Browne for *Magill*, the current-affairs magazine. Browne was a Leeds fan. He had a cat named Giles. He was supportive of the Rovers project. Browne was smart, one of a small group of journalists John felt comfortable with. In the *Magill* interview, John outlined his ambitions for Rovers: 'I want to see Irish football standing on its own feet, setting standards to be followed by others, rather than for us to be led. We should not worry about England, but set our own standards at League and international level. We must entice young boys to stay at home and create something worthwhile here.'

The interview closed with John going further than he'd ever done before, in public, about his hope for the future: 'Ultimately, I want to win the European Cup with Shamrock Rovers. This may sound fantastic but if you consider the amount of football talent there is in Ireland it isn't all that outrageous an ambition.'

Houlihan was way off the mark. The truth was starkly different. John, Ray Treacy and I had made career sacrifices to come home. As he would later prove, Ray was a very savvy guy, gifted with a shrewd entrepreneurial gene, which enabled him to create a successful business after the Rovers project collapsed. I also managed to make a living in the media after the dream died. In fact, John was by some distance the biggest loser in the doomed Shamrock Rovers project.

When West Brom grasped that John meant what he said about leaving, they offered him a three-year contract worth £75,000. When he decided to come home he seemed certain to claim one of the coveted jobs with one of England's biggest clubs. He had led West Brom from Second Division mediocrity to seventh (and rising) in the First Division. Ron Atkinson, his successor there, built on John's achievement and was subsequently head-hunted by Manchester United. And, of course, John transformed the Irish team from the rabble he had inherited into contenders for qualification for major championships. At Shamrock Rovers he was on £150 per week. If John was on the make, he wasn't very good at it.

The development of young players being the most critical aspect of our plans, I worked hard to build a good relationship with key figures in the schoolboy leagues. I went to the Dublin and District Schoolboys League AGM to speak to the delegates. The idea was to win the hearts and minds of those working at the game's grassroots. They listened politely as I outlined our plans to usher in a new era in Irish soccer. They were not impressed. The vibe in the room was bad. When it was time for questions the Houlihan theory about making money selling players to England got an airing. As for ushering in a new era, what was wrong with the existing era, I was asked.

One hostile delegate made his point rather bluntly by asking, 'Who the fuck do you think *you* are?' This gent went on to remind me of all the great players produced by the DDSL – Giles himself, Liam Brady, David O'Leary, Frank Stapleton. The message was simple: we don't need you. All the talk about Ajax and Celtic and bringing the European Cup home to Dublin was pie in the sky. We're doing all right. Now, would you like a cup of tea before you go home?

I'd gone to the AGM with one specific request: permission to enter the Shamrock Rovers Youth Team in the DDSL's under-18 competitions, League and Cup, the equivalents of the FA Youth Cup in England. We needed our young players to be competing against the best of their contemporaries as they made the transition from schoolboy to senior football. When I broached the issue, the door was slammed firmly in my face. If Rovers wanted to play in the elite under-18 competitions we'd have to start by entering a team in the under-11 league and earn the right to play against the best. 'But that means we'll have to wait seven or eight years to play in the strongest league,' I stuttered.

Correct.

'That's how long it took the rest of us,' I was curtly reminded.

Goodnight, Eamon.

My encounter with the DDSL delegates was a wake-up call, the first inkling that what we had set out to do was impossible. We'd been naïve to the point of stupidity. Like Mormon missionaries on a suburban estate, we were preaching to the unconvertible. Doors were closed in our faces. Sometimes politely.

Our naïvety was laced with an unhealthy dose of arrogance. My meeting with the DDSL was a perfect example of this. My plea that Rovers should be parachuted into their elite competitions, which we hoped to dominate using players poached from other schoolboy clubs, was outrageous.

Our approach to the League of Ireland was similarly disrespectful. 'We know you're doing your best but it's not good enough. The boys are back in town to show you how things should be done.' Nobody was more responsible than me for the hype around the Shamrock Rovers project. To be fair to John, he didn't favour all the big-time talk about European Cups and other exotic ambitions. He felt that by setting the bar too high publicly we'd be putting too much pressure on our own part-time players. He was right about that.

The team we inherited was mediocre by Rovers' traditional standards.

The addition of John, Ray and myself helped, but not enough, for we struggled badly in the early months. Bohemians, coached by Billy Young, and Dundalk, with Jim McLaughlin in charge, were the leading clubs in the League. Billy and Jim were exceptional coaches; both teams were experienced and well organized. Bohs and Dundalk got on with business as usual. We were more inclined to bitch. And there was plenty to bitch about. Many of the pitches in the League were sub-standard. Bumpy bogs. The showers were cold, the crowds small, though animated by the prospect of putting Rovers in their place.

Our own stadium at Milltown was pristine, the pitch beautifully manicured to enable us to play the passing game John wanted, the stands and terraces clean and newly painted. We drew large crowds of Dubliners eager to see the League of Ireland reborn, touched once more by the magic of the fifties and sixties, when Rovers had ruled the roost. We couldn't deliver. If anything the buzz of large, expectant crowds inspired our visitors to play above themselves while seeming to inhibit our own players. We dropped too many points at home to be competitive in the League. By Christmas it was clear that Bohs and Dundalk would scrap it out for the title.

Another grave problem surfaced in those early months: John and Barton Kilcoyne fell out. Barton was the eldest of the three brothers involved with Rovers. Louis ran the football club day-to-day. He was married to John's sister Pauline. A rising star in Merrion Square, Louis was a pleasant man. In terms of Irish football, he was what might be called a modernizer. He organized an all-Ireland soccer team to play a ground-breaking international match against Brazil at Lansdowne Road in 1973. This was a daring initiative at the height of the Northern troubles. Derek Dougan and John co-captained the side. Lansdowne was packed for an occasion that captured the public imagination. The idea of an all-Ireland team had been around for ever. How wonderful it would be, many thought, if John Giles, Liam Brady and David O'Leary could play alongside George Best and Pat Jennings, uniting two tribes through soccer, the people's game, with an international team good enough to take on the world.

It was Louis who'd persuaded John to come home. But Barton signed the cheques. Barton the builder was funding our dream. He was also building a house for John. But the price kept moving upwards. A bitter row was simmering away from the public gaze. John had cut his ties to the English game. There was no going back. He felt marooned, distracted.

The football results were disappointing and the John/Barton stuff was no help. Houlihan was sniping. The DDSL weren't playing ball. The League of Ireland was ramshackle: bad facilities, small crowds, too many clubs run by men like Fart Bummings. As the months passed it dawned on me that our mission was impossible.

We won the FAI Cup on a wet Sunday in May 1978. With some justification, our opponents, Sligo Rovers, felt they'd been robbed. We were awarded a penalty just before half-time. It was a dodgy decision. The ref, John Carpenter, was one of the League of Ireland's stars. Perma-tanned, decisive, John reffed with undoubted authority. But I thought he got this call wrong. Ray Treacy slotted home. We hung on to win by that solitary goal.

We experienced some euphoria for a couple of hours, but when the clamour died down we were able to put the victory in perspective. It changed nothing. We had fielded a team with five full internationals in it: John, Ray, Johnny Fulham, Alan O'Neill and myself. And yet all we managed was to tough it out, scrambling over the line to claim our medals. I felt sorry for Sligo. They had a couple of great pros in their team: Tony Fagan and Chris Rutherford, experienced big-hearted fighters, the kind of men I'd laboured with for seventeen years in England. The medal I won that day was my first as a pro. I valued it way below the three promotions I'd been part of in England.

Sean Kilfeather, our friend from the *Irish Times*, was a Sligo man. Sligo, a garrison town, had a great soccer tradition. The legendary Dixie Dean came to Sligo to play in the dying days of his magnificent career in 1939. Dixie still holds the English scoring record of sixty goals in one magical season for Everton. When he came to Sligo he scored ten goals in seven games, including five in one match against Waterford. He was at our game against Sligo. They had never won the cup.

Poor Sean was, like all Sligo fans, distraught after their narrow defeat. A few weeks later I gave him my winner's medal.

38.   The Quality of Mercy

A couple of weeks after the Cup Final, Tim O'Connor invited me to work as an analyst on RTÉ's studio panel for the 1978 World Cup Finals in Argentina. I accepted without hesitation. This was a big break, an opportunity to gain some kind of foothold in the media. In the plan B that was forming in my head as an alternative to football, journalism seemed to be the only thing I was qualified to do. I could write. I knew about football. And for the purpose of television I could talk.

Then Sean Kilfeather asked if I would contribute to the *Irish Times'* World Cup coverage. 'Yes' was the answer, but as Argentina was five hours behind, I would be working for RTÉ until the early hours and would find it difficult to file copy to the paper's deadline. And what about the union problem? Sean had figured both problems out. I could make notes, phone a rough account to him, which he would polish for publication. A byline 'as told to Sean Kilfeather' would satisfy the NUJ.

Nobody watched soccer on RTÉ in 1978, save for those in Single Channel Land, a bleak place in rural Ireland where your rabbit-ears aerial couldn't access BBC and ITV. The English channels featured big-name analysts Jimmy Hill, Brian Clough, Malcolm Allison and any number of former players, my old friend Terry Venables among them. Despite the marquee names and lavish production, the English programmes were, as they still are, banal. The analysis was superficial, devoid of rigour. The kind of passion that informed heated debates wherever football lovers gathered was noticeably absent on the English channels. Television across the water seemed content to follow an agenda set by the print media. Asked for an opinion, most British analysts were coy. 'Football is a funny game' was the stock cliché trotted out to avoid any genuine expression of conviction. Then there was the language: the painful torture of English, creating the impression that to play soccer you had to be semi-literate.

Ironically, my love of sport had been immeasurably enriched by the great sports commentators on British television: John Arlott's quietly evocative cricket commentary; Henry Longhurst's eloquent celebration of golf's great moments, which, remarkably, could be rendered by some metaphysical process even more wondrous by silence as Longhurst let the picture tell the story. When Doug Sanders missed a two-and-a-half-foot putt to win the British Open at St Andrews in 1970, Longhurst on the BBC captured and bottled for ever the anguish and empathy of every viewer with magical simplicity: 'There but for the grace of God . . .' Nothing more needed to be said.

Richie Benaud's cricket commentary in print and on television was gloriously fluent, yet unsparing in its rigour. Benaud took to journalism after he retired from international cricket in 1964. He started as a columnist with the *News of the World*, joining the BBC television commentary team later on. Benaud inspired me in much the same way as Danny Blanchflower did. He wrote and spoke with great authority about the game he loved. He was in the best sense a critic, cutting through the back-page hype to the heart of the matter under consideration. No favours for old pals, no punches pulled, Benaud in print and on air was elegant, incisive, clearly believing that his passion for cricket should be shared with his readers and other cricket lovers who tuned in to the BBC. Critically, you didn't have to share Benaud's passion for cricket to appreciate listening to an intelligent man talk candidly about the thing he loved.

The first thing I noticed when I turned up at RTÉ for my first gig as a television analyst was the tension in the air. Even though RTÉ's audience for football was small, the production was lavish. The set was huge, with two anchormen, Liam Nolan and Bill O'Herlihy. Nolan, a star broadcaster who worked on the BBC's boxing coverage, wore a white suit and a smug smile. He introduced the show, presented some basic facts about the matches we'd be watching before handing over to Bill and the panel of football experts. The experts were two print journalists, me and Liam Tuohy. The two hacks knew very little about football. They were nervous. Liam knew his stuff but he, too, was twitchy as the cameras focused on us. All the jolly pre-show banter dried up when O'Herlihy started posing questions.

I was fine. My determination was to call it as I saw it. It was only a game of football and talking about football was a pleasure. I'd been doing it all my life. There was one problem before the show. I wasn't wearing a tie. I never wore ties. In Makeup before we went on air, someone remarked on my tielessness. I explained my aversion to ties. 'You can't go on without a tie,' I was told. 'Get one in Wardrobe.' I refused. They called Tim O'Connor, who backed me up. No tie! Man on television without tie, shock horror! Tieless anarchist hijacks football show. Now tielessness is a badge of honour, the means by which spivvy businessmen and bent politicians establish their integrity for the viewers. In 1978 not wearing a tie was regarded as an insult to the folks at home. The tie question would arise again from time to time. Tim always supported me but others around the place disapproved of my casual dress code.

The tournament was fascinating. Argentina won the trophy, beating Holland 3–1 after extra-time in the final. Mario Kempes, the host nation's mercurial centre-forward, was the hero, scoring six goals, two of them in a memorable final.

I enjoyed my three weeks' work. Up to a point. I thought our show was flabby. The analysis was passion-free. No real conviction was expressed. The hacks might as well have been watching *Come Dancing*. What was most notably absent was the robust, opinionated argument about players and teams that football fans engage in whenever they gather to watch a match. What we were offering was a sterilized substitute for the real thing; BBC and ITV without the marquee guests. Then when the studio lights dimmed and the cameras stopped rolling, the 'stiffs' I'd been sitting beside for the previous two hours began to talk in earnest about the match we'd just seen.

In the post-game Green Room chatter, the concept of the 'punter' was occasionally invoked, as in 'How do you think the show went down with the punters?' For 'punters', read 'viewers'. In my book, 'punter' was a pejorative term. On the racecourse or in the betting shops I still frequented, a 'punter' was a mug, a loser easily separated from his money.

'Punter' was an insider's word as common in football as in journalism. The idea behind it was clear: fans, viewers, readers or listeners were a lower form of life, the corollary being that the speaker was, well, special. From where I was sitting, the media game required of its practitioners the skills of a circus contortionist. You regard the person who consumes your work with a measure of contempt. At the same time you care about 'what the punter thinks' and endeavour to provide same. But if you really believe the fan, viewer, reader or listener is a mug, why on earth would you want to pander to the creature?

It didn't make sense. But that was how the game was played. It wasn't hard to see how public discourse was cheapened, robbed of nuance and subtlety and ultimately rendered, in many instances, meaningless.

Sean Kilfeather did a great job turning my rough observations into readable copy for the *Irish Times*. We went for a drink after the tournament. I told him that I wanted to get out of football to try to become a sportswriter. He warned that it would be impossible to get work without an NUJ card, and that the union adhered very strictly to the closed-shop rules. It was Catch-22: you couldn't get an NUJ card until you could produce published copy . . . And you couldn't get copy published until you had your card. The *Irish Times* columns wouldn't count because Sean was the writer. He offered to propose me for membership of the Dublin freelance branch of the NUJ if I decided to leave Rovers.

I knew it was time to get out of football. My back continued to plague me. I was picking up injuries, muscle strains and other niggling knocks on a regular basis. My body had had enough. The years of toil had stretched my spirit to breaking point. I didn't look forward to matches any more. Even a Cup Final – a winning one – failed to lift my spirits.

I told John I was going at the end of the coming season. He was fine with that. He was beginning to feel stretched himself. He was managing the Irish team, he'd spent the summer earning a few bob in Philadelphia, and it was clear now that the League of Ireland was never going to be the launch pad for an assault on Europe. Worse, Rovers didn't look like a launch pad for the League of Ireland.

Still, we kept trying. I came up with the idea of nicking Mick Byrne from Bohs, where he was physio and right-hand man to Billy Young. Mick was working in the ESB, part-time for Bohs. We offered him a full-time gig, which he jumped at. He was enthusiastic, good with players and willing to work day and night.

Eoin Hand called me one day from Portsmouth, where his career was coming to an end. Did we have a job at Rovers? Yes, I assured him, he'd be welcome.

I was helping John with the Irish Youth team. One day I went to a trial game between Munster and Leinster Youth teams. Jim Beglin was playing for Munster. A central defender, Jim looked all class. Soon after, he signed for Rovers.

The Kilcoynes learned that I was leaving at the end of the season.

Barton summoned me to his office in town to find out why. I was coy over my misgivings about the original project. I told him I was 'gone' as a player. I wanted to try journalism. He wanted to talk about John. I didn't. He was probing, wondering about John's commitment to Rovers. I played dumb. So did he: no mention of his own dispute with John. He knew about my interest in politics. The subject came up when he asked me what I thought of Charlie Haughey. I told him I thought Charlie was a chancer.

Barton agreed, but he added, 'He's brilliant, the brightest of them all.' Barton knew him well. He'd contributed to Charlie's campaign funds. 'You don't have much choice.' He laughed. I asked Barton about the rumours that swirled around Haughey, suggesting he was corrupt, that Abbeville, his north Dublin mansion set in 250 acres, had been bought with 'hot' money. 'Jealousy,' Barton replied. 'This town is full of begrudgers.'

Barton was a fully paid-up member of Dublin's business class. A Blackrock College boy made good. A master's in business from Harvard, a member of Fitzwilliam Lawn Tennis Club. And Portmarnock Golf Club. An accountant by trade, a builder by calling. Like many others, and not only of his class, Barton seemed tolerant of Haughey's roguery. 'He may be dodgy, but he's brilliant' seemed to be the message. 'Charlie gets things done.' He'd been an outstanding minister in Justice, Finance and Health. He was a man of destiny, the leader Ireland needed and soon would have.

Barton was by no means alone in being beguiled by Ireland's most charismatic public figure. Journalists I was acquainted with, Vincent Browne and Michael Hand, were charmed and intrigued by Charlie. His first name was enough. Charlie was a star. They might wonder about his money, be sceptical about his integrity, but there was warmth in the voices of even hardened journalists when they spoke about him.

A few weeks after my chat with Barton, a crisis hit the football club. Our bookkeeper discovered that four of our young players' expenses claims didn't match the receipts handed in. We were talking small sums, petty cash, a misdemeanour in my view. But when the matter was drawn to Barton's attention, he demanded a penal sanction. The lads were to be fired, contracts cancelled.

I asked John to intervene. He did, but to no avail. Barton wanted 'to draw a line in the sand'. For fuck's sake, I thought, you're going to shame these kids, ruin their football careers, for one foolish mistake. I went to see Barton in his mansion on Shrewsbury Road, Dublin's most desirable residential retreat. I took a copy of *The Merchant of Venice* with me. I pleaded with Barton to give the boys a break. To bolster my case, I quoted from Portia's 'quality of mercy' oration, one of Shakespeare's best-known speeches. The idea is that one who shows mercy is 'blessed', that bestowing forgiveness on the sinner 'becomes the throned monarch [Barton!] better than his crown'.

'Mercy,' I argued, quoting from the speech, 'should season justice.' Barton listened politely. But his mind was made up. It wasn't the money, which he conceded was small, it was the principle. 'We've got to keep our standards high,' he explained. 'We've got to set an example.'

As I drove away from the imposing façades of Shrewsbury Road, heading for the bleak urban ghettos to tell the youngsters and their families that there would be no reprieve, I experienced a chilling anger that I had never known before. I also felt foolish, and more than a little ashamed, for buying into Project Barton. As for my melodramatic introduction of Shakespeare, I could only hope that it remained a secret. A couple of months later, I was out of football, and out of work.

39.   Family

My father did not approve when I walked out of Shamrock Rovers. A couple of times a week we'd meet for a drink after work. During my first summer at home, Kevin, Paddy and I went to all the big Gaelic matches, the Dublin footballers and Kilkenny hurlers remaining our abiding passion. We didn't have to bunk in any more.

Kevin was working as a plumber. He never married. Although he could have earned much more in the building industry, he preferred the stability of his job as a maintenance man in the Rotunda Hospital. He continued to live with Peg and Paddy.

He'd won his schoolboy cap for Ireland but that was it, as far as serious football was concerned. He knew the League of Ireland was a waste of time. Like many other gifted young players – Dessie Toal among them – the squalor, conceit, in-fighting and thieving of the League of Ireland did not appeal to Kevin. The Golden Age of the domestic game had passed. Too smart to be beguiled by that bullshit, Kevin played junior football with his friends. At weekends he enjoyed dancing and a few pints with my dad, after a match on Sunday.

The first big game after I came home in 1977 was the Dublin–Kerry all-Ireland football semi-final. I got us tickets for the Hogan Stand. Two great teams produced a memorable game. Kevin Heffernan's Dublin won easily in the end. It was a blistering display of power and skill. Paddy was overjoyed. It was almost twenty years since we'd all been together at a big match in 'Croker'. In the fifties, Dublin (and Kilkenny) were commonly roughed up by counties playing a more physical game. The footballers of Kerry or Meath would brush the Dubs' challenge aside in much the same way that Tipperary could intimidate Kilkenny's more stylish hurlers. 'Blackguards,' my father would mutter bitterly as we trudged disconsolately back to Fagan's after our team was whipped again.

Kevin Heffernan played in those fifties Dublin teams. A delightfully gifted, intelligent player, 'Heffo' transformed the Dublin team when he took over as manager in 1973. He seemed to share Paddy's analysis. With

Brian Mullins, Pat O'Neill and Kevin Moran around, nobody was going to muscle Heffo's team out of any game. We had our own 'blackguards' now and Paddy relished the awesome physicality of Mullins and O'Neill. Kilkenny also acquired some steel in the seventies. The Henderson brothers, John, Pat and Ger, and a force of nature called Brian Cody ensured that the days of pushing 'the Cats' around were over.

There was a spring in our step as we walked back up Drumcondra Road to Fagan's for a drink after Dublin's great win over Kerry. Paddy talked of his deep admiration for Heffo, a great player in his day, now a mighty leader of men. Larry Gaynor was with us. He and Paddy remained friends despite their differing politics and Gaynor's shocking (to me) betrayal that had forced my father to choose between the Soldiers and the dole. Heffo was a pal of Charlie Haughey's, Gaynor reminded Paddy, who laughed, remarking, 'Nobody's perfect.' Sport meant more to him than politics, his summers defined by the fortunes of the Dublin footballers, the Kilkenny hurlers and the joys or sorrows that victory or defeat would bring. He was a fan. A 'punter', in media-speak.

This was a happy time in Paddy's life. He loved his job as an orderly in Richmond Three, the trauma ward in the hospital. The hardship of the building sites, the 'broken time' and the perpetual insecurity was history now. His pension was secure. Ten years after I left for Manchester, Paddy was tipped off by a friend that Dublin City Council were offering low-interest mortgages for pleasant semi-detached houses on Collins Avenue in Whitehall. For once he beat the system. The Room was evacuated for the heaven of a semi-d. The Dubs and the Cats were on a roll. Life was good.

I was his greatest concern. Paddy and Kevin thought the Shamrock Rovers project was hare-brained. I soon came to the same conclusion. When I quit without a job to go to, my father reproached me for not biding my time. Of course, he knew the horror of life on the dole with a family to take care of. Worse, my reputation as a troublemaker meant that I was virtually unemployable. Paddy knew this only too well. He'd never been overjoyed by my propensity for shooting my mouth off, agitating about apartheid, wearing black armbands, advocating justice for the Old Bailey bombers, or railing against the Blazers in Merrion Square. I was, he thought, putting myself in the line of fire, maybe even attention-seeking. I understood his reservations. Paddy had paid his own price for resisting Fianna Fáil's advances and was wary of the prospect of my wilfulness leading to the kind of pain he had endured. From where he stood, the possibility that my ambition to be a journalist might be realized seemed remote.

Kevin was more supportive. We were close. Although two years younger than me, he was more mature, sturdy where I was mercurial, content where I was restless, prudent where I was impulsive. The good son and the wild son. The months after I left Rovers were hard. Kevin knew that. He often enquired if I needed money. I always said no, I was grand. In a hole of my own making, I resolved to dig my way out.

Peg was as worried as my father. I'd go and see her during the day when her men were at work. 'Are you all right, boy?' was always the first question. She loved the new house, got on wonderfully with the neighbours, most of whom were young families setting out on the road she had travelled so courageously. The sound of kids playing on the street outside the house brought a smile to her face. Often she went outside to give them sweets or a few pennies.

Like Paddy she was unimpressed by Eamon the Agitator. One night, waiting for Paddy and Kevin to arrive home from work, we were watching the evening news on television. I popped up on screen in an item about football's neglect of young players. The subject was the education scheme we'd put in place for young Shamrock Rovers players. My passionate advocacy caused Peg to laugh. 'You're always giving out, boy.' She chuckled. 'I think there's two Eamons, that fella,' she pointed at the telly, 'and you.' At heart Peg didn't like 'that fella'. Although she didn't put it into words, there was, Peg thought, something immodest about the kind of public advocacy I occasionally engaged in. Some vulgar conceit was always in play on the public square where politicians, priests and other chancers were, in Peg's words, 'giving out'. Later when, in her eyes, I became a professional pontificator, Peg regarded it as a bit of a joke. To be famous you had to be some kind of fraud.

Paddy and Kevin arriving home was still the most thrilling moment of her day. The deep bonds forged in the Room were as strong as ever. After seventeen years away I felt like an interloper. An interloper with a big mouth. And no job. In my father's eyes, 'that fella' was threatening to consume Eamon.

The letter from the building society was blunt. Failure to pay the mortgage for three months meant that repossession proceedings would begin immediately. There was nowhere to go for help. Mr Bigshot had played his last card. I didn't sleep for a week. I knew my father had inherited a few thousand pounds from an uncle in Kilkenny. I took him for a drink. I was mortified, but desperate. Could he lend me £500 to get the building society off my back? The answer was no. The money in his savings account could not be accessed on demand without a penalty he wasn't prepared to pay. I was on my own.

40. Survival

My first application to join the National Union of Journalists was turned down. Like Barton Kilcoyne, the Dublin branch of the NUJ had principles and standards, which were rigorously applied. To join you had to prove that you earned more from journalism than any other source and that the work you were proposing to undertake would not deprive an existing member of income. This was an exacting test.

For several months I earned no income at all. When I first appeared before the branch with my sponsor, Sean Kilfeather, the members suspected that I was lying about my income. On the question of depriving existing members of work, a number of speakers referred to the already significant number of unemployed sports journalists. Somebody else mentioned that I was a footballer, not a journalist, and that there was no precedent for giving NUJ membership to footballers. Sean and I were asked to leave the room while the committee considered my case.

When we were called back in I was informed that my application was refused. No explanation was offered. I was devastated. There seemed to be no way out of my Catch-22 situation. No newspaper would employ me without an NUJ card, and no NUJ membership would be granted until I could show earnings. My situation was desperate, with an overdue mortgage and no social insurance stamps.

Tim O'Connor came to the rescue. Renowned for his mastery of the bureaucracy that governed RTÉ, he had acquired the respect and resources to allow television sport to punch way above its weight or its budget. A Clark Gable lookalike, he possessed in equal measure charm and steel. He deployed the charm across the world of broadcasting to access television rights to prestige international events such as the Masters golf from Augusta, the Olympic Games, Wimbledon tennis and Cheltenham racing at a price RTÉ could afford. Through his extensive contacts in the European Broadcasting Union, Tim competed with giants like the BBC and ITV for major soccer championships, international rugby and anything else coveted by the serious players in sports rights. Charm secured the rights; steel was necessary to persuade the

RTÉ hierarchy that sport other than GAA mattered and deserved a prominent slot in the schedule.

Tim came from a newspaper background. Like his father before him he'd worked for Independent Newspapers. While working for RTÉ he operated a lucrative sideline supplying all the sports content for the *Sunday World*, which was a publishing sensation when it launched in 1973. Ireland's first tabloid broke all circulation records to become the country's most popular newspaper. Sport and sex were key ingredients. Tim supplied the sport.

The only income I was earning at this point was a small monthly sterling cheque from *Time Out* for contributing previews of the big English League games. One Friday the postman walked past our house. No cheque. No money in the bank. No credit card. Two children to feed. In desperation I swallowed my pride and phoned Tim O'Connor. He lent me fifty pounds. When I explained the NUJ impasse he came up with a solution. Although the *Sunday World* was a union house, the closed-shop rules did not apply to the sub-contracted sport Tim was supplying. I could write a weekly column for the *World* without breaching union rules. There was no regular soccer programme on RTÉ television, but he assured me he would use me whenever possible.

I was in survival mode and Tim's generosity sustained me, making the kind of difference that Mr Hayden and Dessie Toal had made in times long past, but not forgotten.

After my rejection by the freelance branch, I had to wait twelve months before renewing my application. My *Sunday World* job didn't earn me much money, but the experience of writing 800-word pieces for a tabloid format was invaluable. Every word had to count; verbosity, to which I was prone, was not an option. Some weeks I slogged for two days, ripping up my handwritten A4 pages to make the message fit the medium.

Vincent Browne, then publisher and editor of *Magill*, the current-affairs magazine, also offered me the odd commission. Browne was the charismatic star of the Dublin media village, a brilliant, challenging conversationalist with a sardonic sense of humour and an eye for talented writers and reporters. Eamonn McCann, Gene Kerrigan and Mary Holland were among *Magill*'s most renowned contributors. Nell McCafferty, a leading feminist who'd established a reputation for outstanding reportage at the *Irish Times*, also featured in the magazine.

Mary Holland was the most distinguished and respected journalist in the city. Mary's gentle, charming persona belied the remarkable tenacity of her journalism. As the *Observer*'s Irish correspondent, she was the first journalist from Britain to write consistently and in depth about the plight of Northern nationalists enduring some of the most appalling oppression in any Western democracy. Free of rhetoric and hyperbole, her writing in the *Observer* was an unwelcome reminder to the British Establishment that the political slum in the North was their responsibility.

Ironically, it was an Irishman, Conor Cruise O'Brien, who put a stop to Mary's campaign for justice in the North. Appointed editor-in-chief at the *Observer* in 1977, he pursued a policy of harassment that led to Mary's departure from the paper. In an infamous memo to her, O'Brien contended, 'It is a very serious weakness of your coverage of Irish affairs that you are a very poor judge of Irish Catholics. That gifted and talkative community includes some of the most expert conmen and conwomen in the world and I believe you have been conned.'

In the O'Brien/Holland controversy, widely publicized at the time, Mary was cast as the martyr, O'Brien as the villain. From a journalist's perspective, his editorial interference was intolerable. Yet there was more than a grain of truth in O'Brien's depiction of the Irish, and in particular the Southern Irish when it came to the North. At the time I was a non-combatant in that arena. Later, when I came to take sides, I would find myself closer to O'Brien than to Mary.

Bruised from O'Brien's assaults, Mary arrived in Dublin at the same time as me, in 1977. We were slightly acquainted from my Millwall days. Eamonn McCann, who would later marry Mary, was someone I greatly admired. He was a genuine radical of the left, and a very nice person with a wonderful Derry sense of humour. Unusually for a 'lefty', he was – indeed still is – a knowledgeable football fan, who enjoyed the company of those working-class people whose rights and interests he championed.

While I was waiting to submit my second application for an NUJ card, Mary Holland was elected chair of the freelance branch. She immediately introduced a policy of liberalization. I was one of a number of people to benefit. Shortly afterwards, Vincent Browne approached me with an offer of regular work for *Magill*. Unfortunately, there was a bizarre catch.

In exchange for £7,500 per year, I would contribute a column for each issue of the magazine, which was growing in reputation and circulation. The catch was that Browne insisted he would produce my copy. 'You tell me what you want to say and I'll write it up,' he proposed. Needing the money, badly, and the work, I still refused out of hand. Browne was a good newshound, but he was a pretty ordinary writer of prose. I'd been writing columns for years, and had published a best-selling book. Why on earth would I need a 'ghost' now?

Quite apart from the ghosting aspect of Browne's offer, I was wary of him. While I respected him for his editorial flair and ability to hunt stories, he was acquiring a reputation as a difficult man to work for. Even someone of Mary Holland's renown and gentle disposition was not immune when entering the war-zone that was a Browne workplace. Returning from London in 1977, Mary had agreed to join Browne in setting up *Magill*. Her arrangement with him lasted one edition of *Magill*. Their deal was based on an agreement that they would mutually agree the cover story every month. After some preliminary discussion on the cover story for issue one, Browne made a unilateral call without consulting Mary. As Eamonn McCann confirmed to me recently, 'Mary was badly hurt.'

Having turned down Browne's offer, I was still in need of steady work. In early 1980 *Hibernia*, the respected political weekly magazine, ceased publication as a result of an expensive libel action. Rumours soon surfaced that *Hibernia*'s publisher and editor, John Mulcahy, might replace the magazine with a new Sunday newspaper. Mulcahy confirmed that the paper would be launched as a quality tabloid, the *Sunday Tribune*. Conor Brady, a senior *Irish Times* journalist, would edit the new title. Geraldine Kennedy, a rising star on the *Times*' political staff, was named as the *Tribune*'s political correspondent. Seamus Martin, one of the city's best sportswriters, was appointed sports editor. With some other good appointments, too, the *Tribune* sounded like a goer from day one.

The existing mainstream Sundays, the *Press* and its broadsheet rival the Sunday '*Indo*', were both dull, complacent and, for this reader, there to be taken by a hungry innovative newcomer. My lifelong obsession with newspapers was in no way diminished. But while I would skim the Irish Sundays, it was from the *Sunday Times* and the *Observer* that I got my weekend fix. But Harold Evans's reign as editor of the *Sunday Times* was coming to an end and a twelve-month strike in 1978 had brought the Times Group to its knees. Fleet Street was reaching the end of an era. As indeed was Britain, where Margaret Thatcher was the newly elected prime minister.

I applied for the job of soccer correspondent with the new Sunday paper. But as launch day approached I'd had no reply. I mentioned this to Vincent Browne. Two days later I received a phone call from John Mulcahy. He invited me to come in to see him. The *Tribune*'s offices were in Beresford Place, close to Busáras. Mulcahy's welcome was effusive. 'Vincent Browne tells me I have to hire you as our soccer correspondent. Otherwise we're doomed,' he began. Confessing that he knew nothing about sport, or me, John asked me how much I wanted as salary. Before I could calculate a sum he enquired if '£13,000 a year' would do. This was a vast sum, way over the odds. I was stunned. Mistaking my silence for reluctance to accept, John assured me that this figure 'would be reviewed upwards' if things worked out. We shook hands on the deal.

On learning that I was his soccer correspondent, Seamus Martin appeared to grimace. When he heard about my salary, the pain was evident. An experienced operator working on a tight budget, Seamus was less than charmed with his rookie acquisition. I thought I'd won the pools. Seamus looked like a man who'd lost a winning ticket. 'How the fuck did that happen?' he asked, reaching for a smoke. Giving him a light, I explained about Browne's testimonial. 'Jaysus,' Seamus exclaimed. 'You'll be the best-paid hack in the building. Can you type?'

'No,' I replied. I decided not to tell him about the upwards review.

Seamus Martin was an interesting man, an intelligent, literate journalist, a cut above your average Dublin sports hack. With some notable exceptions, of which Seamus was one, Irish sportswriting was a semi-literate ghetto. 'They think of us as the Toy Department,' Seamus remarked during our first encounter, 'they' being colleagues in politics, features, business and the arts, the more respected walks of journalistic life.

On first glance Seamus could easily be mistaken for a sardonic hack, a hard-bitten observer of the human condition. Given that I'd been sprung upon him in such bizarre circumstances, ours could have been an unhappy relationship. In fact, Seamus proved to be a very good, if exacting, boss. I learned a lot working for him, the first and perhaps most lasting lesson being his admonition voiced on day one that, as far as copy was concerned, 'If you can't tell your story in nine hundred words, you'd better not tell it at all.'

A few days before the *Tribune* was due to hit the streets, Louis Kilcoyne invited me to meet him for a coffee. I liked Louis. He was a gentle soul. Louis loved football. After studying hotel management in Switzerland, Louis took a job as an under-manager at Dublin's Gresham Hotel, the grandest hotel in the city at the time. When the older Kilcoynes acquired Shamrock Rovers, Louis seemed a perfect fit to run the show. He was *simpatico*, always ready with a solicitous word or gesture for those less fortunate. A decent man who might slip you a few pounds for a pint.

Over coffee, Louis wished me well in my new job. He was a big shot now in the FAI, privy to the backstabbing rife in Merrion Square. Knowing my dissident tendencies, he urged me to steer away from confrontation with the Association. 'Stay onside and I will give you as many stories as you want,' he promised. As politely as I could, I declined the special offer.

For the first issue of the *Sunday Tribune* I produced a scoop – a feat I would rarely repeat – which nobody at Rovers was happy with. The club was proposing to sell Pierce O'Leary to Celtic for a fee likely to break the record for a League of Ireland player. It was a good story in its own right. More importantly, it established my independence from old friends, John Giles included. I was determined from day one to live by the American author Joan Didion's maxim that 'Writers don't have friends, only readers.'

The *Tribune*'s birth coincided with Eoin Hand's appointment to succeed John Giles as Irish team manager. I'd known Eoin since we were kids growing up in Drumcondra. He was a year behind me in St Patrick's National School, and lived on Alphonsus Road. My father and his mother were friendly neighbours. We'd played together in the Irish team, and I'd been glad to fix Eoin up with a gig at Rovers when he'd finished at Portsmouth. He was a nice guy. But no way was he qualified to manage Ireland.

Eoin won the League of Ireland in 1979, in his first season as manager of Limerick. A glamour draw against Real Madrid ended their involvement in the European Cup. In 1980 Eoin was voted Soccer Writers Association of Ireland Personality of the Year. Naturally the scribes who'd crowned him now welcomed Eoin's elevation. He'd be more accessible than that bollocks Giles, and more dependent on their goodwill, for Eoin intended combining the Irish job with managing Limerick. I thought the appointment reeked of small-town cronyism.

Writing in the *Tribune*, I remarked upon Hand's inexperience. I questioned the wisdom of appointing a manager with no track record of managing top-class players, men such as Brady, O'Leary, Stapleton, Kevin Moran, Steve Heighway and Mark Lawrenson, all of them playing for great English clubs. Would Hand, with his one League of Ireland title – and his Irish Soccer Writers gong – have the authority to manage Ireland?

My public comment was mild compared to my private opinion. I had journeyed with Eoin in the international team, most recently on the tour of South America. He was a popular lad. He was a good singer. But crucially, in the context of his new job, he exhibited zero interest in football discussion of any kind. As far as the business was concerned, he was an opinion-free zone, a lightweight. I didn't put that in the paper, even though I knew it to be true. The chances of Eoin commanding the respect and attention of the players in an international dressing room were slim.

Leaving aside my private convictions, I confined my newspaper commentary to expressions of relatively mild scepticism. Eoin got off to an excellent start, Ireland beating Holland 2–1 at home in the opening qualifier for the 1982 World Cup. A home draw against a useful Belgian team followed. So far, so good. Maybe my scepticism was misplaced.

A fortnight after the Belgian game, Ireland travelled to Paris to face France and Michel Platini. This was my first trip abroad as an accredited soccer correspondent with the official Irish party. No longer a player, neither was I an accepted member of the accompanying press corps. Seated beside them, I felt very self-conscious. Tom Keogh, the *Irish Mirror*'s man on board, was a cheerful welcoming presence. Frank Johnston from the *People* was another kindly face. But as our Aer Lingus flight sped down the runway, a wag seated in the row behind wondered, 'How will Dunphy send his copy back?' This was a reference to the shocking revelation that I couldn't type, a 'secret' that had caused much amusement in the Dublin media village.

'By carrier pigeon,' was the swift, cutting response. I thought it was a rather good joke and joined the laughter. It was as much a dig at the *Tribune* as it was an attempt to rattle me.

In Paris I ran into Eoin Hand in the hotel lobby the day before the game. I tentatively enquired if there would be any chance of an interview for the *Tribune*. With a withering glance, not breaking stride, his reply was an emphatic 'No.' Although not visibly bloodied, I was most certainly bowed. Retreating to my room I encountered Liam Brady in the lift. Just the two of us, avoiding eye contact as the lift doors closed. A deadly silence. We had never met. The Brady stare is icy. He said nothing. I didn't ask for an interview. When the lift stopped at his floor, Liam made a point of staring directly into my eyes. The look of undisguised contempt cut me to the quick. France beat Ireland 2–0, Michel Platini scoring the opening goal.

After the game I joined Barton Kilcoyne for dinner in the legendary Parisian restaurant La Tour d'Argent. Arthur Gibney and Patrick Guilbaud were the other guests. The purpose of the dinner was to persuade Patrick, a gifted young French chef, to move to Dublin to open a restaurant. Barton was putting up the money and Gibney, a renowned architect and close friend of C. J. Haughey, had agreed to design a grand space for the upmarket diners. It was to be a culinary version of the Shamrock Rovers project, a world-class Dublin eatery.

My role, Barton explained, was to persuade Patrick, a football fan, that Dublin was a wonderful place to live. I was introduced to Patrick as a former Manchester United and Ireland player who was now a leading soccer commentator in print and television. There was no mention of York City, Millwall, Charlton, Reading or my real status at Man U, simply that I'd been a colleague of George Best, with whom I was still allegedly close.

Patrick seemed impressed by this heavily edited version of my CV. Having previously worked as personal chef to Sir Christopher Soames at the British embassy in Paris, he was currently running a fashionable restaurant in Cheshire. He was a United fanatic. Arthur Gibney's résumé didn't need any gilding. He was internationally recognized for his work. And he was, as Barton claimed, one of Charlie's closest confidants. Haughey was now Taoiseach, and as Barton described him to Patrick, a cross between Charles de Gaulle and John F. Kennedy. With a glass or two of wine on board, I was tempted to add the name Al Capone to that hybrid but, good manners being one of my many weaknesses, I went with the flow.

Patrick was a likeable, confident man. He was fed up with England, where industrial chaos had reigned for almost a decade. The Iranian revolution had triggered a crisis in the international economy, Britain as badly hit as Ireland. According to the narrative of the evening, Ireland's economic woes were nothing to do with Charlie or Fianna Fáil policies. *Au contraire*, our great visionary leader was just the man to build the New Ireland that would soon dawn. Patrick's ambition to create a Michelin-starred restaurant in Dublin would be part of the renaissance. As I tucked into my *foie gras* I thought fleetingly of addressing a number of elephants striding around La Tour D'Argent. Barton's thumbnail sketch of Charlie was, like his outline of my career, not quite the whole story.

There was no doubt that Haughey was a gifted politician. He had served with some distinction in a number of cabinet posts. As minister for justice he abolished capital punishment and introduced the Succession Act, which protected the inheritance rights of women and children, an important piece of progressive legislation. In other ministries he'd displayed originality: he had brought in tax breaks for artists and the disabled; he had allowed free travel and subsidized electricity for pensioners; he was the first politician in Europe to countenance government-backed anti-smoking measures. Haughey's capacity for lateral thinking was not in doubt.

There were, though, questions about his political and personal integrity. When Haughey was nominated for Taoiseach in December 1979, Garret FitzGerald, leader of Fine Gael, cited Charlie's 'flawed pedigree' as one reason for opposing the nomination. The most obvious flaw in the Haughey pedigree was the accusation that, as minister for finance a decade previously, he had conspired to channel money and weapons to the nascent Provisional IRA, a crime with which he was charged before the courts in the notorious Arms Trial. Though found not guilty, many believed otherwise.

FitzGerald's 'flawed pedigree' slur, which he came to regret much later, was regarded with contempt by Haughey supporters. The reason for this indignation was not that they thought Haughey was innocent – few believed that – rather that those who'd hung him out to dry had been complicit in the arms plot. They all had flawed pedigrees. Jack

Lynch, the saintly Taoiseach who threw Charlie to the dogs, had known about the arms scam all along. In a classic piece of investigative journalism, Vincent Browne's *Magill* magazine came close to proving that Lynch was cognizant of Haughey's illegal activity.

What FitzGerald regarded as 'flawed pedigree', the Soldiers of Destiny regarded as proof that Charlie was sound on the National Question. That he lived in a mansion set in 250 acres led to speculation about his wealth, but was also a source of pride to his admirers, for wasn't he 'one of our own' made good, a populist hero who might lead the nation to prosperity? The man who'd risen to power on merit, unlike the Blueshirt lawyers and large farmers born into money, who regarded governing as a birthright. Fuck the begrudgers who questioned his wealth. 'Where did they get theirs?' a Haughey worshipper once remarked to me.

Now, after the McCracken and Moriarty Tribunals of the late 1990s, which investigated Haughey's financial affairs, we know much about the graft and corruption that were an ever-present feature of his life. Oddly, there has been little mention of a story told to me soon after I came home in 1977. The source, close to Haughey and still around, pointed to Britain's sterling devaluation as the moment when Charlie landed his first big 'touch'.

The Irish pound was linked to sterling, so when Harold Wilson's government decided to devalue on 18 November 1967, the Irish government was given twenty-four hours' notice. Charlie was minister for finance. He passed the information on to a small group of wealthy Irish businessmen (identified, mostly still alive and living well), who made a fortune on the currency markets. They 'looked after' the Man of Destiny who'd tipped them off.

A year later, with the heat off, Charlie began negotiations to purchase Abbeville, the mansion of his dreams. In 1969, he moved from his semi-d in the modest suburb of Raheny. This story was known around the town. A vigilant police authority, or Revenue investigator, might have made an attempt to follow Charlie's money trail. But this was Ireland, the Land of Saints and Scholars, the fiefdom of the Soldiers of Destiny, whose founding father, the thief Éamon de Valera, was still president and head of state. Haughey, Dev's political offspring, was untouchable.

A footnote to the Arms Trial business suggested that Charlie and his brother 'Jock' had even trousered some of the money meant for the

Belfast republicans. 'Commission', the wags around town called it. The great man's greed knew no bounds. Much later, when wealthy bene-factors contributed to a fund to send his close friend Brian Lenihan to America for a life-saving liver operation, Charlie nicked some of that money as well.

None of this was referred to in La Tour d'Argent. The *Irish Press* journalist Terry Keane was mentioned, as she invariably was, when Charlie was talked about. Terry, the glamorous wife of High Court judge Ronan Keane, was Charlie's mistress. Everybody in Dublin knew about their relationship, not least because neither of the principals ever stopped talking about what was undoubtedly a tempestuous affair.

Patrick Guilbaud seemed very impressed by the sophistication of Charlie's Ireland. Like many strangers, he was under the impression that the Irish didn't do sex. When the Charlie/Terry anecdotes ended, Patrick told us about Valéry Giscard d'Estaing, the incumbent French president, who was a renowned ladies' man. Gibney confided that Paris was Charlie's favourite city, the favoured destination for our own dear leader and his high-society mistress.

By the end of what was a convivial dinner, Patrick seemed certain to be on his way to Dublin. 'It sounds like fun,' he declared. As we sipped our espressos I told him about the Family Planning Act, which Haughey had introduced when minister for health. Birth control had been illegal in Ireland before Charlie drafted his 'reforming' bill, which allowed couples to access contraceptives once they had acquired a medical pre-scription from their doctor. This was, Charlie had proclaimed, 'an Irish solution to an Irish problem'.

'You're joking.' Patrick laughed. Shortly afterwards he arrived in Dublin.

On St Valentine's night in 1981 a fire in the Stardust nightclub in Dublin's suburban northside claimed the lives of forty-eight young people. A further 214 were injured, many of them burned badly in a tra-gedy that shocked the nation. The Stardust was in Haughey's constituency. The club owners, the Butterly family, were well known Fianna Fáil supporters. This terrible story dominated the news pages for several days. Initial reports suggested that an arsonist was responsible for the fire. But victims' families and others who escaped unhurt talked of fire exits that were locked and chained being a vital contributory fac-tor to the numbers of dead and injured.

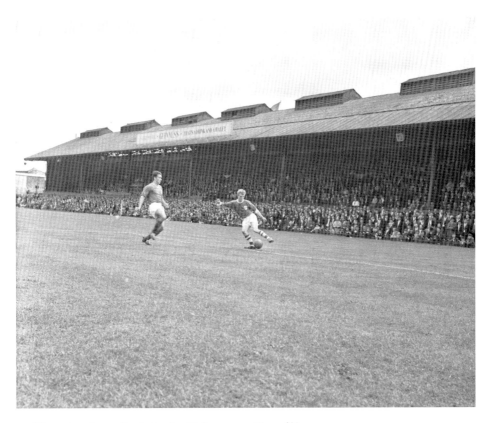

17. Throwing shapes for Ireland at Dalymount. (*Sportsfile*)

18. Terrorizing the Turkish defence at Dalymount Park. (*Sportsfile*)

19. Joy after scoring a goal for Reading, with Robin Friday (*right*). (*Reading Evening Post*)

20. A local farmer promised that if Reading won promotion, he'd slaughter a bullock and give the meat to the players. We were photographed with the chosen beast – but management took the best cuts. 'You'll be all right,' Charlie Hurley (*second from right*) assures the bullock; to his right are Geoff Barker, John 'Minty' Murray and Gordon Cumming. Maurice Evans is at far left, beside me. (*Reading Evening Post*)

21. The Messiah at Milltown: John Giles. (*Sportsfile*)

22. Preparing to conquer Europe: with Ray Treacy and John Giles on our first day at Shamrock Rovers. (*Sportsfile*)

23. With Shamrock Rovers as my playing career came to a close. (*Sportsfile*)

24. Defiant and brilliant, Liam Brady. (*Sportsfile*)

25. With Harry Gregg and Shay Brennan.

26. With Jack Charlton at the launch of *Unforgettable Fire*. (*Derek Speirs*)

27. My brother Kevin.

28. With Bobby Charlton at a charity match in Waterford, organized by Shay Brennan. Bobby helped me with my Busby book, and I got on much better with him than with his brother.

29. Lunching in Dobbins with Eamonn Coghlan, the new world 5,000 metres champion, *c*.1983.

30. Ken Doherty meets his hero, George Best.

31. In studio with Flo McSweeney, Jim Sheridan and Paul Kimmage.

32. Enjoying the sunshine outside Leinster House with three rogues: PJ Mara, Sam Smyth and Shane Ross.

33. The scene in the press room in Palermo, before the Ireland–Holland World Cup match, just after Big Jack walked out in protest at my presence. (*Billy Stickland / Inpho*)

When I reported for work at the *Tribune* the following Tuesday, I was summoned to a meeting with news editor Jim Farrelly. As the fire had taken place the previous Friday night, our weekend paper had focused on the basic news story. Now Farrelly wanted some human-interest copy for our next edition. Darragh McDonald, Emily O'Reilly and I were assigned to go out to the Coolock/Artane area to speak to victims' families. McDonald was an experienced ex-*Irish Indo* news reporter. Emily, who was just starting in journalism, would be well placed to elicit stories from bereaved mothers, Farrelly observed. I was a familiar face from football on the telly and, like the families, working class. 'That will help,' Farrelly noted. 'They'll talk to you.'

'What about the cause of the fire?' I asked, 'Shouldn't we be talking to the emergency services, the guards and witnesses who were in the Stardust on the night?' McDonald and O'Reilly seemed to share my view. What about the locked and chained fire exits and the allegation that bouncers had forced fleeing youngsters back into the inferno? Was arson the cause of the tragedy? No arsonist had been found. The news editor seemed convinced that arson was the cause. If we discovered any evidence to the contrary he would be delighted to publish it. But our task was the human-interest angle.

I then proposed that we arrange to meet the families in the evening when the men were home from work. With a look of exasperation on his face, Farrelly shook his head. 'No, no, you've missed the point. Go out there around eleven in the morning when the mothers are home alone at their most vulnerable, that's when they'll talk from the heart. Go tomorrow.'

We met in the office the following morning. I'd been thinking overnight. I didn't want to do this job. It seemed cruel to exploit people whose lives would never be the same again. Wasn't the pain of bereavement enough? Our mission seemed contrived and prurient. We agreed to travel in my car. A mile up the road I stopped the car. I told Darragh and Emily about my reservations. 'Bottom line, I don't think this is right,' I declared. Emily agreed. Darragh asked what the alternative was. 'We'll tell Farrelly we don't want to do it his way.'

Darragh McDonald was a seasoned pro. Emily and I were amateurs. He understood our concern, but a job is a job. To be fair to Farrelly, he reacted to our pleas of conscience with a wry smile, exclaiming, 'For fuck's sake, guys, get real.'

The Stardust tragedy caused Haughey to cancel the Fianna Fáil Ard Fheis and the general election he was planning to call shortly afterwards, which, opinion polls indicated, he stood a good chance of winning. High Court judge Ronan Keane was to head an inquiry into the fire. Keane's inquiry reported the following November and found that the inferno was 'probably caused by arson'. No credible evidence was presented to support this suggestion.

Those victims still alive and the relatives of those who had perished angrily disputed Keane's 'probably caused by arson' verdict: it implied that someone in their community was culpable for the tragedy while seemingly exonerating the Stardust's owners, the Butterlys.

Keane was critical of the safety standards in place in the nightclub. But following his report, the Butterlys were able successfully to pursue a claim for damages against Dublin City Council. They were awarded £580,000. The victims' families went to the courts seeking compensation, accountability, some form of justice. They received a pittance.

The Stardust Victims Committee campaigned for decades to secure justice and closure. They were largely ignored. The media and the politicians moved on. In 1985 the great singer-songwriter Christy Moore was found guilty of contempt of court after writing and releasing a song called 'They Never Came Home' about the plight of the Stardust victims. Christy's ballad damned the Butterlys and the government.

One verse in particular was deemed libellous.

> *In a matter of seconds confusion did reign*
> *The room was in darkness, fire exits were chained*
> *. . .*
>
> *Hundreds of children are injured and maimed*
> *And all just because the fire exits were chained.*

For this, Christy Moore was prosecuted. It was the only prosecution ever taken in relation to the Stardust tragedy.

On the twenty-fifth anniversary of the fire, the Butterlys applied to open a pub named the Silver Swan on the original Stardust site. Following protests by the victims' families, the licensing authorities turned down the application.

On St Valentine's Day 2006 RTÉ's *Prime Time* broadcast an investigation into the Stardust affair. It demonstrated that Ronan Keane's inquiry was almost certainly fatally flawed. This programme was also a damning indictment of Irish journalism. Based on evidence and witnesses available in the week after the tragedy, when the *Sunday Tribune* and other newspapers were hunting the human-interest angle, *Prime Time* established that arson was far from 'the probable cause' of the Stardust fire.

Most of the salient facts upon which the Keane inquiry relied to produce its findings were wrong. For example, the document plan of the nightclub that Keane used claimed that the storeroom containing a mass of inflammable material was located 'near the basement'. There was no basement in the Stardust. There was a storeroom full of highly inflammable material, floor wax, polishes, cooking oil, which was located in the nightclub's roof space. Witnesses interviewed by *Prime Time* – twenty-five years too late – confirmed that they had seen the fire's flames coming from the building's roof up to eight minutes before anyone in the club knew anything was amiss. Other evidence presented to RTÉ by informed sources claimed that there were several incidents of exceptional relevance to the tragedy in the weeks preceding the deadly fire. Electrical installations in and around the storeroom showed signs of instability before the fatal night. Faulty wiring was suspected to be the cause of the smouldering, smoke and sparking that people had noticed emerging from the storeroom.

Nobody sued *Prime Time*.

A dwindling but determined group of victims' relatives continued to plead for a new inquiry to establish what had happened on the night their children never came home. In 2009 a barrister, Paul Coffey, was appointed by the government to conduct an independent examination of new evidence submitted by the Stardust Victims Committee. Coffey concluded that because of the passage of time it would not be in the public interest to re-open the public inquiry. He did, however, concede that a crucial paragraph from the Keane Inquiry should be revised to state, 'The cause of fire is not known and may never be known. There is no evidence of an accidental origin: and equally no evidence that the fire was started deliberately.'

The Keane Inquiry's finding of 'probable arson' was removed from the public record. The Butterlys kept the £580,000 compensation they received on foot of that now discredited conclusion. And despite the clear breaches of fire regulations at the Stardust, the owners never faced charges.

In the Stardust story, there lie clearly visible the seeds of the myriad scandals to follow that have rendered Ireland a republic in name only: cronyism; the brutal cynicism of all politicians; the callous indifference of a lazy media class; the endless prevarication of authority when faced with inconvenient truth; and the prosecution of the whistleblower.

The ugly defining features of a sick society.

41. Happytown

I first met Michael Hand in London in 1973. He was the star feature writer for the *Sunday Press*. My black armband gesture after Bloody Sunday the previous year had caught his attention. He filed me under possible interviewees for future reference on a low-news week. When Michael eventually got round to profiling me I was at (another) low ebb in my footballing career. His column 'Down Your Way' occupied a prominent back-page slot in what was then Ireland's biggest-selling Sunday broadsheet. It took him around Ireland and as far away as Boston and New York in search of unusual, quirky, colourful stories or people.

Michael arrived at my Catford semi-d with his close friend and colleague the photographer Colman Doyle. Michael was a large, gregarious man with a mischievous twinkle in his eye. Doyle, like many newspaper 'snappers', wore the air of a man who'd seen it all and was not about to be impressed. They were an oddly contrasting couple.

'How's it going, head?' Michael breezily enquired. I was in the Reserves and, thanks to Sam Smyth, banned for life from the Irish team. With a newborn baby boy, an anxious wife, living in a club house and a career on the slide, things were not looking up. 'Great,' I lied.

In an affectionate obituary of Michael, which appeared in the London *Independent*, after his sadly premature death, the journalist Alan Murdoch paid handsome tribute to his journalistic skills: 'His special talent was putting interviewees at their ease, patiently guiding them in a confessional direction, drawing out stories in rich and curious detail.' And so it was in our encounter as Michael gently stripped the veneer of OK-ness in which I endeavoured to cloak my journeyman desperation. As we chatted, Colman Doyle set up his camera shots barely able to disguise the 'What the fuck are we doing here, Mick?' cloud darkening his face.

Draining his cup of tea as the interview drew to an end, he glanced down at his notebook. A moment's pause, a deepening frown, and then, with a dazzling roguish smile, he turned to Doyle: 'I've got her,

Colman. "The Big Man in the Little League".' That was his story, the elusive 'angle'. Colman, unconvinced, merely nodded.

That night my wife Sandra and I took the lads to dinner at a steak house in Blackheath, the plushest enclave on our manor. That Michael possessed a sharp mind behind the genial persona is illustrated by a story Alan Murdoch told in that obituary. When Michael was editor of the *Sunday Independent* he was called before the board for the annual review of the company's titles: 'Hand explained he was wooing a wider readership with expanded arts coverage, led by a competition for poets and short-story writers. When a junior director, keen to impress the chairman, interjected to ask, "And what sort of people entered?" there was a lethal pause as Hand fixed him with a stare and replied, "Mainly poets and short-story writers." '

That mordant wit occasionally landed Michael in trouble. Stopped by a garda patrol car in the early hours, after a long, convivial night, Michael rolled down the window. 'And would it be the case,' the officer ventured, 'that you have drink taken, sir?'

To which Michael replied, 'Ten out of ten, Sherlock.'

We became great pals. There was never much about football or politics. When Michael was off duty, objective number one was a few pints and a bit of fun. He was welcome anywhere, always a source of gossip about Charlie Haughey and Tony O'Reilly, the *Independent*'s new proprietor, and about his brother, Jim, boasting that he provided girls for the big stars who came to Dublin.

I'd mostly see him during the summer when I was home on holidays. There was usually at least one international soccer match in late May or early June. I introduced Michael to John Giles one summer evening in 1974. When he was Irish team manager, John organized music sessions for the team after the matches. He'd hire a room in the Central Hotel in Exchequer Street. Luke Kelly, a big soccer fan, would come to play and talk football. Paddy Reilly, another football-mad musician, was usually there. Ray Treacy, our own banjo player, conducted the session.

The great Irish music revival was in full swing. In venues all over the city, the music lounges were packed out. They were a must-see for tourists, but also hugely popular with a new generation of young Irish people who flocked to see groups like the Dubliners, the Chieftains and great traditional musicians Christy Moore, Dónal Lunny and Davy Spillane. The Clancy Brothers were spreading the gospel in America. Paddy Reilly,

'Pecker' Dunne and the Wolfe Tones were regulars at venues like the Embankment in Tallaght and the Old Shieling in Raheny. O'Donoghue's in Merrion Row was more a tourist haunt, but walking by on a summer's evening the sound of merry-making echoed across the street to Doheny & Nesbitt's, where the civil servants, politicians, journalists and pub philosophers gathered to chew the fat.

The music that had been scorned when I was growing up was now all the rage. As a kid nobody was more dismissive of Aran sweaters, *bodhráns*, banjos and *uillean* pipes than me. I still wasn't buying the Clancys' Aran sweaters, but the voices of Liam Clancy, Luke Kelly and Christy Moore, the melodies and lyrics evoking love and loss, exile and sorrow, now touched a part of me that I hadn't known was there – the corners of my soul, long hidden or suppressed, that reminded me I was the son of Peg and Paddy, the brother of Kevin, the lover of Gaelic games, hurling most of all. In the music and the fun of Dublin summers, I rediscovered the lost dimension of my identity.

I don't think I was alone. One of the ironies of the sessions in the Central Hotel was the differing tastes of the participants. John Giles's father, Dickie, was always there with his friend Sonny Molloy, a well-known rails bookmaker at the racetracks. For those of us lost in exile, Luke Kelly's and Paddy Reilly's were the songs we wanted to hear. But after a while Dickie, a strong-willed character, would grow impatient and demand a culture shift. 'Bing Crosby,' he would shout at Ray Treacy, our MC, 'Johnny Mathis . . . Perry Como . . . Nat King Cole.' Ray kept the peace by mixing things up, one for one, an Irish lament for every American ballad.

Dickie's party piece was 'Underneath The Arches', Flanagan and Allen's music-hall classic. In striking contrast to his dour public image, John was a fabulous singer, a crooner whose *pièce de résistance* was 'The Very Thought of You', recorded by many, but for John at least perfected by Nat King Cole. The last song of the session would invariably be Luke Kelly's rendition of 'Raglan Road', his friend Patrick Kavanagh's lament for love lost. Those were joyous, magical nights for exiles living in England's sober suburbs. Citizens of Happytown, like Michael Hand, Noel Pearson and Tim O'Connor, who often joined us, seemed noticeably less dewy-eyed.

It was a thrill to meet Luke in the intimacy of the Central Hotel sing-songs. He was a truly great singer, capable, like Sinatra, of making any song his own, lending depth, meaning and emotion to the lyrics in a manner that transcended the folk idiom associated with the Dubliners. Luke's poignant version of 'Scorn Not His Simplicity', a song written by Phil Coulter for his Down's syndrome son, was beautiful. 'The Town I Loved So Well', another wonderful Coulter composition, was a further example of a great singer's ability to empathize with and enhance the writer's thoughts. Luke sang 'Joe Hill', the story of the Swedish-American labour activist executed in Utah in 1915 for organizing to defend workers' rights, with quiet, compelling passion.

With his wild red hair and unkempt beard, Luke looked like the devil-may-care Irish extrovert of popular myth. He was in fact a thoughtful, rather shy man. Like me, he was a northside boy who left school at thirteen. He was a voracious reader of books and newspapers. A socialist, he liked to talk about politics, but he was no proselytizer. He listened, laughed and probed in conversation.

When I got to know him better, he talked about his despair with the whole Dubliners phenomenon. In 1969 the group had had some success in England with their version of an old folk song, 'Seven Drunken Nights'. This tale of a drunk cuckolded by his wife reached number seven in the BBC's Top Ten, despite being banned by mainstream broadcasters. Luke hated the song because it branded the Dubliners as wild Irish carousers, the feckless drunken Paddies of ancient stereotype. With that fame came the chance to tour in England, New Zealand, Australia and across Europe – they were particularly popular in Germany – earning good money but they were dying a death as artists.

Luke felt trapped, singing the same set night after night, year after year. By the time I met him, the group had been on the touring tread-mill for several years. A bright, gifted man, he felt the passing of time, acutely aware that the Dubliners were creatively dead – 'Like glorified pub singers,' he bitterly explained over a quiet drink one night. His despair caused him to drink too much. As indeed did the evident absence of love or real friendship in his life.

Driving into town one Saturday night along the airport road, I spotted Luke waiting at a bus stop. I'd been visiting family on the northside, as had he. It was a summer evening, chilly and wet, as is the way in summertime Dublin. I stopped and offered him a lift. He was heading into town, alone, not sure which hostelry to choose for some company and drink. Being as recognizable as Luke was, this was a tricky business. The risk of bores, or worse, someone asking for a song, 'just a few bars', was high. As usual, Luke had a newspaper in hand, a shield to hide behind when drink and the option of solitude were what he wanted.

In a quiet corner of the pub we chose, Luke talked about the vicious cycle he was in. You tour, get big money, adopt a lifestyle compatible with that money. And then it's back on the road to get more money to maintain the quality of life you've become accustomed to. He was not yet forty, yet creatively a 'corpse' in his own description. He talked about John Lennon and Bob Dylan, how they had broken out of their traps, reinventing themselves, taking on new challenges as he believed musicians must.

Another aspect of being a Dubliner that bothered Luke greatly was the notion that, being Irish, the group were often depicted as rebels somehow associated with the sectarian nationalism of the Provisional IRA, who were then engaged in a terrorist war to unite Ireland. This was especially true abroad, where in the seventies rebellion in an Irish context was perceived as violent nationalism and hatred of the British.

Luke had spent much of his early life in England, a country he felt great affection for. Like me, he regarded the idea that you could bomb, murder and maim Northern Protestants into a united Ireland as grotesque. In the split between the Provisional IRA and the Officials, or 'Stickies', as they were known, Luke supported the latter's policy of uniting the working class on both sides of the North's sectarian divide. He regarded Charlie Haughey as a dangerous opportunist.

After Bloody Sunday and the bone-headed British policy of internment without trial, the argument for non-violent resistance was not easily made around Dublin. And, of course, there was the belligerent sectarianism embodied by Ian Paisley to take into account. Many in our republic had, in Seán Lemass's words, a 'sneaking regard' for physical-force republicanism. At best, many of the great and good among them, Haughey and elements in the media and judiciary, were ambivalent about nationalist terrorism.

One night Michael Hand took me to the Old Shieling Hotel in Raheny. A popular music venue owned by a wealthy Kerryman, Bill Fuller, the Old Shieling also served as a refuge for IRA volunteers taking a break from their war in the North. On the night we visited, the Wolfe Tones were topping the bill. They'd had a huge hit record, 'The Men Behind The Wire', in the republic about the victims of internment. Their version of 'A Nation

Once Again' was a naked appeal to the visceral sectarian nationalism that horrified Luke Kelly. They never played across the border in the North. The music worked best before an audience of lounge-bar republicans with a few drinks taken. A kind of creepy populism surged through the room as their set reached its climax.

With Michael that night, I met a number of Belfast Provisionals. I was introduced as the man who'd worn the black armband after Bloody Sunday. Martin Meehan and 'Dutch' Doherty were two of the most celebrated IRA volunteers. Meehan and Doherty had, arguably, earned their heroic status defending their community from deadly assaults mounted by the North's sectarian security forces, the hated B-Specials and the Royal Ulster Constabulary. It was those attacks on nationalist ghettos, which Catholics argued amounted to a pogrom, that acted as a catalyst for the intervention of Charlie Haughey and the Irish government.

John Kelly was the most intriguing person I met in the Old Shieling that night. Kelly was a founder member of the Provisionals. He organized the Citizens Defence Committees to resist the B-Specials and the RUC, and it was Kelly who led the Provo delegation that met representatives of the Irish government looking for money and guns. He was one of the co-defendants, along with Haughey, in the Arms Trial. After their acquittal, Kelly insisted that Haughey was no rogue minister but an honest broker for his government. 'The whole thing was government-sponsored, government-backed, government-related,' he subsequently claimed.

John Kelly was an impressive man. Intelligent, articulate and, in conversation, reasonable. Confidence and determination were his defining qualities. When I expressed my feelings about sectarian nationalism, the folly of worker killing worker as some kind of Catholic/nationalist crusade, he assured me that he felt the same. But he argued: 'Civil rights hasn't worked. We'll have to get the Brits out. Then we can deal with the loyalists.' Listening to the whoops and hollering from inside the room where the Wolfe Tones were finishing their set, Kelly laughed when I referred to the *faux*-patriotism on display at closing-time: 'Don't mind them, they're only useful idiots.'

42.   Beggars Can't be Choosers

John Mulcahy's *Sunday Tribune* was a success. Survival was assured when the early readership surveys showed that we were selling around 110,000 copies per week. And that figure rose in subsequent surveys. Geraldine Kennedy, the political editor, landed a number of major scoops chronicling the woes of Charlie Haughey's troubled government. A divisive figure for the general public, Haughey was also at odds with some cabinet colleagues, notably his deputy leader, George Colley, whom he had narrowly defeated to win the leadership two years previously. In a bizarre arrangement, Haughey allowed Colley a veto over the critical cabinet appointments to Defence and Justice. Despite a televised address to the nation outlining the country's economic difficulties and promising harsh measures to deal with the problem, Haughey was proving to be an indecisive leader.

In 1981 the Northern Troubles were escalating, with IRA prisoners beginning hunger strikes as part of their campaign to be treated as political prisoners. Again, Haughey was seen to be weak and vacillating. Kennedy's news stories enabled the *Tribune* to establish a reputation for strong and credible reportage. She was selling papers. And driving Haughey mad, to the point where he authorized the tapping of her phone and those of two other journalists. His role in the scandal would be revealed a decade later, and ended his political career.

The *Tribune* was a pleasant place to work. Conor Brady was a good editor: calm, hands-off, good-humoured and secure enough to allow strong characters like Kennedy, Jim Farrelly and my boss, Seamus Martin, to do their thing. He was a chairman rather than a dictator. A very good writer himself, Martin was original and daring in choosing contributors to the Toy Department. The chief sports sub-editor, Michael O'Connor, was literate, regarding my more florid copy with nothing more hurtful than a slightly raised eyebrow before simplifying and improving the finished article. I was as content as I had ever been.

I rarely went into the office. But I happened to be in on 29 July 1981, the day of Prince Charles and Lady Diana Spencer's wedding at St Paul's

Cathedral in London. Someone had brought in a portable television to follow this splendid British occasion. Front and centre in the newsroom audience sat Máirín de Burca, socialist and radical feminist. In 1974 Máirín had won a landmark case in the Supreme Court to secure the equal right of women to serve on juries. Máirín, a lively and popular character, laughed when I accused her of heresy. That newsroom scene offered a telling glimpse into the complex relationship between Ireland and Britain.

After the businessman Hugh McLoughlin took a controlling stake in the *Tribune* in 1982 he decided to launch a daily paper on the back of the Sunday paper's success. This was an ill-conceived, badly executed plan. The *Daily News* lasted three weeks. One Friday our pay cheques bounced. I was by no means the worst victim of McLoughlin's harebrained scheme. I had at least been given a chance to prove that I could become a journalist. But for established journalists, like Conor Brady, Geraldine Kennedy, Seamus Martin and Jim Farrelly, all of whom had left secure employment to commit to the *Sunday Tribune*, failure as a consequence of crass stupidity was a real body blow.

I got two calls the following week. One was from Vincent Browne, who was negotiating to buy the *Tribune* title from the receiver, the other from Michael Hand, who'd been editing the *Sunday Independent* since 1976. Browne urged me to wait until his talks with the receiver were concluded. If he got the title I would be his soccer correspondent. Michael had a soccer correspondent but there was a job as a general sportswriter on offer. 'Browne's mad,' Michael argued. 'You'll be at each other's throats every week.' That view of Browne was widely shared in the village of Dublin journalism. Indeed, the news that he was in talks with the receiver to buy the *Tribune* title served only to compound the misery of my more experienced, now unemployed, former colleagues.

Needing work as soon as possible, I went to talk to Michael. He complimented me on what I had done for the *Tribune*. There was a job for me on his paper. But, he explained, the money wasn't great, nothing close to the £13,000 I'd been earning. Independent Newspapers was like the civil service. New entrants came in on the lowest grade. You worked your way up the pay ladder incrementally. Merit, Michael insisted, had nothing to do with your wages. I was in no position to argue. But I did. I was thirty-seven: time was against me. I'd be fifty before I reached the salary of the average *Indo* colleague. I was very fond of Michael, and grateful for his offer, but I told him, 'I'll take my chances with Browne.' We left it at that. No hard feelings.

A week later Michael called again. He thought the pay-grade problem could be resolved. When I arrived in Abbey Street, the Independent Group's managing director, Joe Hayes, was with Michael in the editor's office. When Tony O'Reilly acquired the *Independent* titles in 1973, times were changing but the Indo Group papers weren't. Hayes had been installed to breathe life and energy into a bastion of Irish conservatism.

Michael briefed Hayes on my situation. In shirt sleeves and tieless, Hayes gave the impression of a man who meant business. A can-do Kerry man. A problem solver. After listening to Michael, Hayes turned to me. 'We want you, boy, but we're stuck with these fucking grades.' He blamed the NUJ and the old management. 'Come in on the lowest grade and we'll promote you as quick as we can. Don't worry about the money – we can use the blue dockets.' The blue dockets were for expenses. You filled in the docket, traipsed to a hatch on the second floor, which housed the accounts department, and exchanged the 'bluey' for cash.

'What were you on at the *Tribune*?' Hayes asked. He didn't blink when I told him. He and Michael did a quick sum. The gap between my *Tribune* salary and Grade E, or whatever it was, would be bridged by filing bogus expenses claims. The MD was proposing that I rob the company. The editor was smiling approvingly. It was an Irish solution to an Irish problem. On his way out of Michael's office, Hayes offered a firm handshake and a pat on the back. 'Good luck. Great to have you on board.' Despite serious misgivings I closed the deal with Michael. I was broke and out of work. Beggars can't be choosers.

43. The Decent Skins

The energy and enthusiasm of the start-up *Tribune* was missing when I went to work for the *Sunday Indo*. In Beresford Place, the sense from day one that we were fighting for our lives meant that we were hungry fighters. I was new, but so was everyone else. There was no established hierarchy. The *Indo*, in contrast, was calm to the point of complacency. The NUJ and the print unions were powerful. It wasn't just the grading system, which rendered merit and hard work meaningless, that created a feeling of permanence. Like the civil service, the *Indo* would always be there. The journalists worked to rule, doing things slowly in their own time, secure in their positions. The *Indo* was an institution, its inmates secure, respected members of what they regarded as an honourable profession. They worked their shifts, lunched their sources, made their way, slowly, back to the office to produce sage, judicious commentary for the 'punters'. They were, I thought, smug. The paper, the front-page 'splash' excepted, was generally dull.

As a Grade E former Millwall footballer full of passion, filing robust copy about the Irish soccer team, I was generally ignored. The feeling I detected whenever I went into the office was of what might best be described as indifferent resentment. I'd been parachuted in by Joe Hayes and Michael Hand. I hadn't served my time. As far as the union was concerned, I was barely legal. A bit of a freak.

I wasn't bothered. I had my own ideas about journalism formed by a lifelong addiction to newspapers. I had been what these gentlemen journalists derisively referred to as a 'punter'. I still was, if being a 'punter' meant seeking to be informed and stimulated by newspapers. I was a big fan of the New Journalism, which had emerged in America in the seventies. Hunter S. Thompson, Tom Wolfe and Norman Mailer were heroic figures whose work I'd read and, in the case of Mailer's *Armies of the Night*, re-read. Another Mailer book, *Miami and the Siege of Chicago*, was a seminal influence on me. Published in 1968 after Mailer had visited the Democratic and Republican conventions, the book was a brutally frank report on the pursuit of political power.

Like Thompson and Wolfe, Mailer dispensed with objectivity to tell the story as he saw it. These men weren't striving for sagacity or to be judicious. They were endeavouring to tell their own truth, to take you, the reader, on an amazing journey to the heart of the story. You weren't a 'punter', you were a companion, a co-conspirator.

Thompson invented the concept of gonzo journalism. Commissioned to write an article about the Kentucky Derby in 1970, he produced 'The Kentucky Derby is Decadent and Depraved'. For Thompson and Mailer, sarcasm, humour, exaggeration and profanity were essential tools of the trade. You wrote the way people talked and thought. No gilding of the lily. No objectivity. Well, not too much.

Writing about Richard Nixon, Thompson argued that 'he represented that dark and incurably violent side of the American character'. In an article for *Rolling Stone* magazine in 1973, Thompson reflected, 'If I'd written the truth I knew for the past 10 years, about 600 people, including me, would be rotting in prison cells from Rio to Seattle today. Absolute truth is a very rare and dangerous commodity in the context of professional journalism.'

Kenneth Tynan, the great English theatre critic, was another influence on me. He had raged against the traditional genre of English middle-class drawing-room drama, championing instead a new generation of angry young men challenging convention with a new realism. I knew nothing about theatre, but I admired Tynan's writing. His appeal for me was his desire that things should change, must change. Like my other heroes – Mailer, Thompson, Tom Wolfe and Danny Blanchflower – Tynan was driven. On his desk at the *Observer* he pinned a note to himself: 'Rouse tempers, goad, lacerate, raise whirlwinds.' Another Tynan motto was 'Write heresy, pure heresy.' Which was what I felt inclined to do.

I was a man on a mission when I started at the *Sunday Indo*. I wanted to write what I knew about the clowns running Irish soccer, in so far as I could within the laws of libel. The cosy relationship between the Blazers and the journalists covering Irish soccer was part of the story. In exchange for the kind of snippets of information Louis Kilcoyne offered me to stay onside, most of the hacks refrained from rigorous appraisal. Players were a soft target when things went wrong. You never met them and they were not providers of stories.

I thought Eoin Hand was the big story. Eoin had enjoyed some success managing Limerick in the League of Ireland. He was a good lad, a 'decent skin', as we say in Dublin. But he wasn't officer material. I could see it when I watched the Irish team. Full of talent – Brady, Lawrenson, O'Leary, Heighway and Stapleton – this was the best group of players we had ever had. The results weren't awful at first, but Eoin was failing the ultimate test for managers: he wasn't getting the best out of his players.

My criticism was robust. Sometimes my criticism was absurd. After Ireland lost to Holland at Dalymount Park in a European Championship qualifier, I wrote the following about Liam Brady: 'His performance on Wednesday was a disgrace, a monument to conceit, adorned with vanity and self-indulgence, rendered all the more objectionable by the swagger of his gait'! Writing doesn't get much worse than that. What I was trying to say was that Liam tried too hard. He was everywhere, taking free kicks, corners, getting on the ball all over the pitch, flogging himself to exhaustion. It was an undisciplined performance born out of sheer desperation. A bit like my depiction of it.

I cringed when I read my analysis in the following Sunday's paper. My press-box colleagues attributed Ireland's defeat to the superiority of the Dutch team. I thought Ireland were badly organized. But I went way over the top when I savaged Liam. I tried to learn.

There was plenty to learn. For a brief spell after the *Tribune* closed I was employed as a freelance by the English *Daily Star*, which was based in Manchester. Writing for Sunday newspapers, I could take my time composing my copy. I could rip it up and start again. At the *Tribune*, my Brady rant would have been fixed. At the *Indo*, the rant made it through the system. The *Daily Star* exposed me. Ireland were playing somewhere in Europe. The *Star* wanted copy, a preview of the game. 'Eight pars will be enough,' the salty Mancunian voice at the other end of the phone informed me.

'How many words is that?' I asked.

There was a pause at the other end of the line before an exasperated sub-editor growled, 'Four hundred.'

I was to file my copy the night before the game. Four hundred words seemed very little. I had a lot to say. I divided 400 by eight before writing my preview. Economy of expression was not my forte. After shedding much blood, sweat and tears, I was ready to call Manchester. A woman took the call. She was my first copy-taker. As I began to dictate my words down the line I grew ever more self-conscious. After seven paragraphs I was exhausted. I started the closing one as follows: 'Prognostications about tomorrow's game.'

'Excuse me, luv,' the voice from Manchester interrupted. 'What was the first word in this par?'

'Prognostications,' I repeated.

'Have you ever read the *Star,* luv?' she drily enquired. Before I could reply she got to the point: 'We don't use words like "prognostications" in the *Star*, luv. Have you got another word?' My brain froze. I blushed, breaking out in a light sweat. After a deadly silence she came to my rescue: 'How about "forecasts"?'

'Yes, of course,' I meekly agreed. I never heard from the *Star* again.

For all the pleasures afforded by its intimacy, Dublin was a village where you were likely to meet the victims of your anger. Or someone close to them who would bitterly complain. Everyone knew everyone else. Harsh words had consequences. One day my father met Liam Brady's mother on a bus. They were friends, had sat beside each other in primary school. My dad was very fond of her – she was a lovely lady. 'Paddy, what's Eamon doing to Liam? Would you have a word with him?' she pleaded. He did. I told him I had to do my job. Eoin Hand's family were neighbours too. When they met in a shop one day Mrs Hand blanked Paddy. He was hurt. She was hurt. I was making life uncomfortable for everyone.

I was becoming *persona non grata* with the Irish soccer correspondents. I started pointing the finger at them in my columns, drawing attention to their cosy relationship with Pig Farrell, Fart Bummings and Eoin Hand, their unwillingness to tell the story as it was. On the road I steered clear of the press pack. That was impossible on aeroplanes where the hacks were generally seated in a block at the back. One day I was sitting next to Tom Keogh, the *Irish Mirror*'s correspondent. He was a good journalist, a cheerful, impish character who never wrote a bad word about anyone. We had a couple of beers on the flight. We started talking about Eoin. 'Why don't you lay off him?' Tom urged.

'I don't think he's up to it, Tom,' I told him.

'Give him a break,' Tom suggested. 'He's a decent skin.'

'He's not paid to be a decent skin, Tom,' I laughed, 'he's the fucking manager.'

Nodding at our colleagues, Tom lowered his voice: 'They think you're a little bollocks,' he confided.

'Maybe they're right,' I replied. I liked Tom. We'd worked together for RTÉ. He wasn't trying to get at me, just marking my card.

Shortly afterwards I started writing about 'decentskinsmanship', the means by which mediocrity was insulated from criticism or any public sanction on the grounds that the subject was 'a decent skin'. The English writer Stephen Potter coined the phrases 'gamesmanship' and 'one-upmanship'. 'Decentskinsmanship' was an Irish variation on those themes. It was the curse of a small place. Mediocrity protecting mediocrity; worse, elevating it to a virtue.

A more insidious version of the game was being played in Irish political circles, where journalists played 'footsie' with politicians, a sport from which both gained while the public lost. Charlie Haughey was Taoiseach. He courted influential journalists with what Alan Murdoch described as 'the long-lunch offensive'. Michael Hand and Vincent Browne made no secret of their presence at the great man's table. The economy was in deep trouble. The stench of venality hung over Haughey. Urging austerity on the people, he was living like a prince. The source of his wealth was a mystery nobody seemed too keen to solve.

I was friendly with Browne. We socialized together. He explained Charlie's ineptitude in office as a consequence of trouble in the Haughey/Terry Keane liaison. 'She's driving him mad. He can't concentrate on politics, he's obsessed with her,' Browne revealed, after a long lunch with the Taoiseach. Browne, supposedly the scourge of errant politicians, clearly admired Haughey. When I asked him what he was doing hanging out with Charlie, Browne replied that it was 'fun'. 'He's brilliant, the best and brightest of them all,' he declared. And, of course, the gossip was gold standard.

At the time Charlie was entertaining and dining Browne, his minister for justice, Seán Doherty, was tapping this crusading journalist's phone. We didn't know that, but we might have guessed. Doherty was unfit for any office. That he was minister for justice was beyond a joke. The Dowra affair was public knowledge when Browne was breaking bread, cracking jokes and sharing hot gossip with the Taoiseach.

The scandal broke in September 1982. The brother of Doherty's wife Maura, Garda Thomas Nangle, was charged with assaulting James McGovern, a native of County Fermanagh, in a pub in December 1981. Hours before the case was due to be heard in the district court in Dowra, a village in County Cavan, McGovern was arrested by the Special Branch of the RUC on the basis of false intelligence, provided by gardaí, that claimed he was involved in terrorism. McGovern was therefore unable to make it to court to give evidence. The case against Nangle was dismissed because the principal witness, McGovern, had failed to appear in court.

While Seán Doherty was 'taking care' of his brother-in-law and bugging journalists' phones, he was also sourcing equipment to enable the serving minister for finance and deputy prime minister Ray MacSharry to bug phone calls between himself and former cabinet minister Martin O'Donoghue. The bugging equipment was supplied by Assistant Garda Commissioner Joe Ainsworth. A cursory analysis of the Dowra affair made it clear that very senior police officers had conspired with the minister for justice to pervert the course of justice. It was evident that people occupying the highest offices of the state and guardians of the law at the most senior level were bent. The Soldiers of Destiny were still subversives or, as their esteemed former leader Seán Lemass put it, 'a slightly constitutional' party. This troubled many people, but others merely smiled, shrugged their shoulders and urged Fianna Fáil's detractors to get real.

Influential journalists were courted assiduously, Browne with lunches and gossip. Michael Hand also dined with CJ, as Charlie Haughey was known to intimates. Every Christmas Michael received a bottle of the finest *grand cru* with a specially printed label 'To Mr Michael Hand from his friend Charles J. Haughey'. John Healy, who wrote the 'Backbencher' column in the *Irish Times*, was arguably Ireland's most influential political columnist. He was a wonderful writer, his essays passionate, adorned with wit and flair. My father was a great fan of Healy's anti-Establishment polemics. Healy fell in love with Charlie.

In the febrile seventeen months between June 1981 and November 1982, there were three general elections. I was still a political junkie, although totally confused by the choices on offer to voters. Haughey and his Soldiers of Destiny did not appeal. They seemed more like a sect than a political party, a tribe appealing to the base instincts of the Irish people, the party that had dispatched my father to the dole queue when he refused to join. In the context of the North, the Soldiers still traded on the visceral sectarianism of the bloody past and the murderous present.

The Irish left I regarded as a sick joke: chancers preying on the working class, then betraying them once in office. I noted that Haughey's first two years in the office of Taoiseach were facilitated by the critical votes of the three members of the Workers Party. Unprincipled and opportunistic, the career leftists regarded their constituents with well-disguised contempt.

Garret FitzGerald, the leader of Fine Gael, was by far the most appealing politician in the country. In what was an ugly freak show, FitzGerald stood out. An evidently decent man, he was offering reform. The most important of his ideas proposed reconciliation with the unionist/loyalist minority of the island of Ireland. Before that could be achieved, the republic's culture would have to change. To create the pluralist society that might live in harmony with our Northern neighbours, we would have to address questions about divorce and contraception, challenge Catholic/nationalist orthodoxy and change our constitution, particularly Articles 2 and 3, which laid claim to the six Northern counties, where unionists formed a majority of the population. In short, FitzGerald's big idea was to build a non-sectarian society.

Garret FitzGerald was a liberal. Unfortunately the Fine Gael party he led was, in essence, the same reactionary, conservative entity it had always been. That old Hitler-lover Oliver J. Flanagan still sat on the backbenches. Fine Gael's core support consisted of wealthy farmers and merchants who didn't much care for the kind of reforms FitzGerald was advocating. They tolerated him solely because he might deliver power.

In the *Irish Times*, John Healy mocked FitzGerald mercilessly as 'Garret the Good', the prissy liberal with no grasp of the concerns of the plain people of Ireland. FitzGerald was, Healy robustly contended, a creature of Dublin 4, out of touch with people beyond the Pale. This was a caricature of FitzGerald.

In June 1981, Haughey called a general election in a bid to secure an overall majority in Dáil Éireann. The polls seemed favourable. But he and his Soldiers were carrying too much scandalous baggage and Haughey had failed the economic test he'd set for himself. Fine Gael won sixty-five seats, enough to form a coalition with the Labour Party. 'Garret the Good' was Taoiseach.

He appointed John Bruton minister for finance. The wealthy farmer from County Meath was not the brightest. Seeking the long-cherished Holy Grail of his reactionary party, fiscal rectitude, Bruton imposed

VAT on children's shoes. The government collapsed when the socialist TD Jim Kemmy cast his vote against the budget. Kemmy was unique in Irish politics: a socialist with genuine convictions and a functioning conscience. The government had lasted eight months.

In the ensuing election Fianna Fáil emerged with most seats, but short of a governing majority. When the electoral sums were done it became clear that the next government would be formed by the party that could successfully woo Tony Gregory, the independent socialist from Dublin Central. Charlie pledged £100 million for Gregory's constituency. 'Garret the Good' offered £850,000. Game over. Thanks to a marriage of convenience, Charlie was back where John Healy felt he belonged.

As well as promising a £100 million he had no intention of delivering, Haughey brought with him to the negotiations with Gregory the leader of the Irish Transport and General Workers' Union, Mickey Mullen. Mickey was a decent skin. He witnessed the deal that shafted Garret and the Labour Party with which the ITGWU was nominally aligned. Watching from the sidelines, I thought Irish politics surreal.

I worked as an analyst for RTÉ during the 1982 World Cup Finals. Northern Ireland were one of the big stories of the tournament, reaching the quarter-finals and knocking out the host nation, Spain, along the way. RTÉ's coverage was still fairly conventional. Liam Tuohy, David O'Leary and I were the mainstays of the panel, and Bill O'Herlihy was the anchorman. David was an outstanding footballer but a very average critic. Although not as banal as the BBC and ITV alternatives, we were a long way from where I felt we ought to be.

Italy were among the pre-tournament favourites. But they started badly, failing to win a match in the opening series of games, despite being in the weakest first-round group. After lifeless draws with Cameroon, Peru and Poland, the Italians were available at 25/1 with the bookies, entering the tournament's knockout phase. Having tipped Italy to win before the tournament, I stuck to my guns when they drifted in the betting. Teams grow into tournaments, I argued, and this team was too good to go home.

The Italians were a magnificent team. Dino Zoff in goal. Paolo Rossi up front, Marco Tardelli, Bruno Conti and Claudio Gentile, all great players with the potential to win the World Cup. In a classic quarter-final game against Brazil, Italy prevailed, thanks to a Rossi hat-trick. They beat Poland in the semi-final and West Germany in the final.

I had taken my own advice and backed the Italians at 25/1. The betting shop I frequented was a one-man operation opposite Independent Newspapers in Abbey Street. It was a favourite haunt for many of Dublin's Chinese-restaurant workers. They were crazy gamblers, preferring long-priced outsiders to short-priced favourites. When I went to collect my winnings the bookie looked dazed. The shop was full of happy Chinese punters. Spotting me, the lads crowded round 'the man from telly'. They'd all steamed into the 25/1. I was a hero in my own betting shop.

During the tournament I talked to our programme's anchorman, Bill O'Herlihy, about the turbulent political landscape. Although he was back in office, Haughey's grip on power looked tenuous. The economy was tanking. He remained a deeply divisive figure, not just with the electorate but within his own party. A third election in less than eighteen months seemed on the cards.

Bill was one of a small group of advisers to FitzGerald. His day job was public relations. Pat Heneghan, another FitzGerald adviser, was Bill's co-owner in what was one of Ireland's leading PR companies. Frank Flannery, chief executive of the Rehabilitation Institute, was another key FitzGerald aide. Enda Marren, an old-school Blueshirt solicitor, and Shane Molloy, a senior executive with Unilever, were other influential members of FitzGerald's image-making team.

In his *Irish Times* column, John Healy derisively tagged the group 'The National Handlers', spin-doctors in today's money.

In an idle moment between games, I mentioned my admiration for FitzGerald to Bill. He wondered if I'd be interested in contributing to the Handlers project. If it helped get rid of Haughey and the Soldiers, I was happy to sign on. John Healy's rather facile analysis suggested that the Handlers existed merely to manufacture an image for FitzGerald, an image conceived to disguise the fact that the Blueshirts were still at heart a dark, conservative force.

The truth was more interesting. Yes, the Cosgraves and Oliver J. Flanagan were still around, but FitzGerald was a genuine liberal reformer. He had hijacked the party, much as Tony Blair would the British Labour Party a decade later. New Fine Gael would contemplate reforms that shocked the party's core support. FitzGerald didn't need spin-doctors, it was enablers he required. Hence the importance of the Handlers. They liaised with party general secretary Peter Prendergast to create an election-winning machine. The slogans and scripts produced by the Handlers were less important than targeting winnable seats in the complex multi-seat constituencies across the country.

If FitzGerald and his Handlers had a big idea it was – again like Tony Blair – to ignore the party's traditional supporters, who would vote for them, or against Haughey, anyway. The message was aimed at 'Middle Ireland', at people who belonged to neither tribe, Fianna Fáil or Fine Gael. FitzGerald was more than a poster boy. He was the real deal, a decent man seeking to build a just society. He was the antithesis of Haughey, Seán Doherty and Republican backwoodsmen like Kevin Boland and Neil Blaney, scoundrels with the tricolour in one hand and a bugging device in the other. Compared to his opponents, Garret was better than Good. He was Great.

Frank Flannery was the most influential Handler. As well as a loathing of the Soldiers, Flannery possessed a mastery of the voting system. He knew where the voters were in every constituency in the country, who would be eliminated on which count, on what percentage of the national vote, where the transfers would go. This was science, not spin.

Fine Gael was in election mode when I signed up. Haughey had pulled a clever stroke earlier in 1982 by appointing Dick Bourke, the sitting Fine Gael TD for Dublin West, as Ireland's European commissioner. Bourke came from the Cosgrave wing of the party and FitzGerald had denied him office during his first spell in government. Vacating a seat that Haughey hoped to win was Bourke's revenge. But despite fielding Eileen Lemass, daughter-in-law of legendary former Taoiseach Seán Lemass, Fianna Fáil failed to win it.

Fine Gael morale soared after the by-election victory. Haughey's stock fell commensurately. His government collapsed when Tony Gregory and the other socialist TDs propping it up refused to vote for a tough budget, introducing tax increases and social-welfare cuts. My contribution to the November general election was FitzGerald's campaign slogan 'The Courage to Succeed'. In Ireland's bleak political landscape at this point, courage and success were elusive qualities. Branding FitzGerald with this evocative message seemed rather clever. I was pleased with myself. The Handlers were pleased with their new signing.

Frank Flannery harboured hopes that Fine Gael might win an overall majority for the first time in its history. That wasn't to be, but the seventy seats won represented Fine Gael's best-ever general-election performance, and they were enough to enable them to form a government in coalition with the Labour Party.

In the post-election euphoria I was invited to meet FitzGerald. He thanked me for my contribution to the victory. Maybe I'd be interested in standing for the party some day, he suggested. I assured him I had no such ambition. During our brief conversation I raised the subject of a national lottery, long mooted as a way to raise funds for sport. There would be a massive social dividend if sport and other forms of recreation were properly funded by government, I argued.

Sport, of which he clearly knew nothing, was hugely important to young people in particular. It promoted a sense of community and was a vital element in combating the feeling of alienation that blighted the lives of people who were young, urban, poor or unemployed. For giving people a sense of purpose, sport was character-building. If Fine Gael wanted to build an inclusive society and shed its elitist image, a serious attempt to fund sport through a national lottery would yield a political as well as a social dividend.

He suggested I put my ideas down on paper for him. Shortly afterwards I delivered what was in essence a polemic about sport's enduring virtues. Six months later I was summoned to his house. He was waiting with his wife Joan, a formidable, inquisitive presence. Behind the public image of a slightly nutty professor lay a sharp mind. He was persuaded by the paper I'd submitted to him, particularly by a passage in which I argued that personal development, the formation of character, was much more likely to flow from active participation in sport than from the passivity of looking on. There were, I reminded him, obvious health benefits, which accrued to those playing sport at any level. But more important was the succour to the spirit, intangible but no less potent for that.

It was Joan who pointed out that there would be no short-term political gain from the lottery funding for sport I was proposing. I disagreed, asserting that sport was a national obsession, ranking higher in my opinion than religion or politics. There followed a spirited exchange between husband and wife about the merit of my idea. They forgot about me for a few minutes. The love and companionship between them was evident, the intellectual joust an essential element to their happy marriage.

'It appears you have won the argument, Mr Dunphy.' Joan smiled. 'My husband is converted to sport.' Over a cup of tea, made by the Taoiseach, he asked me to write a couple of paragraphs for his speech to the forthcoming Fine Gael Ard Fheis. We talked briefly about Haughey. Referring to the phone-tapping and the Dowra affair, as well as Haughey's mysterious wealth, I expressed my shock at the amount of political corruption in Ireland.

To my surprise FitzGerald demurred. 'It's much worse in England,' he claimed. 'Look at James Callaghan, with his big farm in Sussex. How could he afford to buy that?'

In his Ard Fheis speech, FitzGerald made a commitment to sports funding as a means to a more socially cohesive society. It would be 1986 before the National Lottery was founded. The money would go to sport. All good intentions dissolved when the Department of Finance intervened shortly afterwards. The lottery money was rerouted from sport to the Exchequer, to be dispersed across government to ministers with muscle in need of funds.

44. Merrion Row

The new *Sunday Tribune* hit the streets in April 1983. Vincent Browne had acquired the title for £5,000. An offer of £17,500 from Noelle Campbell-Sharp, a successful publisher of women's magazines, had been spurned by the court that was processing the receivership. Crucially, the print unions and the NUJ backed Browne's bid. Noelle, a socialite and close friend of Charlie Haughey and Terry Keane, had proven business expertise. Browne, something of a socialist himself, was well acquainted with Haughey and spent a lot of time in bars gossiping about Terry Keane. Dublin was a small town.

Other considerations that came into play favoured Browne. His current-affairs magazine, *Magill*, was highly regarded. He was a journalist of some repute. And wealthy businessman Tony Ryan had pledged support for a new paper edited by Browne. Seasoned Browne watchers were intrigued by the prospect of Irish journalism's *enfant terrible* wielding the power of national newspaper editorship. His track record at *Magill* suggested a bumpy ride for all concerned.

But before publication he head-hunted some very impressive names. Paul Tansey, the respected *Irish Times* business editor, signed on as deputy editor. John Kelleher, controller of programmes at RTÉ television, joined as managing director. In a triumph of hope over experience, Mary Holland forgave Browne his previous sins and agreed to contribute to the new *Sunday Tribune*. Colm Tóibín, then editing *Magill*, was also thought to be on board.

Browne offered me my old job as soccer correspondent. I decided to stay with the *Indo* for a couple of reasons. Job security was one. I was still bearing the financial scars of the sudden demise of the original *Tribune*. I'd only been in Abbey Street a few months and was reluctant to jump ship so quickly. I felt a measure of loyalty to Michael Hand, who'd given me a desperately needed break.

My robust attacks on the FAI, the League of Ireland and Eoin Hand were regarded as a breach of the laws governing 'decentskinsmanship'. The word 'controversial' was beginning to appear next to my name. To

Peter Byrne of the *Irish Times*, the doyen of Irish soccer reportage, I wasn't 'a proper journalist' at all. That sentiment was widely shared, not least by some of my colleagues in Abbey Street. Michael Hand was very supportive though: 'Fuck them,' was his pithy response to readers' letters complaining about my copy's 'unprecedented' attacks on men 'who were only doing their jobs'.

On the downside of life in Abbey Street, the blue-docket pilfering used to supplement my salary was becoming a source of serious embarrassment. My regular visits to the accounts-department hatch were distressing. I hated dishonesty. Yet here I was, an active participant in institutionalized thieving.

On the other side of the hatch, the expression on the faces of the accounts clerks spoke of disdain verging on contempt. The crusading hack fiddling his expenses. I lowered my eyes, took the money and felt sick in the pit of my stomach. Friday, when I delivered my copy, was fiddling day. After leaving my copy at the sports desk, I usually went to see Michael for a chat and a docket. One Friday Michael reached into his desk drawer for the book of blue dockets. He signed one for me, then a second. 'Get this for me,' he said. 'I'm taking Denieffe out to lunch.'

Michael Denieffe was deputy editor. The docket was for thirty pounds. I didn't have the guts to refuse. Making my way down to the hatch, I resolved to stop this shit. I wasn't mad at Michael. He was just working the system. That night I called Vincent Browne to ask if the job he'd offered was still available.

There were no grades at the *Tribune*. There was no graft either. There was no graft because money was tight.

By the time I joined in December 1983 Browne and his patron Tony Ryan were estranged. Browne had assembled an all-star cast of journalists. Andy Barclay, a brilliant designer, had created a really good-looking broadsheet paper. But costs had spiralled and Ryan was unhappy. He installed his own suit, Eugene O'Neill, to keep an eye on costs. And on Vincent.

John Kelleher, hired as MD six months previously, was on his way out. He and Browne were close friends, but the Vincent you encountered in the workplace was a different animal from the laddish, banter-swapping companion you'd enjoy a pint with. In the office the amusing, mischievous Vincent of Doheny & Nesbitt's pub or the Horseshoe Bar vanished. In his place was the brooding, tetchy Browne, a rumbling volcano ready to erupt. On good days an uneasy calm settled round the *Tribune*'s open-plan office. But when Browne was on the prowl the prevailing mood was far from serene.

Nobody could doubt his brilliance as a journalist. *Magill* magazine was his creation. It set new standards, with some great journalists bringing authority, style and wit to the social and political issues of the day. The prospect of Browne editing a national Sunday newspaper was exciting. As the stellar cast of journalists assembled demonstrated, he had a great eye for talent. But, as time would prove, managing his gifted staff seemed beyond him.

The Vincent Browne enigma is one of Irish journalism's enduring mysteries. It is hard to understand his shafting of Mary Holland and Noel Pearson within weeks of them helping him to set up *Magill*. At the same time Mary and Noel remained on good terms with him after the deed was done. He identified and wooed many of Ireland's best journalists. Colm Tóibín, Gene Kerrigan, Fintan O'Toole, Emily O'Reilly: the list is long and distinguished. Yet one by one those to whom he'd offered a chance to make their mark fled Merrion Row, the swanky street in the fashionable part of town where *Magill* and the *Tribune* occupied offices fifty yards apart. Most partings were more in sorrow than in anger.

Most, but not all. Some who left never quite recovered from their trauma. Colm Tóibín and Paul Tansey quit journalism altogether, Tóibín to become a major critic and novelist, Tansey to take an MA in economics and become one of Ireland's most respected economic commentators. Mary Holland eventually found a home at the *Irish Times*, where she emerged as one of the most influential journalists of her generation. Fintan O'Toole also found refuge with the paper of record. Mary Raftery drifted away to the insecurity of freelance print and broadcast journalism. A remarkable woman of deep, enduring conviction, she would eventually expose the cancer of clerical sex abuse eating away the very soul of Catholic Ireland. In death, Mary was celebrated. In life, she was a victim of the endemic mediocrity of Irish journalism. A victim also of the fact that Vincent Browne's *Sunday Tribune* never really happened.

In terms of scale, the difference between running a monthly magazine and a weekly national newspaper was vast. For Browne, with his propensity for micro-management, the adjustment proved impossible. With a handful of writers, *Magill* was relatively easy to control. There were angry exchanges and tiresome conflict, but the day was usually saved. Sadly, the *Tribune* was too big to micro-manage. There were too many strong characters, secure and confident in their specialist subjects. They wouldn't yield when Browne sought to query their copy or their choice for story of the week. That didn't stop him interfering. In all of this, much energy was dissipated and the work suffered.

Most significantly, Browne's work. For in trying to control all around him he squandered time that would more usefully have been spent in being Vincent Browne, the story-breaking journalist. His *Tribune* never sold as many as its ill-fated predecessor.

Like everyone else who worked for him, I had a bumpy ride. Out of the office we got on really well. He'd been generous to me when I was out of work. He was generous with money as well. Soon after I joined the paper I had a major money problem. Between my reluctance to cash blue dockets and tendency for profligacy (and gambling), I was once again in arrears with my mortgage. I went to Browne looking for an advance on my wages. He produced a personal cheque for £1,000. 'Take your time,' he replied, when I assured him I'd repay the debt as soon as I could.

He was passionate about sport. And that caused problems. I wasn't writing much about the League of Ireland, which I considered a waste of time. But I was charged with previewing the weekend games. The League was being sponsored by Pat Grace's Fried Chicken chain of fast-food shops. Together with Paddy Agnew, our sports editor, and Gerry Thornley, who was working as a freelance reporter, I decided to parody what we disparagingly tagged 'The Chicken League'. We decided to take the piss out of the domestic game every other paper was taking seriously. Some of the copy was wild, offensive and, we thought, funny.

Browne was mortified. 'What are you guys doing? . . . You can't say that,' he raged, overcome by agitation. He wasn't into gonzo journalism, not even our minor-league efforts to mimic it. When we defied him, the mood darkened. The buck stopped with Paddy, our boss, a thoroughly nice fellow, now answerable for our sins.

For someone regarded as a radical, Browne was, as this story suggests, very conventional. Another sporting example serves to underline his curious conservatism. John Reason, the *Daily Telegraph*'s highly regarded rugby correspondent, was a regular contributor to *Magill*. Paddy Agnew started using him for the *Tribune*. Reason filed beautifully crafted prose that was a treat to read, even if you weren't interested in rugby. Some Irish rugby followers thought Reason was anti-Irish. He certainly didn't tailor his dispatches to find favour with Irish readers.

One Tuesday when I turned up for the weekly editorial conference I found Paddy at his desk, head in hands. When I asked what the problem was, he told me that John Reason was toast. Having been berated in a pub by a 'rugger-bugger' bank manager, who vowed never to buy the *Tribune* again if Reason's stuff was in the paper, Browne had decided to sack his rugby correspondent. Paddy had been delegated to wield the axe.

Keeping the head down to dodge the critical bullets was virtually impossible, particularly for department bosses. In a profile of Browne published recently, Fintan O'Toole calculated that between 1983 and 1990 the *Tribune* had lost five literary editors, three business editors, two arts editors, three sports editors (including Agnew), three chief subs, one deputy editor, one women's editor and three news editors. At *Magill*, across the road, Browne went through seven editors or managing editors in the same period, Colm Tóibín among them. Again, it should be noted that O'Toole remained on good terms with Browne, even though he was himself one of the 'Disappeared'.

Oddly enough, living on the edge of the Browne volcano fostered a certain camaraderie among the foot soldiers. An occasional contributor to *Magill*, I was particularly fond of Tóibín, who took over as editor when Browne relaunched the *Sunday Tribune*. Tóibín was then a wildly bearded, untidily dressed hippie who didn't bother to disguise his disdain for my sports commentary. I was going through a phase where I tended to contrast the innocent beauty of sport and sports people with the degeneracy of those elsewhere in public life, politicians, churchmen and various weasels in suits. I often described sport as uniquely character building.

A conscientious editor, Tóibín would summon me to his office to go through my copy line by line. Eyes widening, a disbelieving smile slowly forming across his whiskered face as he studied my submission, Tóibín would look up and, struggling to suppress the giggles, ask, 'You don't really believe this stuff, do you?' I did, of course, but I never took offence. He was a dazzling conversationalist with a crazy, brilliant mind, and seemed immune to the terror being waged across Merrion Row by

Browne. In the end his time with Browne would finish in severe trauma, but that, in 1984, was some way down the road.

One summer day, Colm, Fintan and I went to lunch in Bernardo's, an Italian restaurant at the back of Trinity College. I was older than both of them by ten and thirteen years respectively. Hungry for ideas and barely educated in comparison to these two young men, I was intrigued by their take on Ireland. I was happy, too, to talk about something other than soccer, in which neither of them had much interest. We talked about books and politics and, of course, about Vincent Browne and how we might form an 'escape committee'.

As time passed my own relationship with Browne grew more difficult. In the summer of 1984 he sent me to cover the Los Angeles Olympics. The Olympics movement had long since been drained of its original idealism. The LA Games were overshadowed by politics, drugs and the host's insatiable corporate greed. Eight years earlier, Montréal had gone bust hosting the Olympics. Determined not to go down that road, the Americans appointed Peter V. Ueberroth, a corporate titan from the airline business, as president of the LA Games. Ueberroth's stated aim was to make a profit of $15 million. To that end, people were not allowed to take their own food and drink into the Coliseum. Family ice boxes were impounded in what I described in my report for the *Tribune* as 'an act of corporate hooliganism'. Ueberroth insisted that he was merely 'protecting our concessionaires'. The only food available to spectators was hot dogs and burgers washed down with Coca-Cola.

'Hardly the Olympic spirit,' I wrote, 'but the spirit of LA.' The copy I sent back to Dublin was laced with tart observations about America, LA in particular:

Imagine a centre full of high-rise buildings, a massive heart of concrete and steel, into which all the arteries are clogged. Full of exhaust fumes. In the steaming nightmare live those who pursue the materialist dream. There are two million Mexicans, 200,000 Salvadorans, more Koreans than anywhere outside Korea, more Armenians than in Armenia. Thirty thousand of the population are homeless. The downtown faces are sometimes tired, sometimes alive and watchful for a chance to exploit the unwitting. The name of the game is getting out of this motorized slum. To the hills outside from where the better-off look down on their desperate past. On the hills the better-off tend to their insecurities with drugs and status symbols.

Nobody coming to Los Angeles could fail to sniff the toxic scent of the city, to experience some odd moment of fear and resentment. Fear that on the streets the violence that lay barely dormant on the still night air would suddenly erupt in your face, would choose you as a victim. Resentment at being commercially exploited by hoteliers, peddlers of souvenirs or most disgracefully by the Los Angeles Olympic Committee.

Back at the Tribune during a post-Olympic debrief, Browne queried my dispatches from Los Angeles, the criticism of the host city in particular, American values in general. A Mr Plummer from Malibu had written to the paper deploring my 'diatribe' about his homeland. 'Being from Los Angeles and very fond of my ancestral Ireland I was deeply hurt,' Mr Plummer whinged.

We were sitting in Browne's office when he produced Plummer's letter. What did I have to say? he asked.

'Tell him to fuck off, Vincent,' I replied.

This was an action replay of the 'rugger-bugger' bank manager in the bar scenario that had led to John Reason's sacking. I couldn't believe Browne's sensitivity to readers' often idle criticism. He proceeded to interrogate me on the merits or otherwise of American corporatism, liberty and the pursuit of happiness, US style. At some stage or other, every *Tribune* staffer endured his version of Alex Ferguson's hairdryer treatment. I gave as good as I got, but left his office feeling drained and dispirited.

Eight months after joining the *Tribune* I had come to the conclusion that the *enfant terrible* was a sheep in wolf's clothing. And that summer of 1984 I was well placed to distinguish between wolf and sheep.

In the build-up to the European Championship Finals earlier that summer I had discussed RTÉ's coverage with Tim O'Connor and programme editor Mike Horgan. I argued that our coverage lacked rigour. Why not try something original? Get John Giles alongside myself and Bill O'Herlihy and do some in-depth analysis that would engage the soccer community. Let's go hardcore, was the message. Tim and Mike were tough guys, wolves in wolves' clothing. Still, my big new idea was a hard sell. They wouldn't accept John at any price. 'He'll say fuck all,' Tim insisted, instancing John's notorious monosyllabic responses to journalists looking for enlightenment. Mike agreed. I argued that John's knowledge and passion for the game were a vast resource RTÉ could tap into. Bill O'Herlihy was the perfect man to engage with John. I'd provide the showbiz.

The lads weren't buying John. But they agreed to go hardcore with just me and Bill in the studio.

France hosted the tournament. Their captain, Platini, was widely regarded as Europe's best footballer. He had replaced Liam Brady as the sole foreign player Juventus were permitted to sign. I thought Platini was overrated. I'd seen him play for France at Lansdowne Road in a World Cup qualifier in 1981. Ireland had won 3–2. Platini was missing in action. When we previewed Euro '84 on RTÉ I assured Bill O'Herlihy and the viewers that France wouldn't win the tournament. I cited Platini's lack of character as the reason.

'But, Eamon, he's regarded as the best player in Europe, if not the world,' Bill asserted.

'Don't worry, Bill, he'll be found out. That's what happens in major championships. That's what championships are for, sorting out the real great players from the imposters,' said I. This was hardcore, telling it like it was.

Platini scored the winner in France's opening game against Denmark.

'Well, Eamon, what do you make of that?' O'Herlihy wondered.

'Don't worry, Bill, it's only Denmark,' was my smug response. A trickle of complaints began to flow into RTÉ's front office.

Then Platini scored a hat-trick against Belgium to ensure that France topped their group. The RTÉ switchboard was alight with angry soccer fans queuing up to complain. 'He's not being found out, Eamon,' said Bill, putting the boot in.

'Look, Bill, he's a good player, but he's not a great player.' I was sticking to my guns.

Before the semi-final against Portugal I went for broke. 'He'll be found out today,' I predicted to a visibly shaken O'Herlihy, who was bearing witness to a man intent on committing professional suicide.

The semi-final went to extra time. Platini scored the winner in the last minute. Platini had scored eight goals in four games and France would face Spain in the final. The trickle of complaints was now a flood. RTÉ's credibility was on the line.

The decent skins of Dublin journalism were beside themselves with unadulterated joy. The satirist Dermot Morgan was on my case. I had, quite literally, become a national joke. In the dénouement, Michel Platini scored the opening goal in the final against Spain. Game to the end, I persisted with the idea that distinguishing between the good and the great was important. Compared to Cruijff, Beckenbauer, Best, Charlton, Pelé and Maradona, Platini was not a great player.

My spectacular failure to call the European Championship was a source of much amusement in Decentskinsmanland.

Tim O'Connor was brilliant. He laughed out loud at all the fuss. 'You're mad,' he told me, 'but it was great television.' The viewing figures were the best ever for soccer on RTÉ. I should be fair to Vincent Browne here: I was writing the same anti-Platini stuff for the *Tribune* without any recriminations. At that point anyway.

I had a drink with John Giles after the tournament. Was I wrong about Platini? I wondered. 'No, you weren't,' he said, 'but maybe you were wrong to say it on television.'

45. Epiphany

The Platini business taught me a couple of important lessons. If you expressed a forthright opinion and were mistaken, people would give you a break as long as they believed you were sincere. The cute hoors would snigger and mock to the point of caricature, but viewers and readers were smart enough to work you out for themselves. They didn't necessarily want a sage, rather someone telling it as they saw it, with whom they could engage. The other lesson learned was the need for support from your bosses.

Tim O'Connor and Mike Horgan never flinched. RTÉ stood by me on the basis that a singular voice, though challenging, was essential in all forms of commentary and analysis. It was a very different RTÉ back then. On another part of the campus Gay Byrne's *Late Late Show* was breaking all kinds of taboos and doing it with vigour and relish. I was no Gay Byrne, and we were only talking soccer, but the principle was the same. Fear was noticeably absent.

This was quite a contrast to the *Tribune*, where Vincent Browne was fretting about bank managers and residents of Malibu. I took note. Quite apart from his innate conservatism, Browne's biggest problem was the *Tribune*'s lack of financial muscle. When he wasn't fighting with his staff, Vincent was at war with the money men or, worse, pleading for a dig-out with potential sugar-daddies like Martin Naughton or Dermot Desmond. At one stage he is reported to have approached Charlie Haughey for financing. My days on Merrion Row were numbered. With nothing to lose, I decided to go out with a bang.

I wasn't assigned to cover the centenary all-Ireland hurling final in Thurles in September but it was certain to be a great occasion so I went with a couple of pals, Enda Marren, my Blueshirt Handler friend, and Oliver Barry, one of Ireland's leading concert promoters and one of Charlie Haughey's most ardent supporters. It was a wonderful day. Enda regaled us on the way to Thurles with great stories about Ronald Reagan's recent visit to his ancestral home of Ballyporeen in south Tipperary. The US president had charmed everyone he met on the visit.

Everyone except Garret FitzGerald, our esteemed Taoiseach, who had important matters of state to discuss with the most powerful politician in the Western world.

Reagan had no interest in matters of state. Every time Garret tried to raise the issues, the North being top of the list, the former Hollywood idol changed the subject. Garret was trying to reach some accommodation with Margaret Thatcher on the North. He was hoping that Reagan might use his influence with the British prime minister to broker some kind of deal. This was urgent business. But Ronnie wasn't going there.

In Dublin on the final day of the visit, a one-on-one meeting was scheduled between Taoiseach and president. According to Enda the meeting was a disaster. Every time Garret tried to talk politics, Reagan urged him to desist. 'Talk to the guys [his aides] about that,' Reagan insisted. Mr President didn't want to know about politics. Instead he spent the sixty precious (to Garret) minutes telling anecdotes about Hollywood. These were interspersed with risqué jokes and perfectly timed punchlines.

Frustrated, FitzGerald emerged from the tête-à-tête shaking his head in bewilderment. 'Is this guy for real?' Garret asked his advisers from Foreign Affairs. The answer was yes. So three days of bowing and scraping and general paddywhackery had been for nothing.

Oliver Barry was greatly amused by 'Garret the Good's' inability to engage Ronald Reagan. Charlie would have figured that one out, he teased Enda. Joking apart, our trip to Thurles was politics-free. The Blueshirt, the Soldier and the former junior Handler were united in sport. I found the day very moving. Although off duty, I decided to write a piece for the following Sunday's paper. At the end of an often trying summer, Centenary Final day in Thurles helped crystallize my thoughts and emotions about the country I'd returned to after seventeen years in exile. It appeared in the following Sunday's paper under the headline 'Which Ireland was in Thurles?'

Centenary Sunday morning was light grey and peaceful. By half-past eight we were well on the way. The small towns and villages were slowly waking up, women taking in the milk, solitary men walking back from Mass, reading the papers.

Despite my dodgy credentials I always have the feeling travelling down the country of going home. In the lovely curious faces, the sounds of kids laughing in the fields, the imagined whiff of soda bread one recognizes something indefinable from the past. Even if you're Unofficial. So many celebrations of Official Ireland and Official Irishness are, well, bewildering . . .

At half-past ten the town square was crowded but not packed. People walked slowly through the streets looking at other people. This is a peaceful, gentle, good-humoured thing, an extraordinary luxury in our busy lives. There are few days when we have the time to simply stroll. Here we had four or five hours to kill before the match, time to talk and reflect . . .

By matchtime one felt almost official, almost proper. The Soccerman had been recognized but no harm had come to him. 'What are you doing here?' They laughed, but it was a friendly greeting, a parody of the Official Attitude . . .

And then Jack Lynch was called. He was cheered longer, louder and with such deep affection that we wondered why? A great hurler among great hurlers, yes. A Corkman among Corkmen, yes. But so loud, so long, so deep?

Technically, economically, nationalistically speaking he was not a great politician. Lynch, it could be – and was – argued, was one of the principal architects of our economic slump. A man who did, some would say, stand idly by. Yet, astonishingly, through the public persona there filtered from Jack Lynch a sense of . . . decency, tolerance, good humour . . . a sense of simple virtues . . . that separated him from Official Ireland . . . that linked him with the morning scenes in Liberty Square. And this the people understood as he now walked out to join his hurling peers. Unlike Official Ireland, which sat strongly in their Official Box and craved this kind of public response, Lynch wore a sports coat and pants.

He knew something about Ireland that the others didn't. He knew about its decent, non-sectarian human soul.

And then there followed a man who didn't know. The voice of Official Ireland, Ballyporeen Revisited: Fr Leo Ó Moracháin.

We now know his identity, but when he hijacked the proceedings as the teams lined up for the Centenary Final he was only a voice. A strident voice, redolent of Nuremberg. This was the Official Message. 'A toast to memory, Race memory.' The words were shocking, a sickening contradiction of the day we were having. 'Celtic Mists . . . stream of people's history . . . bowed neck, broken treaty . . .'

At first it was a murmur of disquiet, then people started whistling, booing and finally we looked embarrassed at each other . . . and laughed. The great pure song of freedom?

Ho, ho, ho.

'Wherever green is worn.'

In truth we couldn't hear the words . . . but we understood the sentiments. It was the strident, unmistakable voice of fanaticism. There was no place for it at the Centenary Hurling Final.

When the GAA celebrate their second hundred years in Thurles in 2084 they should remember that.

The day belonged to Jack Lynch and the people. It was a celebration of what we really are, not what we are supposed to be.

Nothing illustrated this more than the game, the hero of which was a small fat – yes, fat – Corkman, Seanie O'Leary. If you saw him out jogging you'd laugh and advise him to steady on.

Hurling is a great game because it can accommodate his sort of genius, allow for the nonconformist. There are no Official Hurlers. If there were, little fat Seanie would be . . . Disqualified.

One travelled home joyous with that thought . . . and another. That there are no Official Irishmen either. The people are wiser than their rulers.

Up the Republic!

The derision that greeted the gombeen cleric invoking race memory was the most revealing moment in a beautiful day. (Significantly, no national newspaper reported the crowd's mocking of the priest.) The vestiges of the Ireland of my youth, where you were identified by what sport you played, which church you worshipped in, whether or not you spoke the Language, were still around. People paid lip-service to old shibboleths, but in Semple Stadium on Centenary Final Day the scorn directed at Father Leo Ó Moracháin suggested a certain contempt for those who would divide the nation on the basis of class, creed or race memory.

The people had moved on, were less inclined to genuflect before the iconography of Official Ireland. People, in this instance, from Ireland's rural heartland, where gombeenism was supposed to be alive and well and still as resonant as it had always been.

The reception Jack Lynch got was particularly interesting. A fallen Soldier of Destiny, brought down by his own tribe. A failed politician, in fact. Yet it was Lynch the crowd wished to salute, the decent, tolerant

Cork hurler of yore, who had never roused the rabble or waved the flag of sectarian hatred. People were done with that old cant, even though a few miles up the road in the North, men and women were still dying – and killing – for the cause.

'What's Official Ireland?' Browne asked, when I next saw him in the office.

'You should know,' I replied. 'You're at the heart of it.' I coined the phrase in the Thurles piece to identify the Irish Establishment, all elements of it: political parties, the Catholic Church, the Gaels not just in sport but in the arts and every cultural nook and cranny, including Irish journalism, all celebrating in one form or another a narrow version of Irish identity that was, in essence, bogus.

Unlike the England I'd left, where a new wave of satirists and writers had attacked the Establishment with mocking caricatures and savage invective, Irish intellectuals were tame, compliant facilitators of official cant. They sought not to satirize but to get their hands on Arts Council grants – and to find a little niche in Official Ireland. What Patrick Kavanagh memorably described as the 'Devil Mediocrity' in his epic poem *The Paddiad* stalked the land. Journalists, some honourable exceptions apart, were working off official scripts intent on causing no offence. Browne's *Sunday Tribune* was no different.

Ironically, across Merrion Row, *Magill* magazine was a source of some discomfort to Official Ireland, its bent police force in particular. Under Colm Tóibín's editorship, journalists like Gene Kerrigan, Derek Dunne and Eamonn McCann were given free rein to pursue the corruption endemic in the state. Kerrigan's epic account of the unsolved Kerry Babies case in 1985 was a classic piece of investigative journalism.

It is now part of official Irish mythology that Browne sought to expose Charlie Haughey's corrupt behaviour in the 1980s. This simply isn't true. During the second 1982 election campaign I was present at a Fianna Fáil press conference where Browne interrogated Haughey about the source of his wealth. The myth suggests that Haughey squirmed under questioning. In fact, he sat there laughing at the *enfant terrible*, enjoying nothing more threatening than undergraduate banter. It was a game rather than an exposé.

As the truth about Browne became ever clearer to me – that he was a licensed jester at Official Ireland's court – I made my mind up to leave Merrion Row at the first opportunity.

46. The Horseshoe Bar

Sam Stephenson, an architect friend of Charlie Haughey, designed the Horseshoe Bar in the Shelbourne Hotel. Shaped like a horseshoe with a high ceiling, wide mirrors and low lighting, it is a beautiful room. In the sixties, when they were rising stars in Fianna Fáil, the coming men who would continue Seán Lemass's modernizing project, Haughey, Donogh O'Malley and Brian Lenihan frequented the bar. It is said that the Haughey/Terry Keane liaison began in the Horseshoe over champagne cocktails.

The economic woes of the seventies and early eighties had taken a toll on that part of Dublin, where bright young things with grand ambitions shared gossip and dreams. Grooms Hotel, another Haughey hangout, and the Hibernian on Dawson Street had closed their doors. The Horseshoe Bar remained, but the gilded age was over. In eighties Dublin money was tight. Save for Horse Show week in August, the room was largely empty.

I started drinking there in 1983. The Horseshoe was a three-minute walk from the *Tribune* and *Magill*. Vincent Browne arranged to meet me there to discuss my move to Merrion Row. After we'd concluded our business we were joined by PJ Mara, Fianna Fáil press secretary. In fact, PJ was much more than a press secretary. He was Haughey's aide-de-camp, and even that description does less than justice to PJ's role in the Haughey story.

After the Arms Trial, Haughey became a pariah among senior members of his party. Cast into the wilderness by his peers, yet much admired by the grassroot Soldiers, Haughey began his comeback by touring the country, rallying the faithful to his cause. This was a long, lonely journey in search of redemption. PJ drove the car. No better man. Like his boss – the Boss – PJ was smart and streetwise. He was amusing, a connoisseur of men's vanities and other foibles, quick to spot the right button to press, be it on the Dublin correspondent of the august London *Times* or a low-life cute hoor in deepest rural Ireland. He was a hustler, a charming cynic.

We were long acquainted. He was born in Millmount Avenue, a stone's throw from St Pat's National School which, like me, he'd attended. He was five years older than me, the same age as Dessie Toal, whom PJ knew. Both were striking figures in my Drumcondra. I would often see him when roaming the streets looking for mischief as a kid. Always smartly turned out even in the fifties, PJ was no street kid. He strolled with purpose through the neighbourhood, a man, though young, on a mission, to the tennis-club dances, or maybe a meeting of the local Fianna Fáil *cumann* to hatch election plots or arrange the shafting of dissidents like my dad, occupying jobs that were needed for the more deserving Soldiers. PJ knew my father, Paddy, 'A decent man,' he declared in the Horseshoe Bar the night we met. He knew Sam Prole, the Dump, Father Mac, knew Drumcondra inside out, every lane and alleyway, every house and how they voted.

Because it was close to the *Tribune*, I would pop into the Horseshoe a couple of times a week. I was a modest drinker, a two-bottles-of-Heineken man, three on a wild night. The fun, gossip and, oddly, the tranquillity of that beautifully designed space were the attraction. Years later, towards the end of the eighties, the journalist John Boland wrote an article for the *Independent* about the bar's then well-known regulars. Sam Smyth also wrote a piece depicting a Fianna Fáil salon populated by Dublin's movers and shakers. But in the early days the Horseshoe was mostly empty, an elegant, fading relic of Dublin's glamorous past.

My involvement with the Blueshirts was a source of much amusement to PJ and other Soldiers, like Noel Pearson, Oliver Barry and Michael Hand's twin brother Jim, who drank in the Horseshoe. Jim was in the music business, managing the Dubliners, the Fureys and Johnny Logan, the Eurovision winner. Where Michael was gentle and full of impish fun, Jim was tough, with a scabrous line in put-downs. He was a Haughey fanatic. When CJ, as Jim always called the Boss, lost the November 1982 general election, the allegedly decent wing of the party launched a heave against his leadership. Jim Gibbons, a former Fianna Fáil cabinet minister, was a leading Haughey critic. When Haughey survived the leadership challenge after the lost election, Gibbons was physically attacked and knocked to the ground on the steps of Leinster House by a mob of drunken Haugheyites. Jim Hand was in the mob in scenes that were unprecedented in parliament buildings. He was a rare exception to the rule that decreed you left your politics outside the barroom door. When Jim was holding court in the Horseshoe everyone was fair game.

'Dunphy, you little working-class gurrier,' he roared at me one night. 'What the fuck are you doing with those fucking Blueshirts? You're giving them street cred. They wouldn't know the difference between Millwall and Manchester United, and if they did, they wouldn't have anything to do with you,' he taunted. Jim's devotion to CJ was real; the volley aimed at me wasn't. Five minutes later he was over with a bottle of Heineken. 'Here, you fucking eejit, have a drink.'

Jim's occasional breaches of protocol apart, the Horseshoe was a politics-free zone. PJ was said to be viciously partisan during the internecine warfare that blighted the Soldiers during their eighties years in opposition. But unlike Jim, PJ could 'cool the jets' to present an avuncular persona to the world. 'Now, now, Jim, lay off,' he would chide the bulky, hostile Dubliners' manager when things threatened to get out of hand. 'Leave the man alone.'

As with everyone he came across, PJ knew which buttons to press with me. Drumcondra, the football, the characters . . . Blind Matt . . . Dodgy Father Mac . . . Dessie Toal . . . Tolka Park and the epic battles between Drums and Rovers . . . the girls we'd lusted after in the far-off fifties: all of that now seemed so far away. The dreadful floods of 1954, which had turned his Millmount Avenue and my Richmond Road into a stinking swamp.

We also shared a passion for books. He was a Betjeman fan like me. Unlike me, PJ could recite from memory one of the poet's most popular poems 'A Subaltern's Love Song': with a lusty gleam in his eye, PJ would begin,

> Miss J. Hunter Dunn, Miss J. Hunter Dunn,
> Furnish'd and burnish'd by Aldershot sun,
> What strenuous singles we played after tea,
> We in the tournament – you against me.

'She'd have done for you and me.' PJ would grin at the prospect of a liaison with this iconic English rose. He was an uncommon and hugely enjoyable companion on a quiet Tuesday night in a largely empty bar in a city where recessionary gloom was the order of the day.

Drink was expensive in the Horseshoe, hence the scarcity of

customers. It was PJ's presence and, of course, his proximity to 'The Great Leader in Waiting'. Haughey, that caused other notable Soldiers to gravitate there.

On the subject of Haughey, PJ was discreet. He knew about my antipathy to his boss, but being well-reared northside boys we checked our work in at the cloakroom. On the subject of Terry Keane, PJ made no secret of his belief that she was 'a menace'.

Shane Ross was another Horseshoe regular. A wealthy stockbroker and independent senator for Trinity College, Ross was one of the bar's great stars. He was a public schoolboy (Rugby), married to one of Ireland's great beauties, the talented broadcaster Ruth Buchanan. Along with his fellow Trinity senator Mary Robinson, Ross was a vocal advocate of the liberal agenda in the upper house. He was an Anglican with a large unionist constituency in Trinity.

When the New Ireland Forum called for joint authority in the North, Charlie Haughey's response was to call for a united Ireland. This absurd opportunism by PJ's boss, and other cultural and religious differences, did not in any way damage Ross and PJ's close friendship. 'He's a great chum,' PJ declared, when he introduced me to Ross. They'd served together in the Senate. Despite the public utterings of Haughey, PJ was an Anglophile; the word 'chum' was like his fondness for Betjeman, an indication of his cultural proclivity.

In those days Ross was fond of a drink. So fond of gin and tonic – large – that he'd be three-quarters pissed by sundown. He could be very funny. One night he arrived in good form and spotted me sitting quietly in my usual corner. With no PJ to protect me I was fair game for the senator. 'Jimmy,' he brayed, addressing the head barman, Jimmy Kelly, 'there's a footballer in here, a Millwall footballer. He's lowering the tone, Jimmy, can't we kick him out?'

'Now, now, Senator Ross, we don't want too much noise,' Jimmy cautioned. The moment passed. Save for Jim and Ross, malice rarely featured in the Horseshoe. Over time, Ross and I became great friends. He gave up stockbroking and drinking to become an outstanding journalist.

His friendship with PJ also endured. Years later when PJ was government press secretary he asked Ross to propose him for membership of the Kildare Street Club, a bastion of old Protestant money. Ross was happy to oblige. When summoned before the membership committee to make the case for PJ, Ross cited his important position as government press secretary and his closeness to the Taoiseach.

One esteemed elderly committee man asked Ross who the current Taoiseach was. 'Mr Haughey,' Ross replied.

At which point another member of the committee remarked, 'Does that mean I might come down to breakfast one morning and find Colonel Gaddafi in the dining room?'

Ross allayed all fears and PJ became the first Drumcondra man to join the Kildare Street Club. Maybe the first Drumcondra man who ever wanted to join the Kildare Street Club.

There was always fun of one kind or another in the Shelbourne. Noel Pearson, Oliver Barry, Paul McGuinness, Sam Smyth and John Kelleher were regulars. So was the writer Tony Cronin, Haughey's cultural adviser. He regarded Haughey as the most gifted, imaginative politician of his generation. Rogue he might be, but a cultured rogue and a committed patron of the arts. Colm Tóibín contributed greatly to the fun, his laser gaze scanning the room for the stories incubating in every corner. Scattered along the bar on any given night was a cast of characters who added a comforting frisson of low-life to the scene: the struck-off solicitor; the dodgy bank executive; the man from the stock exchange with a drink problem. And some ladies of a certain age, the unfulfilled wives of merchants out of town. On its better nights, the Horseshoe Bar was full of possibilities.

For a few months before I left the *Tribune* I wrote some television columns for the paper. They were nothing special. But in a couple of them I wrote harshly about popular national characters. Maeve Binchy, then an *Irish Times* columnist beginning to make her name as a novelist, was universally liked. After watching her on Terry Wogan's BBC chat show indulging with the host in a bout of paddywhackery, I wrote a barbed piece about the caricature Irishness of the item. Sister Stanislaus Kennedy, Ireland's favourite caring nun, also got a lash. As did Derek Davis, a self-regarding fixture on RTÉ.

One night in the Horseshoe another regular, Noel Pearson, gave me a pull. His message was blunt: 'Do yourself a favour, stick to the football.' I wasn't too bothered. The iron law of journalism stated that sportswriters should confine themselves to the Toy Department. There was no badness in Noel. He was simply marking my card. In fact, Noel was the last person who should have been proffering advice to stick to what you're good at.

After starting out as a small-time hustler on the Dublin music scene, running dances, managing baby bands, doing whatever it took to avoid the dreaded nine-to-five existence, Noel defied his nay-saying contemporaries by thinking big. While managing the Dubliners at the height of their fame, he was restless to move on.

He took a gamble to invite Diana Ross to Dublin in 1969. He brought the cultish American singer-songwriter Dory Previn to the city for a season at the Olympia. Musicals were expensive and risky to put on, yet Noel mounted his own production of Andrew Lloyd Webber and Tim Rice's first show, *Joseph and the Amazing Technicolor Dreamcoat* with Tony Kenny in the lead role. Against all the odds, *Joseph* was a huge hit in Dublin, running for over a year. 'Mr P' was a sitting duck for Dublin begrudgers. Who does he think he is? Hence, perhaps, his warning to me.

Noel was gruff, shy and soft-spoken. He was very friendly with Haughey and vocal in his dislike for Blueshirts. He lacerated me for my flirtation with FitzGerald. He didn't like Ross. I was very fond of Noel, always glad when he was on the premises. He told wonderful stories about Dublin life, about Behan, Kavanagh and Myles, about theatre folk Micheál Mac Liammóir and Hilton Edwards (in whose grand house he would eventually live), musicians, journos and politicians.

Undaunted by the pessimism of those mid-eighties years, Mr P nursed an extraordinary dream, a movie he wanted to make about the life of Christy Brown, the writer and painter who'd overcome severe cerebral palsy to write the best-selling memoir *Down All the Days*. His left foot was the only moving part of Christy's body. With that left foot he wrote and painted. Christy's was a story of barely believable courage and defiance. Noel was his manager in his final years. They'd talked about the prospect of a film.

The rights to *Down All the Days* were already sold so Noel bought the available film rights to Christy's slender first book, *My Left Foot*. As depicted by Noel, Brown was anything but a victim, his tale no sob story. Christy didn't think of himself as disabled. He was irascible, ambitious, a skirt-chasing man about town. He wanted Marlon Brando to play him in the movie, he told Mr P, or, if not, Robert Redford. Christy Brown died in 1981, his Hollywood dream unfulfilled.

The film eventually appeared in 1989. Daniel Day-Lewis won an Oscar for his portrayal of the indefatigable Christy. Brenda Fricker claimed the Academy award for Best Supporting Actress in the role of Christy's mother. In the movie's credits, Mr P is listed as producer. He was much more than that. *My Left Foot* was, like Pearson's original telling of its hero's story in the Horseshoe Bar, remarkably free of sentimentality.

I first met Mary Harney in the Horseshoe Bar in the mid-eighties, just after she and Des O'Malley split from Fianna Fáil and created a new party, the Progressive Democrats. The PDs promised new politics. They seemed to herald the dawn of a new post-Civil War polity in which ideas mattered more than which side your father fought for in the War of Independence. In the general election of 1987 the new party won fourteen seats. Flush from the success of my U2 book, I wrote a cheque to boost their fighting fund, and found myself the laughing stock of the Horseshoe Bar, where the presiding Soldiers recalled my love affair with Garret the Good.

'When will it be our turn?' Oliver Barry teased me.

'We wouldn't have him,' PJ tartly observed. 'He's no sense of loyalty.'

'How do you define loyalty?' I enquired.

With a devilish grin, PJ put it very succinctly: 'Once bought, you stay bought.' We laughed and ordered another round.

Although in retrospect it seems pathetic to have been bantering about cronyism with Oliver, against whom the Mahon Tribunal made adverse findings, that was the way it was. I wasn't the only fool in town. Sam Smyth and Vincent Browne, two of the country's leading newshounds, were close friends of PJ and Oliver. The truth is, nobody knew how deep the cancer of corruption ran. Yes, rumour abounded, but except for the land rezoning scams taking place in the corridors of Dublin County Council, facts were thin on the ground. And even the bribes associated with planning could be explained away as political donations.

When Joe Joyce and Peter Murtagh published *The Boss* in 1983, it was acclaimed as a classic account of Haughey's nine-month term as Taoiseach in 1982. It was superb reportage but, hamstrung by libel laws and absence of firm evidence, Joyce and Murtagh could do little more than establish Haughey's ruthlessness. In the *Sunday Tribune* Vincent Browne lavished praise on 'by far the best book published on contemporary Irish politics – *but* it does betray a prevalent contempt for Haughey'. The italic is mine. Browne's caveat suggests, though, that he was unconvinced Haughey deserved contempt.

For those of us who claimed to be journalists while hanging out in the Horseshoe Bar swapping drinks and gossip with Haughey's buddies, the findings of the Moriarty Tribunal make sobering reading. Moriarty, a notably scrupulous judge not prone to hyperbole, found that between 1979 and 1986 Haughey was paid more than £8 million by various benefactors and businessmen; £1.3 million was paid by Ben Dunne. In return, Moriarty found that Haughey had arranged a meeting between the businessman and Seamus Pairceir of the Revenue Commissioners, which resulted in an outstanding capital-gains tax bill being reduced by £22.8 million. Moriarty found that this was 'not coincidental' and that a substantial benefit was conferred on Dunne by Haughey's actions.

Nobody could accuse Charlie of disloyalty to Big Ben. Once bought, he stayed bought. It was the citizens who picked up the tab for £22.8 million.

Mary Harney deplored the cute hoorism and corruption associated with Charlie Haughey and his cronies, Ray Burke prominent among them.

She singled out Burke in our first conversation. For at least a decade, Burke had been suspected of corrupting the planning process. Three garda investigations had failed to nail him. Harney confirmed that corruption was rife in Dublin County Council, where she'd served for two years. Developers, builders and councillors from all parties were engaged in a massive conspiracy, she alleged. When I asked why the guards had failed to find the evidence, she shrugged her shoulders and smiled. The implication seemed to be that the police hadn't tried too hard.

Burke's fellow soldiers, Charlie Haughey and Seán Doherty, were former ministers for justice. Burke was currently a cabinet minister, untouchable despite all the rumours about him. No policeman was going to make trouble for Fianna Fáil. Justice was for the little people. This tolerance for corruption clearly frustrated Harney. The Progressive Democrats would, she vouched, be different. I was impressed. An honest politician. Like Garret the Good.

I became friendly with Harney. We socialized from time to time. On the North and the ailing economy, the two big issues of the day, the PDs and the *Sunday Indo* were on the same page, both against high taxation, both uncompromising on terrorism. As with Garret FitzGerald, I made no attempt to hide my infatuation with Harney and Des O'Malley.

The PDs lost eight of their fourteen seats in the 1989 general election. Haughey called the election, hoping to win an overall majority. But voters spurned the Soldiers, who lost four seats. When the votes were counted, no party was in a position to form a government. For the first time in Irish history, no Taoiseach was appointed when the new Dáil assembled. After a month of horsetrading, Des O'Malley's PDs swallowed their principles and did a deal with Haughey. Even those who accepted Bismarck's adage, that politics was the art of the possible, were taken aback when O'Malley and Haughey sealed the deal. Ray Burke was appointed minister for justice in the new administration.

My friend Mary got a junior ministry: Environmental Protection. She was an outstanding minister. Resisting powerful vested interests, some in her own cabinet, she legislated to ban the sale of bituminous coal in Dublin, which eliminated smog from the city. Unlike most politicians, Harney was not diminished by office. She was not intimidated by civil servants telling her what couldn't be done. Smog was a blight on the lives of her constituents in the less well-off areas of Dublin West. I was impressed by Harney's clear-eyed commitment to fulfil her election promises. There was a hint of Margaret Thatcher about her no-nonsense approach to the lobbyists for coal. Privately shy and a touch gauche, she was a formidable public speaker. When discussing the planning corruption with me one night, she suggested telling what she knew to a journalist. 'How about telling me?' I ventured.

'No, no,' she blurted out. 'I mean a proper journalist, someone like Sam Smyth.'

I wasn't offended by her lack of tact. I was no Carl Bernstein when it came to breaking stories.

The government she served in was doomed. Seán Doherty knifed Haughey. Albert Reynolds and Des O'Malley fell out over beef. The government collapsed. O'Malley appointed Harney deputy leader when the PDs returned to opposition. Eight months later O'Malley resigned as leader. He favoured Harney to succeed him. He tipped her off twenty-four hours before announcing his resignation but no advantage was conferred. In fact, O'Malley's clumsy attempt to anoint Harney annoyed other members of the PD parliamentary party who would choose his successor. Pat Cox was her main challenger. Newly arrived in politics from a career as an RTÉ current-affairs reporter, Cox was a wily backroom operator. Harney or Cox? The ten PD TDs would make the call.

A week before the election Harney asked me to meet her for a drink. She told me Cox had the election in the bag. It wouldn't even be close. By Harney's tally, Cox would win 7–3. Harney believed that she was more popular than Cox with the public: the successful anti-smog legislation and her gender were, she felt, major pluses. Ironically she believed there was a bias against electing a woman leader within the parliamentary party. An opinion poll was her only hope, she confided. Could I persuade my editor at the *Sunday Independent*, Aengus Fanning, to commission such a poll for the following Sunday, the day before the leadership election?

Aengus was sceptical. Opinion polls were expensive. A single-issue poll seemed extravagant. I enlisted the help of deputy editor Anne Harris. She backed me. The prospect of the first woman leader of an Irish political party was enticing. It was a good story if the numbers fell right. Aengus yielded. Sunday's paper led with the news that the public preferred Harney, 67 per cent to 33 per cent. Game over.

Harney won easily. The following day she treated me to lunch. She was relieved. And grateful. My reward was an offer to stand for the PDs at the next election. I politely declined. She was remarkably clear-minded about her strategy for what was now her party. She rejected my suggestion that the PDs should broaden their appeal beyond its middle-class base. She would aim for between ten and fifteen seats, which would allow the PDs a decisive say in the formation of future governments. Her vision was uncannily accurate.

One gloomy Tuesday night in the mid-eighties, my *Tribune* colleague Paul Tansey came into the Horseshoe Bar with Paul McGuinness, manager of the rock band U2. The Pauls and Shane Ross had been contemporaries at Trinity College. The two lads were looking for Ross, who was missing in action on this particular night. McGuinness complimented me on my sportswriting. He wasn't into sport, he explained, but he found my stuff interesting. His band were looking for a biographer and he wondered if I would be interested in writing their book. Although flattered, I told Paul that I knew nothing about the music scene. Anyway, I was anxious to get on with writing a biography of Matt Busby, an idea I'd had for some time.

A week later Paul and I had lunch. U2 were planning a new album, which he thought would be a breakthrough record. They had a huge fan base in America, Britain and around Europe. They didn't want what Paul described as 'a rock hack' to do their book. They wanted someone Irish and independent. He promised full access to his 'clients' and no censorship of the finished product.

I agreed to call my London publishers to see if they were interested in a U2 book. The answer was no. An emphatic no, because a recently published rock book, a biography of the superstar Bruce Springsteen, had flopped so badly they couldn't give it away. My advance for the Busby book was £20,000. I offered a £5,000 discount on the U2 book. Still no go, in London.

At Paul's invitation I went to meet his clients. U2 were due to play a gig at Milton Keynes. I travelled with them. We stayed at the Bell in Aston Clinton, a tiny village in Buckinghamshire, about fifteen miles from the venue. The Bell had one of the best restaurants in Britain. Dinner was very much a family occasion. The band's wives and girlfriends, Paul and his wife Kathy Gilfillan enjoyed fine wine and good food at a long, rectangular table.

There was no rock 'n' roll. No drugs. No groupies. Expecting a rather different scene, I'd brought a small stash of hash. But there was no party. Even Adam Clayton, U2's designated hell-raiser, was in bed by half past midnight.

They were up bright and breezy the following morning. We talked about the book, what the research would involve, how long it would take. Bono did most of the talking. He was smart, tough, very much the first among equals. The piece I'd written about the Centenary Final in Thurles, about the fanatic cleric evoking race memory, had caught Bono's eye. He wanted to know if I really believed what I wrote about Official Ireland and the complex question of identity. I assured him I did.

U2 were four Protestants from the Dublin suburbs. Outsiders. 'You don't buy the Official deal?' Bono asked.

'No,' I replied.

I told them about my stash. They laughed. 'Next time talk to Adam. He's in charge of entertainment,' Bono advised.

That night's concert in Milton Keynes Bowl was amazing. I resolved to tell their story. I had no book deal. It would be a small book. I hoped to explore through the U2 story the larger question of Irish identity. I even had a title in mind: *Suburban Heroes*.

47. Big Jack

Eoin Hand finally lost the manager's job in November 1985 after Ireland were humiliated in their final World Cup qualifier, losing 4–1 to Denmark at Lansdowne Road. It was a bad day for Irish soccer. Many fans left the stadium before the end. Those who remained expressed their anger and derision with boos, whistles and slow handclapping. Hand's credibility with players and supporters was shredded. The team won only one of his last twelve games in charge. Even his decent-skin sympathizers in the media were losing faith in their man.

The writing was on the wall at half-time against Denmark. I was having a cup of tea in the press room at the interval with Tom Keogh when Con Houlihan lumbered by. I made some smart-alec remark about the shambles we were witnessing. Houlihan paused and glared at me. Then he lashed out with his elbow, catching me full on the face. My cup of tea hit the deck as I staggered backwards. I was hurt but, sizing up the hulk in front of me, I decided not to retaliate. I was at the same stage of exasperation as most Irish fans: welcoming the result that now seemed inevitable because matters would surely be settled.

Over the next few weeks there was much speculation about the identity of the next manager. Even the most resolute decent skin seemed to accept that something better than being a decent skin was required. Billy McNeill, renowned captain of Celtic's Lisbon Lions, was one of the first people linked with the job. Billy was doing well at Manchester City. Liam Tuohy was doing splendid work with Ireland's junior teams. His name popped up. There were reports that Brian Clough might be interested. Former Irish captain Noel Cantwell was also mentioned, as were John Giles and his old Leeds United team-mate Jack Charlton.

The nineteen members of the FAI Council would decide. That was a terrifying thought. Des Casey, a trade unionist from Dundalk and a wily character, was FAI president. In the event of a tie, he would have the casting vote. The hunt for Ireland's next manager rapidly descended into farce.

The various factions in Merrion Square had differing agendas, none of them to do with what was best for Irish soccer. Some admired Giles, others loathed him. Billy McNeill opted to stay with Manchester City. A faction of delegates representing junior soccer, the grassroots boys, favoured Liam Tuohy. He was a decent skin, respected by all in Irish soccer. He had qualified the Irish Youth team for a number of major international championship finals. His candidacy was certainly credible. I was in the Giles camp, which didn't help his cause at all. Nobody took Jack Charlton's claim that seriously, although he was interviewed by the FAI.

As the weeks passed, no consensus about the best candidate emerged. Sensing a stitch-up, John Giles withdrew his application. Louis Kilcoyne and Dr Tony O'Neill, two of the more enlightened Blazers, were lobbying for John. Fran Fields, a colourful delegate from Donegal, also pledged his support. Des Casey was thought to be in the Giles camp. I flew to John's Birmingham home to persuade him to get back in the race. After a phone call from President Des he reluctantly agreed.

It was 7 February 1986 when the FAI executive finally met to choose Eoin Hand's successor. Des Casey was the kingmaker in circumstances where no agreed candidate had emerged. As FAI president, he owned the goodie-bag containing tickets to big games, trips to exotic locations – like Poland – and appointments to influential Association committees. Tickets for FA Cup Finals, coveted premium seats for big European matches. The goodie-bag was full of sweeteners. And, being an experienced trade unionist, Des knew the price of every vote.

Thus, a quietly confident John Giles travelled to Dublin earlier that day. He was in the Berkeley Court Hotel with our friend Tim O'Connor. I joined them for a drink before heading down to Merrion Square for the eight o'clock meeting. I waited in an ante-room with the rest of the press pack. We were close enough to the council chamber to hear raised voices.

A Blazer emerged. He told us the row was about whether or not to let John Giles back into the race after his withdrawal. We learned later that the dispute was settled in John's favour. So, after weeks of politicking, there were three runners in the race: John Giles, Liam Tuohy and Jack Charlton.

Or so we assumed. After the procedural row over John, President Des produced a rabbit from his hat. He'd spoken to former Liverpool manager Bob Paisley, who'd accepted the job, subject to the executive's rubber stamp. Some rabbit! Paisley was the most decorated manager in English football history. Seven League championships and three European Cups stood to his name. He wasn't looking for a big salary.

Des had organized a quiet coup. He'd secretly opened the goodie-bag to lobby ten delegates to vote for Paisley. The president's good news was greeted with consternation. A frisson of anger swept through the council chamber. This was treachery.

Treachery was a way of life for the Blazers. It was their own grubby little deals involving betrayal and deceit that had earned them the right to sit on the executive, to be wielding power in that room on that important night for Irish soccer. Now Mr President had fucked them. Royally.

In our ante-room, we hacks gazed anxiously at our watches. Deadlines were looming for the daily newsmen.

Inside President Des called for a vote. Paisley received nine votes. Giles got three, Tuohy three and Big Jack the other three. One of the conspirators had reneged. The coup was now a cock-up. Another vote to decide which of the runners-up should be eliminated ended Tuohy's hopes. Giles was binned next, leaving Paisley and Charlton to scrap it out. In the final count Charlton won by ten votes to eight.

While the bewildered delegates briefed the media, Casey excused himself to make an important phone call. Bob Paisley was waiting for the call. The news he got was not the news he'd been expecting. I was disappointed for John. But, setting that aside, I welcomed Jack Charlton's appointment in my *Sunday Tribune* column. He had done outstanding work at Middlesbrough and Sheffield Wednesday. As a television analyst he was provocative and engaging. He was big enough for the job. 'Leadership, a sense of purpose, has been restored to Irish football at international level,' I burbled optimistically in the *Tribune*. 'Decent-skinsmanship has finally been dispensed with.'

The FAI had trouble finding Jack on the night he got the job. No one had his phone number. No salary negotiation took place before he was publicly anointed. Their raids on duty-free were better planned than the Blazers' moves to fill the manager's job.

Jack arrived in Dublin four days later. He was introduced to the media at a press conference in the Westbury Hotel. The large room was packed. A full contingent of FAI luminaries turned out to see the show. There might be canapés and free drink. The media were also out in force. Not just the sportswriters, but the features guys and girls, the heavy-hitters who normally disdained the Toy Department. Jack Charlton was a star. A World Cup winner, a television personality, brother of the legend Bobby.

In contrast to my optimism, most of my decentskin colleagues were cool on the Charlton appointment. But the press conference passed pretty tamely until Peter Byrne of the *Irish Times* posed a question alluding to the Merrion Square cock-up that had led to Jack becoming Ireland manager. The question was directed at President Des, who was sitting beside Jack. Wrong time, wrong place for this to be discussed, Casey replied.

Jack rammed the point home, asserting that Byrne's question was irrelevant and embarrassing. Byrne was no friend of mine, but I thought he was entitled to ask his question. I spoke up, arguing that the public was entitled to know the truth behind newspaper speculation about the goings-on in Merrion Square. Solidarity with a colleague in trouble was my intention. I'd mentioned the public interest.

'Public interest,' Jack exploded. 'Public interest. I know you. You're a fucking troublemaker, you are. I'm not going to argue with you. I'm bigger than you.' He started to rise from his seat at the top table. 'If you want to step outside, I'm ready now.' With an icy glare in my direction he picked up his cap. 'I'm off.' As Jack stormed out, the assembled decent skins, Blazers and hacks, applauded long and loudly.

48. 'Bollocks'

A few months after Jack was appointed, the Professional Footballers' Association of Ireland held their annual dinner in what is now the Conrad Hotel. It was a grand black-tie affair, a gathering of decent skins, with lots of self-congratulatory back-slapping. If the evening had a theme it was that all present were wonderful servants of 'this great game of ours'. I went along reluctantly. John Giles was the guest of honour. My friend and mentor Tim O'Connor sat beside me. As the *Magill* magazine account of the evening confirms, proceedings didn't quite go to plan.

> *All Dunphy said was 'Bollocks.' It was 1986, the year Jack Charlton was appointed as manager of the Irish soccer team, and it was at the end-of-season dinner of the Professional Footballers' Association.*
>
> *John Giles, the guest of honour, rose and spoke about Jack Charlton's accession. There had never been any doubt for Giles but that Charlton was the right man for the job. Nor had there been any doubt for him that the FAI had handled the appointment badly, causing him distress. He wished Charlton well, after he had told the assembled players, officials, journalists and sponsors that the FAI should have had more respect for the people concerned.*
>
> *Alongside Giles at the top table sat Ray Treacy and an FAI official involved in the appointment. Treacy stood up and said a few words of praise for the official, and added that the official was a brave man to come along to the dinner.*
>
> *Treacy's remarks were met by silence. Until, that is, Eamon Dunphy enunciated, loudly and coldly, 'Bollocks.'*
>
> *There was uproar. Tim O'Connor, RTÉ's head of sport, who was sitting at Dunphy's table, got up and walked away. Others hissed and catcalled Dunphy. Dunphy just sat there and said no more.*

The three guys who threw me out on the street were prominent activists in the PFAI, worthies from the 'Chicken League' I'd been writing about derisively in the *Tribune*. I'd ruined the 'grand occasion', now

'Fuck off,' they ordered. I wasn't too bothered. It *was* bollocks. The Blazer was a parasite. Yet there he was at the top table, beaming with pleasure.

Around this time I encountered Eoin Hand in Joys nightclub. I was out on the town with Colm Tóibín. We kicked off in the Horseshoe Bar. Neither of us was a big drinker, but on good nights an hour or two in the Horseshoe could give you a *grá* for more divilment. We moved on to George's Bistro, a piano bar in South Frederick Street. For a while in the eighties, George's was the place to go. The food was pretty average but a couple of torch singers created an atmosphere that was faintly exotic. The newly formed Progressive Democrats had their headquarters round the corner in Molesworth Street. The piano bar was where Mary Harney and Michael McDowell went to let their hair down! On a bad night you might be cornered by Michael D. Higgins, the Labour Party's socialist firebrand, clutching a copy of his collected poems. The poems aside, this titan of the left, now our esteemed president, was great fun. He liked a drink and a soliloquy.

Before the Celtic Tiger, Dublin night-life was limited. No Lillie's Bordello. No Renards. Most people headed for Leeson Street. But there wasn't much on Leeson Street for the discerning night owl, just lots of awful 'clubs' selling plonk at extortionate prices.

Suesey Street, owned by Rhona Teehan, was the exception. Jean Crowley, whose legend would later be forged running the VIP bar in Lillie's, managed Suesey Street. It was a well-run club with a full licence and strict door policy. Colm and I headed to Suesey Street. The music was contemporary pop with a dash of Rolling Stones. The crowd was mostly thirty-something, although older would-be ravers like Noel Pearson, Paul McGuinness and Sam Smyth often dropped in. The trouble with Rhona Teehan was that she obeyed the law. Last orders at one thirty a.m. Doors closed by two o'clock. The night was still a pup and Joys was the refuge of last resort.

It was Sam Smyth who framed the burning question of those innocent eighties years: what becomes of you when you're too old for Suesey Street, yet too young for Joys? In my early forties I ticked both boxes, just about. Colm, ten years younger, was too young for Joys. But we went anyway. Joys was on Baggot Street. It's still there, as weirdly, wonderfully decadent as ever. Run by two Blackrock College boys, Frank and John Conway, Joys had no door policy. Wine could only be consumed with food. There was no food although there was a kitchen where the odd steak sandwich was cooked, for cosmetic purposes.

Joys was favoured by politicians and journalists unable to sleep. Brian Cowen, Enda Kenny and Big Phil Hogan were regulars. Austin Deasy, a dissenting conservative Fine Gael voice when Garret FitzGerald embarked on his liberal crusade, was an amusingly morose fixture in Joys. Most of the regulars from the Horseshoe Bar were Joys patrons. There was a small dance-floor. The music was vintage pop. The clients were generally older, the lost and the lonely: middle-aged men wearing Marks & Spencer jumpers, slightly younger women wearing either cardigans or slightly daring low-cut blouses. Lots of married men prowled the joint, seeking someone who would understand them.

The dissident writer and philosopher Desmond Fennell was an occasional visitor. Sipping red wine and listening to the Hollies, he was an engaging companion. Henry Mount Charles often turned up on his visits to town. The Most Honourable Henry Vivien Conyngham, 8th Marquess Conyngham, to give him his full title, owns Slane Castle. We were acquainted from our time as supporters of Garret FitzGerald's liberal crusade. An Old Harrovian, he reminded me of Mr Michael, the Old Etonian chairman of Charlton.

'Dunphy, you little fucker, what are you doing here?' was his usual opening salvo.

'Planning the revolution, Henry, when we'll confiscate your castle and string you up from the nearest lamppost. Unless you buy me a bottle of champagne.'

Occasionally the cops would raid the club. By some mysterious bush telegraph, Frank and John would learn that a raid was imminent. All the booze was whipped off the tables to be replaced by innocent-looking cups of coffee. The sound of sizzling steaks emanated from the kitchen. The boys in blue would thus be greeted by the improbable sight of a gathering of coffee-drinking music lovers listening to the Bee Gees at four o'clock in the morning, among them a couple of cabinet ministers. No arrests were ever made. Yet another Irish solution to an Irish problem.

Eoin Hand approached our table out of the gloom. He asked if he could join us. 'Sure.' I gestured him to a seat and introduced him to Colm. He was drinking red wine. After a few minutes' small-talk he filled his glass to the brim. With a muttered 'Cheers', Eoin leaned closer to me. Then he threw the wine in my face. It seemed to happen in slow motion. 'I've wanted to do that for a long time,' he said, rising from the table. Colm started remonstrating with my assailant. He made to rise with malicious intent. I urged him to sit down. No point in making an unpleasant situation worse. Eoin was a decent skin. So was Frank Conway. When I suggested that Eoin be ejected for his misdemeanour Frank demurred. 'Didn't you cost the man his job?' He shrugged. 'What was he supposed to do?'

49. Aengus

I first got to know Aengus Fanning during my blue-docket period with the *Sunday Independent*. Aengus was news analysis editor of the daily paper. Before that he'd been the agricultural correspondent. On the few occasions we bumped into each other he was always encouraging about my copy. 'How's it going?' he would ask, guessing, perhaps, that I wasn't exactly the most popular hack in Abbey Street. One day we went for coffee in a little café a few doors down from Independent House. I sang the blues about the expenses scam, my Grade E status and the various conceits of the pinstriped journos in the office.

Aengus was sympathetic. Although news analysis editor was a good job he was less than enamoured of the staid culture in the paper. His boss, the 'legendary' Vinnie Doyle, was highly regarded by his contemporaries in the city. One of this legend's great gifts was for lifting stories from rival papers late at night. Doyle was a dour character. While relishing his reputation as the quintessential newsman, Doyle's newspaper did very little to disturb Ireland's governing elite. When Aengus attempted to inject some originality and contrarian opinion into the op-ed section Doyle would often demur.

I liked Aengus from the first time I met him. He wasn't hard-bitten. He was enthusiastic about ideas, life, sport, which he had excelled at, and music. He played the clarinet. He loved cricket. We shared a fondness for England, its literature and the journalism of English icons like Malcolm Muggeridge, the historian A. J. P. Taylor, Robin Day and Bernard Levin.

Aengus was a free spirit with a wonderful Bohemian streak. He was a Kerryman and therefore shrewd. But there was an innocence about him that was most engaging. As a young man he had worked in the Queen's Arms pub in London's Chelsea, frequented by poets, writers and assorted bums, also by a couple of his sporting heroes, Denis Compton, the great English cricketer, and Johnny Haynes, the first hundred-pounds-a-week footballer. This was, he thought, the best time of his life.

This spirited and deeply intelligent man was restless when we first met. The prevailing mediocrity of Dublin journalism, rendered absurd by the vanities of its practitioners, frustrated Aengus. He did a good job redesigning the *Irish Indo*'s op-ed pages, but there was little he could do with the sterile copy submitted by Doyle's preferred contributors.

When Michael Hand stepped down as editor of the Sunday paper, Aengus was appointed to succeed him. I suspect his fellow Kerryman Joe Hayes steered Tony O'Reilly in Aengus's direction. The call I'd hoped would come did so a couple of months after Aengus got the job. This time there were no blue dockets. And no Grade E. I didn't want to go on staff. A contract was agreed, which paid me well. There was no security of pension, but no need to fiddle at the hatch on the second floor either.

Aengus wasn't a member of any journalistic clique. He was happiest with musicians, show people and sportsmen. The playwright Hugh Leonard, recruited as a columnist by Michael Hand, was a regular lunch companion. Aengus was an avid Liverpool fan, often taking his sons Dion and Evan to Anfield. He played Gaelic football for the Kerry Senior team, so, quite unusually for a national newspaper editor, took an informed interest in the Toy Department.

Journalism was in his DNA since his family owned the *Midland Tribune*. He had learned his craft on provincial newspapers, covering courts, births, deaths and marriages. He was a pro. Above all, Aengus was passionate about journalism, yet there was no sign of the self-importance or myriad conceits that afflicted so many senior members of the Fourth Estate, the mannered gravitas favoured by other sages waltzing around town.

I was fortunate to meet him when I did. Like Mr Hayden, Dessie Toal, Benny Fenton and Tim O'Connor, Aengus believed in me and encouraged me to be myself. Over the years when I came in with copy others would deem outrageous, offensive or, a favourite, 'over the top', he'd laugh and reassure me: 'Great stuff, that's great, Eamon, thanks.'

In the summer of 1986 the World Cup took place in Mexico. I spent months before the tournament trying to persuade Tim O'Connor and Mike Horgan to enlist John Giles for the RTÉ panel. I got no joy. John wasn't a performer. His reasoned, astute analysis would bore the viewers. He'd be reluctant to stick his neck out. His circumspection wouldn't work on television. The case I made focused on John's quiet passion for the game. His forensic mind and unparalleled knowledge of football would enhance RTÉ's credibility, which I had placed in jeopardy with my Platini rants. The World Cup lasts for a month, so we wouldn't be reduced to sound-bites, which weren't John's forte. Bill O'Herlihy's broadcasting skill and my passion would engage John. And, crucially, given time and space, the real John Giles, the man behind the caricature, would emerge. It was a hard sell and I failed.

So I played my last card: no John, no Eamon. Tim and I were very close friends. He was a mentor to me, cool where I was a cauldron of passionate conviction. I generally deferred to him. I owed him a lot, but this time when finally he said no to John I stuck to my guns. Three days before the tournament began the lads gave in.

The new panel worked. There was a certain irony to my campaign on John's behalf. He wasn't all that pushed about being on TV. He wasn't a natural. But Bill O'Herlihy was. Bill is a consummate television pro. Although ostensibly acting the eejit, he knows exactly where the conversation should be heading, knows the right question and how to couch it. John was his project for the '86 World Cup Finals. With extraordinary skill, Bill got John talking about the games as if he were sitting in his own front room. The tentative John was but a memory by the tournament's end. He came across as a man of great character and rare intelligence who happened to have been one of football's great players.

John's contribution to RTÉ's World Cup coverage in 1986 took TV analysis in these islands to a new level. He was articulate, cerebral, the perfect antidote to my driven passion. In four weeks John nailed the lie, long-voiced and deeply felt by Gaels who spoke of 'race memory', that soccer was a gentleman's game played by gurriers. The other big lie, that soccer was a 'foreign' game, seemed equally absurd. There was nothing foreign about John Giles, one of international soccer's greatest exponents, who was born and reared in Ormond Square in inner-city Dublin.

The viewing figures were very good. Reviewers were complimentary, drawing attention to the fact that RTÉ's soccer coverage was superior to that of rival broadcasters BBC and ITV, long leaders in the field.

Maradona was the star of the '86 World Cup. Assisted by 'the hand of God', Argentina reached the final, where they were due to play West Germany. France and Belgium contested the third and fourth place play-off game on the Saturday night before the Sunday final. Bill, John and I were given the night off. When I switched on the play-off game I froze in shock.

The satirist Dermot Morgan and a number of other clowns were seated on our World Cup set. They were having fun taking the piss out of Bill, John and myself. We were depicted as inarticulate cliché-spouting morons. In order to work, parody has to bear some resemblance to the original object it's designed to mock. What Morgan and Co. were parodying was the BBC/ITV football panels of universal ill-repute, which were indeed inarticulate and dismayingly banal. Everyone involved in RTÉ's football coverage worked really hard to offer viewers an intelligent alternative to the dismal British soccer coverage.

In a rage I phoned Mike Horgan. He knew nothing about the Morgan takeover. Tim, I couldn't get. Next morning when I finally got hold of him, I told him I was finished with RTÉ. They had shot themselves in the foot. 'Put fucking Dermot Morgan on your panel tonight' was my parting shot. Vincent Finn, RTÉ's director general, called to apologize and ask me to reconsider. But I was gone beyond recall. At best, those responsible for this travesty were stupid. At worst, Morgan was playing to a nasty cultural stereotype.

50.   Unforgettable Luck

During the World Cup Finals I took a few days off to accompany U2 on the last two stops of a tour they'd undertaken to promote Amnesty International. In a sign of the band's growing status they topped a bill that also included Sting, Lou Reed, Peter Gabriel, Bryan Adams, Joan Baez and the Neville Brothers. This was a rare opportunity to see them play. I was close to the end of my research for the book that no one wanted to publish.

For almost a year the band had lived in seclusion, putting together their new album, *The Joshua Tree*. They worked in Adam Clayton's big house in Rathfarnham at the foot of the Dublin Mountains. I was given full access to watch them both in Rathfarnham and at Windmill Lane studios. Brian Eno and Danny Lanois, a pleasant Canadian, were producing the album. Steve Lillywhite, an old friend who produced some of U2's early work, was also involved. Steve's then wife, Kirsty Mac-Coll, who was later killed tragically in a speedboat accident, was in Windmill Lane for the sessions that produced the finished album.

The atmosphere was businesslike but tense during those final sessions. While we sat in the control room listening to the endless takes of the album's songs, Lillywhite was blown away, as was MacColl. 'This is special,' he confirmed. 'They're going to be the biggest band in the world.'

Amnesty's 'Conspiracy of Hope' tour ended with an all-day concert at the Giants Stadium in New Jersey. From noon till eleven p.m., when U2 were due to bring the curtain down, a galaxy of stars from politics, music, film and sport took to the stage to praise Amnesty International. The holding area was a long, luxurious, purpose-built tented room behind one of the stadium's in-goal areas. Alongside the stars' dressing rooms there was a buffet serving the finest food. Any drink you wanted was available for free. It was a starfucker's dream.

Robert De Niro sat close to Yoko Ono. Miles Davis and Joni Mitchell shared a joke with Bob Geldof, the creator of Live Aid. Daryl Hannah, Christopher Reeve, Carlos Santana, and Peter, Paul and Mary all relaxed nibbling delicious food, waiting their turn on stage. My 'Access All Areas' pass placed me at a designated table next to Muhammad Ali, who was with his two daughters.

Already visibly suffering the effects of Parkinson's disease, Ali was still an awesome presence in that room of exceptionally gifted people. Shaking badly, he smiled in recognition as De Niro, Joni Mitchell, Miles Davis and many others came to his table to pay their respects. Ali greeted well-wishers graciously. His eyes widened and he beamed that famously mischievous smile, reading the sadness in his visitors' eyes yet conveying to them his own message, unspoken . . . I'm OK, at peace, having fun with my daughters. For most who came to see him he produced a little magic trick, which caused him great delight. Holding a small red handkerchief, he clasped his hands together and made it disappear.

Guessing from my place beside Paul McGuinness that I was connected to U2, one of Ali's companions asked if I could arrange for his daughters to meet the band. They were huge fans. Paul quickly responded, taking Ali and the girls to the lads' dressing room. Bono was born in 1960, the year Ali had won the gold medal at the Rome Olympics. The band mightn't have known just how courageously potent this now shuffling giant had once been. But his aura was unmistakable, his radiant spirit filling the tiny dressing room. Standing close by, it was impossible to dispute the often idle notion that there is something we might reasonably describe as greatness. And that possessing greatness was a matter not of power, money or beauty, but of something divine, elusive, beyond the reach if not the comprehension of mere mortals. The brief visit went well. Ali did his magic trick, his daughters lovingly looking on. Bono, the Edge, Adam, Larry and Paul marvelled at his playfulness, serenity, the tenderness and lack of guile. The poise and grace were still evident, though his body, stooped and withered, resembled an oak tree struck by lightning.

On 27 April 1987, U2 featured on the cover of *Time* magazine. This was a major PR coup engineered by Paul McGuinness and Island Records, who released *The Joshua Tree* to extraordinary acclaim. The *Time* cover was beyond price in marketing terms. You couldn't buy that space but you could hustle it if you made the right connections. The strapline over a photograph of the boys looking cooler than cool read 'Rock's hottest ticket'. The fact that this edition of *Time* sold more copies than the ones featuring John F. Kennedy and Marilyn Monroe was the icing on the cake. When the album shot to the top of the charts internationally, U2 were confirmed as the biggest rock band in the world.

My publisher was soon on the phone to ask if I still had that U2 book. Yes, I replied, nothing has changed, except the price. I didn't have to push too hard to secure a strong advance. I was very lucky. If there was any other conclusion to be drawn it surely was to follow your instinct, even if it means making sacrifices.

From the beginning I believed the story of those suburban heroes was intrinsically valuable. Even if they hadn't conquered the world of rock 'n' roll, the experiences of four young Protestants growing up in Dublin's northside suburbs would have intrigued me.

Paul McGuinness, educated by the Jesuits at Clongowes Wood public school, was a fascinating character in his own right. His father, Philip, had volunteered for the Royal Air Force during the desperate days of the Battle of Britain. A profoundly courageous man, he was awarded the Distinguished Flying Cross, the RAF's highest honour, at the end of the war. Like his clients, Paul defied the prevailing caricature of Irishness, which the gombeen men marketing Ireland were still hawking round the world, and killing and dying for at home.

When I finished the book, titled *Suburban Heroes*, Paul and the band didn't like it. They didn't want to be depicted as suburban heroes. In the two years that had elapsed between our original meeting and *The Joshua Tree* the band had evolved, certainly in terms of image, something they were acutely conscious of. In the beginning they had wanted to be portrayed as they were. After reaching rock 'n' roll nirvana, and 'hanging' with Lou Reed, the image they craved was darker and cooler than my book proposed.

After a tense four-hour meeting with the five of them in a hotel suite in Edinburgh before a gig at Murrayfield, we agreed to disagree. They honoured their commitment that I would have the final say on content. But Bono declared they would publicly distance themselves from the book. I gave them manuscripts to read so that they could correct any factual errors.

When I received their corrections I incorporated them into the final text. Through all of this Adam stayed aloof. He was a terrific guy. He said he trusted me, didn't need to read a book to find out about himself. 'Go publish and be damned.' He laughed.

My publishers rejected *Suburban Heroes* as a title and, given their investment, I wasn't going to fight them. They chose instead a title that would explicitly link band and book. *Unforgettable Fire*, the album before *The Joshua Tree*, served that purpose.

Unforgettable Fire was savaged by Irish critics. Reviews elsewhere, in the UK and the States, were mixed. The rock 'n' roll bible, *Rolling Stone*, really put the boot in. U2 were close to *Rolling Stone*.

Despite the criticism *Unforgivable Fire* sold one million copies in hardback and paperback. It topped the bestseller lists in Britain and Ireland and reached number eight in the *New York Times*' prestigious non-fiction category.

The most interesting critical response came from Dave Fanning, the RTÉ broadcaster. Dave was very close to U2. When they were a baby band Dave had championed them. When new albums were released he invariably got to play the music first. He was also top of the list for interviews with the band. Going against the flow, Dave praised my book, adding that he'd read it twice. I never did ask him if that comment was ironic!

51.   Nightmare Fairytale

In May 1984 the New Ireland Forum report was published. The Forum was Garret FitzGerald's idea, its task to seek a solution to the Northern Troubles. In its final report the Forum outlined three possible scenarios in which a 'New Ireland' might be created. A unitary state, in other words a united Ireland, was one so-called solution. A Federal Ireland, which would see the Republic of Ireland and Northern Ireland form a new unified polity, was another option proposed. Joint authority, in which the British and Irish governments would govern the North together, was a third Forum possibility.

I thought the New Ireland Forum was a sinister nationalist conspiracy. It was set up as a response to republican terrorism. The Forum was the brainchild of John Hume, the Northern leader of constitutional nationalism, who persuaded Garret FitzGerald to convene what was in effect a talking shop designed to put pressure on unionism. Most Southern citizens paid no heed to the blather emanating from Dublin Castle, where the Forum hearings were held. There was a very good reason for the general public's indifference: most sensible people knew that a united Ireland, or some variation of such an entity, wasn't possible.

Reflecting on proceedings at Dublin Castle, the unionist historian Graham Walker remarked, 'The Forum Report did reflect a more considered appreciation of the unionists' distinctiveness and their attachment to the Union, but it was also replete with time-worn assumptions and stereotypes, and a partisan historical narrative.' I thought Walker was being too kind. How very decent of Official Ireland to show some 'appreciation' of unionists' culture, religious beliefs and identity! But Walker was spot on when he referred to 'the time-worn assumptions and stereotypes, and a partisan historical narrative'.

The underlying assumptions were deluded. One of them was that unionism was the core problem on the island of Ireland. Another was the absurd assertion that the republic forged in the South on the back of a terrorist Rising in 1916 was in some way superior to 'the sectarian statelet' north of the border.

When deconstructed, stripped of its weasel words, the 'partisan narrative' Walker alluded to proposed that the Easter Rising was a 'Good Thing' and that justice would not be served until Ireland was 'A Nation Once Again'. And, by the way, Catholicism was the one true religion, Protestantism some kind of alien aberration that could be 'tolerated' if the New Ireland Forum report was implemented.

That was the subtext of the New Ireland Forum report. Buying into the report's surreal subtext was the price unionists must pay for peace. This, for me, was Thurles revisited: 'race memory'; the 'great pure sense of freedom'; the malevolent message of the fanatical cleric rendered ostensibly genteel for coming from the mouths of those paragons of Official Ireland, Garret FitzGerald and John Hume.

In Thurles at the Centenary Final, the citizens present jeered and mocked Father Leo Ó Moracháin's reactionary rant. When the rant's spruced-up corollary was published in the guise of respectable analysis in the Forum report, nobody mocked or jeered. On the 'Northern Question', the Dublin media in all its forms were tame to the point of intellectual bankruptcy. Editorials welcomed the report. Unionists would be well advised to pay heed to the reasoned musings of nationalist moderates like FitzGerald and Hume.

Five months after the Forum report was publicized the IRA tried to assassinate Margaret Thatcher. She was attending the Conservative Party Conference in Brighton. A bomb was planted in the Grand Hotel. Thatcher survived. Five Tories died, three of them women. Several more were maimed. Margaret Tebbit, wife of Norman Tebbit, was left permanently disabled. Nobody in Dublin linked the Brighton atrocity to 'the partisan historical narrative' that was guiding Official Ireland along an evil path, marked ambivalence.

By the time I reached the *Sunday Independent* I wanted to dispute a narrative that I believed to be not merely partisan but downright fraudulent. The unionists were bigots, according to conventional Dublin wisdom. Could anybody worshipping at the constitutional shrine of Dev and McQuaid really talk of Protestant bigotry? Could anyone living in this corrupt, sectarian slum of a republic seriously propose that the decent Protestant people of Ulster should share the island with Charlie Haughey, Seán Doherty and mad clerics banging on about race memory? Should they be obliged to share 'the national territory' with a Catholic majority who would deny them the right to practise their religion freely, a Catholic majority bearing a thinly veiled contempt for their cultural allegiance to Britain? A republic where loyalist terrorists were damned as 'death squads' and republican terrorists dignified by the term 'active service units'.

By stripping language of meaning, the morally bankrupt media could report that bombs placed in pubs in Birmingham, Guildford and Woolwich, a part of south London I knew so well, were put there by IRA 'active service units'. The victims of the ensuing carnage were 'killed' rather than murdered. It was innocent Catholics in East Belfast who were 'murdered' by loyalist 'death squads'.

There was something Orwellian about the partisan narrative of the Dublin media/political class. The concept of Groupthink, first identified by an American journalist, William H. Whyte, in *Fortune* magazine in 1952, perhaps best explains Official Ireland's response to the Northern Troubles. In Groupthink, Whyte wrote: 'We are not talking about mere instinctive conformity – it is, after all, a perennial failing of mankind. What we are talking about is a *rationalized* conformity – an open, articulate philosophy which holds that group values are not only expedient, but right and good as well.'

Groupthink Irish-style held that John Hume was a 'Good Thing'. Loyalism was 'Bad'. Unionists were bigots. And these bigots must stop saying no to proposals advanced by what was, in effect, a pan-nationalist front consisting of politicians like Haughey, FitzGerald and Hume, the IRA and the loony left in Britain, where Ken Livingstone was a key Sinn Féin supporter.

Underpinning all of this was the notion that the 1916 Easter Rising defined Irish identity. This was rationalized conformity, the truth passed down through the generations in Catholic colleges and universities, a corrupt set of tribal values to which one had to adhere to get on. Another American, Irving Janis, a research psychologist at Yale University, defined Groupthink as 'a term of the same order as the words in the newspeak vocabulary George Orwell used in his dismaying world of 1984'.

Crucially in the context of Official Ireland, Janis concluded that Groupthink's consequences included 'a deterioration in mental efficiency, reality testing and moral judgement that result from in-group pressures'.

In 1972 Janis published his book *Victims of Groupthink*. His interest in Groupthink led him to study a number of American foreign-policy disasters, notably the Vietnam War, the Bay of Pigs invasion and failure to anticipate the Japanese attack on Pearl Harbor. He concluded that in each of these cases the decisions made were largely due to Groupthink, which prevented contradictory views being expressed and subsequently evaluated.

If a dissonant voice struggled for a hearing in the United States, what chance in Dublin politics or journalism where everyone knew each other and had been educated by clerics, then later at University College Dublin? After ten years back home, it struck me that for many of its principals, public life was an extension of the Literary and Historical Debating Society at UCD. Haughey and FitzGerald were UCD contemporaries. Vincent Browne was a member of the L and H, as they fondly referred to it, at the same time as Ruairi Quinn, the prominent Labour politician.

Politics and journalism were variations of the old games they'd all played at uni. They were privileged posturers educated at the people's expense. Beneath their carefully manufactured public personas, in Browne's case the *enfant terrible*, in Haughey's the noble nationalist chieftain, in FitzGerald's the lofty intellectual, they all sought the same thing: approval in the small provincial city of Dublin. In background and temperament, UCD graduates fitted perfectly the identikit profile of Groupthinkers.

They and the likes of them thought for Ireland. They might quibble among themselves about detail, but on the big-ticket issues theirs was Official Irish dogma. The North was a big-ticket issue.

On the North, the conventional wisdom was out of touch with the feelings of the people. They didn't want a united Ireland on the IRA's terms. There was undoubtedly some residual sympathy for nationalist victims of unionist sectarianism, but the IRA's terror campaign was causing the sympathy to ebb away, not only from the terrorists but from the 'Cause' itself.

The Anglo-Irish Agreement of 1985 was welcomed by Official Ireland as an historic advance for the 'Cause'. For the first time the Irish government would have a say in Northern affairs. The Agreement was a blow to unionism, a victory for Hume and FitzGerald. But Garret FitzGerald's eventual fate at the ballot box confirmed that the North was low on the list of voters' priorities. That was 1987. People wanted work, a halt to emigration, a decent health service, education for their children. In the north unionists in their thousands took to the streets to protest against the Agreement. The pan-nationalist movement had backed them even further into a corner marked 'obsolete'. And their death toll kept mounting as a result of IRA atrocities.

The Fine Gael/Labour coalition managed to double Ireland's national debt while simultaneously, through the Anglo-Irish Agreement, acquiring power and influence over the lives of the people of Northern Ireland. That was some stroke. The ceremonial features of the Agreement provided the ultimate photo opportunity for politicians. FitzGerald, Dick Spring and Peter Barry strode purposefully up Downing Street, men on a mission to make history. Documents were produced and signed with great solemnity by our great statesmen. Cameras clicked to capture the historic scene. This was no B movie, this was the real thing. One almost felt sorry for C. J. Haughey, sulking on his private island Inishvickillane, a symbol of the wealth he had mysteriously acquired.

On Remembrance Sunday 1987 the IRA placed a bomb near the cenotaph in Enniskillen, where a group of Protestant people had gathered to commemorate Britain's war dead. Eleven people were murdered ('killed', in Dublin media newspeak) and sixty-three injured. The Anglo-Irish Agreement was two years old. It wasn't working. Among the dead at Enniskillen was Marie Wilson, a young girl attending the Poppy Day ceremony with her father, Gordon.

In a television interview with the BBC, hours after Marie's murder, Gordon Wilson described his last conversation with Marie as they both lay buried in the rubble. 'I bear no ill will, I bear no grudge,' this decent Protestant man declared. He became a peace campaigner. Later the *sleveen* Fianna Fáil government made Gordon Wilson a senator. They saw some political mileage in this gesture. The Irish media welcomed the appointment. Official Ireland felt good about itself.

I thought Official Ireland complicit in the Poppy Day massacre. There was a big story here, which the Dublin media refused to cover. The story was Groupthink, the ancient claim embedded in our constitution to the 'whole national territory', the fairytale turned nightmare of 1916 and the 'nobility' of unmandated physical-force republicanism. Sly ambivalence in the face of obscenities like Enniskillen, the use of weasel words like 'killing' to describe murder.

Aengus Fanning agreed. Indeed, when editor of the *Irish Independent* news-analysis pages he had encouraged some dissenting voices to challenge the partisan narrative. John A. Murphy, a historian from University College Cork, Shane Ross, Eoghan Harris and Conor Cruise O'Brien were also prepared publicly to challenge the prevailing consensus about Irish unity and the legitimacy of the 1916 Easter Rising. Kevin Myers was courageously voicing similar objections in the *Irish Times*. Murphy, O'Brien and Myers were damning of the IRA, but they extended the logic of their critiques to include constitutional nationalists, North and South, whose ill-disguised hostility to unionism gave some comfort to the gunmen.

Mary Robinson, the Trinity College senator, was another dissenter. She resigned from the Labour Party over the Anglo-Irish Agreement. Unionists had no say in the text formulated for this now sacred document. Although Robinson had consistently disputed the partisan narrative, some sceptics believed her resignation from the Labour Party was prompted by another matter. Labour leader Dick Spring had overlooked Robinson for the position of attorney general in the coalition government. Instead he appointed John Rogers, a former student in Robinson's Trinity law class. Robinson was so miffed she resigned from Labour, the Anglo-Irish Agreement her pretext. But we hadn't heard the last of Mary.

52. Controversy

The Island – Paul Brady

They say the skies of Lebanon are burning,
Those mighty cedars bleeding in the heat,
They're showing pictures on the television,
Women and children dying in the street,
And we're still at it in our own place,
Still trying to reach the future through the past,
Still trying to carve tomorrow from a tombstone . . .

But hey! Don't listen to me!
This wasn't meant to be no sad song,
We've heard too much of that before,
Right now I only want to be here with you,
Till the morning dew comes falling,
I want to take you to the island,
And trace your footprints in the sand,
And in the evening when the sun goes down,
We'll make love to the sound of the ocean.

They're raising banners over by the markets,
Whitewashing slogans on the shipyard walls,
Witchdoctors praying for a mighty showdown,
No way our holy flag is gonna fall,
Up here we sacrifice our children
To feed the worn-out dreams of yesterday,
And teach them dying will lead us into glory . . .

Now I know us plain folks don't see all the story,
And I know this peace and love's just copping out,
And I guess these young boys dying in the ditches
Is just what being free is all about,
And how this twisted wreckage down on Main Street

Will bring us all together in the end,
And we'll go marching down the road to freedom . . .
Freedom

Like other great native-born singers and composers – people like Luke Kelly, Christy Moore and Liam Clancy – Paul Brady inspired some pride and deep affection for Ireland, the real Ireland, as opposed to the shoddy construct proposed by our national iconography. His song 'The Island' is one of the great anti-war or, more specifically, anti-terror songs.

Paul Brady is a Northern nationalist. He was born into a Catholic family in Strabane, a border town, and educated at John Hume's alma mater, St Columb's College in Derry. Strabane was one of the towns most affected by the Troubles. The British army base and the RUC barracks ensured that Strabane was a regular target for IRA 'active service units'. When Brady, with restrained anger, evokes the 'twisted wreckage down on Main Street' bringing us 'all together in the end', he is writing from direct experience.

Brady's final verse is the most damning of Official Ireland, its sly politicians and their media cronies, the sages endeavouring to retail the bogus narrative upon which they wish our national identity to be shaped. 'Freedom . . . Freedom' – the song's end sardonically captures the anguish, futility and despair so many 'plain folk' felt when they saw victims of terror stumbling dazed from the rubble of the latest atrocity.

Under Aengus Fanning, the *Sunday Independent* set out to challenge terrorists, their political fellow-travellers and the ambivalent tendency in the media who were marching us down the road to 'freedom . . . Freedom'. This was campaigning journalism. The campaign lasted for years. Official Ireland was the target. Official Ireland and its icons.

By this time the staid, conformist paper Aengus had inherited was no more than a memory. He and his deputy, Anne Harris, had created a superb Sunday newspaper. There was a vitality about the *Sunday Indo*, strikingly absent from its two main broadsheet competitors, the *Sunday Press* and the *Sunday Tribune*. The *Press* was boring, the *Tribune* a bastion of right-on types – *Irish Times* lite. The other broadsheet in the market, the *Sunday Business Post*, was excellent. Among its founders and contributors were Damien Kiberd, Frank Fitzgibbon, Aileen O' Toole, James Morrissey, Matt Cooper, Frank Connolly and Tom McGurk. Its writing was first class, but it was a niche newspaper. Its politics were

Republican with a capital R, hence the soubriquet the '*Continuity Business Post*'.

I still loved newspapers. Aengus and Anne's paper reminded me of the *Evening Press*, edited by Douglas Gageby, which had hit the streets when I was a kid in the 1950s. Even though I worked for the paper, I was still excited when I bought it on a Saturday night.

Aengus bust budgets to hire the best writers he could get. Colm Tóibín, Anthony Cronin and Gene Kerrigan contributed to a paper full of fine writing. Geoffrey Wheatcroft, a London journalist who worked for the *Spectator*, the *Guardian* and the *Daily Telegraph*, filed wonderfully erudite pieces offering a British perspective on the North. Aengus bought in Jeffrey Bernard's low-life column from the *Spectator*. That was daring in any context. We also had two great young sportswriters, David Walsh and Paul Kimmage.

On the big issues of the day, the paper was radical. Conor Cruise O'Brien offered his unique perspective on the national question. Unionists were regularly given space to argue their case. Shane Ross and the Trinity transport economist Sean Barrett challenged the prevailing orthodoxy on the ailing Irish economy. Barrett was particularly interesting on the state monopolies, Aer Lingus being the most notorious. Ross had given up the drink and Joys. The nights were duller. But journalism was the winner. He began to write about cronyism in the banks and usury in the financial-services sector. He wasn't afraid to name names, of individuals and institutions. He was the first to identify the rot in the banking culture that would destroy the country two decades later.

It was expensive to hire all those out-of house contributors. Aengus was conscious of the budget, but brave enough to stand up to the suits in Accounts. Fortunately our readership began to grow.

I was the paper's soccer correspondent. I also wrote a column for the back page on any topic that took my fancy. Once a week I went into the office to see Aengus. We'd chat about sport, politics and the various crooks, chancers and poseurs jinking their way across the landscape of Irish public life. I was always badgering him about setting up an investigative-journalism unit to tackle corruption. One day, tired of being pestered, Aengus reminded me that such a unit – I'd cited the *Sunday Times*' legendary Insight model – might want to start by examining Fitzwilton, Tony O'Reilly's holding company, our parent. Laughing, he wondered when the *Irish Times* were going to launch an investigation into the Irish Times Trust, the working of which remained shrouded in secrecy. The libel law was *the* major obstacle facing any journalist seeking to expose corruption.

On Europe and the burgeoning EU project, we were both sceptics. Aengus had spent a lot of time in Brussels when he was agriculture correspondent for the daily paper. When I speculated that we'd end up being governed from Brussels, he agreed, though added, 'We'd probably be better governed.' He was a romantic about journalism, but realistic about what his paper could do. One day when we were chatting I suggested that Kevin Myers would be a great signing for the paper. Aengus agreed. Myers wrote well. He was passionate. I didn't always, or even often, agree with the views he expressed but I admired his courage. Aengus suggested I take Myers to lunch to sound him out.

I booked a table at Dobbins, a favourite haunt. Dobbins was the creation of John O'Byrne, a delightful rogue, full of gossip and mischief. Johnno lived by his wits, as did many of his clients. Dobbins was the Horseshoe Bar with food and expensive wine. There was no natural light. The room was long, sawdust on the floor, candles on the tables. Dobbins was popular with Fianna Fáilers. John was a Haugheyite, many of his customers rakes around town. Lunches tended to be long. Noel Pearson christened Dobbins the 'Gluepot': it was very hard to leave this refuge from respectability. Michael Fingleton lunched there every Friday – 'Fingers' had his own table. Paul McGuinness, Oliver Barry, PJ Mara and Gillian Bowler, Haughey's friend and protégée, were regulars.

Over lunch I pitched the *Sunday Indo* to Myers. He seemed pleased to be courted. I assured him the money was good. Aengus was great to work for. I mentioned all our outstanding contributors, Tóibín, Cronin, Kerrigan, Conor Cruise O'Brien among them. And, working for a Sunday paper, he'd have to deliver only once a week. Kevin listened politely but he didn't seem convinced. I ordered a second bottle of wine. It was Friday: work done, we could relax. In the context of Dublin journalism, Myers was an exotic creature. He'd grown up in England, and had campaigned courageously for the Irish who served Britain in the 1914–18 war. They'd been written out of Irish history. He wanted their sacrifice recognized and honoured. Myers was an outsider. Perfect for the *Sunday Indo*. Perfect for journalism, especially in a small town like ours.

Sadly, while happy to be wooed, Kevin wasn't going to leave the *Irish*

Times. He agreed our paper was successful, with a large and growing readership. But he felt the *Irish Times* was *the* paper. 'They read the *Sunday Indo*,' he conceded, 'but they listen to us.' The 'they' he was talking about were, it appeared, politicians and civil servants, the people who made decisions.

Much as I respected Myers, I thought he was mad to believe that the nonentities in government buildings were 'listening' to anybody other than lobbyists from industry or the trade-union movement, their paymasters. After a pleasant lunch we parted amicably.

When I reported back to Aengus he laughed at the idea that Official Ireland didn't take the *Sunday Indo* seriously. 'We must be doing something right,' he said. Right or wrong, the paper was attracting hostility from journalists on more respectable papers. I was partly to blame. I was being tough on the wrong people, launching what were increasingly described as 'diatribes' at national heroes such as John Hume and Big Jack.

John Hume, the leader of constitutional nationalism, appeared to stand for peace and reconciliation. He was certainly a masterly politician. His analysis of the Northern problem set the agenda whenever, wherever solutions were sought. Hume had wooed and won over the political/media class in Dublin. He'd pulled the same stroke in Europe and, most potently, in Washington. You didn't question John Hume.

When I began to do so, the word 'controversial' was bandied about. I didn't question his character or personal behaviour, just his politics. Aengus allotted me the back page of the *Sunday Indo* to write about the great statesman. One particular piece caused ructions in the Dublin media village. It followed a TV interview given by Hume to Anthony Clare, who had recently returned to Ireland after nineteen years in England. It was a fawning, uncritical performance by the celebrated psychiatrist and broadcaster:

> *When asked what his aspiration for the future was, Hume replied as follows: 'I want to see the unionist people coming to terms with the rest of the people on this island.' The clear implication of that remark was that* they *were the problem. Anthony Clare settled for that. He didn't ask the obvious question which was, how the unionist people, having been subjected to a murderous 20-year campaign waged by Irish nationalists, could*

conceivably 'come to terms' with the community that had given birth to such terrorism.

Nor did our recently returned emigrant confront his hero with the republic's constitution which denies the Protestant community down here their Civil Rights . . .

John Hume closed his 50-minute monologue by placing himself alongside Tone and Parnell, both of whom, he claimed with characteristic disingenuousness, had sought nothing more than him. An end to the link with Britain. Unity 'for all the people on this island'. The plea surely of a man whose respect for the past has paralysed his attitude to the future.

If John Hume thinks that we don't understand him he is mistaken. To watching unionists I offer that consolation. To Dr Anthony Clare I can only say welcome home.

By the time that piece appeared the Hume/Adams talks had been going on for a year or more. I wrote tougher polemics about John Hume before and after his encounter with Anthony Clare. What I wanted to challenge was the morality of engaging with the IRA while their campaign of terror continued. Before talking to Gerry Adams, constitutional nationalists must insist that 'young boys' stop 'dying in ditches' and there be no more 'twisted wreckage down on Main Street'.

At the 1981 Sinn Féin Ard Fheis, Danny Morrison had famously declared that 'with a ballot paper in one hand and an Armalite in the other we will take power in Ireland'. Hume/Adams seemed to be a manifestation of Morrison's outrageous proposition. The *Sunday Independent* rejected the idea that terrorism and democracy were compatible. This was deemed controversial.

While Hume was talking to Gerry Adams, he was trying to get me kicked out of my job. He contacted Aengus and Tony O'Reilly to complain about my attacks on him. I was, he claimed, putting his life at risk. The paper was placing the peace talks in jeopardy. The leading Irish-American newspaper accused the *Sunday Indo* of 'McCarthyite' tactics. I was singled out for my abuse of Hume and other peacemakers. O'Reilly was CEO of the Heinz Corporation. He was a leading light in the Ireland Fund, a grouping of Irish-American business people who'd raised tens of millions of dollars to support peace and reconciliation in the homeland. These were heavy hitters with plenty of political muscle.

John Hume was their hero. The *Sunday Independent* became the focus of their ire. O'Reilly began to feel the heat from his corporate buddies.

Aengus never flinched. Nor did Willie Kealy, our news editor, who frequently found himself fielding calls from Hume on a Saturday night when the early edition of the paper hit the streets. But, ultimately, Tony O'Reilly would make the call on my future and the paper's campaign.

Eventually O'Reilly summoned me to a meeting. His biographer and friend the journalist Ivan Fallon was with him. O'Reilly wanted to know what was driving my writing. Hadn't I worn a black armband after Bloody Sunday and campaigned to have the Old Bailey bombers repatriated to serve their sentences? Yes, but that was almost twenty years ago. I was sympathetic to nationalists enduring oppression in a sectarian statelet. Bloody Sunday was state terrorism. I'd wanted to show solidarity with the victims. And remind Millwall fans of what was being done in their name. Back then, nationalists and republicans were victims. But as a consequence of the IRA's campaign the victims now were very often innocent people, Protestants, unionists. I thought we in the South should be vocal in our solidarity with today's victims. Ambivalence towards terror was a cancer in Dublin, I argued. We must expose it.

Behind the charming, urbane persona, O'Reilly was a cool, calculating character. Fallon was from the North; he knew the journalism game. I knew they were sussing me out to see if I was sincere or the grandstanding controversialist of, by now, widespread ill-repute.

I didn't make a plea. I argued my case. Fuck them, I thought. If they don't believe, too bad. Back to the Toy Department, which I hadn't really left. After the gentle but searching interrogation, O'Reilly told me to keep going.

53. George

I'd wanted to write a biography of Matt Busby for a long time. I began to research it when he agreed to co-operate. That was vital. He was a very private man. Over the decades few journalists had breached the charming persona to glimpse the steel that lay beyond. Now retired, though retaining a plush office at Old Trafford, he was viewed by the media as the father of British football.

But you don't build the greatest football club in Europe on charm. His was a rich and complex story, not all of which was glorious. Armed with his consent, I was able to talk to former players, friends and family. I took an apartment in Manchester for three months to work on the book.

Bobby Charlton was my first port of call. For obvious reasons, I was apprehensive about approaching him. Like Busby, Bobby was careful with the media, rarely giving much away, unwilling to talk about the Busby Babes and the devastation of the Munich plane crash.

Jack and Bobby had a somewhat strained relationship. They were very different men. Bobby was reserved and thoughtful, Jack the public curmudgeon, the brash Geordie character of TV panel shows and countless 'Evenings with Big Jack', his main source of income before the Irish job. Jack was closer to his mother, Cissie, than Bobby was. Cissie was from the Milburn clan, a renowned football family from the north-east of England. Cissie liked the media limelight. According to those who knew Bobby, among them Shay Brennan, a very close friend, Cissie's public profile bugged Bobby. In an infamous sound-bite Jack told a journalist, 'Our kid was a better footballer but I'm a better person.' The reason being, it was said, that Jack visited Cissie more regularly than Bobby.

Bobby agreed to help me with the book. He was a partner in a successful business in Manchester, and an influential member of Manchester United's board. When Alex Ferguson struggled in his first three seasons as manager, Bobby saved him while fans were calling for Ferguson's dismissal. Martin Edwards was chairman and Bobby had Edwards's ear. One of the reasons for this was Bobby's clear-eyed take on Matt Busby.

In Manchester United mythology, Busby was the hero, Louis Edwards the villain. The truth was more complicated. In the myth, Edwards betrayed Busby by breaching an agreement that his son Martin and Matt's son Sandy would both join United's board. The fact that Sandy was a bookmaker and was therefore not permitted to be a football-club director enabled Louis to give the club to his son.

But Matt was just as ruthless with many who'd served him and the club, notably his right-hand man, Jimmy Murphy. Matt shafted Jimmy when it suited him. Louis did the same to Matt.

I spent three hours interviewing Bobby in his office just outside the city centre. He was thoughtful and candid, and at times emotional. When he recalled the days of glorious innocence between 1955 and the crash in which he lost his boyhood friends at Munich in 1957, the tears welled up in his eyes. He'd rarely spoken about the crash in public. Enquiring journalists knew it was a no-go area in the few in-depth interviews Bobby gave. He trusted me enough to speak on the record.

Matt was hard, he told me, illustrating the point with a story that involved himself, Denis Law and a fiver a week. When Denis signed for United in 1962, his salary was a matter of much speculation in the dressing room at Old Trafford. It cost a new British transfer record of £115,000 to sign Law from Torino, where wages were much higher than at United. When the maximum wage was abolished in 1961, Busby was loath to loosen United's purse strings. Johnny Haynes at lowly Fulham was on a hundred pounds a week. Busby offered his stars twenty-five, thirty with appearance money.

Bobby had accepted on the understanding that if anyone breached this wage-cap Busby would ensure that nobody was earning more than him. When he learned that Denis was on a fiver more than him, Bobby felt badly let down. Almost thirty years later this still rankled.

So did Busby's shabby treatment of Jimmy Murphy. Bobby believed Jimmy was integral to everything United had achieved before the Munich disaster. Nobody helped Bobby become the great player he did more than Jimmy. But towards the end of his time at Old Trafford Jimmy Murphy was marginalized. The cruel final blow was a decision, sanctioned by Busby, to stop the three-pounds-a-day taxi allowance Jimmy, who didn't drive a car, availed himself of to get to work.

There was a stark contrast between Busby's neglect of Jimmy and the indulgence shown to George Best. Towards the conclusion of my interview with Bobby he reflected sadly on the tragedy that was George. Although they'd never been close, Bobby was inclined to reproach himself for not doing more to help George: 'Sometimes I'd see him looking as if he'd been out all night and part of me would be outraged, yet at the same time part of me wanted to put my arm round his shoulder and offer him advice. But everyone was doing that and I just couldn't bring myself to make the gesture.'

Over the years I'd met George occasionally on his visits to Ireland. His public persona was the stuff of tabloid legend: according to that folklore he was a lush, an inveterate womanizer, the wife abuser in a bad marriage, a genius, once beautiful, now sliding into the gutter. After my U2 book was published we met on one of his trips to Dublin. Over dinner we talked about the possibility of me writing his biography. I wanted to do it. He was agreeable. There had been books written about him, some of which he had co-operated with. But the books weren't very good. Even one of Fleet Street's best sportswriters, Joe Lovejoy, had failed to reach beyond the 'Bestie' of tabloid notoriety. *The Good, the Bad and the Bubbly* was little more than a catalogue of George's female conquests and more outrageous falls from grace.

The book I had in mind would dig deeper, something George didn't really want. On the surface he revelled in the caricature 'Bestie', George the 'character', savouring a life consumed by sex, booze and rock 'n' roll. Yet, interestingly, no drugs. Over our Dublin dinner I broached the subject of hash as a substitute for the alcohol that was clearly killing him.

Although publicly stating that he was off the drink, George ordered a glass of white wine before we ate, then a couple more during the meal. We were haggling good-naturedly over money, how we'd split a publisher's advance for our proposed book. Eighty-twenty in his favour was his opening gambit. 'How much did you give U2'? he enquired.

When I replied, 'Nothing,' he seemed puzzled.

'I did the work, George, they just told me their story.'

'What's the point of doing a book for no money?' he wondered.

'To tell your story, George,' I replied. 'To tell the real story, not that shite about birds, booze and your ten greatest games.'

The real story would involve his mother's alcoholism and his father Dickie's membership of an Orange Lodge, which was not, as conventional prejudice suggested, the same as being a bigot. Dickie was a fabulous, utterly decent man, who'd stuck stoically by George through all the awful public shame. George himself was brave enough to face down loyalist terrorists who threatened to kill him when he declared himself in favour of a united Ireland soccer team.

George was ultimately the victim of the 'Bestie' caricature as well as being the most significant contributor to it. Shortly before I interviewed him for the Busby book, he had appeared drunk on Terry Wogan's prime-time television talk show. Playing the 'Bestie' character he went on a riff about his love of 'screwing'. He was promoting a book about a guy who likes to screw and drink. In a later interview with Wogan, when George was sober, the TV host claimed that George had been fine when he'd left him in the green room three minutes before the show. 'You'd be surprised how much an Irishman can drink in three minutes,' George glibly responded. He got a laugh. But he was the victim, as was his watching father, Dickie, who, George confessed, hadn't spoken to him for months after the débâcle. Trying to be Oliver Reed, Richard Harris or Peter O'Toole, noted hellraisers of those days, George looked foolish. And, to those who cared for him, rather tragic.

Yet, as he unwittingly revealed at dinner that night in Dublin, the wannabe hellraiser was, beneath it all – and not too far beneath – a very conventional person. After our meal he ordered a double brandy. I settled for the wine still in the bottle. He'd been in and out of rehab at the Priory. Officially he was on the wagon.

'For fuck's sake, George, you're killing yourself,' I chided. 'Have you ever smoked dope? You get the same buzz without the deadly damage.'

'Never,' he replied. 'I hate drugs of any kind.' He was genuinely shocked later when I smoked a spliff. A few brandies later we hit the Dublin nightclub scene – Lillie's – where he pulled a local good-time girl to take back to his hotel.

He was very helpful with my research for the Busby book. As Manchester United spiralled into decline in the post-Busby years, George had fought courageously to save the team. Despite the drinking, gambling and womanizing, he was still magnificently committed on the pitch. But fame was detaching him from reality.

As I recorded in the book:

> *. . . insidiously, through the years '65 to '71/72, the intelligent, gentle athlete known to David Sadler and me and the youngsters he'd grown up with at Old Trafford, lads like John Fitzpatrick, Bobby Noble and Jimmy Ryan – the real George Best – was isolated from the people he was fondest of and the game he loved. Fame allowed him to indulge some fantasies but it also detached him from the friends of the bowling-alley, snooker-hall days. Others got married and settled to suburban existence, George hung out in town. A first team player, he was not ever really regarded as a senior pro. He fell into a void somewhere between the factions at United. The younger players, his old buddies, found it hard to identify with the legend Georgie, yet at the same time the senior players didn't take him seriously in terms of his opinions about important matters. George Best was carrying them every week for four seasons, yet he was never in on the politics of Old Trafford the way 'Sir' Willie and Alex Stepney were. A 'bimbo' outside, George was something of a 'bimbo' within as well.*
>
> *He was only the greatest footballer in the world, European Footballer of the Year in 1968, yet nobody consulted him about training or tactics. And George was too timid to get involved without invitation: 'I knew the club was a mess. It was burning me up inside but I suppose I didn't have the guts to tell the great man to his face.'*

The Busby book consumed eighteen months of my life. Sport was my passion and Busby was one of English soccer's great stories. English reviewers were kind. In Dublin, the reception was mixed. Working for the *Sunday Independent*, attacking Jack Charlton, John Hume and other national icons, I was damaged goods. Small towns don't forgive.

After the book was published, George invited me to London to re-open the discussion about his own book. I arrived at his Chelsea apartment one Monday morning around ten thirty. He claimed he was getting his act together. He had a weekly gig doing commentary for Sky Sports and was drinking moderately, only white wine and champagne. Mary Shatila was the new woman in his life. An attractive, strong and sensitive woman, Mary was no bimbo. She was now managing his business affairs. Mary had her own heartache: a daughter she'd had with a previous lover had been snatched and taken to Lebanon by the father.

When I arrived at their apartment Mary answered the door. George was in the shower. It was eleven o'clock when he emerged looking his old boyish self. Most days he hung out in a pub in Chelsea. We should go there, he suggested. But, first, a glass of champagne. He took a bottle from the fridge and set out three glasses. We sat and talked about the book and Mary's problem. At twelve thirty we took a taxi to the pub. They had to make a detour on the way, though, to Fleet Street to pick up a package. Mary did the picking up. We resumed our journey. George asked the cabbie to stop at a branch of WH Smith. A few minutes later he was back with a copy of the *Mastermind* quiz book. The popular TV series hosted by Magnus Magnusson was one of his favourite programmes. We'd do the quizzes in the pub to pass the time, George suggested.

He ordered white wine. This was his local, George explained. Nobody bothered him. For the purposes of the quiz I was Magnus Magnusson. 'Ask me anything,' he challenged, an impish smile on his face. Over a sandwich lunch and long into the afternoon he answered nearly every question: current affairs, history, geography, sport. His knowledge was astonishing. In the section of the book that measured IQ he took a particular delight in scoring high. Two numbers either side of a vacant bracket: invariably he supplied the missing number. Insert the missing word: no problem. All the time he sipped his wine, clearly relishing the demonstration of his extraordinary intelligence. 'It's usually my job,' Mary wryly remarked, about my quizmaster role. When the tables were turned, with George posing the questions, I was hopeless.

It was a lovely, funny, innocent day. The lunchtime rush came and passed. Dusk fell late afternoon. We were pleasantly tipsy. Nobody paid any attention to George. He was at his usual table. This was how he spent most days, he told me: consuming enough white wine to get what he described as 'that glow', enough to stave off boredom and loneliness, I thought, as late afternoon gave way to evening. Around six o'clock Denis Compton came into the pub. The great former English cricketer (and Arsenal footballer) came over to greet George. Two sporting geniuses, they shared another distinction: Compton was the first English cricketer to exploit his renown by endorsing commercial products. In Compton's case, the product was Brylcreem. The poignancy of seeing them together in that anonymous London pub was almost painful. They'd captured hearts and minds more than any of their peers, yet in this setting the sense of glory past, never to return, was almost palpable.

Around seven, we left for Soho to have some dinner. There was an Italian restaurant George regularly frequented. We'd talk about the book, he promised. When our starters arrived he excused himself to go to the bathroom. Ten minutes later Mary glanced at her watch. 'He's not coming back, Eamon,' she concluded wearily. He didn't.

Mary explained the stop in Fleet Street: the package she'd picked up was cash. Ten grand paid by a Sunday newspaper for a 'Best and the Barmaid' story. It was a scam, Mary explained. There was no barmaid, not in any meaningful sense. Yes, there would have been a woman. Perhaps one of the many who targeted George, according to folklore. George would contact an eager hack with the story. A compromising picture was staged. The exposé would be 'splashed' on a low-news Sunday morning front page. Ten grand was currently the going rate. There was a time when the price had been five times as much.

On this occasion the money was supposed to be for a private investigator Mary wanted to hire to find her missing daughter. But George had done a runner. 'He's gone to the casino,' Mary said, sadness in her eyes. 'He'll be home later, broke.' Loving George was a bumpy ride.

Yet he was capable of great generosity. In his glory days, George appeared in many testimonial games for old footballing pals who'd fallen on hard times. His presence guaranteed a bonanza. He took no fee. When my Busby book was published, Gay Byrne offered a priceless publicity slot on *The Late Late Show*, subject to George appearing with me. He came to Dublin for nothing more than a two-night stay at the Westbury Hotel. No fee, no hassle, George turned up on time and charmed the audience for half an hour.

For all the crazy things he did, the alleged abuse of women being the most unforgivable, and to those of us who knew him, the most inexplicable, I never heard George swear.

I last saw him about a year before he died. He was coming to Dublin to do a 'gig' at the Towers, a super-pub in Ballymun. The format was a question-and-answer session. He rang to ask if I'd sit beside him on the stage: 'You can talk.' He laughed. The agent laid on a limo, Celtic Tiger style. His wife Alex was with him. When we arrived at the Towers the room was less than half full. The MC urged people to push up to the front to create some atmosphere. George looked worn out.

The anecdotes about Miss Worlds and all the times he had 'scored' on and off the pitch were stale from being recycled too often. The audience, bored, could deliver the punchlines long before George got there. George was drinking. He began to slur his words. People drifted off to the bar, embarrassed for him. The 'Evening with George', as it was billed, mutated into an evening with the ghost of George, a parody that only served to underline how far from grace he'd fallen.

Afterwards we went to the bar. There was a pool table nearby. George suggested a game. Alex was growing restless, desperate to leave. A young Down's syndrome boy approached George for an autograph. George was gentle with him. 'Would you like a game of pool?' George asked the boy. They started to play. A small group gathered round the table. George didn't let him win. Wistfully the youngster asked to go again. 'Okay, best of three,' George promised.

At that moment Alex snapped. She wanted to go. Now. 'Take the car, we're staying,' George responded curtly. Best of three stretched to best of five. The boy gazed dreamily at his dad standing proudly watching. It was a very touching moment. The boy will never forget the night he played the great George Best at pool. Where other personalities would have made a meaningless gesture before leaving, George surrendered completely to the moment. The car returned from town. We dropped George at the Westbury. He died a year later.

54. Mob Rule

After our Westbury confrontation John Giles arranged peace talks between Jack and me over a few drinks at the Airport Hotel, the team's headquarters. Shay Brennan, an old friend of Jack, joined us. It was a convivial evening. With his droll sense of humour, Shay could have melted a furnace. John and Jack had shared a dressing room at Leeds for eleven years. Although they didn't agree on very much, certainly not about football, the bond between Leeds United old boys was very strong. At Elland Road Jack was regarded as eccentric: stubborn, very fond of money, a big baby, in John's description, when not getting his own way. Still, there was no badness in him.

Over a few pints John, Shay and I filled him in on the crew at Merrion Square, the Blazers' idiocies and their capacity to fuck things up. Jack had run into trouble shortly after his appointment. In a very good exposé of the Charlton era published in 1994, Paul Rowan wrote an account of Jack's first crisis. Liam Tuohy was the victim, as Rowan told the story:

> *As one of the most respected figures on the domestic scene, Tuohy was seen as the ideal figure to act as Charlton's assistant manager. And when Charlton came to Dublin as Irish manager, Tuohy had been asked by an FAI official to meet him at the Westbury. In his hotel room, Charlton said that he hadn't asked to see Tuohy, but they would have a chat anyway. Tuohy filled Charlton in about his job as youth manager. Charlton told him that he hadn't yet decided what he was going to do about his support staff. Tuohy told him of his team's efforts to qualify for the European Youth Championships, and both men agreed that Tuohy would at least see out the last couple of matches.*
>
> *Three weeks later, the youth team, attempting to qualify for their fourth European Championship, found themselves in Yorkshire on a foggy, freezing day, for a match against England. Charlton arrived unexpectedly at the team's hotel on the day of the match and told them he would be at the game as another one he had been planning to watch had been cancelled because of bad weather. He joined them for lunch, taking issue with the team's selection from the menu.*

'We had a chat during lunch, but I felt that he was in a bit of a tetchy humour,'
says Tuohy. 'He made observations about the meal – the boys were having steak. I
said, well, it hasn't done them too badly because they've reached three European
Cups and a World Cup Finals. He made this observation about the pasta, and
about what the new thinking in the game was. So I wondered was he spoiling for
something.' . . .

Ireland, a small team who played neat football, were 2–0 down at half-time.
Charlton didn't like what he saw. It was a freezing cold evening, so cold that the
water in the doctor's bucket was turning to ice. But, as the doctor observed, it got
very hot in the dressing-room at half-time . . .

'In comes Jack, walks directly in front of me, not a "by your leave" or "excuse
me, Liam". He just ignored me as if I wasn't there. I couldn't believe he had the
bad manners to do a thing like that. He was quite forceful in his comments and
some of the things he said were very negative. Everything he said was very nega-
tive. He wanted the long ball.' . . .

When the team got back to Dublin, Tuohy handed in his resignation to the
FAI. His assistants, Brian Kerr and Noel O'Reilly, went with him.

Jack mentioned this at the Airport Hotel. As John would later explain, the
Elland Road incident was vintage Jack. He was totally out of order, yet it
was 'Liam Tuohy who caused me more aggravation than anyone else'!

The day after that meeting, Ireland played Wales at Lansdowne Road.
Ian Rush scored the only goal of a dour match. It was an inauspicious
start for Jack. That Sunday in the *Indo* I rationalized the defeat as follows:

Jack Charlton's Ireland will be as stubborn as Ramsey's England and as
admirably honest as he himself has been these past few weeks. Although he
has upset a few people behind the scenes, posed a permanent threat to jour-
nalists who ask questions he doesn't fancy, committed an almighty blunder
by picking a player he had never seen, can't remember players' names and
probably wouldn't recognize the national anthem if he heard it on the car
radio, Jack Charlton has gone a long way towards proving he is the right
man for the job of managing Ireland.

Against Wales, the Irish team was organized and committed. OK, they
lost, but it was only a friendly, the beginning of the project, not the
end. But I was proving that I could give Official Ireland a run for its
money when it came to false narratives. I believed in Jack. I'd played

against his Middlesbrough team that was promoted to the First Division with a record number of points. Graeme Souness was a pivotal figure in that team. Bought cheaply from Spurs, Souness flourished under Jack's management. With outstanding players like Liam Brady, Frank Stapleton, Mark Lawrenson, Paul McGrath, Ronnie Whelan, Ray Houghton, Kevin Moran and John Aldridge, Jack would surely succeed with Ireland. That was my attitude.

So I didn't tell the story I knew about Jack's shabby treatment of Liam Tuohy, Brian Kerr and Noel O'Reilly, good Irish football men who were very badly hurt by Jack's behaviour at Elland Road. He might have 'upset a few people', I'd written, not even giving them a name. John Reason's phrase, 'fans with typewriters', comes to mind when I reflect on my initial response to Big Jack.

I also suspended my disbelief on Jack's treatment of David O'Leary. Jack didn't fancy David. A cultured, swift centre-half, David was one of the best defenders in Europe. He read the game perfectly. He hardly ever had to make last-ditch tackles because his forward rarely reached the last ditch. David used brain instead of brawn. He played in Jack's first game against Wales. Jack blamed him for Ian Rush's goal. Jack, a centre-half himself, couldn't grasp the subtleties of David's game. The brawny physical presence of Mick McCarthy was much more Jack's cup of tea. Bye-bye, David.

Ireland's next assignment was an end-of-season triangular tournament in Iceland. Czechoslovakia and Ireland were the host nation's opposition. When Jack named his squad, David's name was missing. Following a number of last-minute withdrawals from the original squad, he named David as a replacement. Having booked a family holiday, David refused to alter his arrangements. He wasn't the only player who declined to travel for what was, in essence, a Mickey Mouse tournament. Ronnie Whelan, Mark Lawrenson, John Aldridge and Ray Houghton, all Liverpool players, also chose to go on holiday.

Ireland won the tournament, making history of a kind. As important from Jack's perspective, the O'Leary issue was put to bed. He'd refused his country's call. End of story. Nobody mentioned the Liverpool holiday-makers. Being now a decent skin, I kept quiet as well.

Ireland began the 1988 European Championship campaign with a 2–2 draw away to Belgium. Next up was Scotland at Lansdowne Road. A no-score draw. The match was painful to watch. It was Jack football:

pressing high up the pitch, fighting for every ball, making life hell for the opposition. In possession, Ireland pumped long balls deep into opposition territory, then hunted in packs trying to force a mistake. Jack's football was premised on two basic principles: foreigners didn't have the stomach for a war of attrition; his own players weren't good enough to play a passing game.

Whatever about the first element in that equation, the second was dubious to say the least. This was the best Irish team ever. The idea that his players couldn't play was absurd. At the press conference after the abysmal Scottish game, reporters challenged Jack. Bill Kelly of the *Sunday Press* put it to him that players should be allowed to think for themselves rather than sticking to his game plan. Jack gave Bill the evil eye, picked up his cap and walked out, his parting words, 'Half of you don't know what I'm talking about.'

The reverse fixture against Scotland at Hampden Park provided vindication for Jack's methodology. Of a kind. Ireland had one shot at goal, which Mark Lawrenson tucked into the corner of the net. What was most extraordinary about the evening was the team that Jack selected. David O'Leary, widely believed to be one of the best central defenders playing in England – he would have been a certainty for the England team, most observers agreed – watched the game from his London home. Ronnie Whelan, an attacking midfielder coveted by every club in the British Isles, played left full-back. His Liverpool colleague Lawrenson, vying with O'Leary for best central defender in the game, operated in midfield. And Paul McGrath, the legendary centre-half, played right full-back. With Mick McCarthy and Kevin Moran actually playing as central defenders, Ireland fielded four centre-halves and denied Scotland a sniff at goal. Bill Kelly wasn't the only one who didn't know what Jack was doing. But it worked at Hampden.

Next time out, Ireland lost 2–1 to Bulgaria in Sofia. Then another goalless draw at home to Belgium was followed by an embarrassingly narrow 2–1 win at home to Luxembourg's part-timers. The Belgian and Luxembourg games were played on a Lansdowne Road pitch with grass too long; it was bumpy because it hadn't been rolled after the most recent rugby match. That was Jack's idea. Although his team contained some of the best footballers in Europe, who might have relished a good playing surface, Jack was focused on making life difficult for Johnny Foreigner.

Ireland's final qualifying game was against Bulgaria at Lansdowne Road. We swarmed all over them to win 2–0. The Bulgarians were still hot favourites to qualify, needing only a point from their home game against Scotland in Sofia. With three minutes to go, Bulgaria had their precious point. Then Scotland's substitute, Gary Mackay, scored the goal that saw Ireland qualify for their first major championship finals. History by osmosis. For a nation enduring a desperate economic recession, the news from Sofia provided a welcome tonic. The 'foreign game' was about to be adopted in a big way. Soon a new slogan would emerge. It read 'Go On, You Boys in Green.' With the slogan, there came a new hero: Big Jack.

Jack had eight months to prepare for the European Finals in West Germany. Ireland played five friendlies, winning them all, conceding only one goal. The idea of the Irish soccer team making the big-time after all those miserable decades of failure captured the public imagination. For a nation blighted by economic woe, unemployment, emigration, health-service cuts, a general sense that Ireland was always destined to fail, success on the sports field offered a glimmer of hope.

When Eamonn Coghlan won the 5,000 metres at the World Athletic Championships in 1983 he instantly became a national hero. After Stephen Roche won the Tour de France in 1987, Taoiseach Charles Haughey flew to Paris to greet our hero on the Champs-Élysées. These were good news stories but they were few and far between.

Big Jack was a very good news story. He, rather than the players, was the focus of attention. He charmed Gay Byrne on *The Late Late Show*. He endorsed breakfast cereals, motor-cars and savings accounts. Nobody does flattery like the Irish. The love affair between Big Jack and an adoring nation was swiftly consummated. As the championship finals loomed ever closer a wonderful sense of anticipation developed, taking our minds off the horrors of the economy and the terror up North. When the draw for the finals pitched us against England in the opening game, interest reached fever pitch. In the rush to interview Big Jack, those of us in the Toy Department were swept aside by our betters in Features. Special supplements featuring Big Jack and his men dominated newspaper coverage. There was no talk now of 'foreign games'. Celebrities and the nation's commentariat, most of whom thought the offside rule was a metaphor for adultery, disclosed a lifelong love of soccer. The *Irish Times* told us what all of this meant. Official Ireland was on board, paying homage to the Boys in Green.

From a purely footballing perspective there were a couple of troubling matters to reflect on. Liam Brady would miss the Euros. He'd been sent off in the final qualifying game against Bulgaria and the two-match ban he received meant he wouldn't be picked for the finals. The other pressing matter was the make-up of Big Jack's squad, specifically whether or not David O'Leary would be selected. To go to a major championship finals without one of the best defenders in Europe, who was playing superbly for Arsenal, seemed crazy. As well as England, we were due to face the Soviet Union and Holland. Jack had blanked David for two years, and the case for ending this vindictiveness seemed unanswerable. But Jack left David out. And nobody, myself included, made a fuss about the hero's decision.

June the 12th was a Sunday. I wrote my preview for the paper and settled down to watch the England game on telly. I was planning to travel to Hanover for the Soviet Union game on the Wednesday. After six minutes, Ray Houghton put Ireland ahead with a looping header. It was a wow moment, still etched in Irish folklore. For the next eighty-four minutes Ireland hung on, defying extreme English pressure in the game's closing stages.

On any objective reading, an unforgettable emotional experience for a nation badly in need of a happy pill was a pretty average game of football. England deserved something from the game but Gary Lineker had left his shooting boots at home, while Packie Bonner and the Irish team defended stoutly. Next morning nobody wanted objective analysis. Big Jack's bandwagon was rolling and every chancer in the country was looking to hitch a ride. Beating England was a big deal. For Jack, the win was special for another reason: ten years previously he'd applied to the Football Association for the job of managing England. He had received no letter of acknowledgement.

Three days later we were in Hanover for the game against the Soviet Union. Irish fans occupied the city centre in the hours before the match. They were partying with *bodhráns* and fiddles, laughing and singing, charming the natives in that sober university city. These scenes of peace and joy stood in stark contrast to the spectre of football hooliganism, which, pre-tournament, had cast a cloud over the championship. For this, a minority of English fans were responsible. I got no kick from beating an average England team in Stuttgart, but it was a source of some patriotic pride to witness the good humour and innocent gaiety radiating through downtown Hanover before the Soviet Union game. Thurles revisited.

The team played really well against the Soviet Union. Ronnie Whelan scored a spectacular goal to put Ireland in front. We played a passing game against a very good side who would go on to contest the final. It was a beautiful summer evening. The Soviets equalized with fifteen minutes to go, but the draw was, in footballing terms, more satisfying than the win over England.

Back in the hotel afterwards people were in good humour. Ireland had arrived on the international stage as a footballing nation. After decades of looking on from afar we were part of a great occasion. And that night there were signs that Jack had allowed his players to escape from the crude tactical straitjacket they'd been imprisoned in.

I was standing in the hotel lobby when Jack walked in, a big smile on his face. I congratulated him on the performance. He invited me to join himself, Maurice Setters and Mick Byrne for a drink. I never socialized with people I wrote about. But between the fans in the city earlier and the team's outstanding performance I was in good form. Why not? After a couple of drinks Jack suggested we have dinner. 'Come and eat with us,' he said to me.

'No, Jack,' I replied. 'I'm fine, thanks.'

'Come on, we've got the private dining room.'

'No, Jack, that wouldn't be a very good idea. I've got history with those players. I don't think they'll want me in the room.'

'Fuck them, you're with us.' He steered me down a corridor, Maurice and Mick trailing in our wake. I knew Mick well from Shamrock Rovers. He knew this wasn't a good idea. But neither of us said no to Jack. I was weak. I'd been a player. I knew what was coming.

When we walked into the private dining room, the murmurings of conversation stopped. The lads were seated at two adjoining tables. We sat at a table laid for four.

Frank Stapleton was first on his feet to lead the walk-out. Mick McCarthy was up next. Frank was an arsehole. McCarthy I could understand, for I'd never hidden my belief that he was David O'Leary's poor relation. To be honest, I thought the players were entitled to be annoyed. Or worse. This was their space. I was an unwelcome invader. I wanted to leave. Jack wouldn't have it. After an uncomfortable hour I escaped.

The final group game against Holland was played in Gelsenkirchen. Holland had beaten England comfortably but had lost to the Soviet Union. This meant Ireland needed only a draw to progress to the tournament's knockout phase. In those days only eight nations contested the European Championship Finals, so a draw against the Dutch would see us in the semi-final of a major championship. Jack and his team were on the cusp of something quite remarkable.

The match was a scrappy affair. This was an outstanding Dutch team. Marco van Basten, Ronald Koeman, Ruud Gullit and Frank Rijkaard were among the best players in Europe. Their coach, Rinus Michels, was world renowned for his concept of 'total football', the classic attacking game that distinguished teams he created at Ajax and later with the national team. As usual Ireland pressed in a pack, denying their technically superior opponents time and space. In possession of the ball we were profligate, a shadow of the team that had played so constructively against the Soviet Union.

As the match reached its decisive phase, the cumulative consequence of giving the ball away cheaply allowed Holland to camp in Ireland's half. The goal, when it came in the eighty-second minute, seemed inevitable. A crazy deflection fell to Wim Kieft, whose header spun past a helpless Packie Bonner. It was a cruel end to an astonishing week.

Objectively speaking, it was hard to pin the blame for Kieft's goal on any individual. But sitting in the press-box preparing to file my match report I was in no mood to be objective. Two things had been bugging me for a couple of years: Mick McCarthy's presence in the team ahead of David O'Leary's; and Big Jack's perverse decision to pretend that David didn't exist. The report I now dispatched to Dublin was highly subjective, coloured by my feelings about the McCarthy/O'Leary business.

I identified McCarthy as the defender responsible for costing Ireland the game. Kieft, his man, scored the goal, I argued. We had paid the price for O'Leary's exile. Big Jack was guilty of vindictiveness, which was taking its toll on the Irish team. On this matter I had been mute for long enough.

Twenty-five years later, in 2013, the *Irish Daily Mail*'s experienced soccer correspondent, Philip Quinn, described Jack's treatment of David as 'brutish, unashamedly personal and callous'. My timing was off, and on reflection I was much too tough on McCarthy, but in terms of justice for David O'Leary, the piece I filed from Gelsenkirchen raised an issue that had to be addressed.

In the corridor outside the Irish dressing room after the game, Jack and FAI secretary Tony O'Neill were talking intensely as I passed by. Jack beckoned me over, knowing nothing at this stage about the report I'd filed. 'They're talking about a civic reception in Dublin tomorrow,' he told me. 'What do you think? We've won nothing, we just got beat.' Tony had conveyed the news to the slightly bemused Englishman.

'I think you should do it,' I told Jack. 'You've had a great week. People at home want to express their appreciation. Go for it.' Tony was giving the same advice. Reluctantly Jack agreed, adding ruefully that in England 'they'd be fucking moaning'.

What happened next is chronicled from Jack's perspective in Paul Rowan's book:

> As the players were returning from Germany, Dunphy launched his fiercest attack yet on McCarthy in the Sunday Independent. The paper was handed out to the players on the plane. Charlton was reading the article when McCarthy leaned over his shoulder. 'I don't think you should see this,' Charlton said to him. 'It'll ruin your day.' McCarthy insisted and Charlton then apologized to him for having inflicted Dunphy on him back in the hotel in Hanover.
>
> At the airport hotel, Charlton spotted Dunphy. 'I got hold of him, and I said: "You little cunt. I tell you something. I've gone along with you and I've tried to help you. But now you can fuck off. Cos I'm joining their fucking ranks. I want fuck all to do with you."'

Taoiseach Charlie Haughey greeted Jack and the team at Dublin Airport. After the fawning, Big Jack and the Boys in Green took an open-top bus to the city centre. An estimated 200,000 people lined the streets. Only the Pope in 1979 and John F. Kennedy in 1963 had drawn such a crowd. As with the Pope and Kennedy, people travelled from rural Ireland just to be there on that sunny evening in June 1988. Although the players mattered, Big Jack was the star of the show. As the cavalcade glided slowly towards the city centre, the star acknowledged the cheering throng, a broad, slightly bemused smile lighting his big Geordie face.

I made it home in time to watch this extraordinary story unfold on television. What, I wondered, would the Gaels make of this celebration of the 'foreign' game, a large English national treasure at its heart? I viewed all of this with mixed emotions. On the positive side I was pleased for the players who had battled so gallantly at the championships. They had beaten England. The performance against the Soviet Union was as good as any I could recall since Ireland had beaten the same opponents 3–0 in Dalymount Park when John was manager in 1974. And there was no shame in losing to a freak goal against the outstanding Holland team that went on to claim the title.

The warmth of the crowd's greeting for Paul McGrath, Kevin Moran, Packie Bonner, Ronnie Whelan, Ray Houghton and John Aldridge, all the players, even Mick McCarthy, was wonderful to behold. And as the main man, Big Jack, stepped forward to frenzied acclaim, I temporarily laid aside my misgivings to reflect on his contribution to our communal joy. From the shambles he had inherited, Jack had built a disciplined, professional team. From day one he had worked diligently to recruit players like Houghton and Aldridge, born elsewhere but qualified to play for Ireland. The net result was the team we had seen in the Euro Finals, reflecting, as many teams do, the character of their manager: in this case, stubbornness; no frills; taking no prisoners but playing within the laws of the game. Also, to his credit, Jack was as bloody-minded with the Blazers in Merrion Square as he was with the working press.

When he took over in 1986, Peadar O'Driscoll, the Association's general secretary, ran the show. Having a drink at the Airport Hotel one night in the early days, Jack told John, Shay and me a story that even we, with all our surreal FAI experiences, found hard to believe. For his first few matches Jack had given his squad selection to O'Driscoll. When the squad was released to the media, Jack discovered that O'Driscoll had added the names of a couple of players he fancied. Jack decided he wouldn't do business with the general secretary. As he subsequently told Paul Rowan, 'I would only phone Merrion Square between twelve and two o'clock when I knew the secretary wouldn't be there.'

Big Jack put a shape on the team and manners on the lads in Merrion Square. For those things alone many of us who had lived through the pantomime would have granted him the freedom of the city. But that took a bit of time. The crowd gathered in the city centre for the homecoming were there to celebrate Ireland's arrival as participants in a major championship in the world's most popular sport. To paraphrase Robert Emmet, Ireland had finally taken her place among the (footballing) nations of the earth.

This was a big deal. For youngsters and their infatuated parents there was plenty to celebrate. For Haughey and all the corporate hustlers on the make and the media looking for a feel-good story there was plenty to exploit. Big Jack and our soccer players had traced the footprints of our *Eurovision Song Contest* heroes, of Stephen Roche and Eamonn Coghlan. An informed critique suggesting that the hero might have feet of clay was bound to spoil the party.

To mention David O'Leary and Big Jack's 'brutish, highly personal and callous' treatment of him was, thus, deemed controversial. And Liam Tuohy, Brian Kerr and Noel O'Reilly, arguably treated worse than David, were now written out of the script. The people out cheering on the streets didn't want to know the whole story. Shamefully, the media didn't want to tell that story. Groupthink was back in town with a vengeance.

For the small football community I belonged to, steeped in Irish soccer lore, Liam Tuohy was a hero from Shamrock Rovers in that fifties golden age of League of Ireland. When Jack walked into the Elland Road dressing room and pissed over Liam Tuohy, he was pissing over all of us. And the reason? Liam was encouraging his youngsters to play a passing game, to develop good habits even if it cost you on the night. They were kids. They were learning to play the game the way Irish players had always played it. Smart. Brain trumping brawn. (Later, post-Jack, Brian Kerr returned to groom Robbie Keane, Damien Duff and Richard Dunne triumphantly in Irish youth teams.)

Jack's behaviour with David O'Leary triggered another culture clash. David's exile had had nothing to do with a holiday, as Jack claimed. The four Liverpool lads, Whelan, Houghton, Aldridge and Lawrenson, had taken time out too. No, Jack didn't appreciate David's style. David was a classy footballer. More brain than brawn. The O'Learys were a respected Dublin soccer family. As were the Gileses, the Whelans, the Lawlors, the Bradys and the Martins, Con, Mick and Con Junior. Our roots went deep, our traditions and native football culture gave us an identity that was distinct. Icons like Johnny Carey and John Giles were wonderful, cultured footballers. It was that culture Liam Tuohy was nurturing. It was that distinctly Irish culture that David O'Leary honoured every time he laced his boots.

None of this, the great back-story of Irish soccer, meant anything to Jack, Big fucking Jack. As his story developed, as he trampled on everything sacred to those of us in the Irish football community, I met Kit Lawlor on the street one day. By then I was public enemy number one. Kit was a savvy man: he dressed as he played the game, stylishly. He was a hero.

'What do you think of yer man?' I asked Kit.

'I don't even watch it, Eamon.' He smiled, a look of resignation on his streetwise face.

The mob scene that was the homecoming of 1988 was only the beginning. Some degree of suspended disbelief allowed me – and John Giles, with whom I talked a lot about the emerging story – to retain a measure of objectivity.

Jack's football philosophy was crude. The basic principle was to eliminate risk while maximizing the pressure on your opponents. This was an English concept in vogue in the lower divisions of the Football League, where I had plied my trade for all those years. Alarmed by the technical deficiencies of a generation of young English footballers, a man named Charles Hughes had come up with a solution.

As director of coaching for the Football Association, Hughes developed a theory that rendered talent largely irrelevant. He was a boffin, a mad scientist and a deeply controversial figure in his own country. After studying hundreds of football matches, Hughes concluded that most goals were scored from moves involving less than three passes. In his published work he emphasized the importance of particular areas of the pitch where goals were most often scored. He named these areas Positions of Maximum Opportunity, or POMO for short. Hughes also stressed the importance of set-pieces and crosses into opponents' penalty areas.

Although Hughes and his POMO were derided by sophisticated football men, he had some disciples in England's lower leagues, forced by circumstances to work with limited players. Graham Taylor was by far the most successful Hughes disciple. Deploying POMO, Taylor guided Lincoln City to promotion from Fourth Division in 1976. The Reading team I played in was promoted that same year. I knew Taylor. I knew POMO. It was hell to play against. In the lower leagues.

But Taylor really put himself and POMO on the map at Watford, a small club that rose dramatically from the Fourth Division to the First in five glorious years. In 1983 Watford finished runners-up to Liverpool in the First Division. The following year POMO arrived at Wembley for the FA Cup Final. The long-ball game might be sneered at by purists, but it got results.

Jack Charlton's successful Middlesbrough team won the Second Division by a record fifteen-point margin playing POMO. The blueprint was designed to get the best out of ordinary footballers. Allowing them to pass the ball in order to create danger was risky. As Jack would argue, they can't play, so why not take Route One? John and I knew all this stuff when Jack arrived. The fascinating question was how he might adapt his version of Charles Hughes's philosophy to the skill-set in the Irish team.

Big Jack's unseemly behaviour towards Liam Tuohy and David O'Leary provided a clue. I was not looking for a fight so it took me more than two years to draw attention to the prejudice that had cast David into exile. By the time I'd got my act together and started behaving like a journalist, the mob was on the march.

With expectation now high, Ireland began the qualifying series for the 1990 World Cup Finals with two mediocre performances. We were drawn in a five-nation group that looked relatively easy on paper: Northern Ireland, Malta, Hungary, ourselves and Spain. Two nations to qualify. Our first game against Northern Ireland in Belfast ended in an excruciating 0–0 draw. The football was shocking. Then we lost 2–0 to Spain in Seville.

Although fit to play, Liam Brady had been bombed out by Big Jack. After a successful career in Italy, Liam was back in England playing for West Ham in the Second Division. He'd lost a year's football with a career-threatening cruciate-ligament injury. But many of us felt his guile and big-match experience were still valuable assets. Liam played all eight games in the European Championship qualifiers and played really well. There were calls for his return to the squad after our modest start to the Italia 90 campaign.

When Jack was asked about Liam at a press conference, he snapped, 'What Brady can't do at thirty-three is give me ninety minutes of football at a pace and work-rate our style demands.'

Brady, a strong character, highly respected by everyone in football, rarely broke media cover but, responding to Jack's dismissive remarks, he told a journalist: 'I don't like stupid quotes like that. I take exception to those remarks.'

There was some history between Jack and Liam. Although he was outstanding in the Euro qualifiers, Liam consistently defied Jack's orders to knock long balls behind opposing defences in the manner demanded by POMO. Jack kept quiet because the results were good. But his resentment was obvious from his attitude to Liam in the dressing room. A row was brewing.

Meanwhile, Ireland won three home games against Spain, Malta and Hungary. World Cup qualification now seemed probable. The home victory against Spain was critical. On a windy April afternoon, on a rugby pitch, bumpy as Jack ordered, Ireland tortured the Spanish with biting tackles and long, high balls. Trapped in their own half for much of the game, most of the Spanish players packed it in. After an own goal gave us a 1–0 lead the result was never in doubt. Liam Brady was on the bench. He recalls the visitors' whingeing in the tunnel after the game: 'Rugby, rugby,' they taunted, a reference to the Lansdowne Road pitch and the long-ball game they'd failed to cope with.

The same tactics saw off Malta and Hungary in the following weeks. Italia 90 beckoned. A home win against Northern Ireland would seal the deal. Four weeks before the Northern Ireland game, Ireland played West Germany in a friendly at Lansdowne Road. Jack was already mulling over his squad selection for the World Cup Finals. He didn't want to select Liam Brady. By his own admission, in public to Paul Rowan for his book *The Team That Jack Built*, and in private to John Giles, Jack hatched a cunning plan to shaft Liam:

> *'With Ireland, you see, they don't give up their fucking heroes easily, so you've really got to show 'em. If I don't pick Liam to play or I don't pick Kevin Moran to play or I don't pick somebody that's Irish and been there a long time, they want to know why you didn't fucking pick him to play. And you say, "Well, he's too old, he's not fast enough now. I want somebody who can do better for us in the years to come and I've got to reshape the side." So what I did was I put 'em on display. I had three of them – Liam, Frank and Tony Galvin – who were coming to the end of their time and I put 'em on display to the public.'*
>
> *Charlton's public display didn't go exactly to plan, as Stapleton scored after 10 minutes to put Ireland in the lead and was having an excellent game. His goal shook up the Germans, and they began dominating the game. 'Jack was totally absorbed in the game,' said one of his coaching staff, Noel King, 'and he was becoming more and more frustrated. He was roaring at Liam to pick players up.'*
>
> *'We were getting run to death across midfield,' Charlton says. 'And it was obvious that Liam had had his day. He wasn't tackling anybody. He wasn't getting away from anybody like he used to.'*

The Germans equalized after half an hour and three minutes later Brady was replaced by Andy Townsend. At half-time, Brady remonstrated with Charlton in the dressing room, telling him that he had been humiliated by being replaced so early and it could have waited till half-time. The match finished 1–1. In the hotel afterwards, Brady announced his retirement from international football.

In that passage from Rowan's excellent exposé, Jack reveals quite a lot. About himself. It's clear he wanted to get rid of Liam, Frank Stapleton and Tony Galvin. All he had to do, if he really was Big Jack, was drop them from his squad. Instead he opted for putting them 'on display' against a strong West German side in the hope – and expectation – that they would be humiliated. When Rowan put it to Jack that he deliberately set out to strip Liam of his dignity, the big man denied it:

'Hey, I didn't do it to embarrass Liam. If I thought I was embarrassing Liam I would have left him on. I am a fuckin' pro at the business. That's my job, to get results for Ireland. I'm not going to give up a result against the West Germans for Liam or anybody. I could never give Liam another game. He was a national hero. In my opinion he was gone, he had had a bad leg for a long time, he just wasn't the fuckin' Liam we knew and loved. They would expect me to call him up for every international match in spite of the fact that he's not quick and not playing, so I put him on display. And then after that Liam disappeared off the scene.'

After a comfortable 3–0 victory over Northern Ireland, our qualification for Italia 90 was assured. Jack was now a national hero and the Irish wouldn't give up on him easily.

After decades of striving, the prospect of Ireland playing in the World Cup Finals was enchanting. Even those of us with reservations about Big Jack's long-ball game laid them firmly aside to savour the experience in the months leading up to Italia 90. We remembered the agony of John Atyeo's last-minute goal for England in Dalymount in 1957, which denied us the dream cherished for so long. The narrow defeat by Spain in Paris on the night I made my debut, so painful at the time, was now forgotten. A sense of joyous anticipation gripped not just the soccer community, but the whole country. Songs were composed about the history being made. The media celebrated our heroes, the players, of course, and Big Jack, the man who had delivered the dream. Credit unions were besieged by fans seeking loans to make the journey to the finals.

New heroes emerged. Mick McCarthy became Captain Fantastic. That was a bitter pill to swallow. Still, David O'Leary was included in the twenty-two-man travelling squad. Arnold O'Byrne became a star. Arnold was the managing director of Opel, the team's sponsor. Arnold was on *The Late Late Show* telling Gay Byrne how he'd done it. And, of course, Big Jack was lionized in every newspaper, radio show and television show in the country. *My Left Foot* had conquered Hollywood, U2 were the world's biggest rock band and the Boys in Green were off to Italia 90.

By some metaphysical process those three cultural accomplishments were deemed to have restored the nation's confidence. 'We're all part of Jackie's Army' was the *de facto* national anthem. The mob was larger and louder than ever before.

Liam Tuohy, Brian Kerr, Noel O'Reilly, Liam Brady? Men overboard, forgotten heroes of a bygone age.

I was invited back to work for the RTÉ television panel. I was happy to return, although my commitment to the *Sunday Independent* meant I would be going to Italy for some of the matches.

When the draw was made for the finals we found ourselves in the same group as England, Egypt and Holland. England up first. Again. On a wet and windy night in Cagliari, England took the lead when Gary Lineker gave Captain Fantastic the slip to score a simple goal. But Ireland battled bravely, forcing England to retreat deep into their own territory. It was like a pretty ordinary English League match, lots of effort, rare glimpses of skill. High balls rained on England's defence. Irish forwards scuttled after the scraps. A nation waited anxiously for a break, any stroke of good fortune to even the scores.

When it came, Ireland's goal was sublime. A deflected long ball fell to Kevin Sheedy, who struck it perfectly past Peter Shilton from eighteen yards. The dream was still alive. Thanks to their remarkable resilience, the Boys in Green had done the nation proud.

Egypt was next, the following Sunday. The Boys in Green were now the biggest story in the country. Everyone was engaged with the team. The story dominated all conversations. People made plans for the Sunday game against Egypt, with parties, barbecues and gatherings in community halls around Ireland. Not just in the old soccer strongholds, the garrison towns where shoneen men once played a 'foreign' game, but in bastions of Gaeldom, places like Kerry, Kilkenny and

Meath, where the soccer man had long been scorned for the vice of playing the imperialist game.

Bowing to the mood of the nation, the GAA rescheduled their Sunday-afternoon fixture to facilitate those wishing to watch the next chapter of a wonderful story. This really was something special, an end to sporting apartheid, the moment when our beautiful game of soccer would be recognized, and those who loved it would finally be assimilated into Irish culture.

I recall that Sunday morning very clearly, as if it were yesterday. Driving across the city to RTÉ there was a stillness in the air. Flags and bunting sticking out of windows, adorning shop fronts, pubs and lamp-posts, kids skipping happily in their green Opel shirts, being Paul McGrath, Kevin Sheedy, Captain Fantastic. Today was soccer's great day – more than that, a day when all who loved sport would join together in a celebration of a shared identity based on something real. The old, fraudulent divisions were finally buried in the grave.

Egypt had drawn with Holland in their opening game. England and Holland had drawn the day before. A win meant Ireland would top the group. An hour before the game, news filtered through that Jack had omitted Ronnie Whelan from the team. Ronnie, captain of the Liverpool side that had just won the English First Division, on the bench! That was a very strange decision. Ronnie was a classy player, a goalscorer and goalmaker.

The game against Egypt was a horror show. Seeking Positions of Maximum Opportunity, Ireland humped long balls at the Egyptians for ninety minutes. Tony Cascarino lumbered around up front, like a drunk at a Communion mass. We never attempted to play a passing game. Long after it became clear that some quality was required to break Egypt down, Jack stuck to his game plan. With twenty-five minutes to go John Aldridge was taken off. No Ronnie. Alan McLoughlin was the journeyman sub. With five minutes to go Cascarino was replaced by Niall Quinn.

Jack's attempt to bully the Egyptians was an abysmal failure. In our studio analysis I described the football played as 'rubbish'. And I contended: 'Anyone sending a team out to play that way should be ashamed of themselves.'

Jack's post-game television interview was also, I thought, deeply embarrassing. He didn't know the names of the Egyptian players (the running joke in the Irish camp suggested he sometimes didn't know his own players' names) so he attempted to distinguish between them on the basis of the colour of their skin. Thus, there were references to 'the light-skinned lad' and 'the one with darker skin'.

Sitting in the studio, aware that the nation was watching, I winced in embarrassment. John and I exchanged knowing glances. This was an OMFG moment. I repeated my assertion that Ireland's football was shameful. Then I dropped my pen on the studio desk and sat back with a sigh of resignation.

Within minutes the RTÉ switchboard lit up with complainants. At least two thousand people rang to voice their anger. The fuss was only beginning. With little that was printable to say about the game, the media decided that I was the story. I had, they wrote, declared that I was ashamed to be Irish before flinging my pen across the studio in disgust. The mob began marching. And they were marching in my direction.

The following day I travelled to Italy to cover our final group game against Holland for the *Sunday Independent*. The morning papers were full of reports about the public reaction to my remarks on RTÉ the previous day. At the airport I bought a copy of the *Evening Herald*. A poll they had commissioned showed that 97 per cent thought my robust criticism was wrong. The airport terminal was packed with travelling Irish fans. It was an afternoon flight. Drink had been consumed. A group of young fans spotted me having a coffee. As they closed in around me they began to chant: 'If you hate Eamon Dunphy, clap your hands. If you hate fucking Eamon Dunphy, clap your hands.' It was borderline dangerous, with the drink and high emotion whipped up by the morning tabloid reports fuelling what was in effect a battalion of 'Jackie's Army'. Other travellers averted their gaze as the mob closed in around my table. A security man arrived. Assessing the situation, he offered me an escape to a quiet room beside the gate we were to board from.

I was shaken. The press reports stated as a matter of fact that I had said I was ashamed to be Irish. I had thrown my pen across the RTÉ studio. The mob chanting outside must have seen the match on television. They must have known the difference between what I'd actually said and what the press was reporting. What, I wondered, would await me in Italy, where the news reports would doubtless be gospel?

As we waited to board, the chanting continued. More security arrived at what was now an ugly scene. I was seated halfway up the plane. The

Aer Lingus hostess checked my ticket as I stepped aboard. She seated me in the front row. 'You'll be OK there.' She smiled. This touching act of kindness almost made me cry. The flight was uneventful, an opportunity to reflect.

Tim O'Connor and Mike Horgan were brilliant in the face of ·the unprecedented hostility RTÉ had encountered the previous night. Tim assured me they would replay my comments to establish the truth of what I'd said. There was no question of RTÉ giving in to demands that I be dropped from the World Cup panel. Aengus was equally supportive. 'Call it as you see it. That's why we employ you,' was his answer to the periodic outbursts of indignation when I wrote something deemed controversial by others.

I'd arranged to meet Colm Tóibín in Palermo, the venue for the Ireland–Holland game. Colm was on assignment for *Magill* magazine to report on the now extraordinary cultural phenomenon that was 'The Boys in Green'. It was more than a sporting story. The whole country was engaged. Mary Harney, now a government minister, phoned after the Egypt game to advise me to lay off Big Jack: she thought the team were doing great!

When I went to Jack's pre-match press conference I didn't anticipate trouble. That was naïve. Jack believed the reports that stated I had declared myself ashamed to be Irish. In that context my presence was provocative. When I posed a question he refused to answer, saying that I 'wasn't a proper journalist'. It was, Jack insisted, his press conference and it would be conducted on his terms.

His success with the Irish team was big news in England. A number of British journalists were present along with the Irish press corps. Ian Ridley from the *Guardian* argued that it was absurd to suggest I wasn't a proper journalist. Jack lost his cool. He walked out, beckoning the Irish scribblers to follow. A row flared between the English and Irish pressmen. Ridley was verbally abused by Cathal Dervan, a young tabloid gunslinger: 'Why don't you fuck off back to England?' Dervan told the *Guardian*'s esteemed football correspondent. In an instant the tension evaporated as I and my English colleagues started laughing at the surreal implications of Dervan's intervention. The Irish journalists repaired to a private room, where Jack provided his pre-match briefing. The Englishmen stood by my fight to be treated as an accredited journalist. It was a rare example of water proving thicker than blood.

Colm Tóibín and I got a taxi to the stadium. I gave the press-box a swerve, opting to buy two tickets for Colm and myself in the regular grandstand. Our taxi dropped us about two hundred yards from the stadium at a car park where Irish and Dutch fans were being deposited from their coaches.

As we began our walk to the stadium we bumped into the economist Colm McCarthy. 'What have you done?' he asked me. I gave some shorthand account of the mood back home, the fuss generated by my post-match comments. It was dark. The street was a mass of green and orange, the Dutch being as famously fervent as our own travelling fans. Then a group of Irish fans spotted me. 'Dunphy, you bastard,' one guy erupted. He was joined by his mates, who crowded round as we attempted to keep moving. The chant began: 'If you hate fucking Dunphy, clap your hands.' Suddenly we were surrounded by hundreds of men (and women) wearing the green, chanting feverishly, pushing ever closer. A few Irish voices offered some support, but 'Leave the man alone' was a minority opinion. The potential for something nasty hung in the air on the final stretch of road between us and the stadium. The two Colms were shocked. I was too. This wasn't the Irish way. Sport was celebrated at Croke Park, Lansdowne Road or any other arena when people gathered to follow their team. There was something loutish about Jackie's travelling army, the kind of vibe familiar to those who visited English soccer grounds.

Before the game we knew that Ireland needed at least a draw to progress to the tournament's knock-out phase. The draw would do both sides if England beat Egypt in their match, which was being played simultaneously. Ruud Gullit gave Holland the lead after ten minutes. The European champions oozed class. They stroked the ball around with great confidence. A second goal would be fatal. But Ireland dug in, defending all around the pitch with incredible determination. Defiance was a defining quality of this team. For this Jack Charlton deserved credit. For our failure to be more constructive with possession he deserved criticism. Watching with Colm Tóibín, I gave him a tutorial on the beautiful game. A great writer, he sensed the drama, in the arena and outside it.

With twenty-five minutes to go, Jack made a couple of substitutions. Tony Cascarino came on to join Niall Quinn up front. Ronnie Whelan replaced Kevin Sheedy. Ireland needed a break. Route One, a long, high ball as prescribed by POMO, was the way Jack chose to go. In the seventy-first minute, goalkeeper Packie Bonner launched a guided missile in the direction of Ireland's twin towers, Quinn and Cascarino. For all their sophistication, the Dutch couldn't cope with the sheer force and physical presence of our two strikers, who were, in the argot of the game, 'putting themselves about'. A stressed Dutch defender misjudged an attempted back-pass to his keeper, allowing the Mighty Quinn to pounce for a magnificent equalizer. Five minutes later, news filtered through that England were 1–0 up on Egypt. A draw would see Holland and Ireland qualify for the last sixteen. Both sides settled for that.

Jack and his army moved on to Genoa to face Romania in the first knock-out round of the tournament. I retreated to the relative safety of the RTÉ studio in Dublin. As a result of the media firestorm I felt very lonely. In shops and on the streets around town people stared, nudged each other, saying, 'Look, it's him.' Kids were particularly alert, unable to disguise their hostility to the pantomime villain from the telly: 'Watch out, he's behind you!' At the taxi-rank outside the Westbury Hotel the five drivers on duty all refused to take me in their taxis.

The story I was trying to tell simply wouldn't wash. Ireland were making history, reaching the last sixteen at their first World Cup. We'd drawn with England and Holland, the European champions. This was substance: I was whingeing about style. In the media village the consensus was that I was trying to make a name for myself by blackguarding Big Jack and 'The Boys in Green'.

Romania were a very good team. Their main man, Gheorghe Hagi, was one of the best players in Europe. In Genoa, Hagi hardly got a look in. Denied time and space to move the ball, hounded across every blade of grass on the pitch by a pack of green shirts, and desperately defending the long balls bombed in behind their defenders, the Romanians looked demoralized long before the final whistle blew. After ninety minutes and extra time, the score read 0–0. Ireland were heroic. Paul McGrath, Kevin Moran, Steve Staunton, Ray Houghton, Niall Quinn and, yes, even Captain Fantastic McCarthy had fought with extraordinary tenacity. John Aldridge hunted every long ball.

One of the few players to break ranks, Aldridge offered a clue to the Irish players' true feelings about Jack's POMO football. A prolific goal-scorer throughout his career at Oxford and Liverpool, he remarked wryly in an unguarded moment that 'My legs will be worn down to stumps,' chasing lost causes up front. Aldridge scored one goal in his first twenty-three games for Ireland. But he served Jack's cause.

It is no exaggeration to say that the whole nation watched the penalty shoot-out against Romania. Everybody remembers where they were, how they felt, who they were with. Daniel Timofte missed Romania's fourth penalty. Jack left the decision on who should take Ireland's penalties to the players, who huddled in the centre-circle as the drama unfolded. Timofte's miss meant we were one accurate strike from the World Cup quarter-final. David O'Leary broke from the centre-circle huddle and strolled slowly towards the penalty spot. A centre-half. Exiled by Big Jack. Only on the pitch as a substitute. Never taken a penalty kick before, or not, at least, that anyone could remember. In the studio I looked at John. I didn't fancy David's chances. Everything riding on it. All the stuff with Jack over the years.

In what seemed like slow-motion, David carefully placed the ball on the spot. As he set himself to begin his run-up, George Hamilton in the RTÉ commentary box voiced his memorable sound-bite: 'The nation holds its breath.' With unerring conviction, David struck his shot high and true to the Romanian keeper's left. The net shook. The country went wild with joy. In pubs and offices there was an explosion of happiness, a moment of pure, unadulterated pleasure, temporarily lifting even the meanest spirit. Strangers hugged each other on the streets of the towns and cities into which they had spilled, leaving all inhibitions behind. In the RTÉ studio, watching the pictures beaming in from around the country, informed analysis was forgotten. The story of Big Jack and 'The Boys in Green' was no longer a football story. Tactics and team selection were irrelevant.

One image confirmed the wider significance of this wonderful afternoon: a shot of John Healy, the *Irish Times'* splendidly sceptical political columnist, watching the game on a screen at the EU summit in Dublin Castle. An ardent Gael, Healy was no soccer man. Now, as he watched the Irish players jubilantly acknowledge the applause of Jackie's travelling army in Genoa, Healy, gazing intently at the big screen, began to weep. He clapped his hands, slowly, pausing only to wipe away the tears of something more profound than momentary pleasure. Some corner of his West of Ireland soul was touched by the sight of an Irish victory on an international stage that saw us through to the quarter-finals of the world's most prestigious sporting festival.

Healy was the author of a celebrated book, *No One Shouted Stop: The Death of an Irish Town*. Published in 1968, the book described the economic and social decline of rural life in the West of Ireland during the fifties, a time of dreadful poverty and mass emigration. This man had seen the worst of Irish life, the terrible consequences of a dysfunctional, corrupt political and social order, the pain and enduring misery of the ordinary people of Ireland.

In Healy's time, the emigration that cursed the West of Ireland in particular tended to be for ever. Few came back. I can only guess what prompted the tears that flowed in the RDS. Emigration may have been at the heart of it. And on that day, with the team that Jack had built, emigration was a significant part of the story. Playing for Ireland were the sons and grandsons of Irish emigrants: Andy Townsend, Mick McCarthy, Ray Houghton, John Aldridge, Kevin Sheedy, Chris Morris and Tony Cascarino. As he wept, brushed away his tears and gazed far beyond the big screen in front of him it was maybe this aspect of the story that had touched his Mayo spirit.

Attempting rigorous football criticism in a country surfing unprecedented waves of communal joy was a rather futile exercise. When my ten-year-old daughter, Colette, ran out to join her friends on the street celebrating David O'Leary's winning penalty, the neighbours' kids chased her back indoors, unpleasant taunts ringing in her ears.

There was a football context to all of this that did not resonate among the foot-soldiers of Jackie's Army. The 1990 World Cup was the worst in living memory. Fewer goals were scored per game than ever before or since. A record sixteen players were sent off. The scourge of negative defensive football, which had afflicted the international game for a decade, was now at crisis point. Both semi-finals were decided by penalty shoot-outs. West Germany beat Argentina 1–0 to lift the Jules Rimet Trophy. Even FIFA, football's notoriously conservative governing body, were forced to respond when the tournament ended. Fearful for the future of the sport, FIFA subsequently introduced a rule change to discourage back-passes to the goalkeeper, a favoured method of slowing down the play. Playing for a draw was also discouraged by awarding three points for a win.

To bring attention to this reality, as soccer analysts around the world were doing, was regarded in Ireland as provocative, or worse. Unwelcome facts would not be allowed to interfere with one of the great modern Irish stories. As the nation prepared for the quarter-final encounter with the host nation, Italy, anyone brandishing facts was barking up the wrong tree. With regard to 'The Boys in Green' and Italia 90, the salient facts were: no games won; rubbish football played; two goals scored in four matches, both created by long punts downfield from Packie Bonner's boot.

I travelled to Rome's Olympic Stadium for the quarter-final. Again I avoided the press-box to sit in the stand with Colm Tóibín. Among the many famous Irish faces present were U2 and Charlie Haughey. Gina Lollobrigida sat alongside Henry Kissinger close by. The stadium was packed, the pitch pristine, the football rubbish. Tentative at first, an ordinary Italian side slowly got a grip on the game. Gifted possession easily, the Italians upped the tempo with growing confidence. The Irish players grafted as always, but there was a weary look about them. In the end, even the bucket containing Irish blood, sweat and toil empties.

In the thirty-eighth minute, Roberto Donadoni struck a speculative, swerving shot from twenty-three yards. Packie Bonner was fooled by the flight of the ball. Packie could only parry the ball to the edge of the six-yard box. 'Totò' Schillaci pounced to score the goal that secured an Italian victory. Jack had no plan B. The Italians, master defenders, coped easily with Packie Bonner's bombs. There was one obvious substitution crying out to be made, but Ronnie Whelan sat through the ninety minutes without ever being asked to take off his tracksuit.

Ronnie was one of Ireland's greatest ever players. He had an impressive record as a big-game goal-scorer. His goals helped Liverpool win Wembley Cup Finals. He really should have started the match. But the Liverpool captain, an independent-minded character, had fallen foul of the regime after a training-ground row. Tony Cascarino and John Sheridan were Jack's preferred subs on the night.

A wonderful adventure was coming to an end. The 15,000 Irish supporters in Rome's Olympic Stadium rose to Jack and his players as they walked a slow lap of honour. They would go home as heroes. Charlie Haughey joined the heroes for a valedictory lap of the Olympic Stadium.

At Rome airport the following morning I met Ronnie Whelan's mother and father. Ronnie Senior was a hero from my childhood. Like his son, he had been a goal-scoring forward for St Patrick's Athletic in the League of Ireland's golden age. He had played his schoolboy football for Father Mac's Stella Maris. He confirmed what I'd been writing in the *Sunday Independent*, that his son was fit to play in the tournament. But Ronnie wryly remarked: 'He doesn't follow Jack's orders.'

Ronnie Senior had no time for Jack's Route One football. It was a foreign game to those of us who belonged to the now ever-diminishing original soccer community. How ironic that soccer's emancipation in the Land of Saints and Scholars should coincide with the isolation of people like Ronnie, Dessie Toal, Frank O'Neill, the Bradys, Gileses, O'Learys, Whelans, Liam Tuohy, Brian Kerr and Noel O'Reilly. The mob stole our game. Now we watched helpless, and largely voiceless, as they paraded round the world, led by Big Jack.

Our plane landed at Dublin one hour before the team's. Flying in over the city we could see the vast crowd, an estimated 500,000, gathered for the homecoming party. There were no taxis at the airport. The drivers couldn't get there through the crowds ringing the approach roads. I had my car. Greg Sparks, an accountant and member of Labour Party leader Dick Spring's kitchen cabinet, wondered if I could give him a lift into town. 'No problem, hop in,' I told him.

As we moved slowly along the slip-road towards the roundabout, a couple of hundred yards from the airport, we noted the raucous crowd awaiting the heroes' return. There was a whiff of hysteria in the air as men, women and children pressed excitedly forward. At the roundabout we had to stop briefly. A few young men spilled onto the road alongside my Honda Civic. One of them spotted me: 'It's him,' he roared to his mates.

'Dunphy, you fucking bastard,' another yob screamed.

There wasn't a policeman in sight. We were stalled, the car quickly surrounded. They started to rock the car. Greg and I were in trouble. I suggested he go along the road to find a cop. I managed to get out of the car, which was now completely stuck in a mass of bodies. Drink was being consumed from cans. I needed a stiff one myself. But I kept smiling. People were taking photographs. The mob was split 50:50: some wanted the car turned over, others wanted me left alone. Horns hooted behind us.

During the five minutes while Greg found a guard, I sat back in the car. Two middle-aged women with cameras approached, urging me to wind down the window. 'Can we take a picture, Eamon?' they asked.

'Sure,' I replied.

They took the picture. Then, as they went to leave, one woman turned. 'You're a little fucking bastard,' she snarled. I was genuinely frightened.

Greg returned with a garda superintendent. At the sight of the uniform the mob backed off. He was a decent man. 'We weren't prepared for this.' He gestured at the throng. 'The city's even worse. Don't go down the main airport road, you'll get more of it,' he advised. 'Go round by Portmarnock and in by the coast road. You should be OK on that route.' Shocked by the incident, we made our circuitous journey to the safety of Dublin 4.

I watched the homecoming on television. Jack and the players waved from the open-top bus. Opel's Arnold O'Byrne waved from his pitch alongside the heroes. And downstairs on the bus's lower deck I spotted the mentors from Merrion Square and the decent skins of the Irish Soccer Writers' Association. They'd hitched a lift on the heroes' chariot. Now, like 'The Boys in Green', Big Jack, Captain Fantastic and Arnold from Opel, mentors and hacks coyly waved to the frenzied mob as the bus snaked down O'Connell Street. Happy days.

After the parade, viewers returned to the RTÉ studio, where John Giles, Martin O'Neill and Bill O'Herlihy were in great form. They agreed that this was a great day for Ireland. The Boys in Green had done us proud. 'Magnificent,' Martin thought they were.

John concluded, 'Jack should be proud of the team and the players should be proud of the football they played.'

I punched the off button.

Next day I went to see my friend Patrick Guilbaud. His restaurant was a wonderful success. He had a coveted Michelin star. The first few years in Ireland had been hard for Patrick. Restaurant Patrick Guilbaud offered *nouvelle cuisine*, a simple, elegant alternative to classic French cooking. The dishes were light, the emphasis on fresh produce, lightly sauced. *Nouvelle cuisine* was a long way from the meat-and-two-veg feed of Irish or British tradition. Patrick did not put salt and pepper on the tables. The flavours created in the kitchen by his chef, Guillaume Lebrun, did not require seasoning. Salt and pepper were redundant.

Arthur Gibney had created a magnificent room for Patrick's restaurant. When he had opened in 1981 the restaurant had been the talk of the town. Well, the part of town that talked about fine dining. Charlie Haughey, a Francophile, was a regular. The early reviews, though, were savage. *Nouvelle cuisine* was characterized as a gimmick devoid of substance. The absence of salt and pepper was noted. Prices were extortionate, it was claimed. Portions were too small. 'You'll leave feeling hungry with a lighter wallet,' one well-padded reviewer remarked.

Patrick stuck to his guns, except on the salt-and-pepper issue. If the idiots wanted to spray Guillaume's creations with 'shit', Patrick said, that was their problem. Patrick showed extraordinary fortitude through the early years, and slowly the tide began to turn. Without yielding on price or the kind of food he wanted to serve, he acquired a loyal following. With the award of his Michelin star, triumph was assured.

He loved Ireland. When I drew attention to the country's defects he shrugged his shoulders and laughed. 'You're crazy!' He liked Irish people, liked the informality, liked the wonderful fresh produce his kitchen team could source. He also liked the taxes, which were low, relative to France: 'There you work for the government, I want to work for my family.'

Patrick loved football. He was a Manchester United fan. He loved Big Jack and the Boys in Green. Feeling bruised and lonely after the Italian adventure, I got no comfort from the Frenchman. Like everyone else in the country, Patrick thought getting to the World Cup quarter-final was incredible.

'You're not Brazil or Italy, or even France.' He laughed. 'The whole country is happy. It's about results, and Jack is getting them.'

Like my family and other friends, Patrick was concerned for me. But the truth of the matter was that for me soccer wasn't simply about results. Football had reached a low ebb – exemplified by the brutally cynical final between West Germany and Argentina – and Jack's Ireland team was part of that malaise. I just couldn't see it as Ireland's finest hour. Everything that was glorious about our game was being swept aside to worship at Big Jack's shrine. It was sacrilege.

'Patrick, I need to get out of town,' I told him. 'I need to go somewhere I won't meet Irish people.'

'You like horses,' he said.

'Yes.'

'Okay, go to Deauville for August. There's racing every day, nobody will know you, you'll enjoy it.' Patrick had trained as a chef at the Hôtel Normandy, where he suggested I stay.

Deauville sounded perfect. I booked the Rosslare to Cherbourg car-ferry, and the Normandy for a few weeks' anonymity. When I arrived in Rosslare and joined the queue for the ferry, hundreds of Irish holiday-makers were waiting to board. I tried to keep my head down. I was alone. But within minutes someone had spotted me. As we inched closer to the boarding ramp I was conscious of people staring and pointing. In the ship's reception area, as I waited for my cabin booking, I was surrounded by whispering Irish travellers: 'It's him, Dad,' a youngster exclaimed. 'Dunphy.' A group of young men started singing 'Olé, olé, olé, olé', the anthem of the Boys in Green. Jesus!

The girl on Reception gave me my cabin key. And a warm smile. Down in my cabin I contemplated the sixteen-hour journey. I'd have to eat in the ship's restaurant. I braced myself and went back upstairs. There was a queue for the buffet. More staring and whispering. I was close to tears. The maître d' approached. 'Eamon, come on with me.' He beckoned. 'I've got you a quiet table in the corner. You'll be left alone over there,' he assured me. 'We'll take your order, you won't have to queue.' He brought me a bottle of beer and a menu.

This small act of kindness released a cascade of tears. I sat in my corner for ten or fifteen minutes weeping. I'd been putting a brave face on things for several weeks, pretending not to give a fuck. The tears told a different story.

Notoriety itself didn't really bother me. But I felt remorse for the collateral damage inflicted on my family. On the night of the Home-coming, with the country in carnival mode, my seventeen-year-old son Tim was roughed up in a disco. He was a lovely, popular boy. Now Tim was the son of 'that bastard' Dunphy. My daughter Colette was getting serious grief in school and round the neighbourhood. I had become an embarrassment to my family. I was running away to France while they were living with the consequences of having a dad who seemed to many of their friends and neighbours to be an attention-seeking freak. For my mother and father, decent, private people, being associated with a freak show was unpleasant. Kevin was great. Like many in the football community he thought the Big Jack circus a joke. But, as he reminded me, it was only a game of football, not life or death. Alone in my cabin, I reflected on all of this. I was overwhelmed by a wave of guilt and shame. The kind of journalism I favoured came at a price. Those I loved most were picking up the bill. I was fucking off to France. Good man, Eamon.

Index